VIETNAM: THE WAR IN THE AIR

Other Books by Gene Gurney

THE AIR FORCE MUSEUM

AMERICAN HISTORY IN WAX MUSEUMS

AMERICANS INTO ORBIT

AMERICANS TO THE MOON

ARLINGTON NATIONAL CEMETERY

BEAUTIFUL WASHINGTON, D.C.

THE B-29 STORY

CHRONOLOGY OF WORLD AVIATION

COSMONAUTS IN ORBIT

FIVE DOWN AND GLORY

FLYING ACES OF WORLD WAR I

FLYING MINUTEMEN—THE STORY OF THE CIVIL AIR PATROL

GREAT AIR BATTLES

HIGHER, FASTER AND FARTHER

HOW TO SAVE YOUR LIFE ON THE NATION'S HIGHWAYS AND BYWAYS

JOURNEY OF THE GIANTS

KINGDOMS OF EUROPE

THE LIBRARY OF CONGRESS

MARYLAND

MONTICELLO

MOUNT VERNON

NORTH AND SOUTH KOREA

THE PENTAGON

THE PICTORIAL HISTORY OF THE U.S. ARMY

PRIVATE PILOT'S HANDBOOK OF NAVIGATION

PRIVATE PILOT'S HANDBOOK OF WEATHER

THE P-38 LIGHTNING

ROCKET AND MISSILE TECHNOLOGY

THE SMITHSONIAN INSTITUTION

TEST PILOTS

UNIDENTIFIED FLYING OBJECTS

THE UNITED STATES COAST GUARD

WALK IN SPACE—THE STORY OF PROJECT GEMINI

THE WAR IN THE AIR

WOMEN ON THE MARCH

VIETNAM: THE WAR IN THE AIR

A Pictorial History of the U.S. Air Forces in the Vietnam War:
Air Force, Army, Navy, and Marines

By Col. Gene Gurney, USAF (Ret.)
Foreword by
General William C. Westmoreland, U.S. Army (Ret.)

CROWN PUBLISHERS, INC.
NEW YORK

Published by Crown Publishers, Inc., One Park Avenue, New York, New York
10016, and simultaneously in Canada by General Publishing Company Limited
Manufactured in Hong Kong

Library of Congress Cataloging in Publication Data
Gurney, Gene.
   Vietnam, the war in the air.
   Includes index.
   1. United States.   Air Force—History—Vietnamese
Conflict, 1961–1975.   2. United States.   Navy—Aviation—
History—20th century.   3. United States.   Army—
History—20th century.   4. United States. Marine Corps—
History—20th century.   5. Vietnamese Conflict, 1961–
1975—Aerial operations, American.   I. Title.
UG633.G794   1984   959.704′348   84-11327
ISBN 0-517-55350-3

10 9 8 7 6 5 4 3 2 1

First Edition

Contents

Acknowledgments

My personal thanks to the many military and civilian personnel of the U.S. Armed Forces, both active duty and retired, who helped produce this overall airpower treaty on the Vietnam War. I am especially grateful to General William C. Westmoreland, Jr., for his faith and trust in me ("I am pleased that you are now writing about Vietnam for I know your portrayal will be characterized by facts and objectivity—not sensationalism") and for writing the foreword for the book.

For the photographs on the jacket of the book, I am indebted, as I have been so many times with past books, to Bettie Sprigg, the photograph research expert in the Office of the Assistant Secretary of Defense for Public Affairs in the Pentagon, and to Marie Yates, in the ready access photograph office of the Defense Audio Visual Agency.

Also, to Paul Stillwell, editor, *Naval Review,* United States Naval Institute, Annapolis, Maryland, for permission to reprint the articles, "U.S. Marine Corps Aviation in Vietnam, 1962–1970" by Lt. Gen. Keith B. McCutcheon, U.S. Marine Corps, Retired, and "U.S. Navy Task Force 77 in Action Off Vietnam" by Vice Adm. Malcolm W. Cagle, U.S. Navy, Retired. I attempted to use great care to preserve the integrity of the two articles when I cut the length of them to fit our printing limitations.

My thanks, also, go to the Department of the Army for use of the Vietnam study, "U.S. Army Airmobility, 1961–1971" by Lt. Gen. John T. Tolson, U.S. Army, Retired. General Tolson had been involved with the airmobility concept since June 1939 when he participated in the first tactical air movement of ground forces by the U.S. Army. He also, further into his career, served as Commanding General, 1st Cavalry Division (Airmobile) in Vietnam. No more qualified person could have "written the chapter on the Army's Airmobility" for this book on the air war in Vietnam. Again, in reducing the length of the original monograph to fit the publisher's requirements, I aimed to preserve the integrity of General Tolson's study on airmobility.

Also, my thanks to Lawrence J. Paszek, Chief, Editorial Branch, Office of Air Force History, for his guidance in obtaining the permissions to reproduce the U.S. Air Force material that was used in the book *The United States Air Force in Southeast Asia, 1961–1973,* and to the Office of the Secretary of the Air Force for the use of the material.

My thanks, also, go to the Government Printing Office for their kind and courteous attitude in supplying the positive film for *The United States Air Force in Southeast Asia.*

For the U.S. Air Force chapters in this book, I am grateful to the historians in the Office of Air Force History, Headquarters USAF, and in such field organizations as the Strategic Air Command, Air Force Logistics Command, and the Military Airlift Command, who wrote and otherwise contributed to the preparation of those parts of the book. Many military and civilian personnel of the Air Force, Army, Navy, and Marine Corps, Office of the Joint Chiefs of Staff, and the Office of the Secretary of Defense read and commented on the manuscript. Most of these reviewers possessed expert knowledge of the specific aspects of the war, acquired through personal participation in it or years of research and writing on the subject.

Gen. William M. Momyer, USAF, Retired, who served as commander of the Seventh Air Force in Southeast Asia (1966–1968), provided an especially helpful commentary on the U.S. Air Force material. Others who offered significant comments included Samuel A. Tucker, Office of the Secretary of Defense;

Charles B. MacDonald, Chief, Current History Branch, U.S. Army, Center of Military History; and several faculty members of the departments of history of the Air Force Academy, Annapolis, and West Point; and special thanks to Capt. Robert H. Whitlow, U.S. Marine Corps, who kindly provided a portion of his manuscript concerning the attempts to recover several downed aircraft which clarified an air rescue mission in the book.

Work on the U.S. Air Force portion of this book began in August 1973 under the direction of Brig. Gen. Brian S. Gunderson, Chief, Office of Air Force History. Mr. Max Rosenberg, Deputy Chief Historian, prepared the plan for writing the Air Force portion of the book and helped shepherd the manuscript through several stages of writing and production. Mr. Rosenberg and Dr. Stanley L. Falk, Chief Historian of the U.S. Air Force at the time, also reviewed drafts of those portions and suggested revisions which substantially improved them. Carl Berger, Chief, Histories Division, served as overall editor and authored three of the chapters. Mr. Paszek prepared the U.S. Air Force manuscript for publication. He and Mr. Deane J. Allen of the Editorial Branch collected and selected most of the illustrations. Their sources included the photographic collections of the Air Force, Army, Navy, and Marine Corps, as well as other government agencies. Mrs. Frances Lewis and Mrs. Mabel B. Sneed, 1361st Photographic Squadron, Aerospace Audio-Visual Service, provided substantial research assistance in this effort. Mr. Andrew Poggenpohl, art editor, *National Geographic* magazine, kindly supplied a number of color and black-and-white photographs. Several other private sources also loaned illustrations from their collections for use in the book. Acknowledgments are as follows (in order of first use): Ministère des Armées "AIR," U.S. Air Force, Dwight D. Eisenhower Library, United Press International, John F. Kennedy Library, Maj. Thomas A. Dwelle, U.S. Army, U.S. Air Force Art Collection, *National Geographic* magazine, U.S. Information Agency, U.S. Marine Corps, Maj. Donald J. Kutyna, Capt. Ray DeArrigunga, Lt. Col. Billy Keeler, U.S. Navy, Capt. Donald W. Randle, Capt. Keith Grimes, Col. John S. Wood, Jr., Army (of) Republic of Vietnam, Teledyne Ryan Aeronautical, Sgt. John J. Frerich, the White House, *Life* magazine, NBC: Huntley Brinkley Reports and Brig. Gen. A. R. Brownfield (U.S. Army, Retired).

The original U.S. Air Force casebound book containing the U.S. Air Force portions with the accompanying battle area maps and more than 600 photographs was designed by Dudley Kruhm, Typography and Design Division, Government Printing Office.

The reproduction of paintings (illustrations) are from the originals in the official U.S. Air Force Art Collection, administered by the Office of Information, Office of the Secretary of the Air Force.

Foreword

United States military operations in Vietnam were conducted to block Communist aggression in Southeast Asia, but this aggression was only the tip of the iceberg of the Communist threat to United States security interests in the Pacific. Less obvious components of the total Communist threat were manifested by the provocative actions of North Korea, the mounting pressures of the North Vietnamese presence in Laos and Cambodia, and the rising level of Communist-inspired insurgency in Thailand and Burma. These situations required careful and continuing evaluation to ensure the most efficient allocation of available resources in the U.S. Pacific Command to conduct the war in Vietnam and, at the same time, the protection of vital United States interests in an area stretching from the Bering Sea in the north to the eastern Indian Ocean in the south. Toward this end the United States (and South Vietnamese, and other Free World) forces went into battle to defeat the Communists and their organizations in South Vietnam; there, ground actions were confined by political authority to the territory of South Vietnam and the defense of an unprecedented hostile front of almost 900 miles.

Viewing the conduct and achievements of the military services in Vietnam in an overall context, the record was remarkable: the mammoth logistical buildup; various tactical expedients and innovations; the advisory effort; civic action programs; but, perhaps most impressive of all, the accomplishment for the first time in military history of a true airmobility on the battlefield.

The ability of the Americans to meet and defeat the best troops the enemy could put on the field of battle was once more demonstrated beyond any possible doubt, as was the validity of the Army's airmobile concept.

The military man of the future will perforce truly think, live, and fight in the three dimensions of ground, sea, and air. An excellent example for this kind of three-dimensional thinking in the future is Khe Sanh. The key to our success at Khe Sanh was firepower, principally aerial firepower. For 77 days Air Force, Navy, Marine, and Army aircraft provided round-the-clock, close-in support to the defending garrison and were controlled by airborne forward air controllers or ground-based radar. Between 22 January and 31 March tactical aircraft flew multiple sorties daily. At the same time, increasing numbers of the Strategic Air Command's B-52's were demonstrating their devasting ability to neutralize a large area and were instrumental in preventing the enemy from assembling in large formations. Marine and Army artillery fires supplemented this awesome quantity of aerial firepower. Marine howitzers within the combat base and sixteen Army long-range 175-mm artillery pieces located to the east fired thousands of rounds into the area during the siege.

This tremendous firepower prevented the two NVA divisions directly confronting Khe Sanh and a third in the immediate area from massing their forces to mount a major attack. Their supplies were destroyed, their troop formations shattered, and their antiaircraft fire rendered ineffective.

GENERAL W. C. WESTMORELAND
U.S. ARMY, RETIRED

VIETNAM: THE WAR IN THE AIR

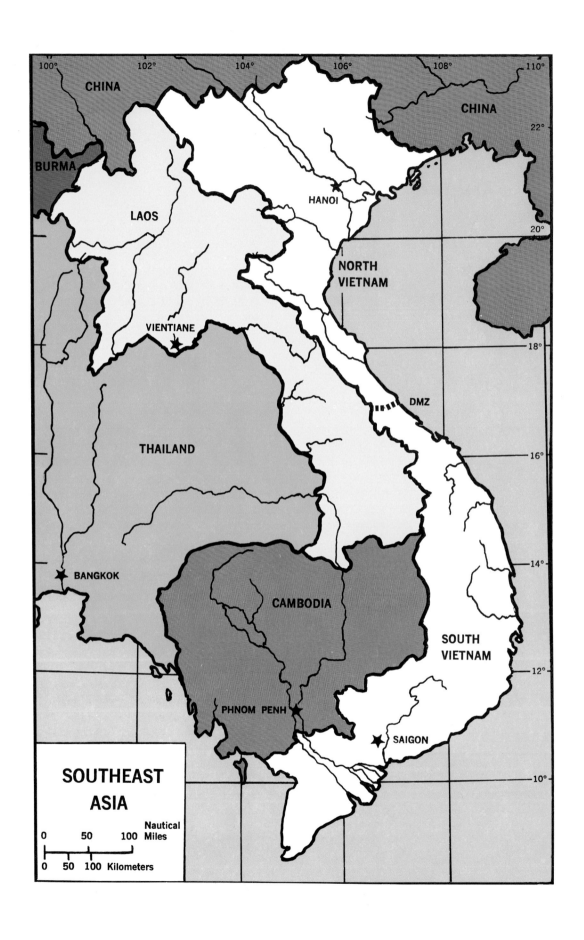

SOUTHEAST
ASIA

Nautical
Miles

0   50   100

0   50 100 Kilometers

I Introduction to the Air War

U.S. Army Air Force fighters and bombers flew their first combat missions in Southeast Asia during World War II. From bases in India, China, and the Philippines, they went into action against Japanese land, sea, and air targets throughout the area, including those in enemy-occupied French Indochina. Among targets attacked by Air Force planes in 1942-1944 were Haiphong harbor, Hanoi's Gia Lam airfield, and Japanese shipping in the Gulf of Tonkin. Beginning in June 1944 B-29 crews joined the air campaign. Flying from Indian bases, they bombed Japanese ammunition and supply dumps, oil storage facilities, naval installations, and other targets at Saigon, Phnom Penh, Bangkok Rangoon, and Singapore. The Superforts also mined nearby Cap St. Jacques (Vung Tai), and Cam Ranh Bay. In the spring and summer of 1945, Philippine-based fighters and bombers swept the coastal railroad, hitting targets at Phan Rang, Nha Trang, Tuy Hoa, and Tourane (Da Nang). On 15 August 1945, following the atomic bomb attacks on Hiroshima and Nagasaki, Japan surrendered.

Sixteen years later Air Force crews returned to several of the places bombed during World War II—to Thailand and the territory of the beleaguered Republic of Vietnam (South Vietnam). The latter for several years had been subjected to guerrilla attacks supported by its northern neighbor, the Democratic Republic of Vietnam (North Vietnam).From bases in Thailand and South Vietnam, Air Force pilots during the early 1960's began flying the first of thousands of combat missions over the Republic of Vietnam and southern Laos, the latter the location of the famous Ho Chi Minh trail. In time this new war spilled over into North Vietnam and Cambodia. For some of the participating airmen, Southeast Asia became the scene of the third war they had fought in less than a quarter of a century.

However, for most members of the U.S. Air Force who served 1-year tours of duty (many of them had multiple tours) in the area, the war against the Viet Cong and North Vietnamese was their first experience in combat. Along with air veterans of World War II and Korea, they were ordered into combat by three Presidents of the United States. The first of these chief executives—John F. Kennedy—had concluded that the United States should provide additional military assistance to South Vietnam and the Royal Laotian Government (RLG) to prevent their takeover by Communist forces. His successors, Lyndon B. Johnson and Richard M. Nixon, also reaffirmed their support for the preservation of non-Communist governments in the area. Initially backed wholeheartedly by Congress and the American people, their decisions ultimately resulted in the longest, most controversial, and financially most costly war in the nation's history.

Origins of the War

The conflict in Southeast Asia had origins in the Vietnamese nationalist movement going back to the end of World War I, aimed at ending French colonial rule. The government of France, however, resisted all Vietnamese efforts to achieve their independence. Following Nazi Germany's conquest of France in 1940, Japan moved in on Indochina intending to incorporate that territory into its empire. But after the defeat of Germany in 1945,

3

the French determined to reassert their colonial rule. However, President Franklin D. Roosevelt in 1943 had urged the freeing of all colonial peoples, including those of Indochina, in the postwar period.

During the last months of the war, U.S. agents had been parachuted into the hills of Annam where they joined up with insurgent forces led by Ho Chi Minh. These local forces, known as the Viet Minh, included both Communist and non-Communist elements, all united in their desire for independence. The Americans brought with them a small supply of rifles, mortars, machineguns, grenades, and bazookas and began training Ho's troops to use them against Japanese occupation troops. On 15 August 1945, following Japan's surrender, President Harry S. Truman issued General Order No. 1 governing procedures for disarming Japanese forces in the Far East. In the case of Indochina, he designated the 16th parallel as the line north of which Chinese Nationalist troops would disarm the Japanese. South of that line British forces were to accept the Japanese surrender.

On 9 September 1945, when advance elements of about 200,000 Chinese troops arrived in Hanoi, they found that Ho Chi Minh's forces had already taken control of the northern region, replaced all French street signs with Vietnamese ones, and issued a Declaration of Independence on 2 September establishing the Democratic Republic of Vietnam. On 12 September British Commonwealth forces landed at Tan Son Nhut airfield outside Saigon accompanied by a detachment of 150 French troops. Three weeks earlier British authorities in London had determined to restore France's administration of Indochina. By 23 September the French, with the help of the British, reassumed control of Saigon. The French subsequently began negotiations with the Chinese to permit French military forces to move into the northern part of Vietnam. An agreement was reached and, in March 1946, a French military force arrived at Haiphong to relieve the Chinese Army of its responsibilities under General Order No. 1. The French commander, Gen. Jacques Leclerc, began negotiations with Ho and, on 6 March, an accord was reached. Under its provisions, the French agreed to recognize the Democratic Republic of Vietnam "as a free state, having its Government, its Parliament, its army, and its finances, and forming a part of the Indochinese Federation and the French Union."

Further negotiations spelling out details of Vietnamese independence got under way in the spring of 1946 at Dalat, at a time when Vietnamese guerrilla warfare was under way in southern Vietnam (Cochinchina). But the discussions foundered on the issue of Vietnamese autonomy, whereupon the French announced the establishment of an "independent" Cochinchina within the French Union. This act only exacerbated the situation and stimulated guerrilla warfare in the south. Another attempt to reach an agreement came during the summer of 1946, when Ho and a Viet Minh delegation travelled to France for 2 more months of discussion of the issue. Once again, the talks failed over the issue of Vietnamese independence. The Viet Minh delegation returned home and, shortly after, forces commanded by Gen. Vo Nguyen Giap launched a series of attacks on French posts and truck convoys, inflicting heavy casualties and provoking general hostilities.

While these events were unfolding in Southeast Asia, Washington's attention was focused on a divided Europe whose eastern half was firmly under Soviet control. An additional cause for worry was the substantial political support the Communist parties of France and Italy began winning during the early postwar years.

American officials felt it was essential to restore France so as to enable her to reassume her historic role in western Europe. Support of French policy in Indochina followed. Thus, the United States accepted the French proposal to give limited autonomy to the Associated States of Vietnam, Laos, and Cambodia. A number of Vietnamese—such as Emperor Bao Dai—went along with the French and he emerged as head of the new State of Vietnam (which incorporated Cochinchina). The United States recognized the Bao Dai government on 3 February 1950.

Meanwhile, the guerrilla war had spread and France found it necessary to send more military resources to Indochina. Exacerbating the French situation was the arrival of Mao Tsetung's victorious troops on the northern border of Vietnam in December 1949. Ho's Viet Minh immediately recognized the new Chinese Communist government, was recognized in turn by Peking, Moscow, and the satellite regimes of Eastern Europe. On 16 February 1950 France formally requested American military and economic assistance in prosecuting the Indochina war.

At this point the Truman administration undertook an evaluation of the situation in Southeast Asia. It concluded that "the threat of Communist aggression in Indochina is only one phase of anticipated Communist plans to seize all of Southeast Asia." In National Security Council Memorandum 64, dated 27 February 1950, it further stated that "all practicable measures [should] be taken to prevent further Communist expansion in Southeast Asia...The neighboring countries of Thailand and Burma could be expected to fall under Communist domination if Indochina were controlled by a Communist-dominated government. The balance of Southeast Asia would then be in grave hazard.'' Subsequently, on 1 May 1950, President Truman approved an initial allotment of $10 million for French Indochina.

The U.S. Air Force in Indochina

Starting in the summer of 1950 and during the next two decades, U.S. Air Force personnel—military advisors, maintenance and supply experts, combat crews, etc.—were ordered into French Indochina and later to its successor states, South Vietnam, Laos, and Cambodia in support of national policy. Besides serving as members of the Military Assistance Advisor Group (MAAG) in Saigon beginning in July 1950, USAF personnel during the early 1950's were sent to Indochina on temporary duty (TDY) for specific purposes. For example, in January 1953 a Philippine-based Air Force aircraft maintenance and supply detachment was sent to Nha Trang airfield to help the French to maintain C-47 transports lent to them for use against the Viet Minh. The detachment completed its work and withdrew in August 1953.

In February 1954, several months prior to the crisis surrounding the battle of Dien Bien Phu, several hundred USAF mechanics were again sent to Indochina to help keep other U.S.-loan aircraft in flying condition. In the early spring of 1954, at the request of the French the Air Force helped fly in troop reinforcements from North Africa and France to bolster the deteriorating military situation at Dien Bien Phu. Just prior to the climax of the battle in May, President Dwight D. Eisenhower and his advisers mulled over U.S. intervention in the form of a possible Air Force and U.S. Navy tactical strike, to include the use of B-29 bombers—to relieve the enemy's pressure on the French garrison. In this regard, Brig. Gen. Joseph D. Caldara, commander of the Far East Air Forces Bomber Command in Japan, in April 1954 reconnoitered the Dien Bien Phu

2

(1-2) The U.S. government loaned France a number of Air Force C-47 transports to bolster French Air Force airlift operations against Viet Minh forces. (3-5) Air Force C-123's, converted into spray aircraft, were employed to defoliate jungle vegetation which provided cover for guerrillas who ambushed military and civilian traffic in South Vietnam. (4) An Air Force Forward Air Controller discusses a mission with his Vietnamese counterpart. (6) President Eisenhower (l.) and Secretary of State Dulles (r.) confer in the White House with President Ngo Dinh Diem of the Republic of Vietnam, 8 May 1957. (7) Viet Minh prisoners captured by the French unload military supplies from a USAF C-54.

1

3

4

5

6

7

battlefield in a B-17 and concluded that a B-29 strike would be successful.

However, in Washington key ·members of the Congress balked at U.S. military intervention unless the British agreed to participate. When Prime Minister Winston Churchill refused to go along, the President dropped the idea of an air strike. On 7 May 1954 the French were overwhelmed by Viet Minh troops under General Giap, his victory in effect marking the end of nearly a century of French rule in Indochina. The very next day, at a previously scheduled international conference in Geneva, Switzerland, representatives of the major powers and of the Indochinese people met to discuss a cease fire agreement, which was subsequently approved on 20-21 July 1954.

The conferees recognized the independence of Vietnam, Cambodia, and Laos. They agreed that Vietnam would be temporarily divided at the 17th parallel pending nationwide elections to be held in July 1956 to unify the country. Under terms of separate agreements signed by the French and the Viet Minh, France agreed to withdraw her forces and presence over a period of several years. The Geneva Protocols prohibited the reinforcement of local military forces or reequipping them with improved armaments beyond what was in the country in mid-1954. The Protocols did not require the U.S. Military Assistance Advisory Group—then at an authorized strength of 342 men—to withdraw from South Vietnam. The Geneva agreement also established an International Control Commission (ICC) to supervise the various agreements.

At the 17th parallel, a demilitarized zone (DMZ) was created between the two Vietnams with people on both sides being allowed to resettle wherever they wished. Some 900,000 Vietnamese in the northern region chose to go south, over 300,000 of them being evacuate by U.S. Navy vessels.

More than 100,000 Viet Minh soldiers and civilians in the south went north, where some formed the military cadres that led the subsequent armed struggle in the south. Meanwhile, in Hanoi, Ho Chi Minh on 11 October 1954 once more proclaimed the establishment of the Democratic Republic of Vietnam. In Saigon the State of Vietnam, originally sponsored by the French, emerged under a new leader, Premier and later President Ngo Dinh Diem. He proclaimed his state a Republic and was immediately recognized by President Eisenhower.

In September 1954 the United States also sponsored creation of an eight-nation Southeast Asia Treaty Organization (SEATO), which threw a mantle of protection over Laos, Cambodia, and "the free territory under the jurisdiction of the State of Vietnam. . ." The Senate ratified the SEATO treaty on 1 February 1955. Meanwhile, the United States transferred its economic and military assistance from France to the new Saigon government and to Laos and Cambodia. President Eisenhower, who accepted the "domino theory" as expressed in NSC 64—i.e., that all of Southeast Asia would fall under Communist rule if Ho Chi Minh's government controlled all of Vietnam—decided to assist Saigon to expand its armed forces.

Thus, he approved Diem's plans to build an Army of the Republic of Vietnam (ARVN), consisting of 4 conventional infantry divisions, 6 light divisions, an airborne brigade-size combat team, 13 territorial regiments, support troops, and limited air and naval forces. The small Vietnamese Air Force (VNAF) was authorized 4,140 men and was equipped with obsolete, non-jet aircraft. It consisted of an F-8F fighter squadron, two C-47 squadrons, two L-19 (liaison) squadrons, and an H-19 helicopter unit. The MAAG took over training responsibility of most South Vietnamese forces after France relinquished command authority on

This Soviet Ilyushin transport was photographed dropping supplies to leftist rebels in Laos. President Kennedy told a Washington press conference the Russians had flown more than 1,000 sorties on behalf of the Pathet Lao.

12 February 1955. The French, however, continued to train the VNAF until May 1957.

In 1956, the year when national elections were to be held to unify the country, South Vietnam—which had not been a party to the French-Viet-Minh military agreement or the Geneva Accords and had strongly protested the election provision—decided to ignore the entire matter. Diem argued that the northerners would not be able to vote freely under Ho's one-party rule and that the bloc vote of the North would overwhelm those cast in the South. The fact was, however, that although a Communist, Ho Chi Minh was—as President Eisenhower once remarked—a legendary hero to the Vietnamese people and would probably have won any nationwide election. In any event, the election was not held and for several years the two Vietnams went their separate ways. But in May 1959 the Central Committee of the North Vietnamese Lao Dong (workers, i.e., Communist) Party—having firmly established control over the countryside by suppressing peasant resistance —called for reunifying the country through armed struggle.

Shortly thereafter, a North Vietnamese Army (NVA) transportation group began work on the Ho Chi Minh trail, the infiltration route through Laos to the South. The first of an initial 4,500-man military cadre—most ethnic southerners who had received training and indoctrination in the north—arrived in South Vietnam. These hardcore Viet Cong cadres were funnelled into Communist jungle base areas in Tay Ninh province on the Cambodian border (later designated by American officials as War Zone C), an area northwest of Saigon (War Zone D), and in the dense U Minh forest area of the Ca Mau peninsula.

Meanwhile, Viet Cong terrorism had steadily increased between mid-1957 and mid-1959, and several MAAG personnel fell victim. Thus, on 8 July 1959 a U.S. Army major and master sergeant were killed in a Viet Cong attack on Bien Hoa. Two months later, several Viet Cong companies ambushed a South Vietnamese army force searching for guerrillas in the marshy Plain of Reeds southwest of Saigon. According to the Viet Cong, this incident marked the official start of the armed struggle. Reacting to it, American officials in October 1959 recommended an increase of the strength of the MAAG from 342 men to 685 so as to provide for U.S. Army Special Forces teams to train ARVN rangers for border patrols. Despite Communist protests to the ICC, Washington on 5 May approved the recommendation. The Special Forces teams arrived in South Vietnam by the end of October.

The Eisenhower administration's primary interest at this time was to improve South Vietnam's counterinsurgency efforts. Not until several months later did it give serious attention to the Vietnamese Air Force, after its commander, Col. Nguyen Xuan Vinh, grounded all of his old F-8F fighters because they were unsafe for flight. The United States responded in September 1960 by shipping the first of 25 U.S. Navy AD-6 aircraft to Vietnam to replace the F-8F's. Later, Washington also agreed to provide the VNAF 11 H-34 helicopters. The first four arrived in Vietnam in December 1960, followed by the others over the subsequent 3 months. However, logistical actions to support the AD-6's and H-34's lagged and many of the aircraft soon were out of commission for lack of parts.

Meanwhile, MAAG and Pacific Command (PACOM) officials drew up a counterinsurgency plan which called for providing substantial U.S. aid to the South Vietnamese in dealing with insurgency. The draft plan, completed by the Commander in Chief, Pacific (CINCPAC) in April 1960, was approved by the Joint Chiefs of Staff (JCS). The latter proposed that South

USAF technicians served on temporary duty in Indochina to assist the French Air Force to maintain C-47 aircraft transferred to France.

Vietnam unify its military command, enlarge the army, and augment slightly (by 499 men) the Vietnamese Air Force.

Kennedy Administration Policies

Two weeks before John F. Kennedy was inaugurated as President in January 1961, Soviet Premier Nikita Khrushchev made a speech in Moscow to the Communist Party Congress which had a decisive influence on the new chief executive's view of events in Southeast Asia. Describing various kinds of wars which might occur in the future, Khrushchev announced that the Soviet Union would "wholeheartedly" support wars of national liberation, examples of which were, he said, "the armed struggle waged by the people of Vietnam and the present war of the Algerian people. . . ." Impressed by Khrushchev's speech, President Kennedy indorsed the counterinsurgency plan in principle and ordered his key assistants to undertake a major study of doctrine and force requirements to support it. Almost concurrently, Hanoi announced the establishment within South Vietnam of the National Front for the Liberation of Vietnam (NLF).

Kennedy had scarcely settled in office when he was faced with a series of crises centering on Southeast Asia, including a deteriorating situation in Laos, where the government was threatened by Communist Pathet Lao forces. In a press conference statement on 23 March 1961, the President told the American people that:

> Soviet planes, I regret to say, have been conspicuous in a large-scale airlift into the battle area—over. . . 1,000 sorties since last December 13th, plus a whole supporting set of combat specialists, mainly from Communist North Viet-Nam, and heavier weapons have been provided from outside, all with the clear object of destroying by military action the agreed neutrality of Laos. . .we strongly and unreservedly support the goal of a neutral and independent Laos, tied to no outside power or group of powers. . .

Within South Vietnam, similar forces continued to threaten the Diem government. Whereupon, in May 1961 Mr. Kennedy dispatched Vice President Lyndon B. Johnson to South Vietnam to consult with Diem. Subsequently, President Kennedy agreed to increase U.S. military assistance to South Vietnam. It included, in the case of the Air Force, the dispatch of a mobile control and reporting post (CRP) from the United States to Tan Son Nhut Air Base (AB) outside Sai-

Ho Chi Minh visited Moscow on the 44th anniversary of the birth of the Soviet state, 7 November 1961. Among the Communist leaders present were (l. to r.) Blas Roca of Cuba; Ho; Soviet Premier Nikita Khrushchev; Janos Kadar of Hungary; Soviet President Leonid Brezhnev; Deputy Premier Frel Koslov; Presidium member Mikhail Suslov; and First Deputy Premier Anastas Mikoyan.

gon. A detachment of the 507th Tactical Control Group departed Shaw AFB, S.C., on 26 September 1961. By 5 October the control and reporting post was operational and began providing radar control and warning in the Saigon area while also serving as a facility in which to train VNAF radar technicians.

In 1961, the President also approved "in principle" a 30,000-man increase in South Vietnam's armed forces. The Vietnamese Air Force was authorized its second fighter squadron, a third liaison squadron, and a photo reconnaissance unit. Secretary of Defense Robert S. McNamara directed that the Vietnamese be provided armed T-28 trainer aircraft for the fighter squadron. The U.S. ambassador in Saigon, Frederick E. Nolting, Jr., rejected a separate Air Force proposal to equip the VNAF reconnaissance unit with four RT/T-33 jets, citing the prohibition on jet aircraft in the Geneva Protocols. The third liaison squadron was equipped with L-19's, transferred from the VNAF training center at Nha Trang.

President Kennedy also approved the establishment of a U.S. South Vietnamese combat development and test center in Vietnam, under the direction of the Defense Department's Advanced Research Projects Agency, for the purpose of learning and improving counterinsurgency techniques and tactics. Among the ideas listed for examination was the use of aerial-delivered defoliants to reduce jungle cover along major highways, where Viet Cong units frequently ambushed government troops. That such a project was needed became apparent to two U.S. Congressmen who visited South Vietnam in late 1961 for a firsthand look at the war. Rep. William E. Minshall later reported that 15 miles outside of Saigon the situation remained "very tenuous. . .very strained. The roads are being cut every night. There are road blocks set up every night and you can hear mortar fire every night."

Gen Curtis E. LeMay, Air Force Chief of Staff, responded to the President's interest in having the armed forces prepared to fight guerrilla wars by establishing the 4400th Combat Crew Training Squadron (Jungle Jim) at Eglin AFB, Fla, on 14 April 1961. It quickly attracted highly motivated airmen who were rapidly qualified to conduct sub rosa air commando operations. On 11 October the President authorized deployment of a Jungle Jim detachment to South Vietnam for training purposes. After Saigon approved, Detachment 2A, 4400th Combat Crew Training Squadron—desig-

11

nated Farm Gate—departed the United States for Bien Hoa, South Vietnam. Farm Gate included 151 officers and men and 8 T-28's, 4 SC-47's and 4 RB-26's. The T-28's and SC-47's arrived at Bien Hoa on 4 November 1961; the RB-26's reached Vietnam some time after 18 December 1961. All aircraft carried Vietnamese Air Force markings.

Meanwhile, in the fall of 1961, Communist Pathet Lao forces accelerated their operations against the Royal Government of Laos. At the same time several Viet Cong units of up to 1,500 men began cutting strategic highways in the vicinity of Saigon and other urban areas. This notable rise of insurgent activities led President Diem to proclaim a state of emergency. Surprised by this outburst of Communist activities, USAF advisors asked for the deployment of a detachment of four RF-101's to Tan Son Nhut to conduct reconnaissance missions over Vietnam and Laos. An invitation from the South Vietnamese for the U.S. Air Force to take part in an air show in October 1961 provided the occasion to send these jets into the area. Between 20 October and 21 November, these aircraft flew 67 sorties. Early in November, four RF-101's of the 45th Tactical Reconnaissance Squadron based in Japan were deployed to Don Muang Airport, Thailand, to augment and then replace the Tan Son Nhut-based detachment. By the end of 1961, the 45th had flown some 130 missions.

President Kennedy—concerned about a lack of confidence in Saigon resulting from the recent Viet Cong successes—on 13 November 1961 approved recommendations made by Gen. Maxwell D. Taylor and Dr. Walt W. Rostow, his national security advisor, both recently returned from a visit to South Vietnam. To increase Vietnamese military mobility, the President authorized deployment of three U.S. Army H-21 helicopter companies (40

aircraft), a USAF squadron of 16 C-123 assault transport planes (code name Mule Train), and the loan to the VNAF of 30 T-28 aircraft. On 30 November the President permitted an aerial spray flight of six C-123's (Ranch Hand)—which had arrived at Clark AB in the Philippines— to continue on to Vietnam to undertake "carefully controlled" defoliation operations. Most of the USAF units were in place in South Vietnam by year's end. They came under the command of Brig. Gen. Rollen H. Anthis, who landed at Tan Son Nhut on 20 November to assume command of four numbered detachments, three located in South

USAF spray missions to defoliate jungle vegetation, to eliminate ambush sites, generated much controversy during the war.

12

(Above) Dr. James W. Brown (2nd from left), a civilian expert assigned to the Pentagon, directed the initial defoliation tests in South Vietnam.

Forward Air Controller (FAC) in a L-19 and two VNAF AD-6's flew overhead. The operation resulted in 2 Viet Cong killed, 1 wounded, and 46 suspects captured. The Viet Cong radio transmitter went off the air and was not located.

The U.S. military units dispatched to South Vietnam—initially viewed by President Kennedy as serving in a combat "training" role—were authorized to "fire back if fired upon." A major prohibition on their operations was to avoid injuring or killing noncombatants. As a consequence, although Air Force reconnaissance planes discovered many Viet Cong targets and President Diem urged vigorous air action against them, USAF pilots did not attack because of concern over possible harm to Vietnamese civilians. In December 1961 Secretary McNamara authorized, and the JCS directed Gen. Emmett O'Donnell, Commander in Chief, Pacific Air Forces (CINCPACAF), to deploy a tactical air control system (TACS) to South Vietnam to provide "cooperative" use of VNAF and USAF strike, reconnaissance, and transport capabilities.

On 26 December 1961 Washington issued a new directive prohibiting Farm Gate aircraft from engaging in combat operations over South Vietnam except when a Vietnamese crewman was aboard or when the VNAF lacked the ability to perform certain missions. In the months and years that followed, those simple rules of engagement grew into many pages of detailed operating instructions telling Air Force pilots what they could or could not do in combat. The President and his chief advisors through much of the war retained tight controls over aerial operations in Southeast Asia. Their reasons were clear—to avoid the military intervention of Communist China, as had occurred during the Korean War, or that of the Soviet Union.

Vietnam, and one in Thailand. His initial organization was designated as 2nd ADVON.

During the waning days of 1961, the first combined U.S.-South Vietnamese air mobile operation was launched against the Viet Cong's War Zone D headquarters northeast of Saigon. Its purpose was to locate and capture a clandestine Viet Cong radio transmitter. Two newly arrived U.S. Army helicopter companies lifted 360 Vietnamese airborne troops to five landing zones in the area on 23 December. Additional troops were brought in on the 27th. During the critical phases of these helicopter lifts, a Vietnamese

II Air Operations in South Vietnam

1962–1964

In January 1962 the Farm Gate detachment began training 25 VNAF pilots to fly T-28's of the newly organized 2d Fighter Squadron. It set up several classes for the Vietnamese and taught them methods of day and night bombing, rocketry, and gunnery. Other USAF personnel instructed Vietnamese ground crews T-28 maintenance and supply procedures. By March 1962 all 25 pilots had been checked out in formation flying, tactics, and instruments, and shortly after, the squadron was declared operational. The Americans found that the VNAF airmen were excellent pilots, although few had night flying experience. One reason for this was that some of the U.S. aircraft provided under the Military Assistance Program —particularly the 1st VNAF Fighter Squadron's obsolete AD-6's—lacked landing lights or serviceable artificial horizon instruments.

Because the Viet Cong became active mostly after dark, the Americans emphasized the importance of night operations. Thus, shortly after their arrival in South Vietnam, the Farm Gate crews began experimenting with aerial flares, dropped from an SC-47, to light up a target for night strikes by the Vietnamese Air Force. The technique worked well and was quickly adopted by VNAF airmen, who began flying their own flare missions on 5 February 1962. The success of the flare-and-strike technique—the Viet Cong would break off their attacks when the flares ignited—led Secretary McNamara to direct that Vietnamese

villages be equipped with radios to facilitate calls for air support. By June 1962 more than 520 radios had been distributed.

In the early weeks of 1962 USAF crews also began test defoliation flights along the highway between Bien Hoa and Vung Tau in an effort to destroy the heavy jungle vegetation, perfect cover for enemy troops. These operations stirred the Viet Cong into denunciations of the United States for resorting to "chemical warfare." As it turned out, the initial defoliation spray was dispensed too thinly and the vegetation was unaffected. On 2 February, during one of these spray flights, a C-123 crashed, killing the crew of three. It was the first Air Force plane lost in South Vietnam.

Nine days later a second USAF aircraft—an SC-47—also crashed while flying a psychological warfare leaflet dispensing mission near Dalat. Six Air Force personnel, two U.S. Army men, and one Vietnamese airman died. In subsequently criticizing the operation, Secretary McNamara reemphasized that U.S. forces were supposed to be training the Vietnamese and not engaging in combat activities.

Early in 1962 the Air Force also began to assist the Vietnamese in setting up a Tactical Air Control System (TACS). It initially relied upon USAF radars at Tan Son Nhut and Da Nang and a Vietnamese-operated radar at Pleiku. This radar network, which provided limited aircraft control and warning coverage over all of South Vietnam, soon began picking up

T-28's over South Vietnam.

15

tracks of numerous unidentified aircraft. Some of these later proved to be U.S. Army helicopters or light planes, which had arrived in South Vietnam beginning in late 1961. Ironically, the TACS was first tested operationally on 27 February when two disaffected VNAF pilots strafed and bombed the presidential palace in Saigon. One plane was shot down and the other escaped to Cambodia.

The system was next exercised during the night of 19 and 20 March 1962 when unidentified low-flying aircraft were detected over the Central Highlands. Concerned about them, Diem requested—and Ambassador Nolting quickly arranged—the deployment of USAF jet interceptors from Clark to Tan Son Nhut. On 22 March four F-102's began flying missions over South Vietnam. After flying 21 sorties, they were relieved a week later by U.S. Navy interceptors on a rotational basis. USAF and Navy crews failed to find any enemy aircraft.

Subsequently, the Tactical Air Control System was refined and expanded to provide the communication network which enabled the Seventh Air Force commander to exercise centralized control over his forces and to monitor the air/ground situation. Within this system, the Tactical Air Control Center (TACC) at Tan Son Nhut allowed the air commander to plan and coordinate the diverse operations of his tactical forces within the four nations of Indochina. A number of Control and Reporting Centers came directly under the Center and supervised activities of subordinate radar elements known as Control and Reporting Posts.

While work on the Tactical Air Control System proceeded, USAF advisors were encouraging VNAF airmen to attack Viet Cong jungle sanctuaries in an effort to keep the insurgents off balance. In this regard, in 1962 Adm. Harry D. Felt, Commander in Chief, Pacific, proposed that Saigon's

ground forces undertake offensive operations to root out the enemy from those areas and pacify the countryside. A pacification program was subsequently drawn up, based on a proposal made by Robert G.K. Thompson, head of the British Advisory Mission in Saigon (1961-1965). Drawing upon Britain's experiences with Chinese terrorists in Malaya in 1948-1959, Thompson recommended the South Vietnamese undertake a strategic hamlet program. The idea was to build fortified hamlets in relatively safe "white" areas. From there ARVN troops would move farther and farther into Viet Cong "red" areas—"like a spreading oil spot"—thus presumably driving the insurgents out of the country entirely.

On 16 March 1962, in a much publicized start of the strategic hamlet program, the ARVN 5th Division launched Operation Sunrise. It began with a motorized deployment of ARVN troops to the southern fringes of the Viet Cong's Zone D sanctuary in Binh Duong province. Once there, the soldiers moved out to uproot Vietnamese peasants—believed to be supplying the insurgents with food—to relocate elsewhere in fortified hamlets they were compelled to build. Following the success of this initial operation, President Diem ordered a rapid expansion of the strategic hamlet program.

Meanwhile, U.S. Army advisors were working to develop ARVN airborne helicopter assault tactics, using equipment of two U.S. Army companies which had arrived in Vietnam in late 1961. Almost at once a problem arose over fixed-wing/air-ground coordination. According to directives issued by the newly organized U.S. Military Assistance Command, Vietnam (USMACV),* all helicopter operations into areas where enemy opposi-

---

*Established on 8 February 1962 with Gen. Paul D. Harkins, U.S. Army, as commander.

tion was expected were required to have fixed-wing tactical air cover. U.S. Army corps advisors who controlled helicopter usage, however, tended to ignore the requirement.

In April 1962, during a visit to South Vietnam, General LeMay learned that Army advisors were not calling for fixed-wing air support, that only about 10 percent of ARVN heliborne operations were accompanied by VNAF aircraft, and that the Air Support Operations Center and Joint Operations Center at Tan Son Nhut frequently were not informed about such operations. Concerned about this situation, LeMay subsequently obtained permission to assign air liaison officers (ALO's) to all ARVN corps and division headquarters and USAF forward air controllers to augment VNAF liaison squadrons. Moreover, soon after the Viet Cong succeeded in shooting down four Army H-21 helicopters, Admiral Felt directed General Harkins to make maximum use of the fixed-wing aircraft during offensive operations. This produced an immediate increase in the number of ARVN calls for fighter cover. For example, whereas during the first 5 months of 1962 only 81 fighter flights supported helicopter assault operations, during July alone there were 139 sorties. Between 1 May and 12 August 1962, approximately 40 percent of all ARVN operations employed fixed-wing air support.

Meanwhile, the Viet Cong continued to exploit the jungle environment with great skill to interdict South Vietnamese road and rail traffic. On 16 June two enemy battalions ambushed an ARVN convoy south of Ben Cat, killing 23 Vietnamese soldiers and 2 U.S. Army advisors. Following this incident and a rash of lesser ones, General Anthis recommended—and General Harkins approved—the mandatory use of air cover over all Vietnamese road and train convoys. The Vietnamese Joint General Staff issued the necessary directive. There followed a com-

plete turnaround in the number of enemy ambushes. During the first 8 months of 1962, the Viet Cong ambushed convoys on 462 occasions; thereafter, for more than a year, no air-escorted convoy was hit.

On 23 July Secretary McNamara—mindful of President Kennedy's policy that the major task of U.S. advisors was to prepare Republic of Vietnam Armed Forces (RVNAF) for combat—ordered an increase in the training of their troops and delivery of additional equipment so as to phase out U.S. combat, advisory, and logistic support activities. At the same time, he honored General Harkins' request for two more U.S. Army helicopter companies to support the ARVN's expanding ground operations. Harkins and McNamara initially delayed acting on a request from General Anthis to augment Farm Gate with 5 T-28's, 10 B-26's, and 2 C-47's to enable him to meet the support requirements. The delay resulted from the fact that the request had not been presented to the JCS and was contrary to the President's policy. It was not until November 1962 that CINCPAC recommended the measure to the Joint Chiefs, who spent another month studying the proposal before recommending it to the Defense Secretary. Not until the proposal was cleared by the State Department 2 weeks later did McNamara recommend the President's approval. Another 11 days elapsed before the White House gave the "go-ahead."

Aerial reconnaissance was another area where the Air Force could not keep pace with expanding combat operations (see also Chapter XII). In 1962 the Vietnamese Air Force possessed two camera-equipped C-45's to conduct photo reconnaissance flights; at the same time, its visual reconnaissance activities had been reduced following transfer of L-19 pilots to fighter cockpits. The few RF-101's at Don Muang were heavily involved in meeting intelligence requirements in both Vietnam and Laos. All combat film was processed in Saigon or at an Air Force laboratory at Don Muang. However, the time between receipt of a request for aerial photos and their delivery proved much too lengthy in a situation involving fast-moving, elusive guerrilla troops who could hide in jungle growth.

To correct this situation Harkins proposed—and Admiral Felt authorized—equipping the VNAF with a tactical reconnaissance squadron composed of 4 RT 33's, 3 RC-47's, 18 RT-28's and several field processing centers. McNamara eliminated the RT-33 jet aircraft and approved the squadron. In September the VNAF activated the 716th Reconnaissance Squadron at Tan Son Nhut with two RC-45's while awaiting delivery of the other equipment. Meanwhile, Farm Gate crews obtained two RB-26's to meet the growing needs for reconnaissance photography.

In early 1962 the Joint Operations Center Airlift Branch—manned by Air Force personnel—prepared daily schedules for the C-123's. Inadequate aerial port and mission control facilities caused serious inefficiencies, however. To overcome these problems, MACV in September organized a theater-level managerial apparatus known as the Southeast Asia Airlift System (SEAAS). It consisted of C-123 units, aerial ports, and countrywide control detachments, which operated in support of MACV J-4 workload allocations. Meanwhile, a second C-123 squadron arrived in South Vietnam to beef up the airlift system. In April 1962, to stretch the scant aircrew resources of the VNAF, 30 USAF pilots (who became known as the Dirty Thirty) were detailed to serve with the Vietnamese C-47 squadrons, allowing transfer of some Vietnamese pilots to T-28 units (see also Chapter IX).

Meanwhile, after several U.S. Army light transport aircraft were lost to enemy fire in Vietnam, General Harkins recommended deployment of the Army's Hu-1A (Huey) helicopter gunships to provide local fire support for air mobile operations. The Joint Chiefs of Staff recommended and Secretary McNamara approved the additional deployment in order to test under field conditions the concept of armed helicopters. In September, 15 Huey gunships arrived in South Vietnam. They were joined later by six OV-1 Mohawk turboprop observation aircraft, equipped with .50 caliber machineguns as well as cameras.

The National Campaign Plan

During the late summer and fall of 1962, General Harkins' staff drafted a National Campaign Plan (NCP) designed to defeat the Viet Cong. Under this plan the Vietnamese armed forces would be reorganized preparatory to launching a three-phased military operation. Initially, their mission was to drive the enemy back into his base sanctuaries inside South Vietnam. This done, the Vietnamese would launch a general offensive or "explosion" of all their forces in all corners of the country to destroy the enemy. Finally, it would be followed by a consolidation phase during which Saigon's authority would be extended throughout the Republic. Harkins proposed the general ARVN offensive begin in early 1963, after the Buddhist Tet holiday; he thought it could produce a military victory by year's end.

On 8 October 1962 he briefed Secretary McNamara on the plan and secured his approval to submit it to the South Vietnamese. President Diem endorsed the concept and on 26 November issued orders to reorganize the Vietnamese armed forces. Vietnamese Army, Navy, Air Force and Special Forces commands were subsequently activated as major operational components serving under a

Joint General Staff (JGS). Beyond the Capital Military District, the country was divided into four corps tactical zones (CTZ's). A new Joint Operations Center, set up to serve the Vietnamese General Staff, impacted upon the existing VNAF-USAF Joint Operations Center. The latter, twice redesignated, eventually emerged as the Air Operations Center (AOC).

Meanwhile, Admiral Felt and General Anthis alerted Harkins to the fact that there was a serious shortage of fixed-wing aircraft to support the nationwide offensive and reminded him of long-pending Air Force requests to strengthen Farm Gate units. Whereupon, on 7 November 1962, Harkins authorized an increase of 5 T-28's, 10 B-26's, and 2 C-47's. There was a delay in receiving approval from Washington, and it was not until 31 December 1962 that President Kennedy authorized the increase in the number of USAF aircraft in South Vietnam.

Although the additional aircraft arrived at South Vietnam in January 1963, General Anthis was worried about the national campaign plan. He thought it would place demands upon the Vietnamese Air Force far beyond its capability, especially since its scheduled expansion and training would be taking place during the "explosion" phase of the plan. Citing the sizable gap between expected requirements and available air assets, he asked for the interim deployment of one USAF T-28 squadron, one B-26 squadron, two RF-101 reconnaissance aircraft (bringing the total to six), and two RB-26's for local photographic services at Da Nang and Pleiku. General Harkins' headquarters, then completing detailed studies on several parts of the three-pronged NCP, did not immediately respond.

A highly relevant aspect of the campaign involved the movement of essential supplies to support it. MACV proposed using U.S. Navy ships to de-liver supplies to five other major port centers in South Vietnam. From there USAF C-123's would airlift the cargo to airfields in the four corps tactical zones, from where U.S. Army aircraft would deliver the war materiel to frontline units. To support this plan, Harkins requested deployment of two more C-123 squadrons and one CV-2 Caribou unit to join one recently deployed to the theater.

While the buildup of offensive forces got underway, the South Vietnamese launched a series of ground-air operations in support of the strategic hamlet program. In October U.S. Army Huey gunships began working with the ARVN 21st Division in the Ca Mau peninsula. Elsewhere, northeast of Saigon, C-123's and C-47's on 20 November dropped 500 ARVN paratroopers into the eastern fringes of the Viet Cong's Zone D sanctuary. From this base of operations, Vietnamese rangers on 19 December launched a nighttime drive through the jungle accompanied by B-26's and T-28's overhead. U.S. Army advisors reported general-purpose and napalm bombs dropped by these aircraft had penetrated the jungle cover with good effects.

Elsewhere, an ARVN heliborne operation was launched just before Christmas Day 1962 near Tuy Hoa in the II Corps Tactical Zone. Twenty-nine U.S. Army H-21's were committed to the operation without fixed-wing air support. The first three helicopters safely landed the Vietnamese troops, but six others were suddenly hit by hidden Viet Cong automatic weapons, which inflicted a number of casualties. A U.S. Army company commander told the famous war correspondent, Richard Tregaskis, the casualties were caused by the fact that "there had been no softening-up" attack at the landing zone (LZ) before the helicopters went in.

No such error was made on the morning of 2 January 1963 when the

JGS committed the entire VNAF-USAF force at Bien Hoa to Operation Burning Arrow, a maximum hour-long air strike against pinpoint enemy targets in the Tay Ninh area. The preliminary fixed-wing bombardment apparently surprised the enemy and was followed by air drops and a landing of helicopters carrying paratroopers and rangers who seized their objectives against very light resistance. Subsequent intelligence received from Communist safe havens in Cambodia revealed that a number of NLF leaders had been killed and wounded.

Unfortunately, within hours of this success the ARVN 7th Division suffered a major defeat in an operation to seize a Viet Cong radio transmitter near the village of Ap Bac, approximately 15 miles northwest of My Tho. The division commander believed a Viet Cong company was encamped at Ap Bac. His plan called for heliborne troops to land in an arc north and west of Ap Bac and then sweep south to meet an armored M-113 amphibious vehicle company moving to the north.

Although informed that no tactical air support was available (all strike aircraft having been committed to the Tay Ninh operation), U.S. Army officials agreed to use Huey gunships for cover, escort, and fire support. Unknown to the division commander and his senior U.S. Army advisor, Lt. Col. John P. Vann, a well-armed Viet Cong battalion—equipped with several heavy machine guns and automatic rifles—was dug in under tree lines adjacent to the planned helicopter landing zones. As the heliborne force went in, it came under heavy fire which the Huey gunships were unable to suppress. Five helicopters were destroyed and nine others damaged.

At mid-morning, the Air Operations Center received emergency calls for help and diverted two AD-6's to the scene. Unfortunately, friendly artillery firing through the air space forced the AD-6's to hold up their attack against plainly visible enemy positions. A B-26 replacing them arrived after the artillery stopped firing and dropped napalm; two additional AD-6's and six T-28's also provided air support. Later, another B-26 and two AD-6's were dispatched. The B-26, although striking with accuracy, was finally forced away by artillery fire. To add to the general confusion, Vietnamese FAC's were unable to direct air strikes with any accuracy. The enemy's fire continued to range freely over the rice paddies, inflicting telling losses on crews of the armored personnel carriers. In the late afternoon, six C-123's arrived overhead with three companies of ARVN paratroop reinforcements but the IV Corps commander, Brig. Gen. Huyn Van Cao, ordered them dropped west of Ap Bac even though the Viet Cong were withdrawing to the east. During the night the enemy escaped, while confused ARVN troops engaged each other in firefights.

Friendly casualties at Ap Bac included 65 Vietnamese troops and 3 U.S. advisors killed and 100 Vietnamese and 6 U.S. advisors wounded. According to the Viet Cong, this victory was a major turning point in their war effort. It rejuvenated their flagging morale and taught them tactics which were described in a new slogan, "wipe-out-enemy-posts-and-annihilate-enemy-reinforcements." Highly critical American press coverage of the battle for Ap Bac left President Diem festering with bitterness.

During a visit to Saigon several days later, Admiral Felt strongly criticized MACV for having allowed the Ap Bac operation to proceed without fixed-wing air support. He asked the Vietnamese JGS to require the mandatory employment of tactical air units in all future heliborne operations. Subsequently, when briefed on the extent of air cover required to support the National Campaign Plan, Felt bluntly labeled the plan infeasible and called for its revision. He urged sup-

Battle of AP Bac
Jan 1963

port of General Anthis' earlier request for two liaison squadrons but only one of two C-123 squadrons, and also acknowledged the Air Force's need for two additional RF-101's and two RB-26's. He also recommended to Washington that Farm Gate strength be increased to permit the Air Force to fly more sorties with existing aircraft. Shortly afterwards, the Air Force was directed to double Farm Gate's strength. Admiral Felt also indorsed Harkins' request to bring in a second Caribou squadron, plus 8 U-1A liaison aircraft, and 10 UH-1B's for use by U.S. Army senior corps advisors.

In Washington, however, senior officials still hoped to limit U.S. military involvement. On 25 March 1962 McNamara decided to send the C-123 squadron recommended by Felt but only one USAF liaison squadron and one U.S. Army O-1A squadron. He directed that they be operated no more than 1 year, after which they were to be turned over to the Vietnamese. Subsequently, the Air Force deployed an additional C-123 squadron to Da Nang, where it arrived on 17 April. The Army Caribou company reached Vung Tau in July. O-1 assets of another

Army company were divided among U.S. Army senior corps advisors. On 8 July 1963 the Air Force activated the 19th Tactical Air Support Squadron at Bien Hoa; it became fully operational in mid-September.

Meanwhile, General Anthis had readied an air strike team of B-26's at Pleiku and a similar T-28 strike unit at Soc Trang to support the impending ARVN ground operations in the II and IV Corps areas. The Pleiku airstrip had been upgraded but the improved 3,200-foot Soc Trang runway could accommodate only the T-28's. Even these planes had difficulty landing at Soc Trang at night or when rain slicked the short runway. Under these conditions, the T-28's could take off but were unable to land safely and normally would head for Tan Son Nhut. In addition to the Farm Gate units, the VNAF maintained an A-1H detachment at Pleiku and also operated eight T-28's at Da Nang in support of I Corps operations.

On 22 February 1963 the Vietnamese JGS issued a general offensive plan, closely patterned after MACV's suggested national campaign plan. It called for corps commanders to begin initial operations against the Viet Cong by mid-March 1963, to be followed by a general offensive on a date to be announced by the Joint General Staff. The freedom accorded the corps commanders, however, resulted mostly in uncoordinated operations. For example, air liaison officers in I Corps reported that the ARVN 1st and 2d Divisions in the north—content to control the coastal plains—followed a live-and-let-live policy with the enemy forces in the mountains to the west. The corps commander kept tight control on air strikes in his area, requiring prior authorization from himself or his chief of staff. Unfortunately, there were times when the operations center received requests for emergency air support but the two officers could not be located.

(1) A1C Norman L. Morgan inspects AC-47 miniguns. (2) The first AC-47 gunship and its crew. (3) Gunship interior. (4) F-100 releases its ordnance on a bombing mission over South Vietnam. (5) An Air Force bomber unloads a phosphorus bomb on enemy forces dug in along a river bank in South Vietnam. (6) Maj. Robert P. Knopf, a gunship commander, relaxes between missions. (7) Gunship at Nha Trang Air Base, South Vietnam. (8) SSgt Allen D. Niehaus loads ammunition into a minigun. (9) USAF O-1E pilots on a FAC mission. (10) side-firing mini-guns.

1

2

3

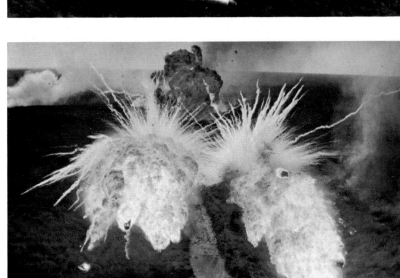

In the II Corps area, the ARVN 22d Division—which had deprived the Viet Cong of food sources by resettling many of the Montagnard tribesmen—policed the Central Highlands. Elsewhere, along the coast the 9th Division undertook clear-and-hold operations in Binh Dinh and Phu Yen provinces. The 25th, which became operational in January 1963, undertook to pacify guerrilla-ridden coastal province of Quang Ngai. Both the 9th and 25th asked for deployment of air strike teams at Qui Nhon and Quang Ngai City, but the limited resources made this impossible . Instead, VNAF T-28's and FAC's were sent to nearby airfields whenever ground operations were planned.

Unfortunately, even when given advance notice of up to 48 hours, Nha Trang-based T-28's were seldom able to react on time. During a month-long campaign launched by some 10,000 Vietnamese Army and Marine troops on 24 April 1963 against the Do-Xa mountain redoubt, the VNAF moved a forward echelon of the Air Operations Center to Plateau Gi and launched a heavy 3-day preliminary bombardment of enemy strongpoints. The combined ground-air assaults enabled Vietnamese troops to overrun the Do-Xa area. Elsewhere, Viet Cong troops, taking advantage of the 25th Division's preoccupation at Do-Xa, attacked Quang Ngai hamlets. However, provincial defense units inflicted heavy casualties on them and drove them off.

In II Corps, pacification appeared to be a complete success, with the Communists clearly thrown on the defensive by mid-year. At this point, General Harkins recommended—and the JGS approved—redeploying the ARVN 9th Division southward to the Mekong Delta, where the enemy had maintained a strong presence for many years. However, the Viet Cong's decline in II Corps proved transitory. During the last half of 1963, South Vietnamese military effectiveness declined—apparently due to the government's disarray during the Buddhist crisis (see discussion below)—the Viet Cong returned to their Do-Xa mountain stronghold.

In the III and IV Corps, the Communists continued to dominate large parts of the countryside despite ARVN efforts. Factors inhibiting successful air operations there included inadequate air-ground communications and a shortage of VNAF forward air controllers. In Tay Ninh province bordering Cambodia, the ARVN 5th Division came to rely more and more on U.S. Army helicopter gunships to provide local air support, primarily because it could not get in touch with the air operations center. When fixed-wing air support was finally provided, ARVN forces were able to penetrate into Zone D and the enemy's headquarters plus several camps along the Ma Da river. This success, however, also proved to be transitory. The Viet Cong later returned to their burned-out Zone D headquarters, dug deeper into the earth, and built stronger log-covered bunkers which enabled them to survive all but direct air strikes.

In the IV Corps area, the battered ARVN 7th Division—still recovering from its Ap Bac defeat—showed little initiative against the enemy, even though it had good intelligence on Viet Cong activity. Captured documents disclosed that the enemy was moving rice from the Delta through the 7th Division's area to feed his troops in Zones C and D. To stop these shipments, Col. Winston P. Anderson, the 2d Air Division's Director of Operations, in March 1963 obtained MACV and JGS authorization to undertake quick reaction air surveillance and strikes in the 7th Division area, using ARVN personnel as forward air guides to mark targets. However, VNAF officials refused to accept targets marked by ARVN troops, rather than by forward air controllers.

In the lower regions of the Delta, the ARVN 21st Division frequently called upon five USAF T-28's at Soc Trang to provide air cover and support for helicopter operations, often launched on the spur of the moment against relatively well armed Viet Cong. However, both T-28's and B-26's were too vulnerable to enemy ground fire. In February 1963, after two B-26's were shot down, Lt. Col. Miles M. Doyle, the Farm Gate detachment commander, requested additional aircraft for his unit. But General Anthis did not have the aircraft to give him. Indeed, in March 1963 the Air Force was able to honor only about 60 percent of the requests from Delta-based units for immediate air support.

Effects of the 1963 Buddhist Troubles

During the spring of 1963 there was a notable cooling of American-South Vietnamese relations against the background of growing Buddhist opposition to President Diem. The problem surfaced in May 1963 when the Buddhists—disaffected by Diem's policies—organized street demonstrations in the ancient capital of Hue. When civil guard troops fired upon them, a riot ensued. During the next 2 months the unrest spread to Saigon, which witnessed the self-immolation of a Buddhist priest in the heart of the capital. This incident shook the government—as well as television audiences around the world—and brought down upon Diem's head a torrent of international criticism. As the political situation deteriorated, so did the morale of the Vietnamese armed forces and their effectiveness in the field.

Viet Cong troops cross an improvised foot bridge in South Vietnam.

While the Buddhist crisis continued to dominate the headlines, the Viet Cong increased their attacks against the strategic hamlets during June and July 1963. Their tactics were shrewd and effective. If a probing showed South Vietnamese defenses were "soft"—as in the Ban Me Thuot area—the Viet Cong launched sudden night attacks which were successful. Where hamlets were well-defended, as in I Corps in Quang Ngai province, the enemy sent in infiltration teams to urge the people to join "the struggle of the Buddhists." The effects of the crisis were soon reflected in the decline of VNAF-USAF tactical sorties during the last half of 1963.

Thus, VNAF flights fell from a high of 1,013 sorties flown in May to 736 in September and 831 in October. As for the Farm Gate detachment—succeeded in the summer of 1963 by the 1st Air Commando Squadron—it had planned to double its combat sorties. However, its intentions were thwarted by aircraft losses to enemy fire and declining aircraft serviceability. The latter situation was highlighted on 16 August when a wing broke off a B-26 and its crew died in the crash. By 11 October the squadron was down to 9 T-28's and 12 B-26's, with the latter under flight restrictions to avoid undue wing stress.

After mid-1963, calls by embattled Vietnamese outposts for air support increased noticeably. In June the Air Force flew 70 flare and 40 strike sorties, in July 75/52, and in August 79/62. C-47 pilots were swamped with many other unanswered calls for help. In September the 2d Air Division placed some C-123's on flare duty and managed to provide 172 flare/132 strike sorties. During this period no outpost or hamlet assisted by a flare-and-strike team was ever overrun; others went under because of lack of such support or because their calls for help were never received by the Air Operations Center.

During the period May through August 1963, the VNAF-USAF force was unable to fill 534 preplanned air support requests from III Corps alone—167 for lack of aircraft and 244 for lack of VNAF forward air controllers. It was not suprising that III

25

Corps ARVN commanders gave up and turned to the more readily available U.S. Army gunships.

The gravest situation was in the southernmost regions of the Delta, where during the late summer of 1963 the Viet Cong launched open field warfare with well-armed, highly motivated battalion-sized forces. On the night of 10 September enemy mortar squads laid down a barrage on the Soc Trang airstrip while other troops attacked two district towns some 70 miles to the southwest. During the Soc Trang attack, four American pilots managed to get airborne in two T-28's and helped beat off the enemy. These USAF airmen later received commendations for their initiative and a reprimand for engaging in combat without the required VNAF crewmen aboard. After 4 days of continuous fighting, heliborne Vietnamese marines defeated the enemy around the two district towns, helped by paratroopers dropped from C-47 and C-123 aircraft. The towns, however, were reduced to rubble. During the fight a Viet Cong .50-caliber machinegun downed an Air Force T-28.

On 19 October the ARVN 21st Division was ambushed near Loc Ninh in Chuong Thien province. Responding to this emergency, the Air Operations Center committed two A-1H's, one B-26, and five T-28's—the only aircraft available--to cover Army helicopters sent to the scene. All aircraft expended their munitions by mid-morning in a futile attempt to silence enemy guns, which downed one helicopter. Other aircraft from Bien Hoa and several T-28's managed 31 more sorties before the day's end. The Viet Cong, however, held their positions, withdrawing after dark. Friendly losses were 41 personnel killed and 84 wounded ((including 12 Americans). In addition to the downed helicopter, enemy fire damaged two B-26's and six T-28's. The Viet Cong hailed Loc Ninh as another victory equal to that at Ap Bac 10

1

2

months before.

In late September Secretary McNamara and General Taylor, Chairman of the JCS, visited South Vietnam. McNamara urged Diem to deploy additional troops to the Delta and to slow construction of strategic hamlets until existing ones could be protected. While in Saigon he also reviewed the Southeast Asia airlift system which-- under the management of Col. Thomas B. Kennedy, a veteran airlift commander--had met all requirements with capacity to spare. Since logistic requirements had never reached MACV's estimate of 34,000 tons a month to support the general offensive, McNamara ordered the return to

(1) An A-1E *Skyraider* attacks enemy supply areas.
(2) An A-1E assigned to the 602nd Air Commando Squadron.

(1) B-57 Canberra tactical bombers on a mission over the Mekong Delta. (2) The last VNAF graduating class trained to fly the A-1E by USAF crewmen.

tember 1963 the President commented publicly that the Saigon government had "gotten out of touch with the people" but that there was still time for it to regain their support through policy and personnel changes. By this time, however, dissident Vietnamese officers under the leadership of Gen. Duong Van Minh had begun to plan a military coup to overthrow Diem.

Departure of the ARVN 9th Division to the Delta and the relocation of the IV Corps Tactical Zone south of the Mekong, effective 1 November, insured the success of the coup. These actions upset the delicate balance of military forces maintaining Diem in power. On 1 November 1963 the coup leaders launched their revolt. To forestall intervention by the Vietnamese Air Force, they seized its commander. His deputy sided with the rebels and sent four A-1H's and two T-28's against the presidential compound in Saigon. A move by loyal Diem troops to Saigon was deterred by the threat of air attack. On 2 November Diem and his brother Nhu surrendered to the rebels and were killed. The same day a Military Revolutionary Council of ARVN generals and colonels led by General Minh formally took over the government and began the wholesale removal of Diemist officials. This action, together with their lack of administrative experience, soon produced governmental paralysis.

Reacting to Diem's overthrow and the governmental disarray, the enemy launched numerous attacks throughout South Vietnam. During this emergency USAF and VNAF pilots flew 284 flare and 298 strike sorties during November in defense of threatened hamlets and outposts. However, the demoralized ARVN ground forces were no match for the enemy and, before month's end, Viet Cong forces had captured enough weapons to arm five 300-man battalions. Thus, in IV Corps, the ARVN 21st Division was

the United States of one Army CV-2 Caribou company by December as part of a planned 1,000-man U.S. force reduction. He also called for an accelerated buildup of the South Vietnamese armed forces to allow the early withdrawal of the remaining 15,640 American military men in the country.

Back in Washington, McNamara and Taylor reported to President Kennedy that Diem's repressive measures against the Buddhists would likely affect the Allied military effort. The new U.S. Ambassador to Saigon, Henry Cabot Lodge—he replaced Nolting on 22 August--concluded that Diem and his brother, Ngo Dinh Nhu, head of the secret police--were hopelessly alienated from the people. On 2 Sep-

ambushed in an Xuyen province on 24 November as it mounted a heliborne attack against a Viet Cong battalion at Chu Lai. The hidden enemy force, equipped with five 7.9-mm machine guns and a twin .50 caliber weapon, shot down 1 helicopter and 1 T-28 and damaged 10 helicopters, 2 VNAF A-1H's, and 1 T-28.

In III Corps, the failure of an ARVN 5th Division officer to use fixed-wing air support apparently contributed to another major defeat on 31 December. The unit involved, the 32d Ranger Battalion, was surrounded west of Ben Cat. The Division's G-3—instead of asking a VNAF forward air controller and two A-1H's orbiting overhead with full loads of 100-pound bombs to provide assistance--called for and used three flights of Huey gunships which proved ineffective. The rangers took heavy casualties in a battle which might have produced an ARVN victory but instead ended 1963—the year of the general offensive—with another disheartening defeat.

Earlier, President Kennedy--in his last public statement on Vietnam before his assassination—on 14 November reiterated America's pledge to continue to assist the South Vietnamese to maintain their independence. His successor, Lyndon B. Johnson, reaffirmed that commitment. On 21 February 1964, in one of his first public comments on the war, President Johnson warned Hanoi to end its support of the insurgent forces in South Vietnam and Laos. Although he appointed a committee of State and Defense Department representatives to study ways to increase pressure on North Vietnam, he reiterated the past policy that the South Vietnamese and Laotian people were primarily responsible for their own defense. Thus, on 3 December 1963 the first 1,000 American military men departed South Vietnam in accordance with McNamara's previous announcements. Among them were members of the famed Air Force "Dirty Thirty" C-47 pilots and the U.S. Army's lst Aviation Company.

Efforts to Revitalize Military Operations

When General Minh's junta assumed power in November 1963, it announced plans to improve the effectiveness of the armed forces by placing them directly under the four corps commanders. The latter were made responsible for carrying the war to the enemy. Subsequently, the ARVN on 18 January 1964 launched the largest helicopter operation ever undertaken in South Vietnam up to that time. It involved 115 helicopters which airlifted 1,100 troops into Zone D. The operation went smoothly but unfortunately not a single Viet Cong could be found in the area.

Unsuccessful operations such as these, combined with continuing political instability, sparked yet another coup on 30 January. Maj. Gen Nguyen Khanh, commander of I Corps, flew to Saigon, ousted General Minh's council, and stated his intention to increase operations against the enemy. On 22 February, he issued his "Chien Thang National Pacification Plan," a modification of Thompson's "spreading oil stain" proposal. It called for launching a series of clear-and-hold operations in relatively secure areas. From there the Viet Cong would be rolled back while simultaneously a "new life development program" would get under way to raise the people's standard of living. Khanh gave the four corps commanders complete responsibility for the clear-and-hold operations and follow-up actions in their respective areas. General Harkins thought the plan had a good chance to succeed, providing Khanh's fragile government stayed in power.

On 31 January, Maj. Gen. Joseph H. Moore arrived in Saigon to assume command of the 2d Air Division from

General Anthis. In reviewing Khanh's plan, General Moore was alarmed by a provision in it which called for assigning VNAF units to the corps commanders. However, the new VNAF commander, Nguyen Cao Ky, quickly assured Moore he would not allow his air force to be parceled out. Ky interpreted the plan's wording to require assignment of VNAF units to corps tactical zones, not to individual corps commanders. Subsequently, he organized separate VNAF wing headquarters at Da Nang and Pleiku under the command of two knowledgeable air officers. They became the principal VNAF advisors to the I and II Corps commanders. He also proposed to set up similar wing headquarters for the III and IV Corps in 1965.

In keeping with Washington's policy of expanding VNAF air capabilities so that U.S. units and equipment could be withdrawn, MACV and 2nd Air Division in early 1964 undertook major reviews of the military situation. Although their findings were not encouraging, they prepared plans for the withdrawal of the Air Force's 19th Tactical Air Support Squadron in June 1964, followed in 1965 by the 1st Air Commando Squadron. To make up for this loss, several VNAF squadrons were to be equipped with A-1's, T-28's, and C-47's. Meanwhile, the 2d Air Division's aircraft were taking a beating from the enemy and age. In February two T-28's were lost to machinegun fire and, on the 11th, all B-26's were grounded after a wing failed during a combat flight.

On 17 February 1964, during a MACV meeting, Harkins' new deputy, Gen. William C. Westmoreland (he arrived in Saigon on 27 January), urged something be done to restore the Air Force's "Sunday punch." In Hawaii, Gen. Jacob E. Smart, who succeeded General O'Donnell on 1 August 1963 as Commander in Chief, Pacific Air Forces, reasoned that the Geneva prohibition against introducing jets into Vietnam was no longer pertinent. He recommended deployment to South Vietnam of one of two B-57 light jet bomber squadrons. Secretary McNamara, however, rejected the proposal on the grounds that it not only would violate the Geneva agreement but was contrary to Washington's policy of preparing the Vietnamese to fight their own war. He did, however, agree to further strengthen Saigon's air force and authorized equipping a new VNAF squadron with A-1H's and to replace the 1st Air Commando Squadron's T-28's and B-26's with 25 A-1E dual-pilot attack bombers.

These decisions, unfortunately, came too late for two T-28 Air Force pilots and their Vietnamese crewmen. On 24 March 1964 one plane--piloted by Capt. Edwin G. Shank, Jr.--crashed after its wing sheared off during a bomb run, killing both men. On 9 April a second T-28, piloted by Capt. Robert Brumett, put his aircraft into a dive and failed to come out. Other pilots watched with horror as the wings fell off and the plane plowed into a rice paddy. A few days before this second crash, General Moore had noted that with the loss of B-26 aircraft and suspected weakness in the T-28's, "the 2d Air Division is practically flat out of business." However, by borrowing nine surplus T-28B's from the VNAF, the 1st Air Commando Squadron managed to stay operational but pilot morale sagged.

Meanwhile, the Viet Cong were expanding their military operations, apparently in connection with a diplomatic offensive by Hanoi to neutralize all of Indochina. They began on the Ca Mau peninsula, where the insurgents boasted they could take any district town at any time. They proved their prowess on 12 April 1964 with a dawn attack on the district capital of Kien Long. VNAF A-1H's performed valiantly under flare lights, destroying a Viet Cong 105-mm howitzer and, after

(1) USAF strike aircraft of the 3d Tactical Fighter Wing provided close air support to the U.S. Army's 11th Armored Cavalry which attacked enemy positions northwest of Saigon. (2) Rebellious VNAF pilots, flying AD-6 fighter bombers, attacked President Diem's palace, May 1962. He was unharmed. (3) C-123. (4) Capt. Thomas A. Dwelle, USAF, poses in front of his A-1E at Bien Hoa AB, South Vietnam. (5) A Vietnamese government observation post, 1963. (6) An A-1E Skyraider attacks enemy forces. (7) Capt. Phan Lang Sue, commander, VNAF 516th Fighter Squadron lands at Nha Trang after completing a mission.

1

2

3

4

6

5

7

daybreak, providing relays of close air support strikes. One fighter took out an enemy machinegun set up less than 100 meters from ARVN troops. Despite the valiant air-ground defense of Kien Long, the enemy succeeded in overrunning the city, killing more than 300 ARVN troops. Some 200 civilians also were left dead or wounded. This defeat was followed by widespread terrorist attacks throughout the country. One daring Viet Cong operation took place on 2 May 1964, when an underwater demolition team sank the USS *Card,* which had been unloading helicopters at the Saigon waterfront.

Secretary McNamara, concluding that more aerial firepower was needed, authorized the Air Force to equip a second USAF air commando squadron with A-1E's. Nevertheless, during his next visit to Saigon in May 1964, he reiterated the administration's policy that all U.S. airmen should be out of combat within a matter of months. In addition, he decided that Air Force pilots could no longer fly combat missions, even with Vietnamese observers aboard. They were told to limit their activities to providing bona fide training only. To balance the loss of USAF strike support, he further directed that four VNAF squadrons be outfitted with A-1H's as soon as possible and he authorized VNAF expansion by another two squadrons, which were to take over from the two USAF air units scheduled for withdrawal.

Meanwhile, on 12 March General Harkins submitted a plan to the Pentagon to reorganize the command structure in Vietnam to eliminate overlapping responsibilities between the U.S. Military Assistance Advisory Group (established 12 February 1954) and the U.S. Military Assistance Command, Vietnam (established 8 February 1962). His goal was to eliminate the advisory group as an intervening command so as to be able to respond more directly to Saigon's military requirements. The JCS approved Har-

kins' proposal in April 1964 and it became effective on 15 May. Although Air Force officials felt that USAF doctrines and organizational views were being ignored, the 2d Air Division did gain some strength and stature under the reorganization. The Air Force Advisory Group, formerly a part of the MAAG, was reassigned to the Division, thus bringing all USAF activities in Vietnam under one agency. MACV, which had "coordinating authority" for the Air Force reconnaissance effort over Laos, subdelegated it to the 2d Air Dvision.

Subsequently, changes were made in the top level commanders. On 20 June General Westmoreland succeeded Harkins as Commander, MACV. On 1 July, Adm. Ulysses S. Grant Sharp replaced Admiral Felt as CINCPAC and Gen. Hunter Harris succeeded General Smart as CINCPACAF. Also, 1 July, General Taylor was designated the U.S. Ambassador to Saigon, succeeding Henry Cabot Lodge.

Continuing Military Reversals

After Hanoi's diplomatic efforts to convene an international conference to neutralize all of Indochina had failed—President Johnson termed it "only another name for a Communist takeover"—the Viet Cong turned July 1964 into the bloodiest month to date. On the 6th, enemy troops struck the Nam Dong Special Forces camp in I Corps, killing 55 ARVN troops, 2 U.S. rangers, and an Australian advisor. Although a flare plane illuminated the area, no VNAF strike aircraft were available to respond to calls for help. Fifteen days later the Viet Cong ambushed 400 ARVN troops in Chuong Thien province in the Delta. After the battle only 82 able-bodied survivors could be found. Nearly an hour elapsed before a VNAF forward air

n A-1E at Qui Nhon, May
965.

controller arrived over the battle site. Strike aircraft from Bien Hoa did not arrive for 1½ hours.

With the Chuong Thien disaster in mind, Westmoreland asked General Moore and Brig. Gen. Delk M. Oden, commander of the U.S. Army Support Command, Vietnam, to prepare an agreement to govern coordination of all aviation activity in South Vietnam. They subsequently proposed to collocate MACV's Army Air Operations Section with the Joint USAF-VNAF Air Operations Center at Tan Son Nhut and to collocated air support centers in the corps areas. Henceforth, senior U.S. Army advisors would conduct preplanning conferences on at least a daily basis with their Air Force counterparts to insure full utilization of fixed-wing strike aircraft. The new arrangement became effective in August 1964.

Moore also was authorized to establish a VNAF air request net manned by Vietnamese personnel so as to enable ARVN commanders to flash calls for air assistance directly to an air support center. Intermediate ARVN headquarters, monitoring the requests, could cancel them only if there were more urgent ones. The VNAF net was installed in the four corps areas by the end of 1964. Although ARVN commanders were unhappy with the arrangement, the Vietnamese high command on 1 March 1965 directed that the VNAF net would serve as the primary system for obtaining emergency air support.

The first direct clash between North Vietnamese and American forces occurred on 2 August 1964 when enemy torpedo boats attacked the *Maddox*-while it was on patrol in the Gulf of Tonkin. The attack was apparently in retaliation for U.S. sponsored South Vietnamese raids along the North Vietnamese coast. Two nights later, the *Maddox* and a second destroyer, the USS *C. Turner Joy,* reported additional enemy attacks against them. Whereupon, President Johnson ordered a retaliatory strike against North Vietnamese coastal torpedo bases and an oil storage depot on 5 August. The President then requested and Congress on 7 August adopted the Gulf of Tonkin resolution. It authorized Mr. Johnson to use all measures— including the commitment of the armed forces—to assist South Vietnam to defend its independence and territory. During this crisis two B-57 squadrons were dispatched from Clark AB in the Philippines to Bien Hoa. In addition, USAF F-100 and F-102 squadrons were sent to Da Nang and still other fighters moved into Thailand.

A white paper subsequently issued by Hanoi admitted the North Vietnamese patrol boats had fired upon the *Maddox* on 2 August because of its support of South Vietnamese naval incursions. It denied, however, that NVA boats were in the area where the second attack reportedly occurred. In any event, Hanoi signalled its determination to fight by redeploying 30 MIG fighters from a South China base to Phuc Yen airfield on 7 August. Several weeks later, the 325th Division of the North Vietnamese Army headed down the Ho Chi Minh trail towards South Vietnam. During this period, Viet Cong

regiments in Zones C and D--augmented by guerrillas brought up from the Delta--were formed into the 9th Viet Cong Division. This unit in early autumn began to move to the coastal regions of Phuoc Tuy province, where it was outfitted with Soviet and Chinese weapons apparently brought in by sea.

Meanwhile, Ambassador Taylor sought new ways to shore up the South Vietnamese. On 18 August, he recommended to Washington that further military steps be taken "to gain time for the Khanh government to develop a certain stability." One of his proposed actions called for "a carefully orchestrated bombing attack" against North Vietnam, aimed primarily at infiltration and other military targets. While these recommendations were being reviewed in Washington, dissident ARVN troops from IV Corps-- led by Brig. Gen. Lam Van Phat—in

September moved against Khanh but withdrew from Saigon after General Ky sent his VNAF units over the city. The political crisis was temporarily resolved on 26 October following installation of a provisional civilian government headed by Tran Van Huong, Saigon's former mayor. However, Premier Huong found himself unable to bring order to the administration.

Against this background of continuing governmental instability, the Viet Cong seized additional portions of the South Vietnamese countryside and launched a series of attacks aimed specifically against the Americans. On the night of 1 November 1964, Viet Cong squads easily approached within 400 yards of Bien Hoa's perimeter and shelled the crowded airfield with 81mm mortars. Four Americans were killed and 72 others wounded. Losses included 5 B-57's destroyed and 15 damaged as well as 4 VNAF A-1's destroyed or damaged. At this point, Ambassador Taylor concluded that while a viable Saigon government could not be created through military actions alone, a campaign to reduce or halt the continuing flow of reinforcements to the Viet Cong from the north might resolve some of South Vietnam's problems. He suggested that air operations beyond the borders of the country could contribute to that objective.

In late November, Taylor was recalled to Washington for critical weeklong discussions with the President and his key Defense and State Department advisors on future courses of action. They agreed the political chaos in South Vietnam had to be arrested and further coups avoided. They also agreed that a graduated military response against North Vietnamese lines of communication(LOC's) would help Saigon's morale and the effectiveness of ARVN operations. Whereupon, on 2 December 1964 President Johnson approved a program of controlled air strikes against

enemy LOC's in Laos to "signal" his determination to counter Hanoi's increasing military activities and to strengthen the governments of South Vietnam and Laos. On his return to Saigon, Taylor passed word of these decisions and of U.S. reaffirmation of support of Premier Huong to the South Vietnamese. On 20 December, however, General Khanh's Armed Forces Council withdrew its support of Huong and the governmental crisis remained unresolved.

Meanwhile, good flying weather in December 1964 allowed VNAF and USAF airmen to score heavily against Viet Cong units. On 9-10 December VNAF crews helped in the successful ARVN defense of Tam Ky in Quang Tin province and An Lao in Binh Dinh province, both in I Corps. In the IV Corps area, VNAF A-1H and USAF A-1E Skyraiders inflicted more than 400 casualties and were credited with averting destruction of a regional force company surrounded near Long My after a convoy was ambushed. Altogether, the air forces claimed an estimated 2,500 Viet Cong troops killed during the November-December period--more than 60 percent of all reported enemy deaths.

Despite these successes, South Vietnam came increasingly under enemy attack. On Christmas Eve, the Viet Cong exploded a powerful charge in the Brink Hotel bachelor officers quarters in downtown Saigon, killing 2 and wounding 71 Americans. On 27 December, the Viet Cong's 9th Division attacked Binh Gia village in Phuoc Tuy province, southeast of Saigon, setting off a 6-day battle during which the 33d Ranger and 4th Marine Battalions were virtually destroyed. ARVN armored and mechanized forces sent to their aid also took heavy casualties. The battle of Binh Gia, the Viet Cong later boasted, marked the end of insurgency phase of its campaign and the start of conventional field operations.

35

III U.S. Army Airmobility

1962–1971
(Condensed)

The first few helicopters to arrive "in country" were based at Tan Son Nhut and provided support to all the Army of the Republic of Vietnam (ARVN) units they could reach. Naturally, this support was based on operational priorities—the average Army of the Republic of Vietnam infantry unit saw very few helicopters in its day-to-day operations.

Following the 57th and 8th (to Tan Son Nhut), the 93d Transportation Company (Light Helicopter) arrived off the coast of Vietnam in January 1962. Ten miles out in the South China Sea from Da Nang, the aircraft were flown off the carrier deck of the USNS *Card* to Da Nang Air Base.

To provide better command and control of the Army's growing fleet, the 45th Transportation Battalion was deployed to Vietnam in early 1962 from Fort Sill, Oklahoma, and assumed command of the three Army helicopter companies and the fixed-wing Otter aircraft company. Shortly thereafter two more light helicopter companies, the 33d and the 81st, were deployed and also came under the command of the 45th Transportation Battalion.

The first of "a long line of Hueys" (UH-1A, B, C, D, and H) arrived in Vietnam as part of the 57th Medical Detachment (Helicopter Ambulance) in early 1962. They were shortly followed by the 23d Special Warfare Aviation Detachment equipped with OV-1 Mohawks to provide reconnaissance and photographic coverage in support of ARVN forces.

The first Marine helicopter squadron arrived in country in April 1962 and was established at the old French base at Soc Trang in the Mekong Delta. In June and July of that year the Marines swapped bases with the 93d Transportation Company at Da Nang because of the greater capability of the Marine H-34 helicopters to operate in the higher elevations of the northern region.

The Early Years in Vietnam, 1961–1965

THE ARMY OF THE REPUBLIC OF VIETNAM BECOMES AIRMOBILE

There is no precise method to divide the Vietnam War into convenient phases. However, from the standpoint of airmobility, one can consider the first phase as a learning period—a time when United States Army pilots were teaching Army of the Republic of Vietnam commanders and soldiers how to effectively employ helicopter tactics, while at the same time the pilots were learning by experience, trial and error. As more and more helicopters became available, we built additional aviation units to help the Vietnamese Army become as mobile as the enemy.

This second phase of the war was characterized by battalion-size air assaults of selected Vietnamese units, including the paratroopers, the rangers, and the regular infantry. It was the success of this phase that forced the enemy to increase his effort in South Vietnam. This proved to be something that the North Vietnamese Army was quite ready to do, and the improved capabilities of the Army of the Republic of Vietnam were matched step-by-step with increased resistance of the Viet Cong and

The Chinook helicopter brings in a 105-mm howitzer to an Army artillery unit at FSB Musket.

37

South Vietnamese troops arrive in a CH-47 (Chinook) at base Maureen near Hue during Screaming Eagles of the 101st Airborne Division.

North Vietnamese Army, as additional units and supplies poured down the Ho Chi Minh Trail complex and across the border. It was during this second phase that we made great improvements on our tactical employment of helicopters. It was also during this period that we created our own airmobile division, tested it, and concluded that in terms of ground tactics, airmobility was here to stay.

It was also during this second phase that the Huey came into its own. The turbine engine helicopter, with its great power, its reliability, and its smaller requirement for maintenance, was the technological turning point as far as airmobility is concerned. Actually, the key improvement of technology was the trio of the Huey as a troop lift bird, the Chinook with its larger capacity for resupply and movement of artillery, and the fledgling attack helicopter—these three together allowed us to take a giant step forward at this time.

From the time of the first major commitment of helicopters to Vietnam on 11 December 1961 until the buildup of major U.S. forces in 1965, airmobility was—like diplomacy—confined to the art of the possible.

The advisory task of the U.S. military forces expanded very rapidly during this period. The Viet Cong regular force grew steadily from two to five regimental headquarters, the Viet Cong battalions doubled in the same period, and the quality and quantity of their weapons and equipment improved considerably. This buildup necessitated the deployment of additional U.S. Army aviation units to support Government of Vietnam forces. From a single transportation battalion with three helicopter companies in early 1962, the U.S. Army developed an enormous operational and logistical support complex consisting of many battalions of helicopter companies, fixed-wing units, maintenance units, and special purpose organizations.

THE ARMED HELICOPTER IN VIETNAM

The first element of fifteen armed Hueys was deployed to Vietnam in September 1962. To assure proper employment, General Rowny hammered out a modus operandi with Military Assistance Command, Vietnam, on 29 September 1962, which provided a framework for the forthcoming test. The terms of reference provided that the test activities must not have an unacceptable impact on military operations. Therefore, testing was undertaken only in conjunction with actual operations, and in no case was the test unit required to engage in activities designed solely for test purposes.

More fundamental limitations were the rules of engagement for U.S. Army armed helicopters, which precluded testing of any tactical concepts involving "offensive" employment. Under these rules, the armed helicopters could deliver fire only after they or the escorted transport helicopters had been fired upon. In late February 1963 the rules were modified to permit the armed helicopters to initiate fire against clearly identified insurgents who threatened their safety or the safety of escorted transport helicopters.

The provisional Utility Tactical Transport Helicopter company was based at Tan Son Nhut Airport on the outskirts of Saigon and was under the direct operational control of Military Assistance Command, Vietnam. From this base, it

A UH-1H (Huey) helicopter of the 101st Airborne Division being guided onto a landing pad.

supported transport operations of the 57th, 33d, and 93d Light Helicopter Companies, all equipped with CH-21 aircraft.

The plan of test for this company called for the evaluation of the armed helicopter in the "escort" role. Although "escort" was not defined, actual experience determined that the escort role broke down into an *enroute phase,* that was generally flown at a relatively safe altitude, the *approach phase,* where the heliborne force usually descended to nap-of-the-earth heights several kilometers away from the landing zone, and the *landing zone phase.* It was in the landing zone phase that the armed helicopter proved most valuable.

Prior to the advent of the escort by the Utility Tactical Transport Helicopter company, transport helicopters on the "dangerous" combat support missions were being hit at a rate of .011 hits per flying hour. For similar missions escorted by the Utility Tactical Transport Helicopter company, the rate declined to .0074. During this same period of time, the hit rate for all other flying done by Army helicopters rose from .0011 to .0024. In other words, the Viet Cong effectiveness against unescorted aircraft doubled while the efficacy of their fire against escorted aircraft dropped by 25 percent. Consequently, it was concluded that the suppressive fires delivered by armed escort helicopters were highly effective in reducing the amount and accuracy of enemy fires placed on transport helicopters.

The Utility Tactical Transport Helicopter company flew 1,779 combat support hours from 16 October 1962 through 15 March 1963. Most of the operations were conducted in the III and IV Corps Tactical Zones. Suppressive fire delivered by the escort helicopters accounted for an estimated 246 Viet Cong casualties. During this period, eleven armed helicopters were hit by hostile fire. While no armed helicopter was shot down, one UH-1B was seriously damaged as a result of ground fire. It appeared that the vulnerability of armed helicopters was well within acceptable risk limits.

By mid-1963 the 1st Platoon of the Utility Tactical Transport Helicopter company which worked with the Marine H-34's in the I Corps sector had become adopted by their comrades-in-arms as an integral part of their operations and few, if any, H-34 pilots elected to fly without the armed Hueys nearby. Procedures were developed whereby the armed Hueys picked up the fire support right after the fixed-wing fighter planes broke off their support for safety reasons, and that, in most cases, the last minute reconnaissance by the armed helicopters prevented the Marine H-34 from going into extremely hot ambushed landing zones.

The early tests with the Utility Tactical Transport Helicopter company indicated that a platoon from five to seven armed helicopters could protect a transport helicopter force of from twenty to twenty-five aircraft. The organization of the new airmobile company was a compromise between the requirement to provide organic arms support and the requirement to lift troops and cargo. The armament system brought the armed UH-1B up to its maximum gross weight, thereby eliminating it from a troop or cargo-carrying role. In addition to the integrated machine gun and rocket systems, two door gunners were used on the armed helicopters.

The UH-1B was not designed for an armed configuration and the weight of the armament system reduced the maneuverability of the aircraft and induced sufficient drag to lower the maximum speed to approximately 80 knots. As a consequence, the armed helicopters could not overtake the airmobile force if they left the formation to attack targets enroute. The early armed UH-1B's did an outstanding job in proving the concept of the armed helicopters.

METHODOLOGY OF THE EARLY AIR ASSAULTS

During 1963 the single most important factor in the development of tactics, techniques, and procedures for airmobile units in the Republic of Vietnam was the lack of significant enemy air defense capabilities, either ground or air. The ground-based threat was essentially hand-held small arms and automatic weapons fire. On rare occasions caliber .50 or 12.7-mm machine gun fire was encountered. The lack of heavy enemy air defense had much to do with the selection of flight altitudes. During this time frame, most flights were made at 1,500 feet or higher to reduce the chances of being hit by ground fire. Contour flying was rarely performed. The Viet Cong continued to ambush landing zones, especially in mountains or mangrove areas where there was a very limited number of landing sites. On occasion, they would mine the area or drive stakes to prohibit landing. Most of the resistance, not surprisingly, was in the critical landing phase of an air assault mission.

THE EAGLE FLIGHT

In an effort to reduce the planning time required for executing an air assault mission, some of the earlier helicopter units developed a task force called an "EAGLE FLIGHT." An "EAGLE FLIGHT" was defined by Headquarters U.S. Military Assistance Command, Vietnam, as "a tactical concept involving the employment of a small, self-contained, highly-trained heliborne force. Tactical planning emphasizes the use of this force to locate and engage the enemy or to pursue and attack an enemy fleeing a larger friendly force. As an airmobile force, 'EAGLE' is also prepared to engage an enemy force located or fixed by other friendly forces. The inherent flexibility of the 'EAGLE FLIGHT' as a force ready for immediate commitment either alone or in conjunction with other forces is its most significant factor."

A typical EAGLE FLIGHT would consist of the following: one armed Huey would serve as the command and control ship and would have the U.S. Army aviation commander and the Army of the Republic of Vietnam troop commander aboard; seven unarmed Hueys were used to transport the combat elements; five armed Hueys gave the fire support and escort to the troop-carrying helicopters; and, one Huey was usually designated as a medical evacuation ship.

The EAGLE FLIGHTS were usually on a standby basis or sometimes even airborne searching for their own targets. Not only were these EAGLE FLIGHTS immediately available for those missions which required a minimum of planning, but they also provided the basis for larger operations. Several EAGLE FLIGHTS were sometimes used against targets that, when developed, proved too large for a single unit.

By November 1964, all helicopter companies in South Vietnam had organized their own EAGLE FLIGHTS and each company maintained at least one flight in an alert status on a continuing basis. The Vietnamese troop commanders were particularly enthusiastic about these operations for they provided a very close working relationship between the air and ground elements and a special esprit was built from the day-to-day operations.

Simply stated, the EAGLE FLIGHT was a microcosm of the large airmobile assaults that were destined to take place later. It had all the attributes of a true airmobile force with its self-contained reconnaissance and surveillance ability, firepower, and infantry. Above all, these early EAGLE FLIGHTS were able to capitalize on the element of surprise which so often was lost in the detailed planning cycle with Army of the Republic of Vietnam forces.

THE GROWING AIRCRAFT INVENTORY

At the beginning of 1964 the United States had 388 aircraft in Vietnam including 248 helicopters, too few to accommodate the expanding advisory effort and increasing Vietnamese Army operations. By the end of September 1964, there was in South Vietnam a total of 406 Army aviation aircraft supporting the Army of the Republic of Vietnam. To support this effort, a total of 3,755 Army aviation personnel were provided consisting of 780 officers and 2,975 enlisted personnel. This made it possible to place a U.S. Army aviation company or a U.S. Marine Corps aviation squadron in support of each Vietnamese Army division with additional aviation supporting each Corps.

THE MOHAWK IN VIETNAM

After a storm of controversy in the Pentagon, the 23d Special Warfare Aviation Detachment was deployed to Vietnam in September 1962 for the purpose of providing air surveillance in support of Republic of Vietnam forces. In addition, they were to serve as a test unit for operational evaluation conducted by the Army Concept Team in Vietnam. The 23d Special Warfare Aviation Detachment (Surveillance) was organized in July 1962 as a prototype armed aerial surveillance unit using the OV-1 Mohawk aircraft.

When they were deployed to Vietnam their rules of employment specified that: on all operational flights a Vietnamese observer would be aboard; that the aircraft would be armed with .50 caliber weapons only; and, that this armament would be used only when required to defend against a hostile attack.

Visual and photographic reconnaissance by this twin-turbine airplane produced a wealth of intelligence for supported units. Hundreds of structures, most of them camouflaged, were detected in Viet Cong base areas. Likewise, hundreds of people were sighted in suspect areas and, because of the detailed familiarity of Mohawk crews with the local situation and activity patterns, some of the people sighted could be positively identified as insurgents. One of the unique advantages of the Mohawk in reconnaissance was its speed to noise relationship which allowed the aircraft to get within observation distance of people on the ground without alerting them to its presence.

From 16 October 1962 to 15 March 1963 the 23d Special Warfare Aviation Detachment flew more than 2,000 hours in the performance of 785 combat support missions. It had delivered defensive fire 27 times and had lost two aircraft.

THE CARIBOU IN VIETNAM

On 23 July 1962, the 1st Aviation Company (Fixed-wing Light Transport) was self-deployed from the Continental United States to Thailand. In December the company was moved to Vung Tau, Republic of Vietnam. A second Caribou company, the 61st Aviation Company, was also self-deployed from the Continental United States in July 1963 and based at Vung Tau first. It was not until early 1963 that Commander in Chief Pacific approved the proposed test plan for the Caribou company, but by that time the Caribous had been integrated into most of the daily planning at the corps level.

Another unit which is seldom mentioned in the Vietnam reports (probably because it was so often taken for granted) was the 73d Aviation Company flying the two-place Bird Dog of Korean vintage. That company had arrived in Saigon on 23 May 1962 and its thirty-two aircraft were spread in fifteen separate locations all the way from Hue in the north to Bac Lieu in the south. These O-1's were primarily oriented to the reconnaissance requirement for the Vietnamese advisors but also were utilized for artillery adjustment, target acquisition,

The C-7 (Caribou) being loaded for a combat support mission.

41

command and control, message pickup, medical evacuation, radio relay, and re-supply. By 1964 this unit had set up its own school to train the Vietnamese officers and aerial observers and they had recorded over 41,000 hours of flying time in their first fourteen months in Vietnam.

INCREASING VIET CONG THREAT

From the arrival of the first H-21's in December 1961 up to mid-1965, the U.S. Army had concentrated on developing airmobile operations in support of Army of the Republic of Vietnam forces in an ever-increasing scope. As the Allied tactics and techniques developed, so did the Viet Cong develop counter tactics and techniques. Consequently, there was always a need for innovation. Experience proved that any set pattern for any length of time was extremely dangerous since the Viet Cong were quick to capitalize on these patterns and strike at the weakest point.

The Viet Cong had learned more than a bit about the method of operation of Free World forces and could well determine probable landing zones and the number of troops which could be brought in by one lift. Their antiaircraft weapons were now being centrally controlled and coordinated to deny the use of the most desirable landing zones and thereby channelize the airmobile forces into landing zones chosen and covered by the Viet Cong. In the latter zones, the Viet Cong forces tried to maintain favorable odds of four to one to the amount of Army of the Republic of Vietnam forces available to react against them.

Combat intelligence for airmobile operations was woefully inadequate due to a multitude of inadequacies in Army of the Republic of Vietnam intelligence combined with restrictions imposed in U.S.–Army of the Republic of Vietnam advisory relations. The increased activity of the enlarged Viet Cong forces made the staging areas of airmobile forces increasingly vulnerable to surprise attacks.

A study group highlighted one of the major problems of the early armed heli-copters—the armed Huey because of its gross weight and additional drag was slower than the troop-carrying transport helicopters that it escorted. This meant that either the whole column slowed down or that the assault had to be timed so that the gunships and troop ships rendezvoused just prior to landing. There was an immediate requirement for a faster armed escort helicopter which could maintain a speed of at least 150 knots.

In summary, in June of 1965, the U.S. Army found itself with a large commitment of airmobile resources supporting Republic of Vietnam Armed Forces with an organization that had grown somewhat like Topsy. Tactics and techniques had been generated by the necessity of the moment, procedures had been hammered out of necessity, and equipment had been borrowed and jury-rigged. Airmobility had obviously kept the South Vietnamese forces in being, but the Viet Cong had become increasingly more sophisticated and were reinforced with large numbers of North Vietnamese regular troops.

The Early Years in the United States

FORMATION OF THE 1ST CAVALRY DIVISION (AIRMOBILE)

In March 1965 the tentative decision was made to convert the 11th Air Assault Division (Test) to a full-fledged member of the force structure. General Creighton W. Abrams, who was then the Vice Chief of Staff, said after the decision briefing, "Is it not fortuitous that we happen to have this organization in existence at this point in time?" Those who had been fighting for such an organization for over a decade could not help but sense the irony of this remark. It was decided that the new division would carry the colors of the 1st Cavalry Division which was then deployed in Korea. This decision was made for a variety of reasons, some of them emotional and some pragmatic.

On 1 July 1965 the 1st Cavalry Division (Airmobile) was officially activated. Despite a crippling loss of personnel by reassignment throughout the division, its personnel were able to retrain, re-equip, and deploy this major force to combat in ninety days. This effort is a major story in itself. Almost 50 percent of the original personnel were ineligible for overseas deployment. Replacement pilots had to be trained on new aircraft and new standing operating procedures, and the original structure itself received major modification. For example, the Mohawk attack aircraft had been eliminated. A full brigade of the division were to be qualified paratroopers, the Little John battalion had been deleted, and the aviation group had been drastically modified.

The division staged out of Mobile, Alabama, and Jacksonville, Florida, on the USS *Boxer* and three Military Sea Transportation Service ships.

An advance party landed in the Republic of Vietnam on 25 August 1965 and arrived at An Khe shortly thereafter. The 1st Cavalry Division was about to write a new chapter to its proud history.

The First Airmobile Division and the Buildup, 1965

BUILDUP OF U.S. GROUND FORCES

The United States had already made a large commitment of airmobility assets to Vietnam in support of Army of the Republic of Vietnam forces. Now U.S. ground forces would test the airmobility concept for the first time in combat. Propinquity dictated that the first major combat unit of the U.S. Army to be deployed would be the airborne brigade stationed in Okinawa. On 5 May 1965 the 173d Airborne Brigade, composed of two battalions of infantry and one of artillery, arrived from Okinawa to provide security for the major air base at Bien Hoa and the airfield at Vung Tau. It would not be long before this brigade would be committed to major offensive action.

On 28 June the 173d Airborne Brigade participated in the largest troop lift operation conducted in the Republic of South Vietnam up to that time. Over 144 Army aircraft, including 77 troop transport helicopters, lifted two battalions of the Vietnamese 2d Airborne Brigade and the 1st and 2d Battalions of the 503d Infantry deep into War Zone D. Twenty-five Viet Cong were killed and fifty or more wounded. On D+2, the forces were extracted.

On 6 July the 173d returned to War Zone D and conducted one of its most successful operations since its arrival in Vietnam. In conjunction with the battalion of Australians and units of the 43d Army of the Republic of Vietnam Regiment, multiple air assaults were made just north of the Song Dong Nai River. Some 1,494 helicopter sorties were flown in support of this operation. Fifty-six Viet Cong were killed by actual body count. Twenty-eight prisoners of war were taken and one hundred tons of rice plus literally tons of documents were captured.

The early operations of the 173d demonstrated the absolute necessity of "orchestrating" an air assault operation. An airmobile operation was no simple matter of moving troops from point "A" to point "B" if you really wanted to exploit the potential of the helicopter. It took training and time to integrate tactical air, helicopter gunships, field artillery, reconnaissance, and troop maneuver elements into a single swift operation.

GROWING PAINS

On 20 July 1965 the U.S. Army Support Command, Vietnam was redesignated U.S. Army, Vietnam. This change was indicative of the growing presence of U.S. ground troops and the necessity for better command and control procedures. On 28 July, President Lyndon B. Johnson announced that our forces in Vietnam would be raised from 75,000 to 125,000 and that additional forces would be sent as requested. On 29 July, the 1st Brigade of the 101st Airborne Division arrived in Vietnam following a brigade of the 1st Infantry Division which had arrived a few days earlier.

The problems involved in this buildup can be described by a short review of the deployment of the 1st Brigade of the 101st Airborne Division. During the period 6 July to 29 July 1965 the Brigade moved from Fort Campbell, Kentucky to Vietnam. From 29 July through 21 August 1965 the Brigade manned a defensive perimeter in the Cam Ranh Bay area and began to establish a base camp. From 10 to 21 August the Brigade conducted operations southwest of Nha Trang and on 22 August, the Brigade moved north by sea and air with a mission to sweep clear the An Khe area of Binh Dinh Province to provide security for the arrival of the 1st Cavalry Division (Airmobile).

The movement of the 1st Brigade, 101st, to secure the An Khe base area for the soon-to-arrive 1st Cavalry Division was entitled Operation HIGHLAND and spanned the period 22 August until 2 October. One battalion conducted an airmobile assault in conjunction with a battalion-size ground attack to open the An Khe Pass and to clear and secure Route 19 from Qui Nhon to An Khe. To secure the division base area, the Brigade conducted eight airmobile assaults and many large ground operations. A special task force was organized to secure convoy movement along Route 19. Tactical air cover was provided for all convoys. During this period, enemy losses totaled 692 killed in action as opposed to the 1st Brigade losses of 21.

DEPLOYMENT OF THE CAVALRY

Meanwhile, the newly designated 1st Cavalry Division was feverishly preparing for deployment. The movement of over 400 aircraft, nearly 16,000 personnel, over 1,600 vehicles, and training for combat in just eight weeks was a momentous task. The USS *Boxer* and three Military Sea Transportation Service ships had been designated to move the division.

THE AN KHE HUB

When the ships with the main body arrived at Qui Nhon, the aircraft prepared for flight while on board the carriers. Only the Mohawks and two non-flyable Hueys were off-loaded by floating crane. The Chinooks quickly became the prime movers for troops and equipment between Qui Nhon and An Khe.

Although the Division did not completely reach An Khe until 3 October, it had assumed responsibility for its own security on 28 September, and elements of the division had already seen combat in support of the 1st Brigade of the 101st.

Major General Harry W. O. Kinnard recognized the vulnerability of the base camp at An Khe and consequently made it as small and compact as it could be so that it could be defended with a minimum number of forces.

THE IA DRANG

By mid-October 1965, the North Vietnamese Army had begun its major operation in the Central Highlands. There is every reason to believe that it planned to cut South Vietnam in two at this time, for three North Vietnamese Army regiments had assembled in western Pleiku Province and adjacent Cambodia. On 19 October, the enemy opened his campaign with an attack on the Pleime Special Forces Camp twenty-five miles southwest of Pleiku. On 27 October, General Westmoreland directed General Kinnard to move his 1st Cavalry Division and seek out and destroy this enemy force consisting of the 32d, 33d, and 66th North Vietnamese Army Regiments. This became the month-long campaign known as The Battle of the Ia Drang Valley.

Initially the 1st Cavalry Division reinforced the South Vietnamese Army in relieving the Pleime Camp, and the North Vietnamese Army regiments broke contact and disappeared into the jungle. The 1st Brigade of the 1st Cavalry was given the mission of organizing a systematic search for the elusive enemy.

It was apparent that the Pleime Camp had been hit—and hit hard—by the enemy and it seemed inconceivable to the Air Cavalry Squadron that thousands of Viet Cong and North Vietnamese soldiers could completely disappear. On 1 November, Captain William P. Gillette, the Air Cavalry Squadron intelligence officer, spotted some unusual activity just eight kilometers west of the Pleime Camp and the Squadron was quick to capitalize on this information. Before the day was over, the Cavalry Squadron had committed most of its rifle and gunship platoons into the skirmish that developed. They killed 78 of the enemy and captured 57 prisoners, all of whom were regular North Vietnamese soldiers carrying identity cards issued in Hanoi. During the encounter the squadron lost five troopers killed and another seventeen wounded.

The best estimate was that the major

enemy force had moved along the Ia Drang Valley close to the base of the Chu Pong Mountains and the 1st Squadron, 9th Cavalry was given the mission of establishing an ambush in this area. A site was chosen called landing zone MARY, and the Cavalry Squadron fought its major battle in this area.

Landing zone MARY was unique in that it was the first time that the 1st Cavalry Division had mounted a successful night ambush and reinforced their attack with a night lift of an infantry company. Also, they had developed their fire procedures to the point that armed helicopters were able to fire within fifty meters of the friendly troops during night operations.

On 14 November the 1st Battalion, 7th Cavalry, commanded by Lieutenant Colonel Harold G. Moore, began the pivotal operation of the Ia Drang Campaign. He had chosen landing zone X-RAY out of the possible landing zones as the best potential position for the initial air assault. The cavalry section had confirmed that landing zone X-RAY could take eight to ten UH-1D's at one time. No signs of enemy activity were detected.

Preparatory fire began at 1017 hours precisely where required and was timed with the lead elements of the assault company. The aerial artillery came on the heels of the tube artillery fire and worked over the area for 30 seconds expending half their load, then went into an orbit nearby to be on call. The lift battalion gunships took up the fire and were immediately ahead of the troop transport Hueys. By midafternoon the battalion knew it was in a major battle and fighting for its very existence. The enemy was coming from all sides.

As the lead elements landed, the helicopters took numerous hits, but none was shot down. One radio operator was killed before he could dismount from the helicopter and the door gunner and pilot were wounded. Colonel Moore stopped the other eight UH-1D's from landing by radio. Those who had landed from D Company immediately became engaged

Map of the Ia Drang Valley area.

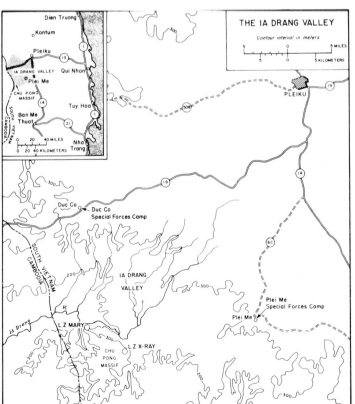

in the fire fight near A Company. The fighting became more intense. Colonel Moore decided to pull back A and B Companies under the cover of heavy supporting fire and smoke to the fringe of the landing zone and set up a tight defensive perimeter for the night. White phosphorus artillery was brought in and caused a temporary lull in the enemy firing that enabled some of the friendly forces to retrieve their dead and wounded and regroup. Both A and B Companies had numerous wounded and killed in action, while C Company had taken a few casualties but was in good shape. Company D had hardly been hit. During the afternoon Colonel Moore asked for assistance. The only company immediately available was Company B, 2d Battalion, 7th Cavalry, which landed in the landing zone by 1800. By 1900, the organization of the perimeter was completed. Units were tied in for the night and defensive artillery and mortar fires were registered.

By late afternoon it had become apparent that the battalion would need a night landing capability. A pathfinder team arrived and cleared a fairly safe zone with engineer demolitions and set up the necessary lights for night landings. This remarkable feat was accomplished under enemy observation and fire.

Early that night the wounded had all been evacuated and the dead had been collected in the command post area. Mortar and artillery fires were registered close to the perimeter and the battalion prepared for night attacks.

At brigade headquarters, Colonel Brown continued to assess the significance of the day's activities. He was pleased that the 2nd Battalion, 7th Cavalry, had been able to hold its own against heavy odds, and with moderate casualties, but was convinced that the fight was not yet over. He radioed General Kinnard for another battalion, and was informed that the 1st Battalion, 5th Cavalry, would begin arriving at brigade headquarters the following morning. In the early morning hours savage close range fighting went on throughout the battalion perimeter.

In his after action report, Colonel Moore noted that aerial rocket artillery had been extremely effective. His commanders had confidence in bringing such fires extremely close to their own positions. He also had noted that tube artillery, aerial rocket artillery, and tactical air can be used at the same time without seriously downgrading the effectiveness of the fire or endangering the aircraft.

All together, the 1st Cavalry Division and Army of the Republic of Vietnam troops killed an estimated 1,800 North Vietnamese troops.

The battle lasted 35 days, and on 26 November 1965, the 1st Cavalry Division had completed its mission of pursuit and destruction.

During the 35 days of the campaign, the aircraft delivered 5,048 tons of cargo from the wholesale terminals to the hands of the troops in the field. In addition, they transported 8,216 tons into Pleiku from various depots (primarily Qui Nhon and Nha Trang). Whole infantry battalions and artillery batteries were moved by air, and approximately 2,700 refugees were moved to safety. In all this flying, 59 aircraft were hit by enemy fire—three while on the ground—and only four were shot down; of these four, three were recovered.

Airmobility Comes of Age, 1966

AIRMOBILITY IN THE DELTA

The 173d Airborne Brigade (Separate) launched the new year on 1 January 1966 with a smoothly executed move into the Mekong Delta. This was the first time an American ground unit had operated in the notorious "Plain of Reeds."

The Brigade had moved from Hau Nghia Province into the Delta by land and air. The air elements, consisting of the 1st Battalion (Airborne), 503d Infantry; the 2d Battalion (Airborne), 503d Infantry; the 1st Battalion, Royal Australian

Regiment; and "C" Battery, 3d Battalion, 319th Artillery, came into Bao Trai airstrip. By 1425 the 1st Battalion of the 503d had the honor of being the first American force to make an air assault west of the Oriental River. This assault, which was preceded by an effective landing zone preparation by Tactical Air, artillery, and armed helicopters, only experienced light opposition which was quickly brushed aside. The Australian battalion established themselves by air assault on the east side of the Oriental River which effectively cut this enemy supply route.

As previously scheduled, the 2d Battalion of the 503d remained at the brigade forward base until the following morning when they conducted a heliborne assault into landing zone WINE. This landing zone was approximately five kilometers south of the Australian position and also on the east side of the river. Here they met very strong enemy resistance and the battalion fought a bitter and fiercely conducted battle throughout the day against a dug-in, well-concealed, battalion-size Viet Cong force. Intense artillery fire, helicopter gunship fire, and Tactical Air pounded the Viet Cong positions continuously. Late in the afternoon a strong coordinated attack behind a wall of artillery fire drove the Viet Cong from his positions. He left 111 dead behind along with considerable equipment.

Operation MARAUDER was terminated on D + 7, 8 January 1966, after decimating the 267th Viet Cong Battalion and the headquarters of the Viet Cong 506th Battalion. The 173d Airborne Brigade, as the first American unit to operate in the Mekong Delta, demonstrated its ability to swiftly co-ordinate the tactical air, helicopter gunships, artillery, and troop maneuvers.

THE 1ST CAVALRY DIVISION IN BINH DINH

During the first half of January 1966 the 1st Brigade of the 1st Cavalry Division conducted Operation MATADOR to find and destroy the enemy in Pleiku and Kontum Provinces. During this operation, the 1st Cavalry saw the enemy flee across the border into Cambodia, confirming that the enemy had well-developed sanctuaries and base camps inside that country.

After Operation MATADOR, the 1st Cavalry Division shifted its weight toward Binh Dinh Province. Some of its forces had been committed into this area soon after its arrival in Vietnam in the summer of 1965, but the major effort in the Ia Drang Valley occupied most of the 1st Cavalry's attention throughout 1965.

The 1st Cavalry's initial major operation in this area was called MASHER in its first phase, and WHITE WING in its second, third, and fourth phases. The fighting covered a full circle around Bong Son. The 1st Cavalry Division, in close coordination with the 22d Army of the Republic of Vietnam Division, began with air assaults into the Cay Giep Mountains, then moved to the Bong Son Plains, the An Lao Valley, the Kim Son Valley, and finally back to the Cay Giep Mountains. As a result of MASHER-WHITE WING, the airmobile division and the Army of the Republic of Vietnam infantry forced the North Vietnamese Army regulars out of the area and temporarily broke their hold on the population.

In the after action report of the 3d Brigade when it concluded Operation MASHER-WHITE WING on 17 February, they were able to report that 893 enemy had been killed by actual body count. A large quantity of equipment and small arms had been captured along with 24,000 rounds of ammunition. Friendly losses were 82 killed in action and 318 wounded.

The Brigade had been supported throughout this operation by the 133d Assault Support Helicopter Company with 16 Chinooks. The CH–47 Chinook had proved essential in moving artillery and resupplying the Brigade with ammunition and supplies. Despite the weather and the enemy fire, the 16 Chinooks assigned to this company during the period 1 January through 31 January flew 526 hours transferring 3,212 passengers and over 1,600 tons of cargo.

THE ROLE OF THE CHINOOK

The story of airmobility is essentially one of men and machines. If the Huey helicopter became the cornerstone of airmobility, then the Chinook must be considered one of the principal building blocks.

Late in 1956 the Department of the Army announced plans to replace the H-37 helicopter, which was powered by piston-driven engines, with a new, turbine-powered aircraft. A design competition was held and, in September 1958, a joint Army-Air Force source selection board recommended that the Army procure the Boeing Vertol medium transport helicopter.

The Army finally settled on a larger Chinook as its standard medium transport helicopter and as of February 1966, 161 aircraft had been delivered to the Army. The 1st Cavalry Division had brought their organic Chinook battalion with them when they arrived in 1965 and a separate aviation medium helicopter company, the 147th, had arrived in Vietnam on 29 November 1965. This latter company was initially placed in direct support of the 1st U.S. Infantry Division.

The most spectacular mission in Vietnam for the Chinook was the placing of artillery batteries in perilous mountain positions that were inaccessible by any other means, and then keeping them resupplied with large quantities of ammunition. The Chinook soon proved to be such an invaluable aircraft for artillery movement and heavy logistics that it was seldom used as an assault troop carrier. The early decision to move to this size helicopter proved to be indisputably sound.

OPERATION CRAZY HORSE

The origins of many of the major op-

erations in Vietnam can be traced to some minor enemy contact which was quickly exploited by airmobile forces. Often this was the only way the elusive enemy could be forced to fight. Operation CRAZY HORSE is a good example of the aggressiveness and determination of our forces in their search for the enemy.

The 1st Cavalry Division was finishing Operation DAVY CROCKETT on 15 May 1966 when a Civilian Irregular Defense Group (CIDG) patrol from the Vinh Thanh CIDG Camp, working the mountain valley immediately to the east, ambushed an enemy force and captured a mortar sight, 120-mm firing tables and a gunner's quadrant, plus some sketches of the CIDG camp and the hamlets in the valley. One company of the 1st Cavalry air assaulted into the hills east of the CIDG camp at 1000 hours on the 16th, to search out the area. At 1100 hours on the 16th, Company B, 2d Battalion (Airborne), 8th Cavalry, made a combat assault into what then was a one-ship landing zone named HEREFORD, a small patch of elephant grass about halfway up the side of the largest mountain east of the CIDG camp.

After a hard climb the company began moving eastward along the razorback. At approximately 1400 hours, the lead platoon spotted what appeared to be a single Viet Cong and opened fire. The fire was immediately returned in volume. The platoon leader radioed that he had encountered stiff opposition. Flanking action by the squad met with an immediate and violent counter-attack by an estimated enemy platoon. All but one man was killed. The sole survivor, badly wounded, wisely feigned death and later escaped. Then the enemy began thrusting at the flanks of the company column. One squad counterattacked, but was beaten back into a position that eventually became part of the company's perimeter.

Under the severe weather conditions, the aerial rocket artillery, the usual savior of an isolated airmobile element, could not be expected to function. However, two birds from the 2d Battalion, 20th Artillery, guided by radio, pressed home salvo after salvo of rockets, some within a few feet of the company's perimeter. One last volley, in conjunction with a violent exchange of small arms and automatic weapons fire, ended the enemy threat for the night. The attacks diminished in strength and intensity and by 2000 hours, all contact was broken. Reinforcements had been landed at landing zone HEREFORD during a brief period when the weather broke. The men of Bravo used the respite to continue digging in.

At 2200 hours, the perimeter was reinforced by some 130 men of Company A, 1st Battalion (Airborne), 12th Cavalry. Alfa had air assaulted into landing zone HEREFORD.

On 17 May, at 0615 hours, Bravo pulled in its listening posts, which had been stationed some 20–25 meters outside the perimeter, and the two companies initiated a "mad minute" of fire—a systematic spraying of trees and bushes in front of the positions. This firing touched off an immediate enemy reaction, and he launched a violent attack at all sectors of the perimeter. The intensity and violence of the incoming fire indicated an assault by at least a battalion-sized unit.

When the smoke cleared, casualties were counted. Bravo had lost 25 killed, and 62 wounded. Alfa had 3 killed and 37 wounded. There were 38 enemy bodies found within or immediately adjacent to the perimeter. Later evidence indicated that as many as 200 additional enemy had died in the fight.

For Bravo Company, the remainder of 17 May was spent evacuating dead and wounded. For the 1st Cavalry Division, Operation CRAZY HORSE had begun.

The rest of the action took place in the most mountainous and heavily forested area in the province, far from the lowlands. Chinooks hovered over the jungle so that the men could climb down swaying "trooper ladders" through the triple canopy. Nevertheless, in the three weeks

of CRAZY HORSE, over 30,000 troops moved by helicopter—an example of the tactical value of airmobility in mountain operations.

In a new plan, the Division marked off the battle area into pie-shaped sectors and moved the airmobile companies to the outer edges on all sides to set up a double row of ambushes. The artillery then began firing 12,000 to 13,000 rounds per day into the enemy concentrations. The Air Force assisted with tactical strikes and also hit the enemy with B-52 raids almost daily. The North Vietnamese, under this pressure, attempted to escape out of the area and triggered several of the prepared ambushes. The enemy's powerful 2d Regiment was disorganized by heavy losses in these ambushes; the survivors evaded to the north into the An Lao Valley and were not in contact again for several months.

Airmobile Developments, 1966

THE CARIBOU TRANSFER

During the spring of 1966, one of the most emotionally packed debates was reaching its final stages. This would culminate on 6 April 1966 in a formal agreement between the Chief of Staff, U.S. Army and the Chief of Staff, U.S. Air Force to relinquish Army claims to the Caribou and future fixed-wing aircraft designed for tactical airlift.

TECHNIQUES OF THE 101ST

The helicopter was probably the only solution to the dense tropical jungle, but even this versatile machine needed some place to touch down. Every unit in Vietnam had to adapt many of its airmobile procedures to fit its mission. The following sample, from the 1966 files of the 1st Brigade, 101st Airborne Division, is typical.

Brigadier General Willard Pearson,

49

An ARVN platoon member rappels from a Huey at Loc Ninh.

Commanding General, 1st Brigade, 101st Airborne Division, had established a training program for helicopter rappelling techniques since his brigade frequently operated in dense jungle terrain which did not have accessible landing zones. Engineer landing zone clearing teams performed a most necessary and dangerous task of going into an unknown and lightly protected area—with equipment that had to be airdropped or sling delivered—and felling enough trees to permit several helicopters to land simultaneously. Vietnam abounds with many large hardwood forests which are extremely difficult to cut, even with the best heavy equipment.

In the 101st operations in the highlands during this period, an airmobile company was placed in direct support of each infantry battalion and the same company habitually supported a specific battalion. The brigade found this arrangement was mutually advantageous; resulted in increased responsiveness; and enhanced the effectiveness of aviation support. By now the use of a command and control helicopter had become routine for each infantry battalion commander and he used this helicopter for liaison, communications relay with subordinate units, assisting units to pinpoint their locations, guiding units to terrain objectives, and locating potential landing zones.

FALL, 1966

Operation THAYER I marked the beginning of the series of battles that kept the 1st Cavalry Division in constant operation in the plains of Binh Dinh for many months. The course of this battle followed the enemy as he drifted across 506 Valley into the Crescent Plains and Cay Giep Mountains.

The Division jumped off in the attack on 15 September 1966, with the simultaneous air assault of two brigades. Three battalions were lifted from An Khe and two from Hammond into the mountains of the Kim Son Valley. The five assaulting battalions secured the high ground all the way around the claw-shaped valley and then fought their way down to the valley floor against elements of the 18th North Vietnamese Army Regiment.

On 20 September, the battle area shifted to 506 Valley as the 18th North Vietnamese Army Regiment attempted to evade to the east and break contact. Three cavalry battalions made air assaults to the east to follow their trail. THAYER came to a close at the end of September with over 200 enemy killed and 100 tons of rice captured.

ARTILLERY IN THE AIRMOBILE CONCEPT

The airmobile tactics of the 1st Cavalry Division, its speed of maneuver, and the distances involved required drastic changes in the techniques and development of fire support co-ordination. For one thing, the air was filled with a number of new objects—hundreds of troop transport helicopters, armed helicopters, reconnaisance aircraft, and tactical air support. Through this same atmosphere thousands of shells from tube artillery had to travel. Fire support co-ordination during the critical air assault phase of an operation was the most difficult to resolve. The tactical air support, tube and aerial artillery, and sometimes naval gunfire and B-52 bombers had to be integrated without danger to the friendly forces and without firepower gaps that would relieve the pressure on the enemy. Only careful planning and carefully worked out standing operating procedures could make this manageable.

As an example, the 1st Cavalry Division had a zone system based on the twelve hour clock superimposed on the map location of each firing position. North was at 12:00 o'clock. Prior to firing, the artillery units announced over the aircraft guard frequencies the danger areas such as "firing in zones three and four, altitude 3,000 feet." It was incumbent on the pilot to check for artillery fire prior to approaching a landing zone.

During MASHER-WHITE WING, the 155-mm howitzer was airlifted for the first time using the CH-54 Sky Crane helicopter. During this same campaign, it became an accepted technique to select hilltops for artillery positions since these were easier to defend and provided open fields of fire.

Close-in fire support has always been inherently dangerous. In the fluid situation of the airmobile battlefield, the ever present danger of the proverbial "short round" is multiplied by all the points on the compass. An error in any direction may well result in friendly casualties. As a result, coordination and control of all fire, the knowledge of the exact location of every friendly element is more important in the airmobile division than in any other combat force. A year's experience in Vietnam had matured the 1st Cavalry Division's fire support techniques and had proven its organization to be fundamentally sound.

OTHER OPERATIONS

The fall of 1966 saw many operations develop as the U.S. strength continued to grow. The newly arrived 196th Light Infantry Brigade ran into a major enemy

A CH-54 (Sky Crane) delivering a 155-mm towed howitzer weighing more than 12,000 lbs. at Fire Support Base Granite.

force south of Sui Da while searching for rice and other enemy supplies on 19 October. When four companies of the U.S. 5th Special Forces Group's Mobile Strike Force were inserted into landing zones north and east of Sui Da, they immediately became heavily engaged. It became apparent that the Viet Cong 9th Division, consisting of three regiments, together with the North Vietnamese 101st Regiment had deployed into the central Tay Ninh Province with the major objective of wiping out the Special Forces camp at Sui Da. The four Special Forces companies were overrun and had to withdraw in small groups or be extracted by helicopters.

General Westmoreland responded to this large enemy threat by committing the 1st Infantry Division, contingents of the 4th and 25th Infantry Divisions, and the 173d Airborne Brigade. Some 22,000 U.S. and Allied troops were committed to the battle which became known as Operation ATTLEBORO. The battle continued until 24 November, during which over 1,100 enemy were killed and huge quantities of weapons, ammunition, and supplies were captured. The Viet Cong 9th Division would not be seen again until the following year.

The 1st Cavalry Division continued its operations in Binh Dinh Province with Operations THAYER II and IRVING. IRVING

51

was a good example of cooperation between U.S., Government of Vietnam, and Republic of Korea forces. The tactical moves and the complicated phasing were carried out with precision, and without any major difficulties.

During the same period, Paul Revere IV was continuing near the Cambodian border in Pleiku Province. The newly arrived 4th Infantry Division carried the bulk of this battle with elements of the 25th Infantry Division and 1st Cavalry Division. By 30 December, 977 enemy had been killed.

Each one of the above operations contained hundreds of examples of the growing capability of U.S. forces to employ airmobile operations with effectiveness and daring.

By the end of 1966, the United States would have a total of 385,000 U.S. military personnel in South Vietnam and would be in a position for the first time to go over to the offensive on a broad and sustained basis. General Westmoreland remarked, "During 1966, airmobile operations came of age. All maneuver battalions became skilled in the use of the helicopter for tactical transportation to achieve surprise and out-maneuver the enemy."

The Peak Year, 1967

PARACHUTE ASSAULT IN VIETNAM

At 0900 hours on 22 February 1967, Brigadier General John R. Deane, Jr., stood in the door of a C-130 aircraft. When the green light flashed, General Deane jumped, leading the first U.S. parachute assault in the Republic of Vietnam, and the first such assault since the Korean conflict fifteen years earlier. This parachute jump of the 2d Battalion, 503d Infantry, signalled the beginning of Operation Junction City Alternate. The original plan, as conceived in November 1966, called for the 1st Brigade of the 101st Airborne Division to make the

parachute assault; but, much to their chagrin, they were engaged in other operations and the honor was to go to the 173d.

Operation Junction City employed the 1st and 25th Infantry Divisions, the 11th Armored Cavalry Regiment, the 196th Light Infantry brigade, elements of the 4th and 9th Infantry Divisions, and South Vietnamese units, as well as the 173d Airborne Brigade. Their target was enemy bases north of Tay Ninh City, in the area the French had named "War Zone C." The decision to make a paratroop assault was based on the urgency to place a large force on the ground as quickly as possible and still have enough helicopter assets to make a sizeable heliborne assault as an immediate follow-up.

The requirement for helicopter lift on D-day was substantial. The 1st Infantry Division had five infantry battalions to put in by air assault and the 173d had three infantry battalions. In addition to the requirement for the Huey slicks, there was a tremendous requirement for CH-47 lift for positioning artillery and resupply of ammunition. The 173d had computed that they would free 60 Hueys and six Chinooks for support of other forces by using the parachute assault technique. The paratroopers were assigned landing zones farthest to the north—areas that would have cost many extra minutes of flying time for lift helicopters.

The 173d was placed under the operational control of the 1st Infantry Division for this operation. Thirteen C-130's were used for the personnel drop and eight C-130's for heavy drop of equipment. Jump altitude was 1,000 feet.

The battalion dropped on schedule and by 0920 hours on D-day all companies were in their locations around the drop zone. Out of the 780 combat troops who made the assault, only eleven sustained minor injuries. The heavy equipment drop commenced at 0925 hours and continued throughout the day. The 1st Battalion, 503d Infantry began landing by helicopter assault at 1035 hours and the entire battalion was in place shortly thereafter. No direct contact with an enemy force occurred during these early hours of D-day. Another infantry battalion, the 4th Battalion, 503d Infantry, conducted a heliborne assault into two other close landing zones at 1420 hours and phase one of JUNCTION CITY ALTERNATE was essentially complete.

During this operation, the 173d Brigade was supported by the 11th, the 145th, and the 1st Aviation Battalions. Over 9,700 sorties were flown in support of the operation and Army aviation lifted 9,518 troops and a daily average of fifty tons of cargo.

As might be expected, some operational problems resulted from this first mix of parachute and heliborne operations. One accident and several near accidents were experienced as a result of helicopters trying to land in an area littered with parachutes. There just wasn't time to adequately police the drop zone. Also there were some problems on Tactical Air coordination. However, the control and coordination procedures began to smooth out after the first few hours of confusion.

This combined operation, which the 173d Brigade had begun so dramatically, continued until mid-May. The enemy lost over 2,700 dead along with vast amounts of ammunition, medical supplies, and more than 800 tons of rice. War Zone C, which had been an exclusive Viet Cong stronghold for many years, was now vulnerable to the allied forces at any time of their choosing. In retrospect, there is no question that the parachute assault which began JUNCTION CITY ALTERNATE was effective. The troopers had been well trained and knew what to expect but, as General Deane stated, "More importantly, they did what was expected of them."

CHANGE OF COMMAND

On 1 April 1967 I assumed command of the 1st Cavalry Division from Major General John Norton.

The 1st Cavalry Division had been operating in the Binh Dinh Province through four successive campaigns since early 1966—Operations THAYER I, IRVING, THAYER II, and the then current campaign, PERSHING. The 1st Cavalry had put intense pressure on the North Vietnamese Army 3d Division and its three main force regiments throughout these campaigns. They had suffered severe logistical and personnel losses. The 2d Viet Cong Regiment as early as mid-October 1966 had retreated north into Quang Ngai Province to avoid the 1st Cavalry. The 22d North Vietnamese Army Regiment also withdrew into Quang Ngai during the month of March. These frequent enemy retreats to the north, to rest and regroup, contributed to the necessity for the 1st Cavalry's participation in Operation LEJEUNE which began on 7 April. The principal reason behind this operation was an urgent marine requirement to free some of their troops in Quang Ngai for movement farther north.

OPERATION LEJEUNE

The boundary between the provinces of Quang Ngai to the north and Binh Dinh to the south established the demarcation line between the I Corps and II Corps Tactical Zones. This same boundary line divided the U.S. military effort, with the III Marine Amphibious Force having the responsibility in the I Corps area.

On the 7th of April an Air Cavalry battalion task force moved into Duc Pho in the southernmost district of Quang Ngai. The Duc Pho area had been effectively controlled by the communists for more than ten years. The legitimate government of Vietnam controlled at most 10 percent of the land area in the district and, in essence, was powerless in the area. On 28 January, the 3d Battalion, 7th Marines, part of Task Force X-RAY, had moved from its base at Chu Lai into the Duc Pho area to alleviate some of the enemy control in that district. The III Marine Amphibious Force had been receiving increasing pressure along the DMZ throughout the early months of 1967 and increased enemy infiltration had forced the Marines to commit the majority of their forces along this line. The Marines were thin on the DMZ and wanted to move Task Force X-RAY north from the southern part of their area of responsibility. The Marine plan included pulling out of Duc Pho as soon as Military Assistance Command, Vietnam, could provide a replacement force. General Westmoreland decided that the most responsive unit available would be the 1st Cavalry Division.

The 1st Cavalry Division was given less than twelve hours to put a battalion task force into the Duc Pho area and less than 36 hours to increase that force to brigade size. In deference to the Marines, the operation was named after Major General John Archer Lejeune, a Marine leader during the Spanish American War and World War I. Most of the landing zones also were given names from Marine Corps history.

It was immediately obvious that the first requirement in this area would be the building of a heavy duty airstrip for support by Air Force aircraft. The decision was made to build a C-7A Caribou strip immediately at landing zone MONTEZUMA which could be expanded to accommodate C-123 aircraft. At landing zone MONTEZUMA there would also be space enough to build a parallel Caribou strip while the first airstrip was improved and surfaced to handle the larger and heavier C-130 aircraft.

Operation LEJEUNE combined the efforts of four military services: The U.S. Army, the U.S. Marine Corps. the U.S. Air Force, and the U.S. Navy. The tactical air force support was substantial. They had only taken over operation of the Caribou since the first of that year and, though slightly leary of accepting the hastily constructed airstrip, they made 159 sorties into MONTEZUMA carrying 1,081 passengers and 229 tons of cargo. During the first eight days of operations, tactical air dropped 115 tons of bombs and 70 tons of napalm. The U.S. Navy provided gun support with a total of 2,348 rounds from its two ships offshore, the USS *Picking* and the USS *Shelton.*

At noon on 22 April, Operation LE-JEUNE was terminated. Although contacts were primarily light throughout the operation, 176 enemy had been killed and 127 captured by the 2d Brigade, 1st Cavalry.

Operation LEJEUNE was unique in many ways. The deployment of the 2d Brigade to the I Corps Tactical Zone was the first commitment of any large U.S. Army unit in that area. More importantly, the engineering effort, including the lifting of 30 tons of equipment to build two tactical fixed-wing airstrips in a matter of a few days, was unparalleled in Army engineering history. Finally, the demonstrated "fire brigade" reaction capability of deploying a large task force in a day and a half to an entirely new area of operations proved again the flexibility of the airmobile division. At Duc Pho the 1st Cavalry left behind two airstrips, an impressive sea line of communications, several critical connecting roads, and a damaged Viet Cong infrastructure. In light of the limited mission, Operation LE-JEUNE was an unqualified success.

Operation LEJEUNE, however, was a relatively short move outside of the Division's area of operations. Much more complex and longer moves were made shortly thereafter which involved Air Force fixed-wing aircraft in addition to the organic lift. These moves demonstrated a technique whereby an Air Cavalry unit was extracted from combat, moved to a landing zone, and the bulk of its equipment flown by Air Force aircraft to a new location. The organic aircraft would then be ferried to the area and join with the unit ready to be employed again.

THE CAVALRY SPREAD THIN

On 23 June 1967, about 0900 hours in the morning, Lieutenant General Stanley R. Larsen told me to have a battalion ready to move by 1300 that afternoon. They would be lifted by C-130's from

54

landing zone ENGLISH in the Bong Son Plain to the Dak To-Kontum area in the Central Highlands where they were desperately needed. It was necessary to pull the 2d Battalion, 12th Cavalry directly out of contact with the enemy and get them to landing zone ENGLISH. Using 24 C-130 aircraft loads and two C-123's, the battalion moved to Dak To by that evening along with an artillery battery. They were almost immediately thrown into combat. The next day, two more battalions followed and the third day, the remainder of the direct support artillery. By now I had my 3d Brigade (—) committed to operational control of the 4th Infantry Division. In the next few days these units would participate in one of the hardest fought battles of the Vietnam war. The enemy had shown unexpected strength and determination.

One airmobile battalion task force was detached under I Field Force control in Binh Thuan Province to support pacification activities around the city of Phan Thiet. A task force was created and moved on 24 hours notice. Although scheduled for 60 days of operation, it stayed in being for 17 months. The task force contained a very significant part of the division's assets. In addition to the 2d Battalion, 7th Cavalry, it included a scout section from the air cavalry squadron, a platoon of engineers, a battery of 105-mm howitzers, a platoon of aerial rocket artillery, lift helicopters, a signal team, and intelligence and civil affairs personnel, plus a forward support element for logistics. This battalion-sized operation, known as Operation BYRD, was especially interesting as a parallel to the Division's activities during this period.

Binh Thuan is located about 100 miles northeast of Saigon, 200 miles south of Binh Dinh and bordering the South China Sea. The principal port city, Phan Thiet, was surrounded by a heavily populated rice-growing area. Forty percent of the Province consisted of forested mountains, which supplied some of the best timber in Vietnam. These woodlands also provided clandestine bases and rest areas for the Viet Cong. Operation BYRD was an economy of force effort, using a minimum involvement of United States ground combat forces, aiming to upgrade capabilities of the armed forces of South Vietnam in that area.

In order to protect the vital port of Phan Thiet and surrounding areas, the Commanding General of I Field Force, Vietnam gave the 1st Cavalry Division the mission of defeating the enemy forces in the BYRD area, in close coordination with South Vietnam forces. The battalion was to assist in opening National Highway #1 as it ran along the coast through this area. Although the composition of the task force varied, the nucleus was the airmobile battalion.

The Task Force ended up with an amazing record. During the 17 months of Operation BYRD, the 2d Battalion, 7th Cavalry had only 34 troopers killed in action while 849 enemy were killed and 109 captured. More important than enemy losses, the Task Force had enabled the South Vietnamese government to spread its control from the province and district capitals to virtually all the population in the area. Agriculture production, commerce, education and medical treatment had increased manyfold.

The small but vitally important air assaults of Operation BYRD not only reproduced the Binh Dinh battle in miniature; they also underscored the significant advantages of envelopment over penetration as a tactic. The air assault concept permits a cheaper, faster, and more decisive vertical envelopment approach, which has made the conventional battlefield more fluid than ever. The great variety of air assault concepts seems to fall under two major headings—each of which is a principle of war—surprise and security. In the Battle of Binh Dinh as well as in Operation BYRD, extensive preparations or detailed reconnaissance, while maximizing security, compromised surprise and often created dry holes, but frequently yielded rewarding results. The choice depends on the enemy situation and the ability of the G-2 to present the proper recommendation to the division commander. The air assault must rely on speed, scheme of maneuver, locally available firepower (aerial rocket artillery), and command and control from an aerial platform.

THE "COBRA" ARRIVES

On 1 September 1967, the first Huey Cobra (AH-1G) arrived in Vietnam. The initial six aircraft were assigned to their New Equipment Training Team, under the supervision of the 1st Aviation Brigade. The Cobra was a major step forward in the development of the armed helicopter.

The Army had long realized that the Huey-gun-rocket combination was a makeshift, albeit quite ingenious, system that should be replaced by a new aircraft specifically designed for the armed mission. Bell Helicopter Company had prudently carried on its own research and development program using proven dynamic components of the Huey. Consequently, they were able to offer, at the appropriate moment, an "off-the-shelf" armed helicopter for just slightly more than the modified UH-1 that the Army was then buying to replace Vietnam attrition. The "Cobra" had enough speed to meet the escort mission; tandem seating; better armor; and a better weapons system.

TAM QUAN

The Battle of Tam Quan, 6 December to 20 December 1967, which was one of the largest battles during Operation PERSHING, was a good example of the "piling on" tactics which had been so successful in the early airmobile reactions to the enemy. The battle began with the fortuitous discovery of an enemy radio antenna by a scout team near the town of Tam Quan and a small force was inserted at 1630 hours on 6 December. Although the original enemy contact had been late in the day, the 1st Brigade reacted by "piling on" with a battalion of infantry and elements of the 1st Battalion, 50th Mechanized Infantry. On the following day, elements of the 40th Army of the Republic of Vietnam Regiment joined the fight and distinguished themselves by their aggressive manner. Throughout the battle, which was characterized by massive use of artillery, tactical air support, and air assaults by both the U.S. and Army of the Republic of Vietnam troops, the allied force held the initiative. There were frequent vicious hand-to-hand battles in the trenches and bunkers. The division used its mechanized forces to fix the enemy and drive him from his fortified positions. The airmobile units hit him when he tried to move. The enemy lost 650 men during this fierce engagement.

The Battle of Tam Quan had a much greater significance than we realized at the time. In that area, it pre-empted the enemy's *Tet* offensive even though the full impact wasn't then realized. As a result, that part of Binh Dinh was the least effected of any part of South Vietnam during *Tet*.

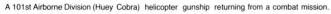

A 101st Airborne Division (Huey Cobra) helicopter gunship returning from a combat mission.

The year 1967 had proved many important facets of the airmobile concept. Perhaps the most important facet that had been demonstrated without question was the inestimable value of the Air Cavalry squadron. This unit, especially in its operations in the I Corps Tactical Zone, had demonstrated its unique capabilities in uncovering the elusive Viet Cong. Practically every major engagement was started with a contact by the 1st Squadron, 9th Cavalry Troop, and the enemy was very slow in discovering means of coping with this reconnaissance in force.

The Air Cavalry squadron success in the airmobile division convinced higher headquarters that more Air Cavalry squadrons should be assigned to the theater to work with non-airmobile divisions.

Tet, 1968

SUMMARY OF OPERATION PERSHING

Operation PERSHING was offically terminated on 21 January 1968, after almost a full year of fighting in, over and around Binh Dinh Province. To most of us PERSHING had come to mean an area of operation rather than a single campaign. During this time the 1st Cavalry Division had been continually fighting at least two different battles, often more.

The primary battle was the tedious task of routing out the Viet Cong infrastructure—that very real shadow government that had been strong in this area even during the French occupation. Working with the National Police Field Force, the 1st Cavalry participated in over 970 combined operations which had resulted in the identification and removal of over 1,600 members of the Viet Cong political and administrative structure. About 200 Viet Cong were identified as key leaders. Under the Cavalry umbrella, the National Police Field Force searched more than 340,000 individuals and 4,300 dwellings. At the close of PERSHING we felt that 50 percent of the Viet Cong cadre had been rendered ineffective. The pessimist would have to conclude that this left half of the infrastructure intact, but the fact remained that the Government of Vietnam had held an election in this troubled province, wherein 96.9 percent of the people eligible to vote, *voted.* This compared with a nation-wide average of 80.9 percent.

The second continuous battle in Binh Dinh was against the regular North Vietnamese Army 3rd Division units. The enemy lost 5,715 soldiers killed in action and 2,323 enemy were captured.

Statistics on relative vulnerability show that out of 1,147 sorties one aircraft would be hit by enemy fire, one aircraft was shot down per 13,461 sorties, and only one aircraft was shot down and lost per *21,194 sorties.* Used properly the helicopter was not the fragile target some doom-forecasters had predicted.

THE ENEMY TET OFFENSIVE

The Communists had hit in a hundred places from near the Demilitarized Zone in the north all the way to the tiny island of Phu Quoc off the Delta coast some 500 miles to the south. No target was too big or too impossible. In peasant pajamas or openly insigniaed North Vietnamese Army uniforms, the raiders struck at nearly 40 major cities and towns. They attacked 28 of South Vietnam's 44 provincial capitals.

TAN SON NHUT AIRPORT

The time was 0315, 31 January. The tower operator at Tan Son Nhut heliport, Mr. Richard O. Stark, had just received a call from an aircraft requesting to know if the field was secure. He replied in the affirmative. At 0325 the aircraft called again saying he had reports of enemy contacts in the area. Mr. Stark recalls, "I noticed sporadic tracer fire northwest of the helicopter tower, but I was not duly alarmed. Minutes later, when a C-47 departed from Tan Son Nhut and drew heavy ground fire, I realized that this was not nervous guards, but actual enemy contact." Tan Son Nhut Air Base was under attack!

Within three minutes after the alert at Tan Son Nhut, two "Razorback" fire teams consisting of four armed helicopters from the 120th Assault Helicopter Company were airborne and attacking the enemy.

There is no doubt that the quick reaction of the armed helicopters saved Tan Son Nhut and Bien Hoa from serious danger of being overrun. In the first few hours they were the only airborne firepower since the Air Force aircraft could not get clearance to even take off. An Air Force sergeant describing the action on a tape recorder at Tan Son Nhut kept repeating over and over, "Oh, those beautiful Huey gunships!" One of the men in those gunships, Captain Chad C. Payne, a fire team leader, said, "I received fire everywhere I turned. My ships received seven hits, but this was nothing considering the amount of ground fire directed toward us. There were hundreds of VC bodies everywhere in the vicinity of the Tan Son Nhut perimeter. I've never seen anything like it."

BIEN HOA AIR BASE

As daylight came over the Bien Hoa Air Base, fighting was still raging around the airfield. Small bands of Viet Cong had managed to penetrate the southeast and southwest areas of the air base. On finding themselves pinned down, the security forces called on the Cobras of the 334th Armed Helicopter Company to suppress the guerrillas. Air Force Second Lieutenant John A. Novak, who was in command of the security force, said, "As the Cobras came to our support they swept down about two feet over our heads and fired into the enemy position, knocking out the enemy who were pinning us down. The Cobras were the turning point in the enemy's destruction."

THE TET OFFENSIVE AT QUANG TRI

At 0420 on 31 January, the 812th North Vietnamese Army Regiment and supporting elements launched a concerted attack on the provincial capital of Quang Tri, a key communications hub in the I Corps Tactical Zone.

The enemy had suffered a terrible mauling from the Army of the Republic of Vietnam defenses within Quang Tri and had been thoroughly demoralized by the air assaults, gunships, and aerial rocket artillery of the 1st Cavalry Division. The aerial rocket artillery and the helicopter gunships experienced unusual success against the enemy troops.

By noon on 1 February, Quang Tri City had been cleared of the enemy and the 1st Brigade immediately initiated pursuit. A Company of the 1st Battalion, 502d Airborne made a heavy contact just south of Quang Tri killing 76 of the enemy with the help of aerial rocket artillery.

In this abortive attack, the enemy lost 914 soldiers killed in action and 86 captured. The city of Quang Tri was without a doubt one of the major objectives of the *Tet* offensive. Its successful defense was one of the highlights of this period.

THE 1ST CAVALRY AT HUE

Volumes have been written about the battle for Hue and the house-to-house fighting that went on until almost the end of February. The 1st Squadron, 9th Cavalry, had been very actively engaged in the outskirts of Hue and the division was given the mission to interdict the routes of egress and destroy the enemy units west of the city. The 2d Battalion, 12th Cavalry began to seal off the city from the west and the north with its right flank on the Perfume River on 2 February. The weather was miserable at this time with ceilings being at most 150 to 200 feet. Nevertheless, helicopters kept flying and placed the troops close to the assault positions even if they could not make an actual air assault. I think it was at this time that General Creighton W. Abrams said that any previous doubts that he had had about the ability of the helicopter to fly in marginal weather were removed.

Two Cavalry battalions were initially committed to the mission at Hue and eventually four battalions were involved in some of the most furious combat that had taken place in Vietnam since the beginning of the war. Air strikes were very difficult to call in because of the bad weather and low ceilings. Most of our helicopter operations were at an altitude of about 25 feet. The Cavalry had cut off one of the enemy's main supply lines and had taken a heavily fortified tactical headquarters at La Chu on the outskirts of the city of Hue. Brigadier General Ngo Quang Truong, Commanding General of the 1st Army of the Republic of Vietnam Division had forecast that "when the Cav reaches the walls of Hue, the battle would be over." He was right. Later, interrogation of prisoners indicated that three enemy regiments had begun moving from around Khe Sanh into the area of Hue between 11 and 20 February to reinforce the weakening local forces. The aggressive actions by the 3d Brigade of the 1st Cavalry around La Chu had seriously disrupted the enemy plans for reinforcement.

SUMMARY OF TET

The *Tet* offensive had hurt the enemy severely. The North Vietnamese Army and Viet Cong had lost some 32,000 men killed and 5,800 detained from the period between 29 January and 11 February 1968. They had lost over 7,000 individual weapons and almost 1,300 crew-served weapons.

Major Operations, 1968

KHE SANH

Weeks before the *Tet* offensive, the eyes of the world had been focused on Khe Sanh as all signs pointed to a major enemy attack on this Marine outpost.

Located some fifteen miles south of the Demilitarized Zone and barely seven miles from the eastern frontier of Laos, the Khe Sanh base functioned primarily as a support facility for surveillance units watching the demilitarized zone and probing the outer reaches of the Ho Chi Minh Trail in nearby Laos. Khe Sanh was obviously an initial objective of the North Vietnamese Army. Its seizure would have created a serious threat to our forces in the northern area and cleared the way for the enemy's advance to Quan Tri City and the heavily populated region. In addition, as General Westmoreland stated, "There is also little doubt that the enemy hoped at Khe Sanh to obtain a climacteric victory such as he had done in 1954 at Dien Bien Phu in the expectation that this would produce a psychological shock and erode American morale."

On the 25th of January I was directed to prepare a contingency plan for the relief or reinforcement of the Khe Sanh Base. This action was the first in a chain of events that was later to emerge as Operation PEGASUS. The mission was threefold: One, to relieve the Khe Sanh Combat Base; two, to open Highway Nine from Ca Lu to Khe Sanh; and, three, to destroy the enemy forces within the area of operations.

In the first weeks of 1968 signs of an impending enemy attack at Khe Sanh continued to mount. As many as four North Vietnamese divisions were identified just north of the Demilitarized Zone.

Convinced that a massive enemy blow would soon fall on Khe Sanh, the American command moved swiftly to strengthen its forces in the area, bringing the troop level at the base to a little less than 6,000 men.

Concurrent with the buildup of the allied forces in the vicinity of the Demilitarized Zone, B-52 bombers began to systematically pattern bomb suspected enemy locations near Khe Sanh and tactical fighter bombers stepped up attacks in North Vietnam's southern panhandle.

In the early morning hours of 21 January the enemy had made his long-awaited move against Khe Sanh. The main base was hit by withering artillery, rocket and mortar fire and probing efforts against outlying defensive positions to the north and northwest. South of the base the enemy attempted to overrun the villages of Khe Sanh and Huong Hoa, but were beaten back by Marine and South Vietnamese defenders.

From these beginnings, the battle lines at Khe Sanh were tightly drawn around the main base and its adjacent mountain strongholds. For the next 66 days worldwide attention would remain riveted on Khe Sanh where the enemy seemed to be challenging the United States to a set battle on a scale not attempted since the great communist victory at Dien Bien Phu.

As the siege of Khe Sanh progressed, air-delivered fire support reached unprecedented levels. A daily average of 45 B-52 sorties and 300 tactical air sorties by Air Force and Marine aircraft were flown against targets in the vicinity of the base. The U.S. Navy provided additional aircraft sorties from carriers. Eighteen hundred tons of ordnance a day were dumped into the area laying waste to huge swaths of jungle terrain and causing hundreds of secondary explosions. In seventy days of air operations 96,000 tons of bombs were dropped, nearly twice as much as was delivered by the Army Air Force in the Pacific during 1942 and 1943. B-52 Arc Light strikes were particularly effective against enemy personnel and had a great psychological impact on their troops.

But even though the allies were successful in keeping Khe Sanh supplied by air and surrounding its defenders with a pulverizing wall of firepower, a deep feeling of apprehension over the fate of this outpost persisted in official and public circles.

OPERATION PEGASUS

This, then, is how the situation stood in

early 1968. Press correspondents began to dramatize the developments. Repeatedly the public was told that Khe Sanh was likely to be a "very rough business with heartbreaking American casualties." The impending battle was seen as a major test of strength between the U.S. and North Vietnam, with heavy political and psychological overtones.

On 2 March, I went to Da Nang to present our plan for the relief of Khe Sanh to General Cushman, Commanding General, III Marine Amphibious Force. In attendance at this briefing was General Abrams, Deputy Commander, U.S. Military Assistance Command, Vietnam, who had his advance headquarters at Hue-Phu Bai. Our plan was approved in concept and provisional troop allocations were made.

The basic concept of Operation PEGASUS was as follows: The 1st Marine Regiment with two battalions would launch a ground attack west toward Khe Sanh while the 3d Brigade would lead the 1st Cavalry air assault. On D+1 and D+2 all elements would continue to attack west toward Khe Sanh; and, on the following day, the 2d Brigade of the Cavalry would land three battalions southeast of Khe Sanh and attack northwest. The 26th Marine Regiment, which was holding Khe Sanh, would attack south to secure Hill 471. On D+4, the 1st Brigade would air assault just south of Khe Sanh and attack north. The following day the 3d Army of the Republic of Vietnam Airborne Task Force would air assault southwest of Khe Sanh and attack toward Lang Vei Special Forces Camp. Linkup was planned at the end of seven days.

It became evident during the planning that the construction of an airstrip in the vicinity of Ca Lu would be a key factor for the entire operation. This airstrip, which became known as landing zone STUD, had to be ready well before D-day (1 April 1968). Calling this a "landing zone" is a gross understatement, for landing zone STUD would have to be a major air terminal, communications center, and supply depot for the future.

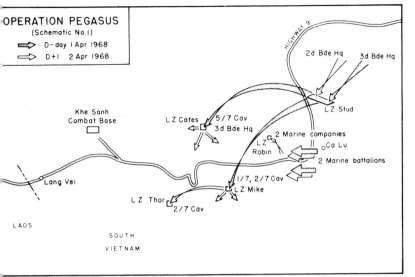

OPERATION PEGASUS
(Schematic No.1)
▭▷ D-day 1 Apr 1968
▷ D+1 2 Apr 1968

2d Bde Hq   3d Bde Hq

LZ Stud

Khe Sanh
Combat Base

LZ Cates   5/7 Cav
            3d Bde Hq

LZ Robin   2 Marine companies   Ca Lu

            2 Marine battalions

LZ Thor   1/7, 2/7 Cav
            LZ Mike
        2/7 Cav

Lang Vei

LAOS

SOUTH
VIETNAM

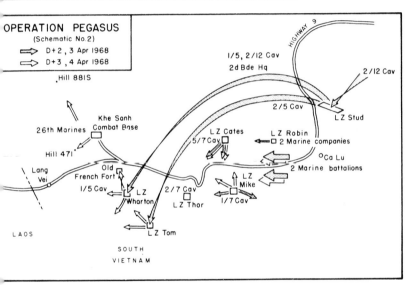

OPERATION PEGASUS
(Schematic No.2)
▭▷ D+2, 3 Apr 1968
▷ D+3, 4 Apr 1968

Hill 881S

1/5, 2/12 Cav
2d Bde Hq

2/12 Cav

2/5 Cav
LZ Stud

26th Marines   Khe Sanh
                Combat Base

Hill 471

LZ Cates   LZ Robin
5/7 Cav   2 Marine companies   Ca Lu

Lang
Vei   Old
        French Fort   2 Marine battalions

1/5 Cav   2/7 Cav   LZ Mike
        LZ
        Wharton   LZ Thor   1/7 Cav

LAOS   LZ Tom

SOUTH
VIETNAM

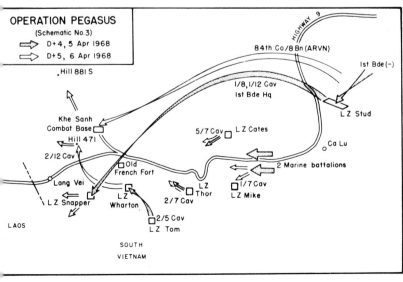

OPERATION PEGASUS
(Schematic No.3)
▭▷ D+4, 5 Apr 1968
▷ D+5, 6 Apr 1968

Hill 881S

84th Co/8 Bn (ARVN)

1st Bde(-)

1/8, 1/12 Cav
1st Bde Hq

LZ Stud

Khe Sanh
Combat Base

Hill 471   5/7 Cav   LZ Cates

2/12 Cav   Ca Lu

                Old   2 Marine battalions
                French Fort
Lang Vei   1/7 Cav

LZ Snapper   LZ   LZ   LZ Mike
            Wharton   Thor
                    2/7 Cav
                2/5 Cav
                LZ Tom

LAOS

SOUTH
VIETNAM

Schematic maps 1, 2, and 3 of Operation Pegasus.

Having established a forward base of operations, the second key element to the success of this plan was the closely integrated reconnaissance and fire support effort of the 1st Squadron, 9th Cavalry and air, artillery, and B-52 Arc Light strikes, during the period D − 6 to D-day. In addition to the aerial observation and daily photographic coverage, General Westmoreland had personally made the decision to divert new acoustic sensors from their intended emplacement along the DMZ to the approaches around Khe Sanh. Through a complex computer system, these devices could provide early warning of any intrusion and were often used to target B-52 strikes.

During the initial surveillance efforts it became evident that the enemy had established positions designed to delay or stop any attempt to reinforce or relieve Khe Sanh. Positions were identified on key terrain features both north and south of Highway Nine. As part of the reconnaissance by fire, known or suspected enemy antiaircraft positions and troop concentrations were sought out and destroyed either by organic fire or tactical air. Landing zones were selected and preparations of the landing zones for future use were accomplished by tactical air using specially fused bombs and B-52 Arc Light strikes. During this phase of the operation, the 1st Squadron, 9th Cavalry developed targets for 632 sorties of tactical air, 49 sorties for the specially fused bombs, and twelve B-52 Arc Light strikes. The thoroughness of the battlefield preparation was demonstrated during the initial assaults of the 1st Cavalry Division, for no aircraft were lost due to antiaircraft fire or enemy artillery.

At 0700 on 1 April 1968 the attack phase of Operation Pegasus commenced as two battalions of the 1st Marine Regiment attacked west from Ca Lu along Highway Nine. The 11th Marine Engineers followed right on their heels. At the same time, the 3d Brigade of the 1st Cavalry was airlifted by Chinooks and Hueys into landing zone Stud in preparation for an air assault into two objective areas farther west. Weather delayed the attack until 1300, when the 1st Battalion, 7th Cavalry air assaulted into landing zone MIKE located on prominent ground south of Highway Nine and well forward of the Marine attack.

The landing zones were secured and no significant enemy resistance was encountered. Bad weather notwithstanding, everything was in place prior to darkness. The major accomplishment of D-day was the professional manner in which this tremendously complex operation, with all its split-second timing and coordination, had to be delayed several hours yet was completed as planned.

Operation PEGASUS-LAM SON 207A from its inception to its final extraction from the area of operations will long stand as a classic example of airmobile operations. The operation dramatically illustrated the speed and effectiveness with which a large force can be employed in combat using airmobile tactics and techniques.

No summation of Operation PEGASUS would be complete without mention of the great team effort of all the Services— Army, Navy, Marines and Air Force. The operation was an ideal example of the synchronization of massive B-52 strikes, tactical air support and artillery firepower with ground maneuver. The South Vietnamese troops gave a splendid performance. The fact that we were able to co-ordinate all of these operations in a single headquarters was a commander's dream.

The success of the PEGASUS operation can largely be attributed to the detailed planning and preparation that occurred prior to D-day and the effective reconnaissance and surveillance of the area of operations provided by the air cavalry squadron. This reconnaissance and its ability to develop hard targets for the tactical air and B-52 Arc Light strikes cannot be overestimated. The concept of building landing zone STUD as a pivot point for the entire operation proved sound. This base provided a continuous flow of needed supplies and equipment to forward elements of the division. The suc-

cess of the initial battalion air assaults was rapidly exploited by aggressive company and even platoon-size air assaults, all supported by artillery and air. The enemy, although well dug in, well supplied, and with an initial determination to deter the relief of Khe Sanh, found himself surrounded with no choice but to retreat in rout order back into Laos, leaving behind 1,304 dead and much valuable equipment strewn over the battlefield.

The total success of the operation can be best measured by the mission accomplished. For the first time, the Cavalry had made an air assault as a division entity; every committed battalion came into combat by helicopter.

9TH DIVISION IN THE DELTA

While the 1st Cavalry Division was occupied in preparation for PEGASUS and in the actual relief of Khe Sanh, the U.S. 9th Infantry Division was pitted against the enemy in an entirely different type of operation in the Mekong Delta. On 1 March 1968, in conjunction with several Army of the Republic of Vietnam units, elements of the 9th Infantry Division began Operation TRUONG CONG DINH in Dinh Tuong and Kien Tuong Provinces in the IV Corps Tactical Zone. By 19 April, they had accounted for 1,716 enemy killed and 999 detained, while the U.S. forces had only lost 57 men. The division, which was operating on water almost as much as on land, saw airmobility in an entirely different light than those troops fighting in the mountains and jungles in the north.

The 9th Division's operations in the Delta proved to be a unique testing ground for certain of the airmobile concepts. To begin with, the Division found itself on the low order of priority for airmobile assets and, consequently, could compare its operations without airmobility to those with airmobility.

The 9th Infantry Division made a study of its operations from March through August 1968 to analyze division operations with and without airmobile assets. They attempted to quantify the division's effec-

tiveness by stripping out all the other variables with the exception of the addition of helicopter lift and the air cavalry. The study considered that the simplest and most relevant statistical index of combat effectiveness was the average number of Viet Cong losses inflicted daily by the unit in question. This criterion had to be adjusted to account for the fact that units do not engage in offensive field operations every day.

An analysis of the Viet Cong losses per field day produced more definitive inferences. With no air assets, the brigade performance averaged 1.6 Viet Cong losses per field day—hardly a creditable return. However, when a brigade was supported by an air cavalry troop and a helicopter company, the brigade performance rose to 13.6 Viet Cong per day—an increase of 850 percent. The study went on to refine its perimeters, but the conclusion was inescapable. There was an astonishing improvement in the combat effectiveness of the 9th Infantry Division when it was supported by airmobile and air cavalry assets.

THE A SHAU VALLEY

On 10 April 1968 at landing zone STUD, General Rosson, the commander of Provisional Corps Vietnam, told me to plan immediate movement of the 1st Cavalry into the A Shau Valley. The following day, we began extracting troops from Operation PEGASUS back into our base areas at Quang Tri City and Camp Evans.

Final preparations for Operation DELAWARE-LAM SON 216 were conducted during the last days of Operation PEGASUS. The 1st Squadron, 9th Cavalry of the 1st Cavalry Division began an extensive aerial reconnaissance of the A Shau Valley to select flight routes, locate antiaircraft and artillery weapons, and to develop targets for tactical air and B-52 strikes. During the period 14 to 19 April, over 100 B-52 sorties, 200 Air Force and Marine fighter sorties, and numerous aerial rocket artillery missions were flown

against targets in the valley. The 1st Brigade of the 101st Airborne Division and the Army of the Republic of Vietnam Airborne Task Force were moved into pre-assault positions ready to make a separate attack on D-day east of the A Shau.

The 101st Airborne Division's role in Operation DELAWARE was to complement the 1st Cavalry Division's assault into the valley itself. The 1st Brigade of the 101st, in coordination with the 3d Army of the Republic of Vietnam Airborne Task Force, was to conduct ground and airmobile assaults to interdict the enemy's routes of withdrawal and infiltration in the area.

Operation DELAWARE was to be a coordinated airmobile and ground attack on two axes using elements of three divisions—the 1st Cavalry, the 101st Airborne, and the 1st Army of the Republic of Vietnam Division.

Operation DELAWARE differed from PEGASUS in that during PEGASUS The Cavalry Division had control of all U.S. ground tactical elements. Operation DELAWARE was under the tactical control of Provisional Corps, and my relationship with the 101st Airborne Division was one of coordination. D-day had been tentatively set for 17 April, but I made the condition that it was really contingent on my having three full days of operations in the A Shau Valley by the 1st Squadron, 9th Cavalry in coordination with tactical air and B-52 Arc Light strikes. The purpose of this effort was to determine and neutralize the heavy enemy antiaircraft concentrations.

On the morning of the 19th of April the 3d Brigade of the 1st Cavalry Division made the initial assault into the A Shau Valley. Prior to the assault, six B-52 strikes had been delivered in the northern part of the valley and two strikes delivered on the main roads to the east. Tactical Air and artillery hit numerous targets just before the helicopters set down. Despite the large amount of preparatory fire, enemy antiaircraft fire was intense.

During the first few days of Operation

DELAWARE, in spite of very low ceilings, thunderstorms, and heavy enemy anti-aircraft fire, the 1st Cavalry Division's helicopters and the U.S. Air Force's C-130 Hercules flew repeated missions into the valley to deliver the required supplies. During the first days of the operation, navigation was strictly by pilotage.

On 24 April the 2d Battalion, 8th Cavalry, led the assault of the 1st Brigade into a landing zone two kilometers south of the A Luoi Airfield.

The 1st Brigade of the 1st Cavalry Division continued their buildup at the A Luoi airfield by flying in heavy engineer equipment, sectionalized in small enough loads to be lifted by crane helicopters. The cranes were fueled with just sufficient JP-4 to make the round trip in order to have sufficient lift capability to sling load this heavy equipment over the ridge lines.

In addition to the superb support of the Hercules pilots, I must mention the 109th Quartermaster Company (Air Drop) at Cam Ranh Bay which rigged 2,212 tons of all classes of supplies for air drop into the A Shau Valley. They and the crews of the C-130's did a tremendous job under extreme pressure.

On the morning of 29 April, elements of the 1st Battalion, 12th Cavalry secured a landing zone in the vicinity of Ta Bat airfield and the 3d Army of the Republic of Vietnam Regiment began its insertion into the valley with the airlift of its 1st Battalion landing at 0830.

While the 1st Cavalry Division was operating in the A Shau Valley, the 101st Airborne Division had been conducting major operations to the east. The 101st had built up two major fire support bases, VEGHEL and BASTOGNE, which would be important throughout Operation DELAWARE.

Operation DELAWARE-LAM SON 216 was officially terminated on 17 May. General Rosson labeled Operation DELAWARE as "one of the most audacious, skillfully executed and successful combat undertakings of the Vietnam War."

The 1st Cavalry Division had gone into the A Shau Valley in the face of the heaviest enemy air defense ever encountered in airmobile operations up to that time. While the 1st Cavalry Division lost twenty-one helicopters in this operation, the fact that they were able to make a major move into such an area in the face of this threat and under the worst possible weather conditions is a tribute of the soundness of the airmobile concept. Some of the helicopters that were lost ignored clear warnings of intense enemy concentrations that had been uncovered by prior reconnaissance. At times the weather gave an additional aid to the enemy by channelling helicopters into certain flight paths to go underneath the clouds. The enemy, of course, adjusted his fire to the obvious approaches.

I believe one of the greatest intangible results of this operation was the psychological blow to the enemy in discovering that there was no place in Vietnam where he could really establish a secure sanctuary. The enemy had always considered A Shau Valley to be his personal real estate and it was a symbol of his relative invulnerability. Operation DELAWARE destroyed that symbol.

Airmobile Developments, 1968

CHANGE OF COMMAND AT MILITARY ASSISTANCE COMMAND, VIETNAM

On 11 June 1968, General William C. Westmoreland passed command of the U.S. forces in Vietnam to General Creighton W. Abrams, who would serve as Acting Commander until General Westmoreland was sworn in as Chief of Staff of the Army on 3 July.

It would be presumptuous on my part to try to give an overall assessment of General Westmoreland's influence on the airmobile concept during his four and one-half years as Commander, U.S. Military Assistance Command, Vietnam; however, there was no doubt that General Westmoreland had set the airmobile stage for his subordinate commanders through his own strategy and example.

For this study, it is important to again note that General Westmoreland believed so much in the potential of airmobility that he was willing to commit the 1st Cavalry to a major operation only days after its arrival—recognizing full well that a failure would have been not only a setback for the war but a disaster for the future of airmobility. Again, his decision to relieve Khe Sanh by a series of air assaults under the scrutiny of the entire world press was solid affirmation of his confidence in the airmobile concept. Appropriately, he would become the first Army Chief of Staff to wear the Army Aviator Badge.

THE SECOND AIRMOBILE DIVISION

On 28 June 1968 U.S. Army, Pacific published General Order 325 which initiated reorganization of the 101st Airborne Division into the Army's second airmobile division. This same order called for the Division to be redesignated the 101st Air Cavalry Division effective 1 July 1968.

Conversion of the 101st to an airmobile configuration had been considered by Department of the Army prior to the deployment of the division (—) in December 1967. However, the continued deficit in aviation assets during the buildup of forces in Vietnam had made such conversion impractical.

On 18 December 1967 the last airplane touched down in Vietnam ending the largest and longest military airlift ever attempted into a combat zone. The move had required 369 C-141 Starlifter aircraft missions and 22 C-133 Cargomaster aircraft missions, ultimately airlifting 10,024 troops and over 5,300 tons of the Division's essential equipment.

During the 1968 Tet Offensive, elements of the Division moved to protect the cities of Saigon, Bien Hoa, Song Be, Phan Thiet, and Hue. The Division Headquarters moved to the Hue area on 8 March 1968. The 101st would remain in this area for the next few years.

General William C. Westmoreland with Lt. Col. Donald A. Yoder, Commander of the 1st Battalion, 101st Airborne Division during a combat field trip.

The Screaming Eagles participated in a series of combat operations in the I Corps Tactical Zone to include Operation DELAWARE near the A Shau Valley. Though the 101st was not programmed into the A Shau Valley proper during this operation, it would be back in force several times in the next few months. When the order came to reorganize as an airmobile division, the 101st was involved in Operation NEVADA EAGLE, a large rice-denial effort in the plains south of Hue. It was determined that a full year would be necessary to convert the 101st to an airmobile configuration. The division would continue to conduct combat operations throughout the conversion period without degradation to its combat posture.

THE CAVALRY MOVES SOUTH

One of the more difficult military tasks is to move a division in contact with the enemy to another area of a combat theater, reposition it quickly, and have it ready to fight. In Vietnam, where there were never any front lines nor truly secure rear areas, such a move had special problems. Operation LIBERTY CANYON, which was the code name given to the move of the 1st Cavalry Division from I Corps Tactical Zone to III Corps Tactical Zone in the fall of 1968, is one of the best examples of rapidly moving an entire division—a move that was made so professionally and smoothly that it even achieved strategic and tactical surprise to a knowledgeable enemy.

The Changing War and Cambodia, 1969–1970

THE CHANGING WAR

Emphasis on the word "Vietnamization" after 1968 has tended to hide the fact that there was a great deal of mutual cooperation, training, and planning all along. In literally hundreds of specific areas, we had already long ago agreed that the Vietnamese should have full control of operations; and, in the Delta, which we will review in this chapter, it had always been the modus operandi. Notwithstanding, we saw the need to do much more. The U.S. Army increased existing programs to train the South Vietnamese in all aspects of airmobility including pilot and crew instruction, joint operations, in many cases from collocated U.S. and Army of the Republic of Vietnam division and brigade bases, and joint logistics. The operation into Cambodia in 1970 was an extremely successful example of what we could do together. The outstanding actions of all Army of the Republic of Vietnam units involved showed us that we were on solid ground in phasing our responsibilities over to the South Vietnamese. This was followed by a successful return to the same area the following year and by an incursion into LAOS–LAMSON 719—in which Army of the Republic of Vietnam forces took on the very best that the North Vietnamese could muster and came out on top. This phase has been marked by the best spirit and mutual cooperation that the war has yet seen and by a dramatic tightening of the airmobile capabilities of Army of the Republic of Vietnam forces.

THE CAVALRY'S CAMBODIAN CAMPAIGN

Probably no single operation better demonstrated the airmobile concept than the 1st Cavalry Division's Cambodian campaign. Here we will highlight this operation to bring out those salient points of the airmobility concept not touched upon earlier. This was the first example of a large-scale U.S. airmobile force in operation outside the borders of South Vietnam. It was the first time our commanders were allowed to cross the frustratingly close borders into the heart of the enemy sanctuary.

Beginning in the fall of 1968 the 1st Cavalry Division had straddled the enemy trails leading southward from the Cambodian border toward Saigon. The Viet Cong and North Vietnamese Army made desperate attempts to reestablish their logistical net in this area, with an obvious aim of repeating the attacks of Tet 1968. Beginning early in 1969 the 1st Cavalry fought a series of heavy skirmishes along these trails as three separate North Vietnamese Army divisions attempted to gain positions closer to the capital. The enemy effort was not successful. The 1st Cavalry's interdiction of the planned enemy operations for Tet 1969 is an untold story that merits much further study; although the enemy force was equally strong as it had been a year earlier during the infamous Tet attacks, the North Vietnamese Army plans were frustrated by the wide-ranging air cavalry surveillance and the superior mobility of the 1st Cavalry.

The enemy attempt during the early months of 1970 was weaker than the previous year. Nevertheless, several battalions did try to operate in force along the trail systems.

On 26 April 1970 Major General Elvy B. Roberts, the Division Commander, received instructions to prepare plans for a coordinated attack to neutralize the Central Office South Vietnam base area in the "Fishhook" of Cambodia. He was told that the 1st Cavalry should be prepared to implement this operation within 72 hours of notification.

This operation, here referred to as the "Cambodian Campaign," was officially entitled "Operation TOAN THANG 43," "TOAN THANG 45," and "TOAN THANG 46." It did not include the Army of the Republic of Vietnam operations in the area of the "Parrot's Beak" to the south which were concurrent and continued after the operations of the 1st Cavalry Division.

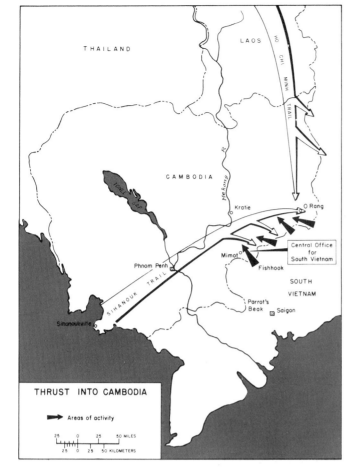

THRUST INTO CAMBODIA

➤ Areas of activity

25 0 25 50 MILES
25 0 25 50 KILOMETERS

A map of the "thrust into Cambodia."

In the early hours of 1 May, six serials of B-52's dropped their heavy ordnance on hard targets within the primary objective area. The last bomb went off at 0545. Fifteen minutes later an intense artillery preparation began with the priority to the proposed landing zones in the 3d Army of the Republic of Vietnam Airborne Brigade's objective area. D-day had arrived.

At 0630 the 1st Army of the Republic of Vietnam Cavalry Regiment began its movement from the northwest of An Loc toward the border. At the same time a *15,000 pound* bomb, with an extended fuse designed to detonate about seven feet above the ground, was dropped to clear the jungle at landing zone EAST. This was followed fifteen minutes later by a similar drop at landing zone CENTER. Shortly after first light, the Forward Air Controllers began directing tactical air strikes on pre-planned targets, shifting to the 3d Army of the Republic of Vietnam Airborne Brigade's objective area during the period from 0700 to 0800.

The enemy reaction to the opening of the Allied offensive took the form of a confused, milling crowd, ill-prepared to deal with the massive onslaught that was unleashed. Tactical surprise was complete. The enemy had not left the area, nor had he reinforced or prepared his defenses. The heliborne assault forces were not greeted with heavy antiaircraft fire but rather only with small-arms fire from a few individuals. Nowhere in evidence were the heavy machine guns from the three antiaircraft battalion-size units known to be in the area. While later evidence showed that while some strategic preparations had been made hedging against a possible allied thrust, the enemy tacticians had not taken steps to counter an air assault. Airmobility had again caught the enemy off balance.

The next few days of operations were characterized by a continuation of maneuvers begun on D-day. The enemy made strenuous efforts to avoid contact and to determine the extent and placement of the Allied forces. His command and control apparatus was completely disrupted and he was caught off guard and ill prepared. The High Command scattered in two's and three's and a large exodus of trucks going in all directions was noted by the 1st Squadron, 9th Cavalry.

Throughout the Cambodian campaign, Allied forces would uncover major caches of equipment which proved that this area was truly one of the most important logistical bases of the enemy.

On the final day of the operation, in the actual crossing of the border by all U.S. troops, every possible precaution was taken to ensure success. Troop ladders, smoke ships, pathfinders, and recovery aircraft were available to cover any contingency. The crossing proved uneventful with the last CH-47 aircraft leaving Cambodia at 1523, 29 June. The honor of being the last U.S. Army aircraft out of Cambodia went to B Company of the 1st Squadron, 9th Cavalry whose screening "Pink Team" reported reentering Vietnam at 1728, 29 June.

The intelligence provided by the 1st Squadron, 9th Cavalry enabled the division to redeploy its assets and effectively destroy many of the enemy's large cache sites. The 1st Squadron proved again during the Cambodian Campaign how invaluable this capability is to any airmobile operation. During the period 1 May 1970 to 30 June 1970 the Squadron had performed intensive ground and aerial reconnaissance operations almost every flyable hour. The Squadron's assets were shifted as necessary, capitalizing on mobility, reconnaissance, and firepower in order to determine enemy locations and escape routes. Using "Pink Teams"—one Cobra gunship and one OH-6A observation helicopter—the Air Cavalry troops were able to cover large areas effectively. When the situation warranted, the aero-rifle platoon would be inserted to face the enemy until a larger force could be committed into the area.

During the Cambodian Campaign, the 1st Cavalry Division (including those units under its operational control) accounted for 2,574 enemy killed in action and 31 prisoners of war. They captured 2,244 tons of rice and over ten million rounds of ammunition.

The 1st Cavalry Division operation in Cambodia far exceeded all expectations and proved to be one of the most successful operations in the history of the First Team. All aspects of ground and air combat were utilized—air cavalry, armor, infantry, and mechanized infantry. The U.S. Air Force reconnaissance, tactical air, and B-52's performed yeoman duty throughout the campaign there.

Organizational Changes and Laos, 1970–1971

ORGANIZATIONAL CHANGES

With the exception of decentralizing its maintenance, the organization of the 1st Cavalry Division had remained essentially unchanged since its deployment to Vietnam. However, after the Cambodian campaign, the ever-increasing area of operation, and the requirement to support more Army of the Republic of Viet-

nam operations, General George W. Putnam, Jr., commander 1st Cavalry Division, was prompted to examine means to increase his air cavalry capability.

During this same period in late 1970 the 1st Cavalry Division introduced new airmobile tactics in using the 81-mm mortar. The 81-mm mortar, long a valuable weapon to the Infantry, was used by the 1st Cavalry to support strike operations outside of tube artillery range. The mortar, which required a smaller security element than an artillery base and could be supported by the Huey, was established in a temporary mini-base located on the periphery of regular artillery range to extend indirect fire in support of ground troops. This became increasingly important as the number of squad and platoon-size operations increased.

After the Cambodian Campaign, it became the rule rather than the exception to conduct small unit operations down to separate squad and platoon-size forces, rather than the multi-battalion operations of previous years. In this way the Cavalry could cover a larger area more thoroughly, but this method of operation brought with it the requirement for a high caliber of leadership at the lowest level.

As an example of the firepower available at this time, the standard armament of the Cobra now included the 2.75-inch rocket with a 17 pound warhead, the very effective 2.75-inch Flechette rocket, and the SX-35, 20-mm cannon. The firepower of the division was enhanced by the intelligence gathering capability of the Seismic Intrusion Devices which were dropped by UH-1H helicopters along known infiltration routes. Once enemy movement had been detected, a small unit was lifted into an area well ahead of the enemy's determined course of movement and established an effective ambush with artillery and gunships standing by.

INTO LAOS

The final airmobile operation was given the code name of Lam Son 719. This combined operation took place in

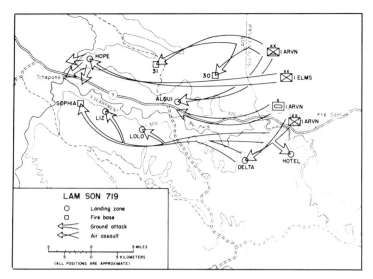

Map of Exercise Lam son 719.

Laos from 8 February to 9 April 1971. LAM SON 719 was unique in many ways, but of principal concern was the impression, generated both in and out of the military by the early reports of severe helicopter losses, that the airmobile concept had "fallen flat on its face"—that airmobility brought unacceptable risks when subject to any threat more than low-intensity antiaircraft fire in the "permissive" environment of South Vietnam. As is so often the case, the impact of the initial headlines remained uncorrected by the later objective review of the facts. Many believed that this operation was nothing short of a disaster when, in fact, it proved again the basic soundness of the airmobile concept and scored a devastating blow to the enemy's logsitics sanctuary in Laos.

For the record, the Army of the Republic of Vietnam fought tenaciously against ever-increasing odds and reached their objective. The Laos operation was a tactical and strategic success, as well as a psychological success, for the Republic of Vietnam.

Before one draws any comparisons between the Laos operations and airmobile operations conducted by the U.S. Army, it must be realized that LAM SON 719 was a very special operation in which strict rules governed U.S. military operations across the Laotian border. While the Republic of Vietnam Armed

Forces could operate freely on the ground and in the air within Laos, U.S. Forces were restricted to air operations under specific rules of engagement and were prohibited from fighting on the ground.

The fact that U.S. personnel were forbidden to go on the ground in Laos required modification of normal procedures for supporting firepower, coordination and conduct of airmobile operations, and rescue and recovery of downed crews and aircraft. The absence of U.S. advisors with the ground forces and the language difficulties added further complications.

By late September and early October 1970 it had become obvious from various enemy actions and intelligence sources that the North Vietnamese Army planned to strangle Phnom Penh and overthrow the Lon Nol Government. At the same time, there was ample evidence that the North Vietnam Army would continue its aggression against South Vietnam and rebuild its bases along the Cambodian border adjacent to III and IV Corps Tactical Zones. The key to these enemy operations was an intensified resupply and reinforcement operation in southern Laos during the dry season which would last from mid-October to mid-April 1971.

December 1970 and January 1971 brought a sharp increase in the amount of supplies moved into the southern Laotian area known as Base Area 604, adjacent to Quang Tri Province in I Corps Tactical Zone. The intelligence community further noted that only a small portion of these supplies had been moved farther to the south. In previous years the enemy had reached his peak efficiency in February and March in moving supplies down the Ho Chi Minh Trail. Accordingly, an attack against the base areas in Laos during these months presented the highest probability of inflicting the greatest damage to the enemy. Operation LAM SON 719 was conceived, developed, and implemented to react to this intelligence information.

Air interdiction of the entry points from North Vietnam into southern Laos had intensified since October 1970 and the 7th Air Force had been very effective in destroying enemy trucks. A new record of kills was reached in December and January. Army of the Republic of Vietnam operations into Cambodia were started in November 1970 with the mission of opening land and water routes to Phnom Penh. The Vietnamese forces had successfully expanded their area of operation and demonstrated their ability to conduct a major campaign without any advisory supervision.

In early February 1971 the Government of Vietnam decided to commit more than three Army of the Republic of Vietnam divisions to interdict the enemy's supply and infiltration routes in southern Laos and to destroy his logistical facilities and supplies. The broad objective was to reduce the North Vietnam Army capability for waging war in the south and to advance the security of the people of the Republic of Vietnam.

The operational area of LAM SON 719 covered an area roughly thirty-five to sixty kilometers. Natural clearings were rare throughout the area and landing zones usually had to be carved out of the dense undergrowth. Intelligence indicated that the natural landing zones would be heavily defended.

THE BATTLE

The attack into Laos was initiated on 8 February from bases established on the Khe Sanh Plain. The Army of the Republic of Vietnam 1st Armored Brigade Task Force crossed the border at 1000 and advanced nine kilometers to the west along Route Nine on the first day. Three battalions of the 3d Regiment, 1st Army of the Republic of Vietnam Infantry Division, air assaulted into landing zones south of Route Nine while two battalions of the 1st Army of the Republic of Vietnam Airborne Division air assaulted north of Route Nine. Some 105-mm howitzer batteries were air-landed in both areas on D-day.

After the attack on 8 February the enemy reacted violently to the allied offensive. He aggressively employed his weapons and troops already present in Southern Laos and he reinforced heavily his forces and committed a variety of weapons including tanks to the battle. Reinforcements came from North Vietnam, South Vietnam, and other parts of Laos.

From 3 to 6 March, the 1st Army of the Republic of Vietnam Division had accomplished a series of airmobile assaults to the west along the escarpment overlooking Route Nine. The first Army of the Republic of Vietnam units air assaulted successfully into landing zones LOLO, LIZ, and Fire Base SOPHIA WEST. After a very effective preparation of the area by B-52's, on 6 March two infantry battalions were lifted by 120 Hueys for 65 kilometers to air assault into landing zone HOPE north of Tchepone. *This large combat assault was carried out in what was considered to be the most hostile air defense environment ever encountered in the entire war, yet only one Huey was hit and it made a safe landing in the objective area.* The Army of the Republic of Vietnam units attacked south and west controlling the town. Tchepone was the objective of the allied drive to the west and was the natural communications hub of the enemy's logistics system in Laos. The enemy immediately increased his pressure in the Tchepone area and attacked the Army of the Republic of Vietnam fire bases on the escarpment viciously.

The I Corps Commander decided that most of the objectives of LAM SON 719 had been accomplished and ordered a timed withdrawal from Laos before weather worsened. During the extraction to the east from the Tchepone area, new enemy forces brought heavy pressure to bear on the Army of the Republic of Vietnam all along Route Nine. Extremely heavy antiaircraft fires were encountered along routes to or from the Army of the Republic of Vietnam fire bases. Enemy pressure was also felt at the primary U.S. Forward Support Area at Khe Sanh which received heavy attacks by fire and sappers. All and all, the enemy used every means at his disposal to make the allied withdrawal as difficult as possible.

The last elements of the 1st Infantry Division were extracted on 21 March and the remaining Vietnamese forces withdrew back into South Vietnam over the next few days. The major airmobile actions in Laos were terminated by 25 March.

Thousands of tons of ammunition, petroleum, oils, and lubricants, and other supplies and equipment were destroyed by LAM SON 719 forces. Initial reports of supplies and equipment destroyed or captured included over 4,000 individual weapons; more than 1,500 crew-served weapons; 20,000 tons of ammunition; 12,000 tons of rice; 106 tanks; 76 artillery pieces; and 405 trucks. The effectiveness of B-52 strikes, tactical air, helicopter gunships, and artillery is further indicated by over 9,700 secondary explosions.

Enemy personnel losses were very heavy. While these losses might eventually be replaced, the requirement to replace losses in such regiments as the 1st Viet Cong, 29th, 36th, 64th, 102d, and 803d would, in all probability, draw off replacement personnel programmed for other units. Combined air-ground operations in Base Area 604 resulted in a reported total of 13,914 enemy killed in action. Air and ground attacks inside the five depot areas reportedly accounted for 5,357 of these casualties. An additional 69 enemy soldiers were captured.

REVIEW OF AIRMOBILE SUPPORT DURING LAM SON 719

The precise impact of LAM SON 719 on the enemy's long-range goals must be left for future studies. The important issue here is whether the airmobility concept failed or succeeded in this important test.

A special aviation task force organization was created to provide the extensive aviation support required by LAM SON 719. This aviation task force was built around the structure of the 101st Airborne Division (Airmobile) by supplementing the division's organic assets with aviation and air cavalry units from other divisions, the 1st Aviation Brigade, and from units scheduled for deactivation or redeployment. The division's 2d Squadron, 17th Cavalry, took operational control of supplemental air cavalry troops. The Division Support Command provided logistic and maintenance support for supplemental and organic units and established forward refueling and rearming points to support the operation. The 101st Division used its command and control structure to command the aviation and air cavalry units and to plan and conduct the airmobile operations in support of LAM SON 719.

With all its limitations, the armed helicopter proved the most important firesupport weapons system during LAM SON 719. Armed helicopters, operating with the air cavalry, aerial rocket artillery, and escorting troop-lift, heavy-lift, and support aircraft, literally covered the battle area with their ability to respond immediately and accurately with their fire against known and suspected enemy weapons and positions. Armed helicopters, particularly those of the air cavalry, played a key role in acquiring targets, directing artillery fire and tactical air strikes against them, and conducting battle damage assessments.

Air cavalry performed two principal missions during LAM SON 719—reconnaissance to the flanks and front of ground operations and reconnaissance and security of landing zones before and during combat assaults and extractions. As the battle progressed it became evident that, because of their great confidence in the Air Cavalry, the Vietnamese units tended to employ the Air Cavalry in the close fire support role rather than in the reconnaissance role.

Upon sighting a tank or group of tanks, the cavalry gunships would engage them to maintain contact, then normally turn the target over to the Air Force and continue reconnaissance missions. If Tactical air was not available, the gunships would engage tanks until their ordance was expended; but they rarely had enough ordnance to destroy every tank in a particular sighting. Between 8 February 1971 and 24 March 1971, the Cavalry *sighted 66 tanks, destroyed (burned) six, and immobilized eight.* Three of the destroyed tanks were hit with flechettes, High Explosive and White Phosphorus; and the other three were destroyed by combinations of flechettes, High Explosive, White Phosphorus, and High Explosive Antitank.

In the context of the enemy's highly developed antiaircraft defense capability, can we make a valid judgment of the airmobile concept from the results of LAM SON 719? Let's be candid. Our total helicopter losses during this operation were 107 aircraft. Taken by itself, that figure seems a de facto indictment of the concept. But the last statistic does not tell the whole story—indeed, it is totally misleading if left unqualified.

The basic fact is: LAM SON 719 would never have been undertaken, much less successfully completed, without the support of thousands of helicopter sorties. *And for every thousand sorties the loss rate was only one quarter of one percent.* Granted, every helicopter loss was regrettable; however, this ratio does show a very high rate of accomplishment versus attrition. Most of these losses were troop transport Hueys—and more than half of these were lost just as they approached landing zones. This again points out in the strongest way that the helicopter is most vulnerable as it comes to a hover over an unsecured or partially secured area.

Not unexpectedly, the older Huey gunships did not fare as well as the Cobra in this intense air defense environment. The higher attrition rate of the armed Huey's proved that the move to the faster and better protected Cobra was timely and necessary. Many of the Cobras were hit by 12.7-mm fire but managed to return to base and, eventually, return to combat.

I recognize that this account of LAM SON 719 focuses on the airmobility aspects and does not pretend to tell the entire story of this important battle, a battle that is perhaps too recent to put into true historical perspective. One thing is certain. Without the air support of the U.S. Army, Air Force, and Marines, LAM SON 719 would never have even been planned, much less would it have succeeded.

Conclusions

The one inescapable conclusion is that the airmobility concept is irreversible. The thousands of officers who have learned to think and fight and live in three dimensions will never allow themselves to be restricted to two dimensions in the future. Airmobility will change and grow, but it is here to stay.

The story of airmobility in Vietnam is almost certainly just the first chapter of a new and dynamic Army. The glamour of airmobility has long passed, but the challenges are as great as ever. Some of the technological forecast, just dimly seen by the early planners, is now reality. If this study has served any purpose besides its bibliography, which I think is most important, it will form part of the corporate memory for those planners of the future who would like not to pay the terrible price of relearning in combat many costly lessons. As the poet-diplomat Paul Claudel once observed, "It is not enough to know the past, it is necessary to understand it."

IV U.S. Marine Aviation in Vietnam

1962–1970
(Condensed)

The Beginning

Marine Corps aviation involvement in Vietnam began on Palm Sunday 1962, when a squadron of UH-34 helicopters landed at Soc Trang in the Delta. The squadron was Marine Medium Helicopter Squadron 362 (HMM-362), commanded by Lieutenant Colonel Archie J. Clapp.

Three U.S. Army helicopter companies were already in Vietnam, and the Secretary of Defense had approved deployment of one more unit to Vietnam. The Marine Corps seized this opportunity to fly toward the sound of the drums and offered to send a squadron. They recommended Da Nang as the area of operations, since it was that area to which Marines were committed in various contingency plans. The Commander, United States Military Assistance Command, Vietnam (ComUSMACV), decreed, however, that the need at the moment was in the Delta since that Vietnamese Army corps area was the only one of the four corps areas in Vietnam that did not have any helicopter support.

Colonel John F. Carey was the commanding officer of the Marine task unit of which HMM-362 was a part. He arrived at Soc Trang on 9 April, and over the ensuing five days an element of Marine Air Base Squadron 16 (MABS-16) arrived aboard Marine KC-130 aircraft from the Marine Corps Air Facility at Futema, Okinawa. Squadron HMM-362, aug-

mented by three O-1 observation aircraft, embarked in the USS *Princeton* (LPH-5) at Okinawa and arrived off the Mekong Delta at dawn on Palm Sunday, 15 April. The squadron's helicopters completed unloading the unit's equipment and were ashore by late afternoon. The Marine task unit which was to be known as "Shufly" was established ashore.

The mission of this unit was to provide helicopter troop and cargo lift for Vietnamese Army units and its first operation was one week later, on Easter Sunday. The squadron continued to operate until August when it was relieved by HMM-163, commanded by Lieutenant Colonel Robert L. Rathbun.

In September 1962, the Marines were ordered by ComUSMACV to move to Da Nang, the high threat area, an area with which Marine planners had become well acquainted in contingency plans, war games, and advanced base problems. Some had been there before. In April 1954, Lieutenant Colonel Julius W. Ireland had landed at Da Nang airfield with Marine Attack Squadron 324 (VMA-324) and turned over twenty-five A-1 propeller driven dive bombers to the hard-pressed French. Now he was back as a colonel. He had replaced Colonel Carey as the commander of "Shufly."

The Marines initially occupied two areas on the air base. The helicopter maintenance and parking area was southeast of the runway. The billeting area was across the base on the western side, about two miles away. In those days there was not much traffic at Da Nang, so the Marines got into the habit of driving across the runway as the shortest route to commute back and forth. Four years later, this would be one of the two or three busiest airfields in the world.

In late 1964, the runway was extended to 10,000 feet, and a perimeter road, half surfaced and half dirt, was built around the base.

EARLY DAYS AT DA NANG

HMM-163 was relieved by HMM-162 in January 1963. Over the next two years other HMMs followed: 261, 361, 364, 162 for a second time, 365, and, finally, 163 for its second tour. Half the Corps' UH-34 squadrons had received invaluable combat experience before the commitment of the Marine Corps air-ground team of division-wing size.

In April 1963, an infantry platoon from the 3d Marine Division (3dMarDiv) was airlifted from Okinawa to join "Shufly." Its mission was to provide increased security for the base. In a modest way, the air-ground team was in being in Vietnam.

Brigadier General Raymond G. Davis, Commanding General of the 9th Marine Expeditionary Brigade (9thMEB), flew to Da Nang in August 1964, shortly after the Tonkin Gulf affair, and completed plans to reinforce the Marines based there in the event of an emergency. He then joined his command afloat with the Amphibious Ready Group of the Seventh Fleet. This Group was to be on and off various alert conditions for some months to come.

Early in December 1964, "Shufly" received a new title by direction of Lieutenant General Victor H. Krulak, Commanding General of the Fleet Marine Force, Pacific (FMFPac). It was now called Marine Unit Vietnam, or MUV for short.

Another aviation unit began arriving at Da Nang on 8 February 1965. This was the 1st Light Anti-Aircraft Missile (LAAM)

Battalion, commanded by Lieutenant Colonel Bertram E. Cook, Jr. The battalion was equipped with Hawk surface-to-air missiles. Battery "A," commanded by Captain Leon E. Obenhaus, arrived by air and was established on the base just to the west of the runway. Within twenty-four hours it was ready for operation. The remainder of the battalion came by ship from Okinawa, arriving at Da Nang later in the month. This battalion had been sent to Okinawa in December 1964, from its base in California, as a result of Com USMACV's request for missiles for air defense. The decision was made to retain the unit on Okinawa instead of sending it to Vietnam, but when the Viet Cong attacked Pleiku on 7 February, the United States retaliated with an air strike in North Vietnam. An order to deploy the Hawks to Da Nang was made at the same time. As in the case of Cuba in

A division of H-34D helicopters of HMM-362, the first Marine Corps helicopter squadron assigned to Vietnam, transported Vietnamese troops on a strike mission against Viet Cong positions in the Mekong Delta in May 1962. Unlike the aircraft of the three Army helicopter companies then in Vietnam, HMM-362 helicopters lacked installed machine guns; their only weapons were the "greasegun" sub-machine guns carried by the copilot and crew chief.

1962, when a crisis situation developed, Marine missile units were among the first to be deployed.

By this time MUV was pretty well established on the west side of the Da Nang air base in an old French army compound. Colonel John H. King, Jr., was in command. The helicopters were moved from their first maintenance and parking area, and were now located on the southwest corner of the field. A rather large sheet metal lean-to had been made available by the Vietnamese Air Force (VNAF) to serve as a hangar. The parking apron was blacktop and was adequate for about two squadrons of UH-34s.

BUILDUP

Late in February 1965, President Johnson made a decision to commit a Marine brigade to protect the air base at Da Nang from Communist attack. On 8 March the 9thMEB, including the 3d Battalion, 9th Marines, was ordered to land. They had been afloat and ready for such an operation for several months. Brigadier General Frederick C. Karch was then the commander of the brigade.

The 1st Battalion, 3d Marines, meanwhile had been alerted on Okinawa for a possible airlift. It, too, was ordered to Da Nang on 8 March because of the congestion which developed on the airfield. ComUSMACV ordered a temporary cessation to the lift. It was resumed on the 11th and the battalion arrived in Da Nang on the 12th.

Squadron HMM-365, commanded by Lieutenant Colonel Joseph Koler, Jr., was embarked in the *Princeton*. Koler's UH-34s were flown to the airfield at Da Nang, but the crews reembarked in the *Princeton* for the voyage to Okinawa. Aircrews and squadron personnel of Lieutenant Colonel Oliver W. Curtis' HMM-162 were airlifted by KC-130 from Okinawa to Da Nang to take over the UH-34s left by HMM-365.

Brigadier General Karch took operational control of all Marine aviation units that were already ashore. He also established an MEB command post in the same old French compound where Colonel King was set up. Colonel King had had the foresight to contact General Thi, who commanded I Corps and the ICTZ, to get permission to use some additional buildings.

The air component of the 9thMEB now included two HMMs and one LAAMbattalion. Colonel King remained in command of the air units. He also received some service support elements from Marine Aircraft Group 16 (MAG-16) based at Futema, Okinawa, and since his command was now integrated into the MEB, the MUV was deactivated and MAG-16(—) took its place. (Marine terminology often describes units as plus or minus to make clear that a unit is missing a capability normally included in the composition of the unit, or it has been given an additional capability not normally part of the given unit.)

Requests for additional military forces were submitted by ComUSMACV. One 15-plane Marine Fighter/Attack Squadron (VMFA-531) was authorized to deploy to Da Nang. VMFA-531 based at Atsugi, Japan, and commanded by Lieutenant Colonel William C. McGraw, Jr., received the order on 10 April. By dusk on the 11th, the aircraft and most of the men were in Da Nang, having flown there directly, refueling in the air from Marine KC-130 tankers as they went. On 13 April, McGraw led twelve of his F-4Bs on their first combat mission in South Vietnam, in support of U.S. Marine ground troops. The F-4 was an aircraft that would perform either air-to-air missions against hostile aircraft or air-to-ground strikes in support of friendly troops.

As the tempo of retaliatory strikes against North Vietnam by the Navy and Air Force increased, the enemy air defense began to include greater numbers of radar-controlled weapon systems. The sole source of tactical electronic warfare aircraft readily available to counter the new enemy defense was Marine Composite Reconnaissance Squadron One

(VMCJ-1) at Iwakuni, Japan. On 10 April 1965, the Commander-in-Chief, Pacific (CinCPac), ordered the deployment of an EF-10B detachment to Vietnam. The detachment, led by Lieutenant Colonel Otis W. Corman, arrived in Da Nang the same day. The electronic warfare aircraft (EF-10Bs and later EA-6As) began to provide support to Marine, Navy, and Air Force strike aircraft. The photo-reconnaissance aircraft (RF-8s and RF-4s) arrived later and performed primarily in support of Marine units, but they also supported Army units in I Corps and flew bomb damage assessment missions north of the DMZ.

Southeast Asia was an area familiar to the pilots of VMCJ-1. Detachments of RF-8As, the photographic aircraft of the squadron, had been aboard various carriers in the Gulf of Tonkin continually since May 1964, when CinCPac initiated the Yankee Team operations to conduct photo reconnaissance over Laos. Detachment pilots were also on hand to participate in the Navy's first air strikes against North Vietnam, and they continued photographic reconnaissance activities as part of carrier air wings until the detachment rejoined the parent unit at Da Nang in December 1965.

Colonel King now had an air group that contained elements of two jet squadrons, two helicopter squadrons, a Hawk missile battalion, and air control facilities so he could operate a Direct Air Support Center (DASC) and an Air Support Radar Team (ASRT). He also had the support of a detachment of KC-130 transports that were based in Japan.

The month of May was one of further growth and change. Several additional infantry battalions arrived and elements of MAG12 landed at Chu Lai to the south of Da Nang. Major General William R. Collins, Commanding General, 3dMarDiv, arrivd on 3 May from Okinawa. He set up an advance division command post, and on 6 May he established the Third Marine Expeditionary Force (III MEF); the 9thMEB was deactivated. Within a few days the title of III MEF was changed to Third Marine Amphibious Force (III MAF).

On 11 May, Major General Paul J. Fontana opened an advance command post of the 1st Marine Aircraft Wing (1st MAW) in the same compound. On 24 May, Brigadier General Keith B. McCutcheon, assistant wing commander, arrived to relieve General Fontana in the advance command post, and on 5 June he relieved him as Commanding General of the 1stMAW. The day before, Major General Lewis W. Walt relieved Collins as Commanding General, 3dMarDiv and III MAF, McCutcheon became Deputy Commander, III MAF, and Tactical Air Commander.

The Marine Air-Ground Team was in place. The 1stMAW now had elements of a headquarters group and two aircraft groups in Vietnam. Additional units were waiting to deploy and still others were requested. It was but the beginning of a steady Marine buildup in I Corps. It was summer and the weather was hot and dry. The heavy rains were not due to start until September.

MAG-11 moved into Da Nang from its base at Atsugi, Japan, in July 1965, and took command of the jet squadrons which up to that time had been under control of MAG-16. Colonel Robert F. Conley commanded MAG-11. The F-8 squadron, Marine All-Weather Fighter Squadron 312 (VMF[AW]-312), commanded by Lieutenant Colonel Richard B. Newport, arrived at Da Nang in December 1965 and occupied the completed northern touchdown pad along with VMCJ-1, which had moved over from the east side of the base.

The MAG operating area for MAG-11 and the west runway were completed late in 1966, and the last Marine flight operations were then moved from the east side of the base to the west side.

A 10,000-foot conventional concrete runway and associated taxiways, high speed turnoffs, and ramp space for two MAGs was begun at Chu Lai early in 1966 and completed that October. Marine Air Group 13 arrived from Iwakuni, Japan, and occupied the new base. This Air Group had been stationed at Kaneohe, Hawaii, as part of the 1st Marine

Chu Lai was not a recognized name on Vietnamese maps when, in March 1965, it was chosen to become the second (after Da Nang) jet base in I Corps; yet, in five years, the SATS concept was proven under combat conditions here. Among the techniques tested at Chu Lai was the modified shipboard arresting gear which can stop a jet—such as this F-4B coming into the cross-wind runway with its arresting hook down—in 600 feet.

so that the LAAM Battery which was still on Da Nang Air Base could be moved to a better tactical location.

Men, Units, and Aircraft

From the time it established its command post (CP) at Da Nang in June 1965

Brigade. It deployed to the Western Pacific with the Brigade and Brigadier General Carl in March, but bided its time in Okinawa and later in Japan, until a base was available for it in Vietnam. Beginning in the fall of 1967, both MAGs 12 and 13 operated from the concrete runway.

As the center of gravity of Marine operations moved north, the helos followed. Late in 1967, Phu Bai was expanded to accommodate a full helicopter group, and MAG-36 moved there from Ky Ha, which was taken over by the Americal Division. Later a base was established at Dong Ha to support the 3dMarDiv's operations below the DMZ. This proved to be a particularly hot area, as it came under fire with some regularity from enemy artillery north of the DMZ. In October 1967, the Quang Tri helicopter base, nine nautical miles south of Dong Ha and beyond the range of enemy artillery firing from the DMZ, was completed in a record 24 days. The helicopters were sent there from Dong Ha and operations were begun immediately. In April 1968, a provisional air group, MAG-39, was established out of 1stMAW resources in order to provide better command and control over the helicopter squadrons based at Quan Tri to better support the 3dMarDiv.

Another formidable construction project was the emplacement of a Hawk missile battery on Monkey Mountain just east of Da Nang. The site selected was over two thousand feet above sea level and about one mile east of the Air Force radar site known as Panama. Naval Mobile Construction Battalion 9, led by Commander Richard Anderson, was given this task. A road had to be built first of all, and then the mountain peak had to be leveled in order to provide a sufficiently flat area to emplace the battery. On 1 September 1965, the site was sufficiently cleared to receive the equipment, and Captain Charles R. Keith's "B" Battery, 1st LAAM Battalion, was emplaced. As in the case of airfields, development of the site continued concurrently with operations. Late in 1966, a similar but less extensive construction effort was undertaken just to the east of Hai Van Pass,

until April 1966, the 1stMAW maintained a rear echelon under its command at Iwakuni, Japan. During this period the 1st MAW had cognizance over all Marine Corps aviation units deployed to the Western Pacific. It rotated jet units between Japan and Vietnam and helo squadrons between Okinawa, the Special Landing Force (SLF) afloat in the Seventh Fleet, and Vietnam. It also reassigned men.

In Vietnam the wing had a Headquarters Group and four aircraft MAGs: MAG-11 and MAG-12, with jets at Da Nang and Chu Lai respectively; MAG-16 at Marble Mountain and Phu Bai with helos; and MAG-36 at Ky Ha with helos. A Service Group, stationed in Japan as part of the rear echelon, did not arrive in Vietnam until 1966, when facilities became available. The Headquarters Group and the Service Group were both reorganized in 1967 by Headquarters Marine Corps into three groups instead of two: a Headquarters Group, an Air Control Group, and a Support Group. This reflected a realignment of functions to provide better management of resources, based on experience gained in the recent move of the 1stMAW from Japan and Okinawa to Vietnam.

The first aircraft squadrons to arrive in Vietnam were from 1stMAW units in Japan and Okinawa. These were "rotational" squadrons. Each had been trained in the United States and deployed as a team to serve a 13-month tour together in WestPac. At the expiration of that tour, another squadron was scheduled to arrive to replace the old squadron on station.

Because all members of the squadron arrived at the same time, it meant they all had to be sent back to the United States at the same time. Likewise, all the men in squadrons that arrived in Vietnam from Hawaii and the United States, whether their units were rotational squadrons or not, would also have to be replaced at the same time.

The Corps could no longer support unit rotation on that scale, so it was forced to go to a system of replacement by individuals rather than by units, except in special cases. This problem arose because the Stateside training establishment became saturated with training individuals as individuals and had no time to devote to team or unit training, except for those units which were reforming with new aircraft. In the latter case, unit rotation was necessary. In order to preclude all of a unit being replaced in one month, the 1st MAW went through a reassignment program in late 1965 in an effort to smooth out the rotation dates of men's tours. All like squadrons, for example all HMMs, had their men interchanged to take advantage of different squadron arrival times in WestPac so that their losses through rotation would be spread over several months rather than one. Short touring a few men helped further to spread the losses. This program was called "Operation Mixmaster." It was a difficult one to administer but it accomplished its objective.

In April 1966, the aviation units in Japan and Okinawa were removed from the 1stMAW and established as a separate command reporting directly to FMFPac. The rotation of aircraft, men, and units in and out of Vietnam then became the direct responsibility of FMFPac in lieu of the 1stMAW. The principal reasons for this were that the 1stMAW was increasing in size to the point that the staff could not manage men and equipment spread all over the Western Pacific, and the units in Japan and Okinawa were under the operational control of the Seventh Fleet rather than under General Westmoreland in Vietnam, who did have the operational control of 1stMAW. So this realignment logically transferred administrative control to FMFPac.

When the war began in 1965, the Marine Corps was authorized 54 deployable aircraft squadrons in the Fleet Marine Forces: 30 jet, 3 propeller transport, 18 helicopter transport, and 3 observation.

After initial deployments to Vietnam in

1965, action was initiated on a priority basis to expand the Corps. Another Marine division, the 5th; one deployable helicopter group consisting of two medium helicopter squadrons; and two observation squadrons were authorized for the duration of the Southeast Asia conflict. The 5thMarDiv was organized, trained, and equipped, and elements of it were deployed to Vietnam. The helicopter group never did become fully organized or equipped. Only one of its helo squadrons was formed. Additionally, two fixed wing and two helicopter training groups, all non-deployable, were authorized for the permanent force structure, but they were not fully equipped until 1970.

The reasons that these aviation units were not completely organized and equipped were primarily time and money. All of the essential resources were long-lead-time items: pilots, technical men, and aircraft. All of them are expensive.

The Reserves could have provided trained personnel, but they were not called up in the case of the Marine Corps. The Reserve 4th Marine Aircraft Wing was not equipped with modern aircraft equivalent to the three regular wings, and it did not have anywhere near its allowance of helicopters, so even if the men had been left behind, it would not have been much help as far as aircraft were concerned.

Two years later the Department of Defense authorized the Marine Corps to reorganize its three permanent and two temporary observation squadrons into three observation and three light transport helicopter squadrons. The net result of these authorization was that the Marine Corps added one medium and three light transport helicopter squadrons, giving a total of 58 deployable squadrons.

THE ARRIVAL OF NEW AIRCRAFT

Aviation is a dynamic profession. The rate of obsolescence of equipment is high and new aircraft have to be placed in the inventory periodically in order to stay abreast of the requirements of modern war. In 1965, the Corps was entering a period that would see the majority of its aircraft replaced within four years.

The A-6a all-weather attack aircraft was coming into the FMF to replace six of twelve A-4 squadrons. (The Marine Corps could neither afford nor did it need to acquire a 100 per cent all-weather capability.) The squadrons retaining A-4s would get a newer and more capable series of A-4. Two-seat TA-4Fs would also become available to replace the old F-9series used by airborne tactical air coordinators.

The F-4b was well along in replacing the F-8 in the 15 fighter squadrons, and in two years, it was to be replaced in part with an even more capable F-4J.

The RF-4 photo reconnaissance aircraft was programmed to replace the RF-8.

The EA-6A electronic warfare aircraft was procured to replace the EF-10B, which was a Korean War vintage airframe.

The O-1 was scheduled to give way to the OV-10A.

The UH-34 medium transport helicopter and the CH-37 heavy transport were to be replaced by the CH-46 and the CH-53, respectively, in the 18 transport helicopter squadrons.

The UH-1E was just coming into inventory to replace the H-43. In a few years, the AH-1G Cobra would fill a complete void. It would provide the Corps with its first gunship designed for the mission. It did not replace, but rather augmented the UH-1E. (The Marine Corps had no AC-47s, AC-117s, AC-119s, or AC-130s. Every C-47, 117, 119, and 130 the Corps had was required for its primary purpose and none was available for modification to a gunship role.)

Only the KC-130 tanker-transport did not have a programmed replacement.

New models were accepted all through

the war. As each was received, a training base had to be built, not only for aircrews but also for technicians. In order to introduce a new model into the 1stMAW, a full squadron had to be trained and equipped or, in the case of reconnaissance aircraft, a detachment equivalent to one-third or one-half a squadron. As a new unit arrived in Vietnam, a similar unit with older aircraft would return to the United States to undergo reforming with new aircraft. After several like squadrons had arrived in Vietnam, they would undergo a "mixmaster" process in order to spread the rotation tour dates of the men for the same reason as the first squadrons that entered the country.

In June 1965, nine of the fixed wing and five helicopter/observation squadrons were deployed to WestPac. By the following June, 12 fixed wing and 11 helo/observation squadrons were in WestPac. A year later the total was 14 and 13, respectively, and by June 1968 it had risen to 14 and 14, essentially half of the Marine Corps' deployable squadrons. Except for one or two jet squadrons that would be located in Japan, at any one time all of these squadrons were stationed either in Vietnam or with the Special Landing Force of the Seventh Fleet operating off the coast of Vietnam.

More squadrons could not be deployed because all of the remaining squadrons in the United States were required to train replacements, either for the individual replacement program or for the limited unit rotation program to deploy new aircraft. Other commitments were drastically curtailed or eliminated. For example, no helicopters accompanied the infantry battalions to the Mediterranean. The capabilities of FMFPac and FMFLant to engage in other operations were substantially reduced.

Employment

ANTI-AIR WARFARE OPERATIONS

Vietnam, at least as far as the war in the south was concerned, was not a fighter pilot's war. There were no air-to-air engagements for Marine squadrons. No aces.

But there was a possible threat. So there had to be an air defense system and capability, and it was exercised under the terms of the agreement signed by Generals Moore and McCutcheon. The Marines provided two battalions of Hawk surface-to-air missiles for close-in defense at Da Nang and Chu Lai, F-4 Phantoms on hot pad alert, and an early warning and control capability through its air control squadron.

The Marine LAAM battalion is part of the overall anti-air warfare function. Its principal role is in close-in air defense. The battalion is normally a subordinate unit of the Marine Air Control Group, because in actual operations it is linked to the TAOC which provides information on friendly and enemy air traffic. The TAOC also normally gives "commence" and "cease" fire orders to the missiles.

One LAAM battery arrived in Vietnam in February 1965 and took position on the airfield at Da Nang. Subsequently it moved to Hill 327 west of the field. The two other firing batteries of the battalion eventually were placed on Monkey Mountain east of Da Nang, and in the Hai Van Pass to the north. Part of one of the batteries, known as an assault fire unit, was emplaced on Hill 55 eight miles south of the Da Nang vital area. The best defense of the installations at Da Nang would call for five battery sites, but adequate real estate did not become available until months later.

The 2d LAAM Battalion landed at Chu Lai in September 1965, and set up its firing batteries north and south of the SATS airfield. There were no elevated positions, but this posed a problem for any potential attacker as well.

Although neither battalion fired in anger, they did conduct live practice firings annually in order to keep their state of training high. In addition to firing at radio controlled drones, they fired at targets towed by manned fighter planes.

The Marine Corps' "air-ground team" displayed its standard, but still virtually unstoppable, power sweep when Marine infantrymen who had just landed by helicopter came under fire in a January 1966 operation. Winging past a bomb explosion from another Crusader, an F-8 from VMFAW-312 went after Viet Cong mortar positions which were firing on the landing zone.

OFFENSIVE AIR SUPPORT OPERATIONS

The main employment of Marine jets was in the delivery of air-to-ground ordnance in direct and close support of ground troops.

In this connection there were some local rules of engagement which had developed over the years, influencing the tactics and techniques to be employed. With very few exceptions, all air strikes had to be controlled by an airborne controller, and most had to have a political as well as a tactical clearance. There was good reason for this. The population was spread out over a considerable area along the coastal region and the U.S. and Vietnamese ground units were operating mainly in the same area. This led to the employment of Forward Air Controllers (Airborne) (FAC[A]). Thus, in a departure from prewar practice, the role of the FAC on the ground was minimized as far as control of air strikes was concerned. However, he had other useful employment.

The O-1 aircraft was used initially for this purpose. The Marine O-1s that were brought into Vietnam were rapidly approaching the end of their service lives, however, and on 1 September 1965, the Marine Corps stopped using them. The OV-10A, which was scheduled to replace them, did not become available until July 1968. To partially alleviate this situation, Headquarters Marine Corps and the Naval Air Systems Command managed to locate about a dozen old O-1s and had them overhauled and airlifted to Vietnam. These were too few, however, so the Marines had to rely on Army observation aircraft and Air Force FAC(A)s for those tactical air control missions demanding an airborne controller. The Air Force used the O-1 initially and later the OV-10A and the Cessna O-2. The latter is a small twin-engine, light aircraft with the engines in line. The one in front drives a tractor propeller and the one in the rear a pusher prop.

In addition to FAC(A)s, the Marine Corps employed Tactical Air Coordinators (Airborne) or TAC(A)s. Whereas FAC(A)s flew low performance aircraft and operated over friendly terrain and within range of artillery support, the TAC(A)s flew high performance jets and operated over territory controlled by the enemy. Their mission was to coordinate various strike aircraft and to ensure they hit the correct targets. In this role the Marines first used the two-seat F-9, but beginning in late 1967 they employed the two-seat TA-4F. These aircraft provided two sets of "eyeballs" rather than one and gave the TAC(A) an increased visual observation capability. The jet performance added a higher degree of survivability to the mission.

The Corps removed one of the two FACs it had in each infantry battalion because of the few opportunities offered them to control strikes and because their aeronautical talent could better be used elsewhere. The one remaining FAC plus the Air Liaison Officer, both aviation officers, continued to carry out their other responsibilities, which included advising their battalion commander on the employment of air support, requesting such support, and controlling helo operations and helo landing zones. This became big business in Vietnam. When the opportunity presented itself, the FAC did control air strikes from the ground.

The arrival of the A-6 aircraft in Vietnam introduced an advanced avionics weapon system. This system was further improved, as far as close air support was concerned, when the Marines deployed small radar beacons for use with their ground FACs. With this beacon, known as RABFAC, a FAC's precise position on the ground could be displayed on the radar scope in an A-6. The FAC could provide the bearing and distance of the target from the beacon, plus the elevation difference between the two, and the bombardier-navigator in the A-6 could enter this data into the weapon system computer, and bomb the target in bad weather or at night with accuracies approaching that of A-4s in clear, daylight deliveries.

The A-6 aircraft displayed great versatility and lived up to the expectations of those who pushed its development after the Korean War. It is the only operational aircraft that has a self-contained all-weather bombing capability including a moving target indicator mode. In this role it was used rather extensively in the monsoon season, not only in South Vietnam but also in Laos and over the heavily defended area of North Vietnam. The usual bomb load was 14,000 pounds.

Both the A-4 and F-4 were used in offensive air support with great success. The average bomb load for the A-4 was about 3,000 pounds, and for the F-4 about 5,000 pounds. These aircraft were generally fragged against planned missions, but they could also be scrambled from the alert pad, or they could be diverted in flight to higher priority targets.

The F-8 was also used during the period December 1965 through May 1968. It was in the process of being replaced in the Marine inventory by the F-4, but while it was in Vietnam it did a fine job in air-to-ground missions.

The F-8 was also the only Marine strike aircraft to be based on board a carrier of the Seventh Fleet during the Vietnam War. Marine All-Weather Fighter Squadron 212 (VMF[AW]-212), commanded by Lieutenant Colonel Charles H. Ludden, was embarked in the attack carrier USS Oriskany (CVA-34) in 1965 when she was operating off Vietnam. The squadron pilots were trained as fighter pilots but, when the carrier arrived in the Gulf of Tonkin, the urgent need was for attack aircraft which could deliver bombs. The primary mission of VMF(AW)212 became the attack of ground targets, and the squadron flew strikes in North and South Vietnam. Both the Navy and Marine Corps would have liked to have had more Marine squadrons afloat, but if they had been afloat, they wouldn't have been ashore and the Corps couldn't do both. Now that we have cut force levels in Vietnam, the Marine Corps has once again deployed aviation units aboard carriers.

During 1965, and into the early part of 1966, there was a shortage of aviation ordnance. Time was required to set up production lines in the United States and get the pipeline filled all the way to Vietnam. In the meantime, the 1stMAW used what was available in contingency stocks, and this included a great number of old high drag "fat" bombs. The old bombs had a much larger cross section than the new ones, hence they added drag to the aircraft and reduced its speed and radius of action. Again because of their cross section, fewer of the old bombs could be loaded on multiple bomb racks. The wing never lost a sortie because of ordnance, but it did have to substitute items on occasion because the preferred store was not available. In order to husband its resources, the wing commander issued a message directing that if ordnance could not be dropped on a worthwhile target, it would be brought back to base, not jettisoned.

By late 1966, a wide range of ordnance was available, including 250, 500, 1,000, and 2,000-pound bombs; 2.75 inch and five-inch rockets; napalm; 20mm. cannon; smoke; and certain other stores for special targets. There is still a requirement, however, for better aviation weapons. We need to get better first pass accuracy to reduce the number of passes over the target. One promising way to improve effectiveness appears to be offered by lasers.

Up to April 1966, ComUSMACV was not involved in the air war in North Vietnam. That war was conducted by the Commander-in-Chief, Pacific Fleet (CinCPacFlt), and Commander-in-Chief, Pacific Air Force (CinCPacAF). 1stMAW electronic EF-10Bs flew missions in the north before this, but they did so in support of the Seventh Fleet or the Seventh Air Force as subordinates of PacFlt and PacAF. On 1 April 1966, ComUSMACV was authorized by CinCPac to conduct air strikes in, and to the north of, the DMZ in what was known as Route Package One. By summer, Marine aircraft were assigned to strike there against artillery and rocket sites as well as other military targets.

With the addition of the A-6A to its inventory, the 1stMAW had the finest all-weather bombing aircraft in the world. Late in 1966, A-6s began striking targets as far north as Hanoi and Haiphong and carried on until the bombing halt in 1968, striking mostly at night. North Vietnam was, of course, heavily defended with antiaircraft artillery and surface-to-air missiles. EA-6As provided electronic jamming in support of the strike birds, and Marine F-4Bs flew cover for them to keep MiGs off their backs. Additionally, the two Marine A-6 squadrons flew strikes in other route packages as directed.

RECONNAISSANCE OPERATIONS

As noted earlier, VMCJ-1 was one of the first fixed-wing squadrons to deploy to Vietnam. In more than five years of continuous operations from Da Nang, the squadron made major contributions in the field of electronic warfare and imagery reconnaissance.

During the opening phases of the air war against North Vietnam, the EF-10Bs of VMCJ-1 were the only jet tactical electronic warfare aircraft available to provide support for U.S. Air Force and Navy strikes. To meet the requirements levied on the squadron, active electronic countermeasures were emphasized. Electronic reconnaissance was conducted enroute to and from the target. In the target area, jamming occupied most of the electronic countermeasure operators' attention. In July 1965, U.S. Air Force aircraft conducted the first strikes in history against surface-to-air missile (SAM) sites. Six EF-10Bs from VMCJ-1 supported the strike. There was no loss of aircraft to radar controlled weapons. The Navy also had an electronic warfare capability, but its EKA-3 was a combination tanker-electronic warfare aircraft and was limited to standoff jamming as opposed to close-in jamming in company with the strike aircraft. The Navy also had some EA-1s, but these were propeller-driven aircraft and were not able to keep up with the jets, hence, they too were used in a standoff role. The Air Force effort in electronic warfare was devoted almost exclusively to larger aircraft and in a "strategic," rather than a tactical, role. After the war in Vietnam got underway, they did modify some B-66 aircraft to the electronic mission.

In November 1966, the EA-6A made its debut in the theater. The quantum increase in electronic warfare capabilty represented by the EA-6A came in the nick of time. The cancerous spread of SAMs throughout North Vietnam made an eventual confrontation between Marine attack aircraft and SAMs inevitable. In April 1967, a Marine A-4 was shot down by a SAM from a site located in the DMZ. In response to the new threat, EF-10Bs began a continual patrol along the DMZ during hours of darkness when the SAMs were prone to fire. The more sophisticated EA-6As provided electronic warfare support for missions against targets located in the high threat areas of the north. Because of the need for electronic warfare aircraft, it was not until 1969 that the old EF-10Bs were at last able to leave Vietnam. As of this writing the EA-6A is the only tactical electronic warfare aircraft in any Service that can accompany strike aircraft to the target and maneuver with them.

In the relatively new art of electronic warfare, aircraft from VMCJ-1 performed in every role: escort for B-52s, support for tactical air strikes, and as intelligence collectors. Lessons learned were documented, tactics became more sophisticated, and hardware was evolved to increase the effectiveness of the electronic warfare capability.

The other side of the VMCJ-1 house, imagery reconnaissance, was equally engaged. Collection of imagery intelligence in the fight against the hard-to-locate enemy of the south varied to a great degree from flights over relatively well defined targets in the north. In the south, the usual imagery reconnaissance mission produced evidence of enemy activity, but the enemy was seldom pinpointed. To determine enemy intentions, reconnaissance flights over the same areas were conducted periodically. Interpreters then looked for telltale indications of change or deviations from the norm that had been established by previous flights. With the RF-8A, the imagery coverage of large areas required by this type of intelligence determination was confined to periods of daylight hours and relatively good weather. Replacement of the RF-8A with multi-sensor RF-4B aircraft, beginning in October 1966, provided VMCJ-1 with an around-the-clock collection capacity. As experience was gained with the new systems, night infrared reconnaissance played an ever increasing role in the overall intelligence collection effort.

TA-4Fs flew hundreds of missions in the Route Package One area of North Vietnam, performing in the visual reconnaissance as well as in the TAC(A) role. They located SAM sites, truck parks, supply dumps, and other targets, and then controlled other strike aircraft against them. They also spotted and controlled naval gunfire for the USS *New Jersey* (BB-62) and other ships that participated in bombarding the north.

Visual reconnaissance by low performance aircraft is still an absolute necessity. Maneuverable, fixed-wing aircraft still have a place in this role, and the OV-10A performed better than expected. However, there is a requirement for a quieter aircraft that can overfly targets without being detected. Had such an aircraft been available, it could have been used very profitably to patrol the rocket belt around the vital area of Da Nang. There is a prototype aircraft designated the YO-3 that gives promise of this capability, but the Marine Corps does not have any.

FIXED-WING TRANSPORT OPERATIONS

Marine transports and helos were not included under single management. The Marines had two models of fixed-wing transports in Vietnam, the venerable C-117 and the work-horse KC-130. The former was assigned only in small numbers, one per group, and was used for organic logistic support. It became apparent in 1965, however, that there were some voids in the Marine capability as far as aircraft were concerned, so the C-117s were rapidly drafted to fill some of these. Examples were flare drops, radio relay, and use as an airborne control center. Later on, US-2Bs and C-1As were assigned to the wing, and sometimes they were also used for some of these tasks.

Marine Refueler Transport Squadron 152 (VMGR-152) was based in Japan when the war began, but it moved to Okinawa late in 1965. It kept a four (or more) plane detachment at Da Nang.

A KC-130 Hercules transport air-drops supplies to the beleaguered Khe Sanh Marine combat base in January 1968. To safeguard helicopter landing of supplies to the garrison, gunships and jets worked the area over with napalm, rockets, 20-mm., and smoke, and as the supplies were delivered, the jets climbed up to waiting KC-130 tankers, were refueled in the air, and returned to their bases.

This little detachment did everything imaginable as far as air transport was concerned. It hauled men and equipment between major bases in Vietnam and to outposts such as Khe Sanh that had suitable airstrips, and it air-dropped to those that did not. It provided aerial refueler service for Marine jets, particularly those that operated up north. In 1965, whenever the strip at Chu Lai was less than eight thousand feet and A-4s were required to take off with reduced fuel loads, there was a KC-130 tanker in orbit to tank them after climb-out. These Hercules also served as airborne direct air support centers and as flareships. They were a reliable and versatile transport.

The KC-130 is getting on in years, however, and in spite of the fact that it was retrofitted with larger engines, the aircraft is only marginally capable of refueling a loaded A-6 or F-4 in flight. Furthermore, a considerable number of them are required to provide refueling service for a fighter squadron ferrying across the Pacific. Because they can't get to the same altitude as the jets, the jets have to descend to receive fuel. This requires blocking off a lot of airspace and frequently this is a constraint on a long trans-oceanic ferrying operation since it interferes with commercial flights.

What the Corps needs is a transport like the C-141, modified to be similar in capability to the KC-130.

The Corps also needs a replacement for the obsolete C-117s and those C-54s still on hand. It is willing to accept a smaller number of more modern aircraft to carry out the missions that are not applicable for the KC-130 or 141. A combination of T-39s and something like the Fairchild-Hiller F-227 would give the Corps a modern high-speed passenger and cargo hauling capability.

HELICOPTER OPERATIONS

Vietnam was certainly a helicopter war for U.S. forces. It is difficult to envisage how we would have fought there without them.

The transition from the UH-34 and CH-37 to the CH-46 and CH-53, respectively, represented a major increase in capability, but, at the same time, there were problems involving acceptance of the new models, shaking them down, training pilots and maintenance personnel, developing techniques and procedures, and establishing an adequate supply posture.

Squadrons equipped with the twelve-year-old UH-34 bore the brunt of helo operations in 1965 and for well over a year thereafter. CH-46s began to arrive in Vietnam in March 1966, when Lieutenant Colonel Warren C. Watson's HMM-164 flew to Marble Mountain from the USS *Valley Forge* (LPH-8). It was not until

1969 that all UH-34s were withdrawn. On 18 August, the blades of the last UH-34s were folded, thus marking the end of an era for Marine Corps helicopters in Vietnam. The UH-34 had performed for over seven years there in an outstanding manner.

A detachment of obsolescent CH-37s arrived from Santa Ana, California, in the summer of 1965 and did yeoman service pending arrival of the CH-53 in January 1967, when Major William R. Beeler brought in a four-plane detachment from HMH-463. By the end of the year there were two full squadrons of CH-53s in Vietnam.

As a matter of necessity the transports were armed with door guns. The H-34s could only take the 7.62-mm. machine gun, and two of these with a gunner (the crew chief manned one gun) reduced the troop carrying capacity by two men. The CH-46 and -53 helos were able to carry .50 caliber machine guns, one on each side, and although their loads were reduced too, the reduction, particularly in the case of the CH-53, was not so noticeable.

The UH-1E has been used by the Marines since 1965 to perform many tasks. They include serving as gunships; as command and control craft for MAF, division, wing, regimental, and occasionally battalion commanders; for liaison, courier, and administrative runs; for visual reconnaissance and observation; as aerial searchlights when special equipment was installed; as platforms for various kinds of sensors; as transportation for VIPs (and this was no small order); for medical evacuation of casualties; and for miscellaneous roles.

In 1965, the Corps was authorized 12 light helos per wing, and these were included in each of the three VMO squadrons. Two additional VMOs were authorized for the war in Southeast Asia and in 1968 the Department of Defense authorized the Marine Corps to convert them to three light helicopter transport squadrons (HML), giving the Corps three VMOs and three HMLs. The VMOs were

to have 18 OV-10As and 12 light helos each, and the HMLs were to have 24 light helos. Two of each kind of squadron were on hand in the 1stMAW by the latter part of 1968. This provided 72 light helos (including gunships) to support two reinforced divisions, but it still was not enough to meet all of the requirements. If there is any lesson that has been learned in Vietnam, it is that the Corps needs more light helicopters. The statistics accumulated over the past several years indicate that on the basis of hours of use there is a requirement for these aircraft nearly equal to the combined total of medium and heavy helicopters.

The AH-1G Cobra was not available for Marine use until April 1969. The gunship was accepted with enthusiasm by the pilots, performed well in a fire suppression role, and was maintained at a rather high rate of availability. Organizationally, they might be in a VMO or an HML. Ideally, 24 of them would form an HMA, one in each wing.

The first UH-34 squadrons were employed in much the same way as they had been during the "Shufly" years. They lifted troops and cargo on either tactical or administrative missions and performed the usual spectrum of miscellaneous tasks. They conducted the first night assault in Vietnam in August 1965. The 2d battalion, 3d Marines, was lifted into Elephant Valley, northwest of Da Nang.

By the end of 1965, Marine transport helos were lifting an average of 40,000 passengers and over 2,000 tons of cargo a month while operating from their main bases at Ky Ha and Marble Mountain.

In 1968, the helicopters carried an average of over 50,000 men and over 6,000 tons of cargo a month. This increase in capacity was due mainly to the substitution of CH-46 helos for UH-34s between 1966 and 1968. The increase in the requirement came mainly because of heavy assault operations against North Vietnamese Army divisions which had invaded the I Corps Tactical Zone. And in the first half of 1970, even after redeployment had commenced, they were lifting more than 70,000 passengers and 5,000 tons of cargo in a month. Part of this increase can be attributed to the increased use of the CH-53 in troop lifts.

Even back in "Shufly" days, Marine helicopter pilots learned to expect all sorts of strange cargo on the manifest. They often had to move Vietnamese units, and this included dependents and possessions, cows and pigs included.

As larger transports entered service, larger loads were carried. And this of course included larger animals. HMH-463 with its CH-53s was tasked to move a remotely located Vietnamese camp. Included in the lift requirement were two elephants. Not big ones, but nevertheless elephants. These pachyderms were tranquilized and carried externally with no problem. The crews named them "Ev" and "Charlie," which proves that they had found some time to read the newspapers sent out from home.

With the CH-53, the 1stMAW could retrieve battle damaged UH-1s, UH-34s, and CH-46s that might otherwise have been destroyed. The CH-53 could not lift another 53, however, under operating conditions in Vietnam. There is a need for a small number of heavy lift helicopters that can retrieve all helicopters and all tactical fixed-wing aircraft except transports. Such a heavy lift helicopter would also be useful in lifting heavy engineering equipment and other loads beyond the capability of the CH-53. The Army's CH-54 Skycrane's lifting capability is not sufficiently greater to make it a really attractive choice. A payload of at least 18 tons is required. Furthermore, the helicopter should be compatible with shipboard operations, and it should be capable of being disassembled and transported in C-5A or C-141 cargo planes.

One of the most hazardous helicopter missions was the evacuation of casualties at night or in poor weather. The problem was twofold: finding the correct zone, and getting in and out without getting shot up. Since most medevacs were called in by troops in contact with the enemy, the available landing zones had no landing aides to help the pilot, and so he had to rely on an accurate designation and visual identification or confirmation. At night a flare aircraft was often required to orbit the area and illuminate the zone so it could be positively identified. Gunships or jets would provide fire suppression, if required, and the evacuation helo would make a fast approach and retirement, making maximum use of whatever natural concealment might be available.

There is no doubt about it, the helicopter saved countless lives in Vietnam. If the casualty could be evacuated to a medical facility in short order, his chances of survival were very good.

Although a small number of helos were fragged each day specifically for medical evacuation, any helicopter in the air was available for such a mission, if required, and many evacs were made by on-the-scene aircraft. These helicopters of course did not carry hospital corpsmen as did those specifically fragged for the mission, but they offered the advantage of being closer, and thus quicker to respond.

The number of medevac missions flown by Marine helicopters is large indeed—in the peak year of 1968, nearly 67,000 people were evacuated in just short of 42,000 sorties—and a great many of the helos sustained hits and casualties themselves in the process of flying these missions. As a group, helicopter crews were awarded a very high percentage of Purple Hearts for wounds received in combat. They were and are very courageous men.

MULTI-FUNCTION OPERATIONS

The majority of operations conducted by III MAF required some degree of air support, and in most cases the support involved two or more tactical air functions. A complete recounting of all these operations is beyond the scope of this article. However, some representative examples are in order so that the reader may appreciate the role of Marine air in MAF operations.

As the MAF units began to undertake offensive operations, helicopters were essential for troop transport and logistic resupply, and jets were equally important for close air support. Operation Double Eagle in late January and early February 1966 illustrates several techniques and tactics that were used quite frequently in later operations. This was a multi-battalion force commanded by the Assistant Division Commander of the 3dMarDiv, Brigadier General Jonas M. Platt. The operational area was southern I Corps. Coordination was required with Vietnamese Army units in I Corps and with U.S. Army units in II Corps, specifically the 1st Air Cavalry Division. One Marine battalion and helo squadron belonged to the SLF and were embarked in the USS *Valley Forge* and other ships of the Amphibious Ready Group. MAG-36 was placed in direct support of Platt's Task Force Delta. Colonel William G. Johnson, Commanding Officer of MAG-36, located his command post adjacent to Platt's. He also established a helicopter operating area with limited maintenance support. This became known as "Johnson City." Logistic support was added: fuel, ammunition, supplies, and a medical aid station. This was in effect a Logistic Support Area (LSA), and it was essential to establish one in order to support mobile ground operations such as those in which General Platt was engaged. As the war progressed, these LSAs would become strategically located throughout the Corps area and close to main roads so that the bulk of supplies could be brought in by truck convoys. If an airfield were near, fixed-wing transport could be used. MAG-36 and Task Force Delta had a mini-DASC located at "Johnson City" through which they could control aircraft assigned to them. Helicopters were immediately available through Colonel Johnson. Jets had to be requested, but the route was direct to the TADC which could scramble A-4s from Chu Lai or F-4s from Da Nang.

Major General McCutcheon was relieved as CG 1stMAW by Major General Louis B. Robertshaw on 15 May 1966. The Struggle Movement within South Vietnam which led to the establishment of the Ky government in Saigon was still unresolved at this point, and an upsurge of political activity forced the cancellation of the planned change-of-command ceremonies. A small impromptu one was held outside III MAF Headquarters.

During General Robertshaw's tenure, the center of action tended to shift north, both on the ground and in the air. In July and August 1966, Operation Hastings produced the highest number of enemy killed to date. The Prairie series of operations, which began shortly thereafter, took place in the same locale, just south of the DMZ. Names like Dong Ha, the "Rockpile," and Con Thien came into prominence. But there was another name which was destined to become even more prominent, Khe Sanh. Late in April 1967, a Marine company made solid contact with North Vietnamese regulars northwest of Khe Sanh. On the 25th, the 3d Battalion of the 3d Marines was helo-lifted into Khe Sanh, and the next day the SLF battalion (2d Battalion, 3d Marines) was heloed into Phu Bai and thence lifted by KC-130 to Khe Sanh. Both battalions took the offensive and attacked the enemy on Hills 881 South and North. In two weeks of bitter fighting, the 1stMAW flew over one thousand sorties in around-the-clock close and direct air support of Marine infantry in the area. Here was an example of the integrated employment of fixed- and rotary-wing transports, close air support, and air control.

Major General Norman J. Anderson relieved Robertshaw on 2 June 1967. His tour was marked with a further buildup of North Vietnamese forces in Northern I Corps and the introduction of single management. The enemy's Tet offensive of

1968, the battle of Hue, and the campaign of Khe Sanh all occurred on his watch. During the Khe Sanh campaign, the entire spectrum of tactical air support was called into play—not only Marine, but also Air Force, Navy, and Vietnamese Air Force. And SAC's B-52s dropped their heavy loads upon the enemy in the surrounding hills.

One example of how all Marine tactical air functions could be coordinated into a single operational mission was the "Super Gaggle." This was a technique developed by the 1stMAW to resupply the hill outposts in the vicinity of Khe Sanh. These hills were surrounded with heavy concentrations of enemy anti-aircraft weapons, and every flight by a helo into one of the outposts was an extremely hazardous mission. Additionally, the weather in February was typically monsoon, and flying was often done on instruments. The "Super Gaggle" was a flight of transport helos escorted by A-4 jets and UH-1E gunships, all under the control of a TAC(A) in a TA-4F. The key was to take advantage of any break in the weather and to have all aircraft rendezvous over the designated point at the same time.

The operation was usually scrambled at the request of the mini-DASC at Khe Sanh on the basis that a break in the weather was expected shortly. The TAC(A) and KC-130 tankers took off from Da Nang, the A-4s from Chu Lai, UH-1E gunships from Quang Tri and CH-46s from Dong Ha. All aircraft rendezvoused over Khe Sanh within a 30 minute period under control of the TAC(A). Instrument climb-outs were often required due to weather. Even the CH-46s with external loads would climb out on a tacan bearing until they were on top. Under direction of the TAC(A), and taking advantage of the break in the clouds if it did develop, the area was worked over with napalm, rockets, 20-mm., and smoke. The CH-46s let down in a spiral column and deposited their loads on Khe Sanh and the hill outposts in less than five minutes and then

spiralled back on top and returned to their bases. The jets also climbed back on top, plugged in to the KC-130 tankers for refueling, and headed back to Da Nang and Chu Lai.

The fourth commander of the 1stMAW was Major General Charles J. Quilter. He relieved Anderson on 19 June 1968. His tour saw a reversal of the trend that started in General Robertshaw's era. The enemy withdrew after taking severe beatings at Khe Sanh, Hue, and elsewhere in ICTZ. The enemy gave up conventional large scale operations and reverted to the strategy of small unit actions and harassment.

III MAF forces underwent an operational change too. Once the 3dMarDiv was relieved of the requirement for a static defense along the strong-point barrier, they were free to undertake a mobile offensive in Northern ICTZ and strike at the enemy in the western reaches. One of the finest example of air-ground teamwork took place during the period of January through March 1969. The code name of the operation was Dewey Canyon. The locale was the upper A Shau Valley and southern Da Krong Valley. This was a multi-battalion operation involving the 9th Marine Regiment, commanded by Colonel Robert H. Barrow, and two battalions of the 1st Vietnamese Army Division.

During the last week of the pre-Dewey Canyon period, Marine attack and fighter-attack aircraft from MAGs 11, 12, and 13 flew 266 sorties over the objective area, dropping over 730 tons of ordnance.

On 21 January, D-1, a "Zippo" team, was formed of representatives of the 1stMAW and 3dMarDiv. Infantry, engineer, helicopter, and observation aircraft specialists were included. This team was responsible to the overall ground commander for landing zone and fire support; base selection and preparation; and coordination of the helicopter assault.

Early on D-Day the initial landing

Since 1965, the UH-1E has served as a gunship, a command and control craft, a liaison, courier, and administrative support craft, a visual reconnaissance and observation craft, a platform for aerial searchlights and sensors, and a means of transportation for VIPs. But perhaps its finest hours were served as, almost without regard to weather, it helped to evacuate casualties such as this Marine (center) wounded near Dong Ha in December 1967.

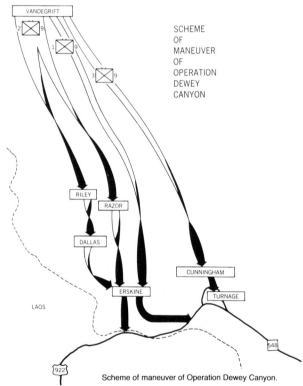

Scheme of maneuver of Operation Dewey Canyon.

zones (LZ) were prepared by fixed wing air strikes (made suitable for helo landings by bombing and strafing to reduce threat of opposition to a minimum), and elements of the 2d Battalion, 9th Marines, landed at 0800. In the rapid buildup that followed, CH-46s, under the control of the division DASC and under the protective umbrella of gunships and observation aircraft, brought 1,544 Marines and 46 tons of cargo into two LZs. By the evening of 24 January, a battery of 105-mm. howitzers from the 2d Battalion, 12th Marines, and the Command Post of the 9th Marines were in place on one of these landing zones, which became known as RAZOR.

The following day, three companies of the 3d Battalion were helo-lifted on to a ridgeline further forward, known as Co Ka Va. It would soon be developed into Fire Support Base (FSB) Cunningham, named for the first Marine aviator. In a few more days, elements of the 2d Battalion from FSB Riley pushed down the ridgeline to establish another FSB, Dallas, to guard the western approach to

the area from Laos. To the east, the two Vietnamese battalions were lifted into two other bases. They would secure the left flank and cut off the enemy escape route to the east.

About the 1st of February, the "Crachin" season really began to make itself felt. This is a period when low clouds and drizzle cover the mountain tops in Northern I Corps and obscure visibility in the valleys.

On 4 February, a company of the 3d Battalion moved into and occupied what was to become the last FSB for the coming infantry advance. Erskine was to be its name.

Marine helicopters continually worked out of FSB Vandegrift carrying essential supplies of ammunition, rations, and water to the various bases. On the return trips they carried wounded back to aid stations. Often the weather precluded access to the area except by flying on instruments. Under such conditions, over 40 pallets of critically needed supplies were dropped by KC-130s and CH-46s under control of the TPQ-10 at Vandegrift.

When artillery was in place on both Cunningham and Erskine, the 9th Marines began moving on foot from their bases into the Da Krong Valley with battalions on line. Their objective was Tiger Mountain and the ridgeline that ran west from it. As they advanced, landing zones were carved out of the jungle with 2,000-pound bombs or, as a minimum, sufficient space was created so that a medevac could be performed by helo hoist, or an external load could be dropped to the troops on the ground.

On 17 February, Marine helicopter resupply during instrument conditions received its biggest boost. Instrument departure and return corridors were established to permit loaded helos to operate out of Quang Tri in support of the operation. The technique was the same as that employed during Khe Sanh operations. During the next month of corridor operation, over 2,000 Marine aircraft were funneled in and out of this highway in the sky to keep Dewey Canyon alive.

Other elements of the air component continued to seek out the enemy and to attack him. O-1, RF-4, EA-6, A-4, F-4, and A-6 aircraft all participated. And when emergency missions arose during darkness, OV-10A, C-117, or KC-130 aircraft were called in to provide illumination by dropping flares.

OPERATION DEWEY CANYON RESULTS

Enemy Personnel Losses
1,617 KIA
    4 POW
   14 Detainees

Weapons Captured
1,212 Individual Weapons
  215 Crew Served Weapons
   12 122-mm Guns
    4 85-mm Guns
   13 82-mm Mortars
   12 60-mm Mortars
   24 57-mm Recoilless Rifles
    4 37/40-mm AA Guns
    4 23-mm AA Guns
   39 12.7-mm AA Guns
   20 7.62-mm AA Guns

The 22nd of February saw the lead element of the 3d Battalion gain the crest of Tiger Mountain. In a few days it became FSB Turnage.

The 24th found the 1st Battalion in possession of the enemy's headquarters at Tam Boi. The 2d Battalion took control of the ridgeline overlooking Route 922, where it crosses from Vietnam into Laos.

The 27th marked the first time a TPQ-10 had ever been emplaced and operated from an FSB. One was placed on Cunningham and remained there for 17 days, controlling 72 air strikes, ten A-6 beacon drops, and three emergency paradrops.

The days that followed turned up masses of enemy equipment and stores, and the quantity accumulated and sent back to our bases was easily the largest amount yet discovered during the war.

The 18th of March marked the final day of operation of Dewey Canyon. On this day virtually the entire resources of the 1stMAW were committed. Over 350 tons of cargo and 1,400 Marines were helo-lifted out of Turnage and Tam Boi without a casualty. These were the last two bases to be vacated. Gunships and jets flew close cover and close air support.

Perhaps the most notable accomplishment of the operation was that only one helicopter was lost in spite of the adverse weather and terrain and the efforts of a stubborn, well-trained, and professional enemy to counter the operation. Lieutenant General Richard G. Stilwell, U.S. Army, commander of all U.S. ground forces in Northern I Corps under CG III MAF, summed it up in a few words when he said, "Dewey Canyon deserves some space in American military history by sole reason of audacity, guts, and team play. I cannot applaud too highly the airmen of the 1stMAW in a variety of roles."

General Quilter was relieved by Major General William G. Thrash on 7 July 1969. Thrash took command when the wing was at its maximum strength and operating a peak number of facilities. The wing was supporting two Army divisions, two ARVN divisions (splitting the helo load with Army helicopters), and the Korean Marine Brigade, in addition to the two Marine divisions. It also flew out-of-country missions. Air-ground team performance reached a new high.

Several techniques that had been in use for several years were further improved during General Thrash's period of command. One of the most interesting was the insertion and extraction of reconnaissance teams. By their very nature, these teams operated well in advance of friendly lines and in enemy controlled territory. Most of the terrain there was high and forested, and there were few landing zones that permitted helos to land. Teams frequently used long ropes and rappelled in.

Getting out was something else. If it was an emergency situation due to enemy contact, it was not feasible to use a one-man hoist. So flexible ladders were employed. These were as long as 120 feet, and 6-feet wide. They were dropped from the rear ramp of a CH-46, and the pilot would hover at a height so that 20 or 30 feet would lie on the ground. The recon team would hook-on individually to the ladder and the pilot would then execute a vertical climb-out. The team would ride back to base hanging on the end of the ladder, 80 to 100 feet below the chopper and 1,500 to 2,000 feet or more above the ground.

During the extraction, a TAC(A) in an OV-10A would coordinate the air effort. Helo gunships would be directed to provide close in fires to protect the reconnaissance team on the ground. A-4s and F-4s were available with larger ordnance if more authoritative action was required.

As soon as the CH-46 pilot cleared the pick-up zone, he would turn away from a planned artillery-landing zone line and call in artillery fire to the zone he had just left. This technique became well known to the enemy, so they did not always come too close. If they did not close, the Cobra gunships would work them over while the actual extraction was in process.

Another operation that was continually improved upon as the war progressed was the Sparrow Hawk or Kingfisher, or, as it later became known, the Pacifier. In any case, the basic idea was the same: find the enemy and preempt his move. A package of aircraft was married up to a rifle platoon: CH-46s to provide troop lift, gunships for close-in support, an OV-10A for visual reconnaissance, and a UH-1E for observation and command and control. The OV-10A and gunships would scout out the target area and attempt to find the enemy, and then the CH-46s would insert the reaction force to cordon off the area and fix the enemy. If heavier air support was needed, the command and control helo could request a scramble. This technique proved to be very profitable, and it was often used to seek out the enemy in areas which fired at Marine aircraft, particularly helicopters. Prompt retaliatory action was one of the best measures to reduce this enemy harassment.

Phase Down

The first Marine aviation unit to come into Vietnam after "Shufly" was a LAAM Battalion. The first aviation unit to redeploy without replacement was also a LAAM Battalion. The 2d LAAM Battalion departed in October 1968 for Twenty-nine Palms, California. The 1st LAAM Battalion followed in August 1969. Even though they had never fired a missile at an enemy aircraft, they had served their purpose.

On 8 June 1969, the President announced his intention to withdraw 25,000 U.S. Servicemen from Vietnam. This increment became known as Keystone Eagle. One HMM departed from the 1stMAW for Futema, Okinawa, and one VMEA departed for Iwakuni, Japan. The 1st LAAM Battalion was part of this increment.

Three months later, on 17 September, another incremental withdrawal was announced, this time 40,500 men from all of the Services—nickname, Keystone Cardinal. The 3dMarDiv was the major unit to leave Vietnam in this increment, and it went to Okinawa. This division plus the 1stMAW (Rear) with headquarters at Iwakuni constituted I MAF. It is to be noted that the 1stMAW (Rear) was not associated organizationally in any way with the 1st MAW in Vietnam. It was simply a temporary title conferred on those aviation units outside of Vietnam that were deployed in WestPac as a component of the Seventh Fleet.

MAG-36 was the largest aviation unit to accompany the division. It deployed to Futema and became the parent group for all Marine helicopter squadrons in 1st MAW (Rear). One HMH, one HMM, and one VMO went to Futema as part of MAG-36. Another HMM returned to Santa Ana, California, to become part of the 3d MAW. One VMA (AW) with 12 A-6 aircraft deployed to Iwakuni and was attached to MAG-15 located there. These moves were all completed by Christmas 1969.

The President announced, on 16 December 1969, his intention to withdraw another 50,000 men. This increment was called Keystone Bluejay. MAG-12 from Chu Lai was the major Marine air unit to leave in this increment. It went to Iwakuni and joined to 1st MAW (Rear). One VMA accompanied it. Another VMA and one VMFA redeployed to El Toro, California, home station of the 3dMAW. One HMH also went to the 3d

MAW. It was then stationed at Santa Ana. Keystone Bluejay ended on 15 April.

Before completing Keystone Bluejay, III MAF underwent a change in organization. Lieutenant General Herman Nickerson, Jr., turned over command, on 9 March 1970, to Lieutenant General Keith B. McCutcheon. At the same time General Nickerson was relieved as the senior U.S. Commander in ICTZ by Lieutenant General Melvin Zais, U.S. Army, Commanding General of XXIV Corps. After nearly five years, III MAF relinquished its position as the senior U.S. command in the area. The XXIV Corps headquarters took possession of Camp Horn, on Tien Sha Peninsula across from the city of Da Nang, and III MAF established a new command post at Camp Haskins on Red Beach, very close to where the 3d Battalion, 9th Marines, had come ashore on 8 March five years earlier. Camp Haskins was a Seabee cantonment, where the 32nd Naval Construction Regiment was headquartered.

On 20 April 1970, the President announced the largest withdrawal yet, with 150,000 to leave by 1 May 1971. On 3 June it was announced that 50,000 of these would be out by 15 October 1970. Keystone Robin was the nickname for this undertaking.

Another MAG was included in this increment. MAG-13, along with one VMFAand one VMA(AW), deployed to El Toro. Another VMFA deployed to MCAS Kaneohe, Hawaii, and joined MAG-24 stationed there. These three jet squadrons flew across the Pacific, refueling from KC-130s and following the general route, Cubi Point in the Philippines, Guam, Wake, Midway, Kaneohe, and finally El Toro. Jet squadrons in previous increments had followed the same route.

The departure of MAG-13 marked the end of an era at Chu Lai. The last Marine jet flew off the concrete west runway on 11 September and headed east. The air base at Chu Lai was taken over by the U.S. Army's American Division.

VMCJ-1 also departed Vietnam and

Type of Marine Squadron	Abbrev	Number of Sqdns End FY		Model Acft In Sqdn End FY	
		1965	1970	1965	1970
All-Weather Fighter	VMF (AW)	8	—	F-8	—
Fighter Attack	VMFA	7	13*	F-4B	F-4B F-4J
Light Attack	VMA	10	7*	A-4C/E	A-1E/F
All-Weather Attack	VMA (AW)	2	6	A-6A	A-6A
Composite Reconnaissance	VMCJ	3	3	RF-8A EF-10B	RF-4B EA-6A
Refueler Transport	VMGR	3	3	KC-130	KC-130
Observation	VMO	3	3	O-1 UH-1E	OV-10A AH-1G
Light Helo Transport	HML	0	3		UH-1E
Medium Helo Transport	HMM	15	12	13 UH-34 2 CH-46	CH-46
Heavy Helo Transport	HMH	2	6	CH-37	CH-53
Total		53	56		

*One Squadron given up in order to retain three HMLs in Force Structure. VMFA-513 redesignated VMA-513 and placed in cadre status 30 June 1970; will become a Harrier squadron in last half FY71.

returned to Iwakuni, where it had been stationed prior to its arrival in Vietnam in 1965.

The other major aviation units included in this package were one HMM, which departed for Santa Ana, and Marine Wing Support Group 17, which was relocated at Iwakuni.

The deployments of units in these four increments reduced the 1stMAW from a wing of six aircraft groups and three supporting groups to a wing of two aircraft groups and two supporting groups. The number of aircraft squadrons was now 10, compared to a peak of 26 in 1968 and 1969.

Shortly after the initiation of Keystone Robin, on 1 July 1970, Major General Thrash stepped down as CG of 1stMAW, and Major General Alan J. Armstrong took command. It was to be his lot to continue the reduction of Marine aviation units in Vietnam.

Retrospect

Marine Corps aviation was in Vietnam in strength for over five years. It was ready when the order was issued to go. The years since Korea had been used to good advantage. New techniques and new equipments were operational. The overall performance from 1965 to 1970 was outstanding.

It was a dynamic period. The Marines deployed to Vietnam in 1965 with UH-34, UH-1, and CH-37 helicopters; A-4, F-8, F-4B, RF-8, and EF-10B jets; and O-1, C-117, and KC-130 propeller aircraft. They added the CH-46, CH-53, AH-1G, A-6, F-9, TA-4F, F-4J, RF-4B, EA-6A, OV-10A, US-2B, and C-1A. From 1966 on they stopped using the UH-34, CH-47, F-8, F-9, RF-8, EF-10B, and O-1. Only the UH-1, A-1, F-4B, C-117, and KC-130 participated in operations from beginning to end.

The year 1965 was one of buildup. Bases had to be obtained and developed, supply pipelines filled, and initial operating difficulties overcome. The sortie rate for jet aircraft gradually climbed to over 1.0, which was the magic figure used by planners to compute sorties. That means one sortie per day per aircraft assigned. In 1966, the rate went well beyond that, and for the entire period the Marines averaged more than 1.0. When the occasion demanded it, they surged to 1.3, 1.4, or even 1.5 for days at a time. The 1st Wing was a consumer-oriented tactical air support command. If the customer had the demand, the wing would supply the sorties.

Twelve of the Corps' total of 27 fighter-attack squadrons were deployed most of the time and 10 or 11 of these were in Vietnam. Fourteen of its 25 helicopter squadrons were deployed—well over fifty per cent. The same airpower was diminished by the following losses in aircraft in all of Southeast Asia in the period starting 25 August 1962 and ending 10 October 1970.

USMC AIRCRAFT LOSSES IN SOUTHEAST ASIA

Helicopter combat losses	252
Fixed wing combat losses	173
Helicopter operational losses	172
Fixed wing operational losses	81

Marine Corps aviation surged for over five years in order to sustain the maximum possible strength overseas. The units overseas in turn exceeded all planning factors in terms of output and productivity, under less than ideal conditions.

Marine Corps aviation left Vietnam with a sense of accomplishment. It performed its mission for nearly six years and carried out every function in the tactical air book. The innovations and developments it had worked on over the years were proven in combat. The new environment created new challenges for men in Marine aviation, and these were met head-on and solved. The war was the longest, and in many ways the most difficult, one in which Marines have had to participate. The restraints and constraints placed upon the use of air power, and the demanding management reports of all aspects of aviation required by higher authority, imposed additional requirements on staffs with no increase in resources, in most cases, to perform the tasks. In spite of these difficulties, Marine aviation performed in an outstanding manner. An analysis of sorties flown compared to assets on hand will prove that no one outflew the United States Marines.

Two A-6A Intruders await clearance for takeoff at Da Nang Airfield. The Viking on the left on another Intruder is the insignia for the Marine All-Weather Attack Squadron 225.

V Air Operations in South Vietnam

1965–1972

As 1965 opened, there was a desperate feeling among American officials in Washington and Saigon that something had to be done to raise South Vietnamese morale and reverse the depressing political and military situation. In early January, General Khanh agreed to continue supporting Premier Huong, but at month's end he ousted Huong from office. South Vietnam's governmental turmoil did not end for another 6 months. During that period the military installed and removed a second civilian premier and, finally, ousted Khanh himself who then went into exile. On 21 June, the Armed Forces Council installed Maj. Gen. Nguyen Van Thieu as the new chief of state and Air Marshal Ky as prime minister.

While the South Vietnamese were still struggling to organize a viable government, the Viet Cong launched a series of destructive attacks on allied facilities. Thus, in the early morning of 7 February 1965, enemy mortar and demolition teams struck with 81-mm mortars against the U.S. advisory compound and airstrip at the ARVN II Corps headquarters in the Pleiku area, killing 8 Americans and wounding more than 100. Five U.S. helicopters were destroyed and other aircraft damaged. An hour later the Viet Cong attacked and set fire to aviation storage tanks at Tuy Hoa airfield. Fortunately, there were no casualties.

These events triggered a meeting in Washington of the National Security Council and President Johnson's decision to order immediate retaliatory air raids against barracks and staging areas in the southern reaches of North Vietnam. That same afternoon, although the target areas were covered by clouds, 49 aircraft from naval carriers struck North Vietnamese Army barracks at Dong Hoi. The USAF-VNAF portion of the retaliatory response was held up because of adverse weather. However, the next afternoon—accompanied by F-100's flying flak suppression missions—30 Farm Gate A-1's hit barracks at Chap-Le. The President, emphasizing that these air strikes (Operation Flaming Dart) were reprisals for the earlier attacks, reiterated that the United States sought no wider war.

The enemy replied on 8 February when the Viet Cong struck Soc Trang airfield without inflicting casualties or damage. Two days later, however, they blew up a U.S. Army enlisted men's barracks at Qui Nhon, killing 23 Americans, 7 Vietnamese, and wounding many others. The Allies responded immediately, launching Air Force, Navy, and VNAF planes against NVA barracks at Chanh Hoa and Vit Thu Lu. Despite these strikes, the enemy was undeterred and announced he would continue to attack U.S. military installations throughout South Vietnam. The reprisal raids, however, did temporarily lift the sagging morale of the South Vietnamese.

In addition to mounting attacks against the Americans, Viet Cong troops managed to achieve impressive gains in the II Corps area. Whereupon, on 19 February General Westmore-

OV-10 Bronco.

(1) Secretary McNamara (l.) and Gen. Earle G. Wheeler, Chairman, of the Joint Chiefs of Staff, visit Saigon on 25 November 1965, where they conferred with Lt. Gen. Nguyen Huu Co and Ambassador Henry Cabot Lodge. (2) Gen. Curtis E. LeMay, Air Force Chief of Staff (l.) consults with Gen. Paul D. Harkins, Commander, U.S. Military Assistance Command, Vietnam, in April 1962. (3) Gen. William H. Blanchard, Air Force Vice Chief of Staff (l.), Secretary of the Air Force Eugene M. Zuckert, and Gen. John P. McConnell, Air Force Chief of Staff.

1

3

1

3

4

2

(1) Prime Minister Nguyen Cao Ky (l.) confers with Maj. Gen. Joseph H. Moore, Commander, 2d Air Division. (2) Gen. John D. Ryan, Commander in Chief, Pacific Air Forces visits Binh Thuy AB in Vietnam, September 1967, and greets Maj. Clifford R. Crooker, an 0-2A FAC pilot. (3) Gen. George S. Brown, Commander, 7th Air Force, accompanies Secretary of the Air Force Robert C. Seamans on a tour of USAF activities in South Vietnam. (4) Gen. John D. Lavelle, Commander, 7th Air Force, greets Gen. Creighton W. Abrams, Commander, U.S. Military Assistance Command, Vietnam.

land—invoking authority given him 3 weeks earlier to use jet aircraft under emergency conditions—sent 24 Air Force B-57's against the Viet Cong 9th Division's base camp deep in the jungles of Phuoc Long province along the Cambodian border. Two days later an Army special forces team and a Civilian Irregular Defense Group (CIDG) company were caught in a Communist ambush at the Mang Yang pass on Route 19. Supported by F-100 and B-57 strikes, which prevented the enemy from overrunning Allied forces, U.S. helicopters moved in and successfully evacuated 220 men who might otherwise have been lost.

The events of February 1965 marked a turning point in the history of the war, although the military situation in Vietnam remained discouraging. In Washington, officials no longer talked about withdrawing American military advisors. Instead, they now recommended deployment of additional U.S. forces to Southeast Asia, proposals which the President generally approved. While a campaign of air strikes against North Vietnam was being readied and launched, Washington also lifted major restrictions on air strikes within South Vietnam. On 6 March, Westmoreland received authorization to use U.S. aircraft whenever the VNAF could not respond on a timely basis. The former requirement that USAF planes carry Vietnamese crew members was dropped.

On 8 March the 9th Marine Expeditionary Brigade landed at Da Nang to secure American installations there. On 5 May the Army's 173d Airborne Brigade arrived at Bien Hoa to defend the military complex there. By the end of May 50,000 American troops were in South Vietnam, 10,000 of them Air Force, and more were to come. On 25 July the President, deciding that an even larger force commitment was necessary to save South Vietnam, authorized an additional troop build-up to 125,000 men.

As the American ground forces increased, so did U.S. air power. In February 1965, the Strategic Air Command deployed two B-52 squadrons to Andersen Air Force Base, Guam, for possible use over South Vietnam. In April the Air Force activated four 0-1 squadrons in South Vietnam. The first U.S. Marine F-4B's arrived at Da Nang on 12 April and immediately began flying close air support missions. A number of Air Force tactical fighter and bomber squadrons also deployed to Vietnam on temporary duty assignments, which were later made permanent. In October 1965 the first of five F-100 squadrons moved to Bien Hoa and Da Nang. They were followed in November by F-4C Phantoms of the 12th Tactical Fighter Wing, which were based at Cam Ranh Bay, and experimental AC-47 gunships at Tan Son Nhut. By year's end, the Air Force had more than 500 aircraft and 21,000 men at eight major bases in South Vietnam.

Other SEATO nations also sent military, medical, or civic action units to South Vietnam. They included a 1,557-man Australian ground-air task force, a New Zealand howitzer battery, a Philippine civic action group, and the Queen's Cobra Regiment from Thailand. The largest third-country contribution came from the Republic of Korea which was not a SEATO member. It initially dispatched one infantry division and a marine brigade totalling 20,600 men by the end of 1965. Later, Korea sent a second infantry division to Vietnam.

Viet Cong-NVA strength also continued to grow and enabled the enemy to retain the initiative and ability to interdict almost any line of communications within South Vietnam they chose. For example, Communist forces during 1965 almost totally isolated the Central Highlands of South Vietnam. To help counter enemy activity, President Johnson on 1 April authorized Westmoreland to employ

Gen. Hunter Harris, Commander in Chief, PACAF, stops at Pleiku AB during an inspection of USAF units.

American troops not only to defend American bases but also to join with the South Vietnamese in taking the fight to the enemy. On the 18th, the giant Air Force B-52's were brought into play for the first time. Flying from Andersen AFB, they struck a suspected Communist troop base area in Binh Duong province north of Saigon. Although the initial attack was unsuccessful—ground patrols could find little damage before the enemy drove them out of the area—the operation marked the beginning of extensive B-52 operations throughout Southeast Asia (see also Chapter VIII).

Aware of the military weakness of South Vietnam, General Westmoreland decided the first phase of Allied operations should consist of a holding action in areas already under Saigon's control. Beyond those areas, he proposed a series of "spoiling attacks" against enemy positions to keep the Communists off balance while the Allied force buildup continued. That is, the emphasis was to be on "search and destroy" operations rather than to seize and hold new territory. Under this strategy, air power was called upon to support all major ground unit actions while also assisting small special forces reconnaissance teams and outposts collecting intelligence of Viet Cong/NVA activity along South Vietnam's Cambodian and Laotian borders.

Gen. Vo Nguyen Giap, North Vietnamese Defense Minister.

The deployment of USAF, Navy, and Marine units to Southeast Asia during the first half of 1965 represented the greatest gathering of American airpower in one locality since the Korean War. More than 142,000 USAF combat sorties of all types were flown and in excess of 56,000 tons of munitions dropped on enemy targets. The joint USAF-VNAF effort alone accounted for an estimated 15,000 enemy dead and thousands of other casualties during the period.

The first major combat action involving American troops came in August 1965 in I Corps. During Operation Starlight, elements of the 3d Marine Division detected and pinned down the 2d Viet Cong Regiment, which found itself trapped along the coastal lowlands of Quang Ngai province, 15 miles from Chu Lai. With their backs to the sea, the enemy fought a bitter 2-day battle during which they suffered more than 700 casualties. Pilots of the 3d Marine Air Wing effectively shut off escape attempts by the Viet Cong.

In the Central Highlands in II Corps, the North Vietnamese launched a large-scale attack against the Plei Me Special Forces camp in October. An enemy regiment of an estimated 2,200 troops began its assault on 18 October and tried vainly during the next 10 days to overrun it in the face of intensive USAF air strikes. On several occasions the ferocity of their attack carried enemy troops to within 20 yards of the stronghold, only to be beaten back. In support of the camp, Air Force pilots flew 696 sorties and dropped more than 1,500,000 pounds of bombs on the attackers.

An even bloodier operation soon followed. Two NVA regiments were found in the Plei Me area, which set in motion a month-long American and ARVN search and destroy sweep which killed an estimated 1,800 enemy troops. This offensive was supported by 384 tactical air strikes, 96 B-52 sorties, and numerous night flare missions. The Communist troops fought hard, giving ground only grudgingly. However, the pounding from the air took a heavy toll, enemy resistance finally broke, and the survivors fled across the South Vietnamese border into Cambodia. But the allied side was not always successful. In November 1965 a South Vietnamese regiment, which had defeated the Viet Cong 281st Regiment, was overrun by the 272d Viet Cong Regiment, suffered heavy casualties and was put out of action. Its Vietnamese commander

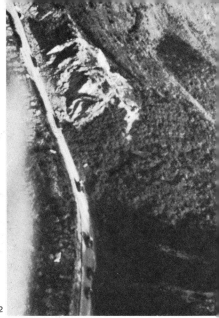

(1) 2d Lt. Edward Ridgley, CO, 3d Battalion, 9th Infantry Division, calls in an air strike. (2) An allied truck convoy heading for the Khe Sanh. (3) Elements of the U.S. Army's 1st Infantry Division arrive at Vung Tau Bay on 13 July 1965 as part of the buildup of U.S. Forces in Vietnam. (4) ARVN troops march to helicopter prior to launching an operation against enemy forces in Can Tho, February 1966. (5) Australian airmen arrive in South Vietnam, August 1964. (6) Troops of the Korean Tiger Division prepare to board a C-130 at Qui Nhon AB for airlift to Phan Rang AB, May 1966. (7) An airman inspects aircraft ordnance prior to a mission. (8) Resupply drop at Ben Het, South Vietnam.

4

5

6

7

8

was killed in the battle.

During 1966 American troop strength continued to grow, reaching a total of 385,000. The allies also were bolstered by arrival of a second Korean infantry division and additional Australian and New Zealand forces. Other air equipment arriving in South Vietnam included an F-5 fighter squadron, two F-4 squadrons, and additional AC-47 gunships.

On 24 January 1966 fierce fighting broke out during search and destroy operations in I Corps involving some 20,000 1st Air Cavalry Division troops in Binh Dinh province and the U.S. Marines in the adjacent Quang Ngai province. Their objective was the 19th and 98th North Vietnamese Regiments and the 1st and 2d Viet Cong Regiments. The operations were highlighted by excellent cooperation between Air Force, Navy, Marine, and VNAF air crews who provided round-the-clock support. AC-47 gunships were especially effective at night in inflicting heavy casualties on the enemy. When the operations ended 6 weeks later, the Air Force had flown more than 1,100 combat support missions.

The only significant enemy success during the year occurred in March in the A Shau Valley when a Special Forces camp was overrun. Located astride a section of the Ho Chi Minh trail, two miles from the Laotian border and 60 miles southwest of Da Nang, the camp was defended by 219 Vietnamese irregulars and 149 Chinese Nung mercenaries, assisted by 17 American Special Forces advisors. Before dawn on 9 March an estimated 2,000 North Vietnamese regulars opened an attack on the outpost. Poor weather limited the number of sorties that could be flown the first day to 29. A CH-3C rescue helicopter managed to land and evacuate 26 wounded defenders that day. An AC-47 gunship reached the scene but was shot down; three of its six-man crew were rescued by helicopter, two were

killed, and one was missing in action.

On 10 March the NVA launched repeated assaults against the camp under cover of a thick overcast which hid the tops of the surrounding hills and mountains. Almost miraculously an A-1E pilot made his way into the valley through an opening in the cloud cover. Other aircraft followed him down and flew 210 strikes that temporarily slowed the enemy attack. According to one American survivor of the battle, tactical aircrews tried to hold off the enemy by flying strikes under such dangerous conditions that they "had no business being there." General Westmoreland later called the air support there one of the most courageous displays of airmanship in the history of aviation. The camp commander, Capt. Tennis Carter, USA, estimated the A-1E pilots of the 1st Air Commando Squadron killed 500 enemy troops outside the camp walls.

During the day's action, Maj. Bernard C. Fisher became the Air Force's first Medal of Honor recipient in Southeast Asia, when he made a daring rescue of a downed fellow pilot, Maj. D. Wayne Myers. Myers' badly damaged A-1E had crash-landed on the camp's chewed up airstrip. Major Fisher made a quick decision to try to rescue Myers. Covered by his two wingmen, Fisher managed to land his A-1 on the debris-strewn runway, taxied its full length, spotted Myers at the edge of the strip, wheeled around, picked him up, and then took off through a rain of enemy fire.

On the evening of 10 March, the camp was abandoned. Strike aircraft forced the enemy back while rescue helicopters went in and picked up the survivors. Of the 17 Americans, 5 were killed and the other 12 wounded. Only 172 of the camp's 368 Vietnamese and Nung defenders survived to be evacuated. The North Vietnamese suffered an estimated 800 deaths, most of them attributed to air strikes. As the last hel-

New Zealand artillery unit arrives in South Vietnam.

icopter departed, the enemy moved in and subsequently began developing the camp as a major logistic base and connecting roads to the Ho Chi Minh trail. Two years would elapse before any allied troops returned to retake the A Shau valley.

In mid-1966 General Westmoreland prepared to begin Phase II operations —a series of offensive actions aimed at blunting enemy advances into the highlands and neutralizing NVA/Viet Cong food and manpower resources in coastal regions. Planned to run through 1967, this phase emphasized Special Forces operations and employment of his fast growing USAF strength, now directed by his new Deputy for Air, Lt. Gen. William W. Momyer* (who also wore a second hat as commander of the Seventh Air Force, which replaced the 2d Air Division on 1 April). Long range ground reconnaissance patrols, working out of fortified base camps, infiltrated into enemy areas seeking weak spots and potential targets. In turn these base camps became the enemy's priority target.

On 2 June 1966 U.S. Army and ARVN elements moved against a North Vietnamese regiment at Tou Monong in the highlands of Kontum province. A vicious battle ensued which lasted 19 days and resulted in more than 500 enemy dead and decimation of the NVA regiment. Air units played a major role during the battle. At times, the opposing forces were so close that strike pilots were forced to try pinpoint bombing well inside the usual strike limitations. In one instance, a company commander called for and received air strikes on his own positions, which were being overrun. The strikes stopped the attack long enough for the Americans to establish a new defense perimeter.

A milestone of significance to General Westmoreland's operations was

Royal Australian Air Force helicopter gunship goes into action against enemy troops.

*He succeeded General Moore on 1 July 1966.

17 June 1966, when the B-52's completed their first year of action over Southeast Asia. Westmoreland later wrote: "The B-52's were so valuable that I personally dealt with requests [for B-52 strikes] from field commanders, reviewed the targets, and normally allocated the available bomber resources on a daily basis." The MACV commander also "continued to urge that action be taken to substantially increase B-52 sorties."

About this time, two actions were taken to enhance B-52 flexibility of operation. The first of these involved introduction of the Combat Skyspot bombing system, whereby ground radar control units directed the big bombers over an enemy target and indicated the exact moment of bomb release. The system reduced planning time and provided a flexibility of operations which allowed diversion of the B-52's to targets of opportunity. The second innovation was establishment of a six-aircraft force of B-52's which was kept on continuous alert on Guam and which could be launched quickly whenever a battlefield situation required their assistance.

Another highlight of 1966 operations was the defeat of the Viet Cong 9th Division, which had an almost unbroken string of victories to its credit. In June and July, the 1st U.S. Infantry Division and the ARVN 5th Division—supported by tactical air units—launched attacks on the 9th, then massing for an attempt to seize the provincial capital of An Loc. In a series of five engagements, they soundly whipped the enemy division, forcing it to withdraw to sanctuaries deep in War Zone C, northwest of Saigon. It left behind more than 850 dead.

Subsequently, the 9th Division was outfitted with fresh troops and new equipment. In October—bolstered by the NVA 101st North Vietnamese Regiment—the 9th returned to action, this time in an operation aimed at a Special Forces camp at Suoi Da. It pur-

sued a classic strategy—initiate an attack with a minimal force, trigger a rescue mission by relieving troops who would then be decimated by the main enemy force through ambushes and counterattacks. Initially, the scenario unfolded as planned. Four companies of U.S. mobile strike forces were heliborne into landing zones south and east of Suoi Da, where they were immediately attacked by the enemy. One company was overrun and the others had to withdraw or be evacuated by helicopter.

Responding to this pressure, Westmoreland committed some 22,000 troops from the U.S. 1st, 4th, and 25th Divisions, and the 173d Airborne Brigade. This triggered a raging 9-day battle with the enemy stubbornly holding his ground. Tactical air strikes came in so continuously that aircraft frequently were stacked 1,000 feet above each other waiting to drop their

bombs. Their pressure, plus the heavy pounding by the B-52's, finally broke the enemy's resistance. More than 2,500 tactical sorties were flown in support of the American troops, including 487 immediate requests for close air support. The B-52's flew 225 sorties. In addition to this strike support, 3,300 tactical airlift sorties delivered 8,900 tons of cargo to the ground forces and transported more than 11,400 men into and out of the battle zone.

By early November 1966, the battle was over. Allied forces had killed more than 1,100 enemy troops and wounded hundreds more and seized enormous quantities of weapons, ammunition, and supplies, including 2,000 tons of rice. The 9th Viet Cong Division was so badly whipped that it was unable to return to combat until the spring of 1967.

Taking stock at year's end, U.S.

A CH-3E helicopter airlifts troops on a mission against enemy forces, June 1968.

An Air Force cameraman photographs a machine gunner strafing an enemy position.

officials estimated that North Vietnam —in order to make up for the huge Viet Cong losses—had been forced to commit more than 58,000 NVA regulars and take over a greater share of the fighting, especially in the two northern corps areas. They estimated this boosted total enemy forces to 282,000—110,000 being North Vietnamese, 112,000 guerrilla troops, 40,000 political cadre, and 20,000 support personnel. That enemy morale was low was testified by captured soldiers who complained about the allied heavy bombardment (especially those by the B-52's) and their personal hardships—inadequate food and supplies and long separations from home and family.

The increasing effectiveness of air power in 1966 was in large measure the result of improved tactics and weapons. Airborne forward air controllers developed an effective system

of visual reconnaissance. Assigned to specific geographic areas, they were able to identify changes in the landscape below which might indicate the enemy presence. Night reconnaissance operations were enhanced by several research and development programs and by refinement of existing instrumentation. A particularly useful device was the starlight scope, developed by the Army, which amplified starlight and moonlight so that its operator could see movement on the ground quite clearly at night. Infrared viewers also facilitated night aerial reconnaissance operations. Munitions introduced into the inventory included cluster bombs, each containing several hundred bomblets, and a delayed-action bomb capable of penetrating heavy tree cover and then exploding on the ground. Another tactic of importance was the routine employment of USAF fixed-wing gunships for night

107

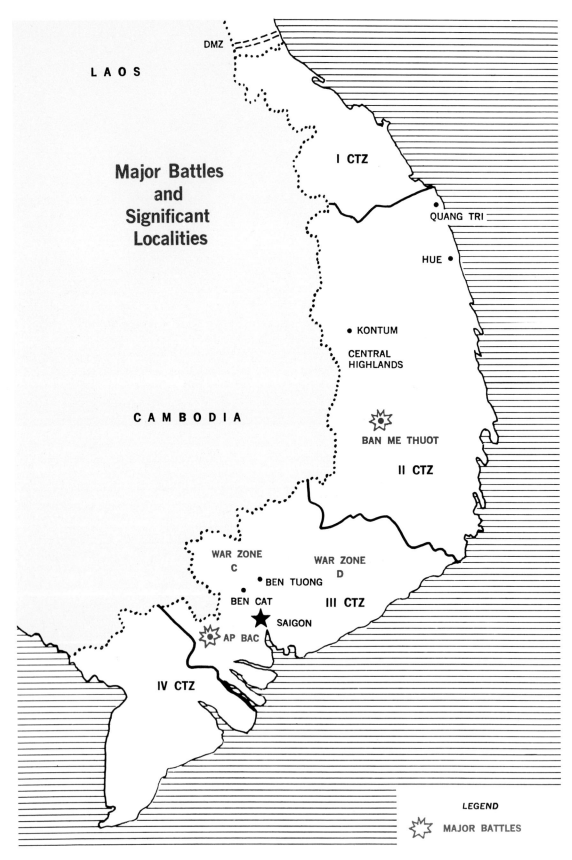

Major Battles
and
Significant
Localities

LAOS

DMZ

I CTZ

QUANG TRI

HUE

KONTUM

CENTRAL
HIGHLANDS

CAMBODIA

BAN ME THUOT

II CTZ

WAR ZONE
C

WAR ZONE
D

BEN TUONG

BEN CAT

III CTZ

SAIGON

AP BAC

IV CTZ

LEGEND

MAJOR BATTLES

hamlet defense. Their ability to remain aloft for many hours and to respond quickly to calls for close air support proved indispensable to hundreds of besieged posts, villages, and hamlets.

The Combined Campaign Plan

During 1967—the second year of the buildup of U.S. forces in Vietnam—American strength in the war zone rose from 385,000 to 486,000 personnel and enabled the allies to continue to pursue the enemy. In accordance with a joint Vietnamese-American "Combined Campaign Plan," ARVN troops were given the mission of pacifying the countryside while U.S. and allied forces conducted combat operations against NVA and Viet Cong units.

A move to root out Communist forces in the Central Highland provinces of Pleiku and Kontum got under way on 1 January and continued periodically throughout the year. During the first 95-day phase, designated Operation Sam Houston, elements of the 4th and 25th Infantry Divisions concentrated on destroying the NVA's 1st Division operating from bases inside Cambodia. This was followed in April with the 6-month-long Operation Francis Marion. Finally, in November, there occurred the Battle of Dak To in Kontum province, supported by massive tactical and B-52 strikes—more than 2,000 in number. At times, the battle was fought so closely that napalm and cluster bomb units fell within 22 and 27 yards of friendly positions while larger 750-pounders were dropped within 77 yards. The Communists broke off the fight after losing more than 1,600 dead and sustaining many more wounded. MACV attributed more than 70 percent of the enemy casualties to air strikes.

In the III Corps area, U.S. and Vietnamese troops on 8 January 1967 launched another sweep into the "Iron Triangle." This 60-square-mile jungle area contained the suspected location of the Viet Cong's 4th Military Region headquarters, which directed operations in the Saigon areas. A 3-week offensive, it involved troops of the 1st and 25th Infantry Divisions, the 173d Airborne Brigade, and the 11th Armored Cavalry Regiment, plus ARVN forces. They succeeded in overrunning a vast "underground city," destroyed the enemy headquarters, and seized enough rice to feed 13,000 men for a year. They also seized almost a half-million pages of enemy documents and captured 213 enemy personnel. According to the U.S. Army ground commander on the scene, the air strikes—1,113 tactical and 102 B-52 sorties—were responsible for the majority of the 720 enemy dead.

The Iron Triangle offensive had barely ended when General Westmoreland initiated the largest operation of the year in the same corps area. It involved 22 U.S. and four ARVN battalions which were set into motion on 22 February against reoccupied enemy bases in War Zone C. It also saw the first American parachute assault of the war aimed at intercepting any enemy troops attempting to flee into Cambodia. Initially, the enemy sought to avoid combat but later began to challenge the American forces, paying heavily for it. According to their own captured casualty lists, the enemy sustained 2,728 deaths and several thousand wounded. The allied troops also captured 600 crew-served weapons, 800 tons of rice, and vast amounts of ammunition, medical supplies, and field equipment.

The Air Force flew more than 5,000 tactical strike sorties and 125 B-52 sorties during the 83-day operation. In all, USAF crews dropped 12,000 tons of munitions, much of it in a softening-up zone just ahead of advancing troops. USAF crews also airlifted 11,307 tons of supplies, in 2,057 sorties. Both officers and men of the

Army's 1st Infantry Division praised the air support in the following words: "We find the enemy, we fix the enemy, air destroys the enemy." High-ranking Viet Cong defectors later reported that the Allied operation was a major disaster for their side. Loss of the base camps in War Zone C led to large-scale deterioration of their forces throughout the III Corps area and a revamping of their operational tactics. Enemy main force units were forced to pull back into Cambodian sanctuaries, taking with them hospitals, supply depots, and training centers.

Military experts from China, Cuba, and North Korea reportedly visited South Vietnam in the spring of 1967 during Operation Junction City and apparently concluded that time was no longer on Hanoi's side. Communist forces had not won a single major battle in almost 2 years. U.S. firepower, especially tactical air, had decimated their main force strength. Desertion was rampant and the Viet Cong infrastructure was being destroyed.

It was against this background that General Giap and other North Vietnamese officials flew to Moscow in March 1967 seeking additional military and economic aid. The Soviets subsequently announced they would send Hanoi "even more planes, high-altitude missiles, artillery and infantry weapons, together with factories, means of transportation, petroleum products, iron and steel and nonferrous metal equipment, food, and fertilizer." Indeed, the number of Soviet vessels reaching North Vietnamese ports rose from 122 in 1966 to 185 in 1967. In September Giap claimed in articles published in his armed Forces newspaper, *Quang Doi Nhan Dan*, that the allied pacification program had failed. He forecast very heavy fighting ahead and a Communist victory. He did so in the context of a strategy which he claimed had drawn allied troops to remote areas, thus enabling Communist guerrilla forces to achieve victory in the heavily populated zones of South Vietnam.

But Giap's statements were an attempt at deception. Instead of relying on the badly battered Viet Cong forces, beginning in the spring and summer of 1967 he deployed 37 NVA battalions into the area just north of

Viet Cong guerrillas fire bolt action rifles against low-flying allied aircraft.

Fire support in defense of an outpost near the Cambodian border.

the DMZ preparatory to launching a full-scale invasion of South Vietnam. The allies detected the threat and hastened completion of a line of fortified bases just south of the DMZ. On 6 April Giap made his first move, launching attacks against Quang Tri City and the neighboring towns of Lang Vei and Hai Lang. The North Vietnamese also opened up intense and continuous barrages of mortar and artillery fire against the allied bases near the DMZ. Shortly after, NVA troops began moving into position around Khe Sanh. On 16 May MACV called in tactical air power to silence enemy artillery in the area. Within 2 days, 30 sites were put out of action. General Westmoreland also deployed Army troops to the northern province of I Corps to support the Marines.

In a further effort to halt enemy shelling of the Marine border base at Con Thien, an air plan was devised and refined under the direction of General Momyer—its goal was the destruction of the Communist positions to the north. Designated Operation Neutralize, it began on 12 September 1967 and employed Air Force,

Navy, and Marine strike aircraft plus off-shore naval guns and Marine heavy artillery. During the 49-day operation, FAC pilots played a key role, flying dangerously close to enemy positions north of the DMZ and pinpointing them for strike aircraft. B-52's saturated NVA troop sites. Special long-range ground reconnaissance patrols were used whenever possible to enter target areas to assess bomb damage and locate additional targets. By the time the operation ended, more than 3,100 tactical and 820 B-52 sorties had been flown. Of these, 916 were under Combat Skyspot control because of inclement weather. The shelling of Con Thien dwindled away after Operation Neutralize succeeded in destroying 146 enemy gun, mortar, and rocket positions, and damaging 83 others.

These American offensive actions succeeded in blunting North Vietnamese efforts to prevent the Allied construction of the line of bases south of the DMZ and capped the failure of General Giap's Phase I strategy. His setpiece battles did not drain off American strength from populated areas, as hoped. Indeed, U.S. air power was more than adequate to defeat the enemy whenever and wherever he massed. The NVA next turned its attention further south to areas closer to its Cambodian sanctuaries, where it could more easily move out and harrass Allied positions in South Vietnam. On 27 November the enemy hit at the village of Song Be in Phuoc Long province and two days later at Loc Ninh near the Cambodian border in neighboring Binh Long province. In both instances, they were soundly beaten.

During a visit to Washington in November 1967, General Westmoreland reported directly to the President and the American people. In an address to the National Press Club, he expressed confidence that the tide was turning and that the allies were winning the war. The enemy, he said, was staking his hopes on a tactical victory to influence American public opinion and force the United States to throw in the towel. By the end of 1967, the enemy had not achieved that goal but evidence was piling up of a noticeable buildup of his forces in their Cambodian and Laotian sanctuaries for yet another try.

The 1968 Tet Offensive

At the beginning of 1968, more than 486,000 Americans—56,000 of them U.S. Air Force personnel—were in South Vietnam. During this climactic year, the Air Force flew 840,117 combat sorties in support of allied ground forces. A new forward air controller aircraft, the OV-10A, made its appearance and night operations were enhanced by introduction of low-light-level television equipment and a laser guided bomb. The year also saw General Giap order implementation of Phases II and III of his offensive plan within 10 days of each other. One of his targets was the Marine base at Khe Sanh, selected—according to General Westmoreland—as the place where

Giap hoped to emulate his great Viet Minh victory over the French achieved 14 years earlier at Dien Bien Phu. Located on a plateau in the northwestern corner of I Corps and commanding the approaches to Dong Ha and Quang Tri City from the west and the coastal corridor leading to Hue, Khe Sanh was an important strategic post. By capturing it, the North Vietnamese would have an almost unobstructed invasion route in the northernmost provinces, from where they could outflank American positions south of the DMZ. Anticipating such an attack, General Westmoreland decided—and the members of the JCS agreed—to defend the base.

On 21 January 1968 the North Vietnamese unleashed a heavy mortar, artillery, and rocket attack on the Marine base and began assaulting outlying defenses west of it. This attack triggered Operation Niagara, an air campaign in defense of Khe Sanh. Nearly 600 tactical sorties (including 49 by the B-52's) were launched against enemy positions. Before the campaign ended 2½ months later, control of all tactical air units—Air Force, Navy, and Marine—had been centralized under General Momyer as the Single Manager for Air, effective 8 March. In the case of I Corps, Momyer made use of the Marines, direct air support center at Da Nang, enlarged it, and assigned non-Marines there. To coordinate tactical air operations, Seventh Air force deployed a C-130E Airborne Battlefield Command and Control Center to the northern corps.

The extensive use of air power at Khe Sanh paid off. More than 24,000 tactical and 2,700 B-52 sorties dropped 110,000 tons of ordnance. The heavy air attacks—averaging 300 tactical sorties a day with a three-ship B-52 cell arriving overhead every 90 or so minutes during the height of the battle—destroyed enemy bunkers and supplies, exploded his ammunition dumps in the area, and caved in his

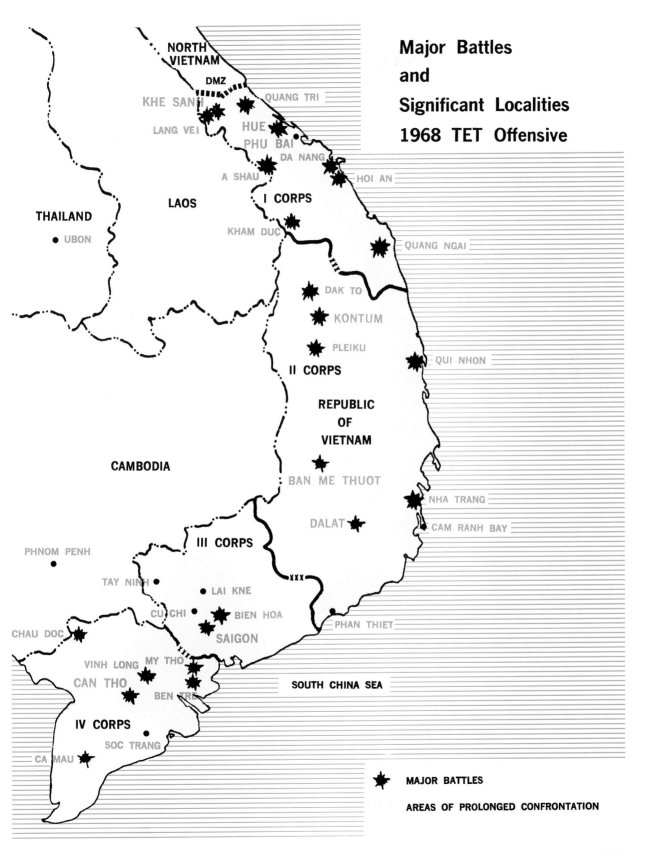

**Major Battles
and
Significant Localities
1968 TET Offensive**

NORTH VIETNAM
DMZ
KHE SANH
QUANG TRI
LANG VEI
HUE
PHU BAI
DA NANG
A SHAU
HOI AN
I CORPS
THAILAND
LAOS
UBON
KHAM DUC
QUANG NGAI
DAK TO
KONTUM
PLEIKU
II CORPS
QUI NHON
REPUBLIC
OF
VIETNAM
CAMBODIA
BAN ME THUOT
NHA TRANG
DALAT
CAM RANH BAY
III CORPS
PHNOM PENH
TAY NINH
LAI KNE
CU CHI
BIEN HOA
CHAU DOC
SAIGON
PHAN THIET
VINH LONG
MY THO
CAN THO
SOUTH CHINA SEA
BEN TRE
IV CORPS
SOC TRANG
CA MAU

★ MAJOR BATTLES

AREAS OF PROLONGED CONFRONTATION

1

ON MARCH 10, 1966 AIRFORCE MAJOR WAYNE
WAS FORCED DOWN ON THE AIRSTRIP AT ASHAU NEAR THE
CAMBODIAN BORDER. THE AIRSTRIP WAS UNDER
V.C. ATTACK. MOMENTS LATER A NAVAL BERNARD FI
LANDED HIS A-1E SKYRAIDER IN THE FACE OF SOME
V.C. TROOPS AND EFFECTED THIS INCREDIBLE RES
A-1 SKYRAIDER SHOT UP FROM THE
FUME AND BURNING AND THEIR CARGO OF GUNS
A DRY FIRE AT THE ENEMY GUNS UPERS AND
THEIR OWN PRECIOUS SECONDS.

3

(1) An RB-66 leads a flight of eight F-4 Phantoms on a bombing mission through a low overcast. (2) This painting depicts the daring rescue by Maj. Bernard C. Fisher of a downed USAF pilot, Maj. D. Wayne Myers, at a Special Forces camp in the A Shau valley, 2 miles from the Laotian border, in March 1966. For his feat, Major Fisher became the first Air Force Medal of Honor winner. (3) An F-100 Super Sabre fires rockets at enemy troops in South Vietnam. (4) An A-1E Skyraider attacks a Viet Cong target wtih a phosphorus bomb. (5) An A-1E attacks Viet Cong forces with 500-lb bombs.

4

5

tunnels near the Khe Sanh perimeter. At night, AC-47 gunships kept up a constant chatter of fire against enemy troops. Because of poor weather, about 62 percent of all strikes were directed to their targets by Combat Skyspot.

Nine days after the siege of Khe Sanh began, NVA and Viet Cong troops launched the Tet Offensive of 1968. In simultaneous attacks throughout South Vietnam, they struck at 36 of 44 provincial capitals, five of six autonomous cities, 23 airfields, and numerous district capitals and hamlets. Saigon and the old imperial capital of Hue were among the prime targets. This nationwide enemy offensive apparently had as its ultimate goal the disintegration of the South Vietnamese armed forces, to be followed—as Communist dogma had it—by the people rallying to the NLF. But that did not happen.

The initial fury of the attack did enable the enemy to seize at least temporary control of 10 provincial capitals, and he succeeded in penetrating Saigon, Quang Tri City, Da Nang, Nha Trang, and Kontum city. However, except for Hue, which took the allies several weeks of rugged fighting to clear, the enemy was ousted in two or three days. Most of 23 airfields attacked by the enemy were soon back in full operation.

Despite the heavy demands placed upon it to help defend Khe Sanh, the Seventh Air Force was still able to provide enough firepower to be a major factor in the defeat of the enemy offensive. Within Saigon and Hue, the Air Force launched carefully controlled strikes against enemy lodgments. Outside the cities USAF crews launched heavy attacks against Communist forces. Forward air controllers remained aloft around the clock directing strikes at enemy storage areas, troop areas, and providing close air support for allied units in contact with Viet Cong and NVA forces. At Hue,

only a trickle of essential supplies reached the besieged NVA troops. B-52's continued saturation raids on suspected enemy areas.

By late February it was evident that the Tet offensive had failed, and Hanoi's dream of a collapse of the South Vietnamese government and armed forces was chimerical. Instead, Viet Cong/NVA troops had suffered heavy losses—an estimated 45,000 men (8,000 of them in and around Hue alone). Unfortunately there also was a heavy civilian toll. More than 14,000 died, some of them (as in Hue) victims of NVA execution squads. Another 24,000 were wounded and 627,000 left homeless.

The extent and nature of the 1968 Communist Tet offensive proved to be a political disaster to the Johnson administration. The American people —who had only recently been assured the allies were winning the war—were shocked by the enemy's ability to strike throughout South Vietnam, even to the gates of the U.S. Embassy in Saigon. News accounts and particularly television films showing the devastation wrought by the enemy seriously hurt the administration. While additional U.S. troops were dispatched to bolster Westmoreland's forces, Washington attempted to speed up the previously planned third phase of American strategy, that is, to turn over most of the responsibility for the war to the South Vietnamese.

As domestic criticism of the administration reached a crescendo against the background of an earlier embarrassing incident—North Korea's seizure of the USS *Pueblo* on 24 January 1968 in the Sea of Japan—President Johnson on 31 March ordered a halt to all bombings north of the 20th parallel. He hoped this action would induce Hanoi to begin peace negotiations. At the same time the President announced he would not run for a second full term of office. Hanoi's leaders agreed to meet in Paris to begin the discussions, but they also continued to pour troops into South Vietnam at the rate of about 22,000 per month.

By mid-April intelligence revealed another enemy buildup in progress around Hue. Accordingly, on 19 April the allies mounted Operation Delaware/Lam Son 216, aimed at destroying the NVA logistic base in the A Shau Valley and denying the enemy an essential source of supply and a line of communication for further operations against Hue. A Viet Cong colonel, defecting to the South the same day, disclosed plans for a terrorist attack against Saigon beginning 4 May. It proved the start of another nationwide wave of assaults against 109 military installations and cities, including 21 airfields. Once again, U.S. air power played a major role battering the weary enemy.

Although visibly weakened, the Communists continued to probe Allied defenses. They established a stronghold at Cap Mui Lay on the coast just south of the Demilitarized Zone, and harassed nearby U.S. Marine positions with mortar and artillery fire. On 1 July a week-long well-coordinated bombardment by air, Marine artillery, and naval guns was begun against enemy positions. Almost 1,800 tactical and 210 B-52 missions saturated the area and destroyed some 2,000 Communist gun positions and structures. Shortly thereafter, alerted that 11 NVA regiments were massing for another assault on Saigon, Gen. Creighton W. Abrams (he succeeded Westmoreland on 11 June 1968) launched a large number of "spoiling operations" and air strikes. Electronic sensors, monitored by reconnaissance aircraft, girded the city to alert the allies of the expected attack. When finally launched in mid-August, the enemy assault proved quite ineffective and was easily repelled.

Three weeks earlier, on 23 July 1968, Maj. Gen. Robert F. Worley, Vice Commander of the Seventh Air Force, was killed when an RF-4C jet he was piloting northwest of Da Nang was hit by ground fire and crashed. The second pilot in the plane ejected safely, however, and was rescued. General Worley became the second Air Force general killed while on an operational mission. The first, Maj. Gen. William J. Crumm, commander of SAC's 3d Air Division, died in a mid-air collision of two B-52's on 6 July 1967 (see Chapter VIII).

As part of Hanoi's continuing effort to influence American public opinion and the peace talks (which began in Paris in May but quickly bogged down), General Giap on 23 August sent 4,000 NVA 1st Army Division regulars against the Duc Lap Special Forces camp, located some 3 miles from the Cambodian border and 15 miles from Ban Me Thuot. The 2,500 South Vietnamese, Montagnards, and Americans defending the camp were taken by surprise and the perimeter breached. However, 30 minutes after the first call for help went out, U.S. Army helicopter gunships arrived in the area, followed 15 minutes later by AC-47 gunships. Placing the attackers under heavy fire, the AC-47's remained overhead spotting and "hosing down" enemy units as they appeared. Their effectiveness drew high praise from the defenders. In all, more than 100 gunship and 392 tactical air sorties were flown in support of Duc Lap. The senior Army advisor on the scene, Col Rex R. Sage, later credited USAF tactical air and gunships with having saved the camp from being overrun.

In October 1968, finally recognizing that it could not occupy and control the South Vietnamese countryside, Hanoi began withdrawing 30,000 to 40,000 troops. On 31 October, after receiving assurances from the North Vietnamese that "serious" talks to end the war would get under way in Paris, President Johnson ordered a halt of all bombings north of the DMZ effec-

1

2

(1) U.S. Army 7th Infantry trooper carries an M-60 machine gun past rubble of a residential section of Cholon, Saigon, following the 1968 enemy Tet offensive, January-February 1968. (2) Hue city officials help prepare victims of the Communist Tet Offensive for burial. (3) A Skyraider approaches Qui Nhon. (4) Smoke and dust obscure part of the Marine base at Khe Sanh, during North Vietnam's unsuccessful attempt to seize in the 1968 Tet offensive. (5) Rocket attack on Duc To, 15 November 1967. (6) Weapons and ammunition seized from the enemy following the battle of Bong Son. (7) Vietnamese marines assemble Chinese-made 240-mm rockets, captured during an allied sweep northwest of Saigon, 1969. (8) A South Vietnamese outpost constructed in a tree-top served as a vantage point for ARVN rangers near Trunglap.

4

5

6

7

8

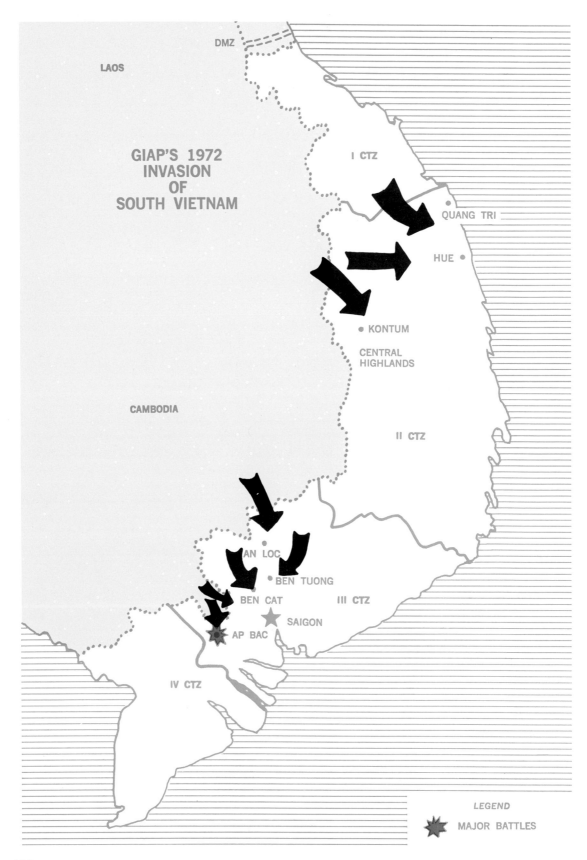

GIAP'S 1972
INVASION
OF
SOUTH VIETNAM

LAOS

DMZ

I CTZ

QUANG TRI

HUE

KONTUM

CENTRAL
HIGHLANDS

CAMBODIA

II CTZ

AN LOC

BEN TUONG

BEN CAT

III CTZ

SAIGON

AP BAC

IV CTZ

LEGEND

MAJOR BATTLES

tive 0800 Washington time on 1 November. Beforehand, the U.S. delegation in Paris explained to Hanoi's representatives that the United States would end "all bombardments and all acts involving the use of force" but that U.S. air reconnaissance would continue. The Americans repeatedly used the above phrase in their talks with the Communists, arguing that reconnaissance was "not an act involving the use of force." The North Vietnamese accepted the phrase and used it in their statement to the international press after the cessation of the bombings.

Vietnamization and Withdrawal

A few days later Richard M. Nixon defeated Hubert H. Humphrey in the 1968 presidential elections. During the campaign Nixon had pledged to bring American troops home while winning an honorable peace. An obvious aspect of this policy was to speed "Vietnamization" of the war effort. In March 1969 Secretary of Defense Melvin R. Laird visited South Vietnam to discuss an accelerated buildup of the Vietnamese armed forces (see Chapter XX). Thereafter, President Nixon met with President Thieu and gained his approval for the buildup. On 8 June Mr. Nixon then announced his plan to withdraw U.S. combat troops. The first of these Americans departed Vietnam in July. By year's end 69,000 had been withdrawn.

Meanwhile, the Air Force not only continued to assist allied operations in South Vietnam against enemy forces in the border regions but soon emerged as the primary military arm to support the policies of Vietnamization and withdrawl. Thus, a multi-battalion helicopter-airborne Marine assault during May-June in the A Shau Valley was preceded by 94 preplanned sorties and 28 immediate sorties which

B-52 Pilot

prepared the landing zone and provided air cover. The Commanding General, III Marine Amphibious Force, was unstinting in his praise of the USAF fighter pilots, air liaison officers, forward air controllers, and other participants. The Air Force also continued to support U.S. Army fire support bases, many of them situated in exposed positions. On 7 June, the enemy tried to overrun one of the bases astride a major enemy line of communication into Tay Ninh province. Responding to a call for help, USAF fighters struck the Communist force with bombs and napalm while gunships supported the action with flares and minigun fire. A subsequent sweep of the area revealed 323 enemy troops killed, all attributed to air power. Friendly casualties totaled seven wounded.

During the same period—between 8 May and 2 July 1969—the enemy launched an intensive attack on the Ben Het Civilian Irregular Defense Group camp. FAC's flew 571 sorties and AC-47's and AC-119's more than 100. Tactical air swarmed overhead in 1,828 sorties and SAC bombers, 804 sorties. Nearly 20,000 tons of bombs assailed the enemy day and night, in all kinds of weather, and finally forced the enemy to retreat.

In August 1969 the Air Force conducted "spoiling operations" in an effort to keep Communist troops off balance. Thus, when intelligence disclosed an enemy troop buildup in Bing Long province near An Loc and Loc Ninh—close to the Cambodian border in III Corps—B-52's struck numerous times and inflicted extensive damage on the enemy force. During the last months of the year, B-52 Stratoforts helped ARVN troops counter a major enemy threat in the Bu Prang and Duc Lap areas of Quang Duc province. In November the B-52's hit 57 enemy targets and struck 24 more during the first half of December. During the next 5 weeks the heavy bombers unloaded more than 30 mil-

1

2

3

4

(1) Damage caused at the U.S. Embassy, Saigon, during the 1968 Tet Offensive. (2) Vietnamese Sgt. Con Nha Tan and USAF Technical Sgt. Richard H. Nelson, a weapons maintenance advisor, load flares aboard a C-47. (3) Damage caused by a rocket attack at Qui Nhon, 18 May 1965. (4) A civilian dashes water on the smoldering remains of his home, following a Viet Cong rocket attack, Aug. 1968. (5) Maj. Bernard C. Fisher, Juna, Idaho (l.) and Maj. Stafford W. Myers, Newport, Wash., following the March 1966 rescue of the latter at an airstrip in the A Shau valley. (6) U.S. and Vietnamese A-1E pilots discuss a mission against the enemy, 1965. (7) An A-1E pulls away after unloading his ordnance on an enemy target.

5

6

7

lion pounds of bombs against enemy troop concentrations, staging areas, and fortifications. Indeed, in 1969 General Abrams came to depend more and more on USAF air power to keep the enemy from massing while U.S. forces withdrew and the Vietnamese armed forces buildup went forward.

In 1970, when the first USAF elements also began to leave Southeast Asia, the VNAF grew to 9 tactical wings and some 40,000 personnel and greatly expanded its training program. Its inventory of nearly 700 aircraft included A-1's, A-37's, F-5's, AC-47's, O-1's, and C-119's. Despite the enemy's reduced activity in South Vietnam, a noticeable buildup was detected in the "Fishhook" area of Cambodia, immediately across the border from Tay Ninh province. In response, the President authorized a major incursion into the enemy's Cambodian sanctuary by allied troops, supported by extensive American and Vietnamese tactical air units (see Chapter VII). However, both the U.S. and Vietnamese Air Forces also continued flying strike missions inside South Vietnam. By the end of 1970 the Air Force had flown 48,064 attack sorties, while the VNAF flew another 28,249—almost 40 percent of the total sorties over Vietnam.

Even as the U.S. withdrawal continued into 1971, the allies laid plans to send an ARVN invasion force into the southern panhandle of Laos to seize Tchepone on the Ho Chi Minh trail, destroy enemy forces, and interdict NVA traffic into South Vietnam and Cambodia. Crossing into Laos on 30 January 1971, the South Vietnamese were supported by a large tactical air fleet. The NVA reacted strongly, sending in large numbers of tanks, artillery, and AA weapons to fight the South Vietnamese. Elements of ARVN forces managed to reach the Tchepone area with the help of massive USAF B-52 and tactical air strikes. Casualties were heavy on both sides. The North

Vietnamese lost about 13,000 men and an estimated 20,000 tons of munitions. The South Vietnamese, having suffered 5,000 dead, retreated from Laos without achieving the initial objectives of the incursion.

By December 1971 the Air Force had reduced its inventory of fighter and strike aircraft in South Vietnam to 277 (from a high in June 1968 of 737). The number of personnel in-country also declined dramatically—from the 1968 peak of 54,434 to 28,791 at the end of 1971. By then the Vietnamese Air Force was responsible for about 70 percent of all air combat operations. The enemy—temporarily put on the defensive by the moves into Cambodia in 1970 and Laos in 1971—began deploying new NVA forces southward in preparation for another major offensive. They deposited a huge amount of supplies in their old sanctuary areas near the Central Highlands. U.S. intelligence detected the enemy buildup but NVA plans for the impending operation were unknown. In an effort to meet the threat, in mid-February 1972 hundreds of sorties were flown against NVA targets just north of the DMZ.

Some 6 weeks later—on 30 March 1972—the North Vietnamese launched a large, three-pronged invasion of South Vietnam, spearheaded by tanks and mobile armor units. One NVA force swept south across the DMZ, its goal apparently the conquest of the northern provinces and the seizure of Hue. The initial NVA surge led to the seizure of Quang Tri City. A second NVA force drove from Laos into the Central Highlands, and a third effort involved a drive from Cambodia into Binh Long and Tay Ninh provinces, northwest of Saigon.

Fierce fighting ensued on all three fronts, with tactical aircraft and B-52's launching repeated strikes against the advancing NVA armored units. The enemy's greatest success was in the northern provinces, but perhaps the

Soviet tanks.

124

most critical and potentially most disastrous battle occurred at An Loc. There, the badly outnumbered and outgunned South Vietnamese stood their ground within the besieged city and survived the heaviest enemy attacks of the entire war. They and the city were saved in large measure by air power, much of it supplied by the Vietnamese Air Force. More than 10,000 tactical and 254 B-52 strikes were flown in support of ARVN forces. Air Force gunships once again proved invaluable at night turning back attacking NVA troops. When the battle for An Loc was over near the end of June, the enemy force there had lost all of its tanks and artillery.

In the Central Highlands, the fight started out well for the Communists. Employing Soviet-built T-54 tanks and heavy armor, the North Vietnamese quickly seized control of much of Kontum province. The Air Force responded to this crisis by redeploying additional strike aircraft to South Vietnam and by considerably increasing fighter strength in Thailand. This bolstered force helped decimate enemy units, with AC-119 and AC-130 gunships being especially effective in the open highland country. By 1 June the North Vietnamese began withdrawing from some of their advance positions.

By the summer of 1972 the battles of An Loc and the highland regions were largely over, and attention turned to the northern provinces where the NVA had seized considerable amounts of South Vietnamese territory. Heavy air strikes had helped stop the enemy advance and destroyed much of his armored forces. But when the fighting wound down, the North Vietnamese were in control of much of the countryside below the DMZ plus a strip of South Vietnam's territory running along the Laotian and Cambodian borders. The major population centers, however, remained under the South Vietnamese. Still, North Vietnam retained substantial lodgements

Demolished VNAF C-47 following an April 1966 enemy mortar attack on Tan Son Nhut.

within the Republic of Vietnam, which posed a continuing threat to the Saigon government.

From the U.S. point of view, perhaps the most heartening aspect of the enemy offensive—which cost North Vietnam an estimated 120,000 casualties and heavy equipment losses—was the performance of the Vietnamese Air Force. VNAF pilots—many of them with 4,000 hours of combat flying under their belts—demonstrated great skill and initiative in attacking the NVA. During 1972, they flew 40,000 strike sorties in support of ARVN ground forces, most of whose troops held on and fought valiantly.Some units did panic and abandoned Quang Tri City during the early phases of the Communist offensive, but the ARVN subsequently recaptured it.

Against the background of the massive NVA invasion of South Vietnam in the spring of 1972, President Nixon ordered renewed bombing of North Vietnam by both tactical aircraft and B-52's. On 8 May he also authorized the mining of the harbors and river inlets of North Vietnam to prevent the rapid delivery of replacement arms, munitions, and other war essentials from the Soviet Union and Communist China (see Chapter IV). This latest interdiction campaign against North Vietnam continued throughout the summer and early fall of 1972.

In October Dr. Henry Kissinger, the President's Special Assistant for National Security Affairs, returned from the Paris negotiations to inform the nation that "peace is at hand," and the bombing of North Vietnam was halted. Unfortunately, at the last moment the enemy balked over some of the ceasefire provisions, that is, Hanoi insisted that the United States install a coalition government in Saigon. A 2-month deadlock ensured, which led the President to order new and more drastic measures to end the war. On 18 December 1972, on his orders, the heaviest air attack of the war were

1

2

3

GIẤY THÔNG-HÀNH

SAFE-CONDUCT PASS TO BE HONORED BY ALL VIETNAMESE GOVERNMENT AGENCIES AND ALLIED FORCES
이 안전보장패쓰는 월남정부와 모든 연합군에 의해 인정된 것입니다.
รัฐบาลเวียตนามและหน่วยพันธมิตร ยินดีให้เกียรติแก่ผู้ถือบัตรผ่านปลอดภัยนี้.

(Front)

SAFE-CONDUCT PASS TO BE HONORED BY ALL VIETNAMESE GOVERNMENT AGENCIES AND ALLIED FORCES

MANG TẤM GIẤY THÔNG HÀNH
nầy về cộng tác với Chánh Phủ
Quốc Gia các bạn sẽ được :
- Đón tiếp tử tế.
- Bảo đảm an ninh
- Đãi ngộ tương xứng

TẤM GIẤY THÔNG HÀNH NẦY CÓ GIÁ TRỊ VỚI TẤT CẢ CƠ - QUAN
QUÂN CHÍNH VIỆT - NAM CỘNG - HÒA VÀ LỰC - LƯỢNG ĐỒNG - MINH.

(Back)

4

(1&2) Propaganda leaflet operations. (3&4) An enemy soldier holds a surrender leaflet. (5) A Vietnamese officer speaks to villagers of Ap Trung, northwest of My Tho. (6) South Vietnamese psychological warfare team hands out leaflets to villagers. (7) A Viet Cong surrenders to government troops after picking up a propaganda leaflet. (8) Airmen loading a leaflet bomb.

5

6

8

7

launched against military targets within Hanoi and Haiphong; on 29 December, the North Vietnamese agreed to proceed with the negotiations. A nine-point agreement was finally worked out and formally signed on 27 January 1973.

Under the agreement, U.S. forces would withdraw from South Vietnam and all prisoners of war would be returned within 60 days. The United States tacitly recognized that the North Vietnamese were in strength within the territory of South Vietnam. Indeed, for the first time, North Vietnam acknowledged that it had 100,000 troops in the northern and western parts of the Republic of Vietnam. Exactly on schedule, on 28 March 1973, the last American military personnel departed South Vietnam, and MACV headquarters was inactivated. Thus, after more than a dozen years, an active American military role in South Vietnam came to an end.

127

VI The Air War Against North Vietnam

As noted in Chapter II, the United States launched its first air strikes against North Vietnam in August 1964 in response to the attack on the Navy destroyer, *USS Maddox*. Navy carrier planes hit four North Vietnamese coastal torpedo bases and an oil storage facility. On 2 December, the President approved a limited Air Force and Navy air campaign against Communist lines of communication used to support the insurgency in South Vietnam. The second air strikes against North Vietnam, nicknamed "Flaming Dart I," was launched by the Navy on 7 February 1965 after enemy mortar and demolition teams attacked U.S. and South Vietnamese military facilities near Pleiku. The following day, as part of this riposte, VNAF A-1 aircraft—accompanied by six Farm Gate A-1E's commanded by Lt. Col. Andrew H. Chapman of the 3d Tactical Group, 2d Air Division—dropped general purpose bombs on the Chap Le barracks. Several of the 20 accompanying USAF F-100's attacked enemy antiaircraft artillery (AAA) sites. Three RF-101's provided photographic coverage. On 11 February, a third air strike ("Flaming Dart II") was conducted by Navy, USAF, and VNAF aircraft against NVA barracks at Chanh Hoa and Vit Thu Lu. It was in response to another enemy attack, this time against U.S. facilities at Qui Nhon which killed more than 20 Americans.

A 19-day pause followed the second Flaming Dart strikes. When air attacks against the North resumed on 2 March 1965, they carried the appellation "Rolling Thunder." On that date, General Moore dispatched 25 F-105's and 20 B-57's—accompanied by KC-135 refueling tankers and other supporting aircraft—hit an NVA ammunition depot at Xom Bong about 35 miles above the DMZ, causing heavy damage.

The Rolling Thunder campaign was substantially different from those of World War I and II, resembling rather the geographically limited air war over Korea. That is to say, President Johnson—determined to avoid a larger conflict with China and the Soviet Union—imposed stringent controls on air operations. The strikes had a threefold purpose: to raise the morale of the South Vietnamese, impose a penalty on Hanoi for its support of aggression in the South, and reduce the infiltration of men and supplies into the South. The air campaign also was based on the hope that the gradual destruction of North Vietnam's military bases and constant harrassment and attacks on its LOC's would bring its leaders to the negotiating table.

The restrictions imposed upon the Air Force made execution of Rolling Thunder strikes very complex. Coordination of USAF and VNAF air operations devolved upon General Moore and his successors. Besides being responsible to Washington authorities and the two unified commanders—Admiral Sharp and General Westmoreland—the 2d Air Division commander also was required to work closely with the U.S. ambassadors in Saigon, Vientiane, and Bangkok. In undertaking air strikes, political considerations were usually paramount. For example, Air Force squadrons based in Thailand could attack targets

Airmen load ammunition on a strike aircraft prior to a mission over North Vietnam.

in North Vietnam and Laos but not in South Vietnam. In June 1965 General Moore was assigned the additional job of serving as MACV Deputy Commander for Air Operations, but it did not greatly increase his authority or alter his responsibilities for three separate but related areas of operations—South Vietnam, North Vietnam, and Laos.

The President retained such firm control of the air campaign against the North that no important target or new target areas could be hit without his approval. His decisions were relayed through Secretary McNamara to the Joint Chiefs, who then issued strike directives to CINCPAC. The latter, in turn, apportioned fixed targets and armed reconnaissance routes between the U.S. Air Force, U.S. Navy, and the Vietnamese Air Force, with USAF crews normally providing air cover for the VNAF, which later withdrew from operations north to concentrate on supporting ARVN forces within South Vietnam. In conducting operations over the North, the American crews were enjoined to minimize civilian casualties as much as possible. This policy—and the overall target restraints imposed by the White House and Pentagon officials—helped avoid in North Vietnam the heavy civilian losses that characterized bombings on both sides in World War II.

The initial air strikes were limited primarily to enemy radar and bridges between the 17th and 19th parallels. Later, the airmen were allowed to hit a number of other military targets below the 20th parallel. The first target hit above the 20th parallel, the Quang Soui barracks, was attacked on 22 May 1965 by Air Force F-105's and the first above Hanoi in late June. After mid-1965, the airmen were authorized to attack important bridges and segments of the northwest and northeast rail lines between Hanoi and the Chinese border. For an extended period, Washington exempted from attack

sanctuary areas around Hanoi and Haiphong, a buffer zone near China, surface-to-air missile (SAM) sites, and MIG bases located within the Hanoi-Haiphong areas. After the first few sporadic strikes, Rolling Thunder pilots on 19 March began flying strike sorties against individual targets and target areas on a weekly basis. Beginning on 9 July 1965, targets were programmed on a biweekly basis; after 1965 new targets were selected periodically.

The first Air Force tactical strikes were by aircraft already in South Vietnam and Thailand. As additional air units arrived, those assigned missions against targets in North Vietnam and Laos—and a portion of the B-52 fleet—were sent to six large airfields, some newly built, in Thailand. USAF strength in Thailand grew from about 1,000 personnel and 83 aircraft in early 1965 to a peak of 35,000 personnel and 600 aircraft in 1968. U.S. Navy aircraft and South Vietnam-based Marine aircraft also flew many missions over North Vietnam and Laos.

The principal Air Force tactical strike aircraft during Rolling Thunder operations was the F-105 Thunderchief. Mass-produced after the Korean War, it served throughout the war in Southeast Asia. A newer fighter, the twin-seat F-4 Phantom, manned by an aircraft commander and a weapon systems officer,* initially was used in a combat air patrol (CAP) role. Committed to battle gradually, it flew its first strike mission at the end of May 1965 and its first armed reconnaissance mission in August. A third Air Force fighter, the twin-seat, swept-wing F-111A, reached Thailand in March 1968, underwent combat evaluation that year, and was withdrawn. Subsequently, in the latter stages of the war, this sophisticated night and all-weather aircraft returned to South-

---

*The latter was trained as a navigator.

east Asia and flew regular combat missions.

A number of older, lower-performance and more vulnerable aircraft were used briefly or sparingly over the North. The F-100 Super Sabre and the F-104 Starfighter saw action chiefly in a support role above the DMZ. Some Starfighters flew strike missions and the B-57 Canberra light bomber was employed largely in night operations. Eventually, all were withdrawn from northern missions, with the F-100 being used primarily for close air support in South Vietnam.

The B-52 Stratofortresses made their debut over North Vietnam in April 1966 with a strike near Mu Gia pass. During the next 6 1/2 years, these heavy bombers were employed against enemy targets in North Vietnam's panhandle, staying far away from the dangerous SA-2 missile sites located mostly in the Hanoi-Haiphong area. Based initially on Guam and later in Thailand, the B-52's were primarily employed to interdict North Vietnamese lines of communication leading to the DMZ and the Ho Chi Minh trail in Laos. On these missions, they normally dropped 25 to 30 tons of ordnance. Gen. John P. McConnell, LeMay's successor as Air Force Chief of Staff, remarked on the irony of the use of these strategic bombers to hit tactical targets. But it was only one of several improvisations introduced by the Air Force in waging the unorthodox air war.

The role played by SAC's KC-135 air refueling tankers proved vital to the execution of Rolling Thunder (see Chapter XI). Prior to 1965 they had been used primarily to refuel B-52's but they also had provided mid-air refueling service to tactical aircraft deploying from one part of the world to another. Gen. William W. Momyer, commander of the Seventh Air Force (1966-1968), observed that few airmen "foresaw that air refueling would become a basic part of the scheme of employment of fighter forces over North Vietnam." Since much of the USAF tactical air fleet was based some 350 nautical miles from their targets in the North, refueling was essential if the F-105's and F-4's were to deliver substantial ordnance loads on their targets. The KC-135's also enabled many fuel-short or damaged aircraft to return safely to their bases.

Among the problems facing U.S. airmen flying over North Vietnam were the heavy forests, the jungle terrain, and the annual northeast monsoon which was most severe from mid-October to mid-March. Both affected operations over the North. They also placed a premium on the ability of reconnaissance aircraft to locate enemy targets and assess bomb damage. To obtain this information, the Air Force employed a number of manned and unmanned aircraft. Perhaps the most famous was the U-2, which first attracted worldwide attention in May 1960, when Soviet missilemen shot one down over central Russia while it was on a high-altitude reconnaissance mission. Later, in the fall of 1962, a SAC U-2 detected the first Soviet strategic missiles deployed in Cuba. In Southeast Asia, the U-2 flew reconnaissance missions over North Vietnam beginning in 1965 (see also Chapter XII).

Throughout the war zone, the Air Force also operated other reconnaissance aircraft, including the RB-57, the workhorse RF-101, the RF-4C, and drones. Some of these aircraft, equipped with infrared and side-looking radar, helped advance the technology of reconnaissance during the war. In 1965, SAC's Ryan 147D (and other model) drones made their initial flights over North Vietnam. Dropped from DC-130 transports, they were able to obtain photo intelligence over the Hanoi area. As North Vietnam began developing a modern air defense system, the Air Force also began using aircraft capable of obtaining

F-105's in Thailand.

FRESCO (MIG-17)

FISHBED (MIG-21)

(1) F-105's in Thailand. (2&3) An Air Force reconnaissance photo of Phuc Yen airfield near Hanoi shows MIG 17's and MIG-21's in revetments. (4) An F-4 Phantom. (5) President Johnson in October 1967 personally approved this first strike against enemy MIG's at Phuc Yen. (6) Kien Am airfield with MIG's in revetments. (7) Gia Lam airfield near Hanoi. It was off limits from attack throughout most of the war.

target data via various electronic methods.

Rolling Thunder, 1965-1968

From the first handful of strikes over the North in early 1965, Air Force and Navy attack sorties rose from 1,500 in April to a peak of about 4,000 in September. In October, with the onset of the northeast monsoon, they declined steeply. While the weather was good, U.S. pilots destroyed or damaged a variety of military targets: bridges, vehicles, rolling stock, barracks areas, supply and ammunition depots, ferries, watercraft, and antiaircraft artillery and radar sites. They bombed railroad tracks and roads to prevent the movement of men and supplies. The results of the air strikes could not be accurately assessed and became the subject of considerable debate. But they reduced or delayed the enemy's operations and infiltration into the South. They led the North Vietnamese to adopt the practice of travelling under cover of night and bad weather —taking full advantage of forested or jungle terrain. They also diverted considerable manpower and materiel to repair their roads, rail lines, and bridges and increased their antiaircraft defenses.

Because of the limitations imposed on air operations, war materiel from the Soviet Union, China, and other Communist countries flowed in easily through Haiphong and other North Vietnamese ports and over rail lines from Kunming and Nanning, China— all of which helped Hanoi to make up for its losses and which facilitated a rapid air defense buildup. During 1965, for example, North Vietnam's AAA inventory expanded from an estimated 1,000 guns to 2,000 pieces and about 400 antiaircraft sites by year's end. These consisted primarily of 37- and 57-mm guns but included a few 85-mm and 100-mm weapons as well.

Smaller but deadly automatic weapons—which inflicted much of the losses and damage to U.S. aircraft—also proliferated.

The Soviet surface-to-air missiles were first detected by a SAC U-2 aircraft on 5 April 1965. By year's end, USAF and Navy reconnaissance had pinpointed 56 SAM sites. The North Vietnamese, who took great pains to conceal them, readily abandoned sites to build new ones. By building a large number of sites, some of them equipped with dummy missiles to deceive USAF crews, they were able to use a "launch and move" tactic. They employed a similar tactic with their AAA guns. Another key element of Hanoi's air defenses was the North Vietnamese Air Force (NVAF), which was equipped with 50 to 60 MIG-15's and MIG-17's plus a few IL-28 bombers. Although the MIG's began challenging U.S. strike aircraft at an early date, they did not become a serious threat until 1966-1967. The sum of the enemy's array of AAA guns, automatic weapons, SAM's, and the MIG force— backed up by an expanding defense radar complex—enabled Hanoi to build one of the most formidable air defense systems ever devised.

On 23 July 1965, after several months of USAF operations against North Vietnamese targets, the first F-4C was downed by an SA-2 missile. Four days later, with Washington's approval, Air Force Thunderchiefs mounted the first strike of the war against the SAM's. In August, a Navy aircraft was downed by a SAM, which led to a series of special U.S. "Iron Hand" missions aimed at North Vietnam's rapidly expanding SA-2 sites. At first, most of them were in the Hanoi-Haiphong sanctuary area and thus could not be attacked, but others were emplaced along major rail and road junctions, bridges, and cities north and south of the North Vietnamese capital. In known SAM areas, Air Force pilots would drop to lower altitudes to

Crews flying strike missions over North Vietnam are continually hampered by heavy flak over the target areas.

avoid the SA-2's but this tactic made them more vulnerable to conventional AAA and especially to smaller automatic weapons. By mid-1965, the latter were credited with shooting down most of the approximately 50 Air Force and Navy aircraft over North Vietnam.

An electronic war subsequently ensued between U.S. tactical aircraft and the enemy's complex of radar-controlled AAA guns and SAM's and other defense radars. The Air Force employed specially equipped aircraft to counter SAM radars. Initially, fighter pilots relied on the electronically equipped EB-66's and "Wild Weasel" F-100's and F-105's to neutralize or warn them of radar emissions from enemy "Fan Song" equipment which signalled that they were being tracked or that a SAM firing was imminent. These countermeasures plus the SA-2's generally poor guidance system kept losses low. Thus, of the approximately 180 SAM's launched in 1965, only 11 succeeded in downing an aircraft, 5 of which were Air Force. Nonetheless, the inhibiting and harassing effects of the SAM's had considerable impact on air operations. After 1967, the fighters carried electronic countermeasure pods of their own. A number of EB-66's and Wild Weasel aircraft continued to be used, however.

The North Vietnamese Air Force, flying from airfields which Washington officials decided could not be hit because of their location in the heavily populated Hanoi-Haiphong area, was not a major threat to USAF pilots during 1965. Although North Vietnamese pilots shot down two F-105's in a surprise attack in April, throughout the year the American airmen clearly held the upper hand in aerial fighting. In June Navy pilots downed two enemy aircraft. On 10 July the Air Force scored its initial kills, when Captain Thomas S. Roberts and Ronald C. Anderson in one F-4 and Captains

Shrike and Bullpup missiles on an F-105.

Kenneth E. Holcombe and Arthur C. Clark in another were credited with the shoot-down of two MIG-17's.

Early in the year, several Air Force EC-121's were deployed over the Gulf of Tonkin to maintain a "MIG watch" over Southeast Asia. Flying off the coast of North Vietnam, these indispensable aircraft not only were able to alert U.S. fighter and support aircraft of approaching MIG's, but also served as airborne radar and communication platforms. They also warned American pilots who flew too near the Chinese border and assisted air-sea searches for downed air crews. Later, the EC-121's equipment was employed in an integrated fashion with the Navy's sea-based radars, enabling U.S. pilots to obtain a variety of additional timely information about the enemy's and their own air operations over the North.

The political restraints placed by the President on air operations over North Vietnam denied U.S. pilots certain advantages of surprise. Another problem was the relatively small geographical area overflown by Rolling Thunder crews. It forced pilots to use certain air corridors going into (ingressing) and departing (egressing) a target, a task made all the more difficult by the need to avoid civilian casualties as much as possible. A third operational factor was the weather cycle in North Vietnam, which generally allowed optimum operations in late mornings or afternoons when clouds and fog were minimal or absent. All of these factors contributed to stereotyped American air tactics which the enemy quickly became aware of and which enabled him to deploy his AAA defenses to great advantage. Also, the relatively short duty tours created much turmoil in air operations. Experienced airmen were constantly departing and less experienced replacements arriving, which diluted both planning and flying expertise in the theater.

1

3

2

(1&2) Maj. Donald J. Kutyna flew missions over North Vietnam in an F-105 which he named the *Polish Glider* (3) F-105 (color painting). (4) F-111's at Takhli AB, Thailand. (5) An F-105 unloads a 750-lb bomb on North Vietnam's Hoa Lac airfield. (6) USAF strike aircraft destroy a North Vietnamese oil storage facility near Hanoi. (7) Captured enemy 37-mm AAA gun. (8) F-4E Phantoms arrive at Korat AB, Thailand, November 1968. (9) A B-66 controls a flight of F-105's on a mission over North Vietnam's panhandle. July 1966. (10) Air Force bombers destroyed more than 30 enemy supply trucks in North Vietnam.

4

5

6

HA NOI 3.7 NM

7

8

9

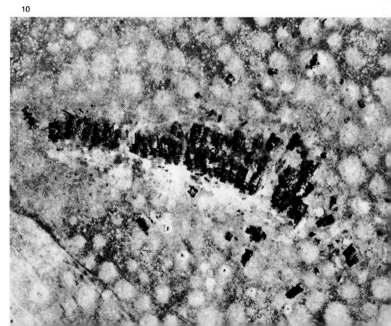

10

Rolling Thunder Route Packages in North Vietnam

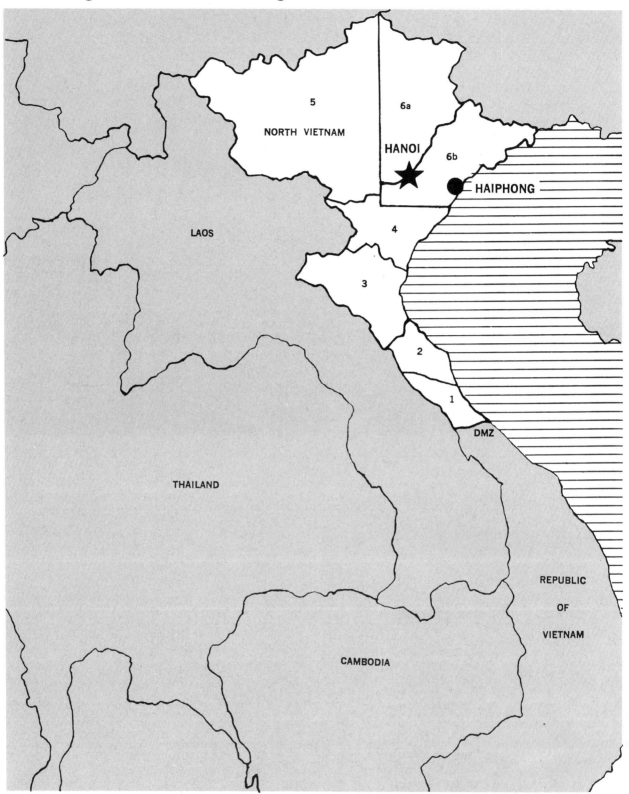

To reduce mission interference between land-based Air Force and Navy carrier aircraft operating over North Vietnam, in December 1965—after consulting with Air Force and Navy officials—Admiral Sharp divided the bombing area into six major "route packages." Generally, the longer-range USAF fighters attacked the inland route package targets while the shorter-range Navy aircraft concentrated on those near the coast. In April 1966, General Westmoreland was given responsibility for armed reconnaissance in and the intelligence analysis of the "extended battlefield" area of route package I above the DMZ as it affected allied operations in South Vietnam.

The Bombing Pauses

During the first 2 years of operations over the North, President Johson periodically ordered bombing pauses in an effort to bring Hanoi's leaders around to discuss a political settlement of the war. The first bombing pause of about 6 day's duration was ordered in mid-May. The second one began on Christmas Eve 1965 and continued until 30 January 1966. In both instances, North Vietnam did not respond to U.S. action and, indeed, used the bombing respites to rebuild its strength and speed the infiltration of men and supplies southward. USAF reconnaissance also disclosed major North Vietnamese efforts to repair damaged roads and bridges and to install more air defense weapons. President Johnson also approved briefer bombing standdowns, to permit celebration of the annual Vietnamese new year ("Tet"), Buddha's birthday, Christmas, and New Year's Day.

When U.S. diplomatic efforts to get the North Vietnamese to the conference table got nowhere, the President in the late spring of 1966 approved a series of heavier air strikes against North Vietnam. Added to the approved target list were POL storage facilities at Haiphong, Hanoi, Nguyen Ke, Bac Gian, Do Son, and Duong Nham. Others included a power plant and cement factory in Hanoi, an important road-and-rail and road bridge on the northwest line, and an early warning and ground control intercept radar facility at Kep. The first major POL strike was conducted on 29 June 1966 when Air Force F-105's hit a 32-tank farm less than 4 miles from Hanoi. About 95 percent of the target area was destroyed. Navy aircraft struck another important POL facility near Haiphong.

Beginning on 9 July 1966, as part of an expanded Rolling Thunder program, U.S. aircraft bombed additional POL facilities, flew extended armed reconnaissance missions throughout the North (except for most of the Hanoi-Haiphong sanctuary area), and began heavier bombing of the northeast and northwest rail lines in route packages V and VI. Admiral Sharp assigned interdiction of the railroads to the Air Force. Additional presssure against the enemy was brought to bear on 20 July when the Air Force and Marines launched a new campaign (Tally Ho) against infiltration routes and targets between the DMZ and the area 30 miles northward in route package I. The U.S. air offensive expanded in the ensuing weeks, peaking at about 12,000 sorties in September.

By that time, Rolling Thunder had taken a heavy toll of enemy equipment, destroying or damaging several thousand trucks and watercraft, hundreds of railway cars and bridges, many ammunition and storage supply areas, and two-thirds of the enemy's POL storage capacity. Many sorties were flown against AAA, SA-2, and other air defense facilities, thousands of cuts were made in enemy road and rail networks. To counter this air campaign, Hanoi was forced to divert an

1   2

ORGANIZATION, 7TH AIR FORCE AND 7/13TH AIR FORCE

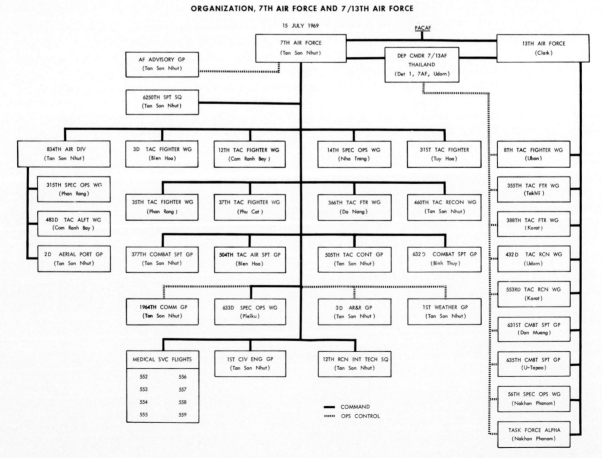

15 JULY 1969   PACAF

- 7TH AIR FORCE (Tan Son Nhut)
- DEP CMDR 7/13AF THAILAND (Det 1, 7AF, Udorn)
- 13TH AIR FORCE (Clark)

- AF ADVISORY GP (Tan Son Nhut)
- 6250TH SPT SQ (Tan Son Nhut)

- 834TH AIR DIV (Tan Son Nhut)
  - 315TH SPEC OPS WG (Phan Rang)
  - 483D TAC ALFT WG (Cam Ranh Bay)
  - 2D AERIAL PORT GP (Tan Son Nhut)

- 3D TAC FIGHTER WG (Bien Hoa)
- 12TH TAC FIGHTER WG (Cam Ranh Bay)
- 14TH SPEC OPS WG (Nha Trang)
- 31ST TAC FIGHTER (Tuy Hoa)

- 35TH TAC FIGHTER WG (Phan Rang)
- 37TH TAC FIGHTER WG (Phu Cat)
- 366TH TAC FTR WG (Da Nang)
- 460TH TAC RECON WG (Tan Son Nhut)

- 377TH COMBAT SPT GP (Tan Son Nhut)
- 504TH TAC AIR SPT GP (Bien Hoa)
- 505TH TAC CONT GP (Tan Son Nhut)
- 632D COMBAT SPT GP (Binh Thuy)

- 1964TH COMM GP (Tan Son Nhut)
- 633D SPEC OPS WG (Pleiku)
- 3D AR&R GP (Tan Son Nhut)
- 1ST WEATHER GP (Tan Son Nhut)

- MEDICAL SVC FLIGHTS
  - 552   556
  - 553   557
  - 554   558
  - 555   559
- 1ST CIV ENG GP (Tan Son Nhut)
- 12TH RCN INT TECH SQ (Tan Son Nhut)

- 8TH TAC FIGHTER WG (Ubon)
- 355TH TAC FTR WG (Takhli)
- 388TH TAC FTR WG (Korat)
- 432D TAC RCN WG (Udorn)
- 553RD TAC RCN WG (Korat)
- 631ST CMBT SPT GP (Don Muang)
- 635TH CMBT SPT GP (U-Tapao)
- 56TH SPEC OPS WG (Nakhon Phanom)
- TASK FORCE ALPHA (Nakhon Phanom)

━━━ COMMAND
┄┄┄ OPS CONTROL

3

(1) Sgt. Leonard B. Williams works on F-100 converters at Phan Rang AB, South Vietnam. Sgt. Philip J. Smith adjusts the drag chute cable (2) Col. Robin Olds, Commander, 8th Tactical Fighter Wing, is carried off by his men after completing his 100th mission over North Vietnam (3) A B-52 drops its bombs on a Viet Cong stronghold (4) F-4 Phantoms destroy 6 of 11 spans of the Lang Giai bridge in North Vietnam, 25 May 1972.

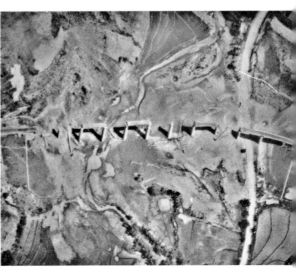

4

estimated 200,000 to 300,000 full and part-time workers to repair roads, railway lines, bridges, and other facilities, and to man its air defenses.

Although infiltration southward could not be stopped, U.S. commanders in South Vietnam credited the bombing with reducing the number of enemy battalion-sized attacks. A new Rolling Thunder program, dated 12 November, added more targets including the Van Vien vehicle depot and the Yen Vien railroad yards, both within the environs of Hanoi. These targets, struck by Air Force and Navy pilots in December 1966, produced collateral damage and civilian deaths which led to a political and diplomatic furor. By the end of 1966, U.S. tactical aircraft had flown about 106,500 attack sorties and B-52's another 280 over North Vietnam, dropping at least 165,000 tons of bombs.

The North Vietnamese accepted the tremendous losses and fought back. By dispersing and concealing much of their POL supply, they were able to reduce the full impact of the air attacks. Bad flying weather and extensive use of manpower enabled the North Vietnamese to keep open portions of the northern rail lines so that some supplies continued to flow in from China. More importantly, Haiphong and other ports—still off-limits to U.S. aircraft—daily unloaded thousands of tons of war materiel. Despite the air attacks, AAA and especially small automatic weapons took a rising toll of American aircraft, downing a total of 455 by the end of 1966 and damaging many more. The number of SAM sites rose to about 150 during the year, but improved flying tactics—plus the installation of electronic countermeasure (ECM) equipment on U.S. aircraft—reduced the effectiveness of the missiles.

Until September 1966 the North Vietnamese Air Force made only sporadic attempts to interfere with Rolling Thunder operations. But on 3 September NVN pilots went on the offensive. Equipped with MIG-21's carrying infrared-homing air-to-air missiles, they operated freely from five bases—Phuc Yen, Kep, Gia Lam, Kien An, and Hoa Loc—in the Hanoi area which could not be attacked. Confronted by daily MIG-21 challenges, General Momyer temporarily diverted Air Force F-4C's from their primary strike mission to exclusive aerial combat against the MIG's.

A favorite MIG tactic was to pop up suddenly and try to force the heavily ladened F-105's to jettison their bombs before reaching their targets. To offset this, Sidewinder-equipped Phantoms flew at lower altitudes to enable their pilots to spot the MIG's earlier and then used their higher acceleration and speed in hit and run tactics. They avoided turning fights because the MIG's had great maneuverability. The EC-121's helped materially by allerting the F4's to the presence of the enemy aircraft. During 1966, U.S. fighters shot down 23 MIG's 17 of them credited to USAF crews, as against a loss of 9 aircraft, 5 of them Air Force.

Early in 1967, Washington officials approved new Rolling Thunder targets closer to Hanoi. To protect vital industrial and LOC facilities, North Vietnamese pilots—operating with nearly 100 MIG's—were thrown into the air battle. To dampen their ardor, General Momyer and his staff devised a ruse nicknamed Operation Bolo. The details were worked out and executed by Col. Robin Olds, Commander of the 8th Tactical Fighter Wing. Baited by what appeared to be a normal Rolling Thunder strike by F-105's, the NVAF on 2 January suddenly found itself engaging F-4's in the largest aerial battle of the war to that time. Colonel Olds and his pilots shot down 7 MIG's in 12 minutes without losing an aircraft. Olds personally downed two of them. On 6 January 1967 the North Vietnamese lost two more MIG's.

Destroyed bridge in Laos, 1965.

Stunned by the losses, the NVAF stood down to regroup and retrain.

The American air offensive continued into March and April. On 10-11 March, F-105's and F-4C's hit the sprawling Thai Nguyen iron and steel plant about 30 miles from Hanoi. Air Force and Navy follow-up strikes also hit portions of the plant. The attacks disrupted but did not completely halt pig iron or steel production. Also, for the first time, Air Force jets struck the *Canal Des Rapides* railway and highway bridge, 4 miles north of Hanoi. Enemy pilots did not attempt to challenge American aircraft again until the spring of 1967, which saw 50 engagements fought in April and 72 in May, the largest 1-month total of the war. During the fierce May battles Air Force crews destroyed 20 MIG's—7 of them on the 13th and 6 on the 20th.

A revised Rolling Thunder target list issued on 20 July permitted air attacks on 16 additional fixed targets and 23 road, rail, and waterway segments inside the restricted Hanoi-Haiphong area. Bridges, bypasses, rail yards, and military storage areas were bombed in an effort to slow or halt traffic between the two cities and to points north and south. On 2 August 1967 Hanoi's famous Paul Doumer railway and highway bridge was hit for the first time. The center span was knocked down and two other spans were damaged. Struck again on 25 October, another span went down and finally, on 19 December, the rebuilt center span was dropped again.

An Air Force reconnaissance plane photographs bomb damage at the Thai Nguyen iron and steel complex, 35 miles north of Hanoi.

Despite these successes, the North Vietnamese during the year managed to inflict a steady toll on the Air Force and Navy, and their MIG's were unusually aggressive. The increasing losses led Washington to approve—for the first time—the destruction of most of the MIG bases. Beginning in April, USAF and Navy pilots repeatedly bombed Kep, Hoa Lac, Hien An and Phuc Yen airfields, destroying several MIG's on the ground in the process.

Except for 18 aircraft left at Gia Lam, which was spared because it was Hanoi's only international airfield, the MIG's flew to nearby Chinese bases. On 16 August 1967, General Momyer told a Senate committee that ". . . we have driven the MIG's out of the sky for all practical purposes. . ." American air supremacy was underscored in 1967 by a record 75 MIG's downed as against 25 losses in air-to-air combat.

However, by early 1968 neither U.S. air superiority, Rolling Thunder, nor air-ground operations within South Vietnam deterred Hanoi's leaders from continuing their efforts to destroy the Saigon government. Although suffering heavy manpower and materiel losses, the North Vietnamese were able to continue the conflict with the help of Moscow and Peking. Washington's military restraints—aimed at avoiding a wider war—permitted foreign military assistance to flow unhampered through the seaports of North Vietnam. In addition, the enemy had almost unrestricted use of Cambodian territory adjacent to South Vietnam for stockpiling supplies (much of it flowing in from Cambodia's major seaport at Kom Pong Som) and for resting and regrouping their troops.

In taking advantage of the opportunities provided by American restraint, the Communists conceived a plan for a major offensive against the Republic of Vietnam in hopes of achieving a dramatic victory—such as they had won over the French at Dien Bien Phu in 1954—which would persuade Washington and Saigon to acknowledge their defeat. Whereupon, in late January 1968 they laid siege to the Marine base at Khe Sanh and then, at month's end, they launched the famous Tet offensive throughout South Vietnam. At Khe Sanh, the allies threw the enemy back with heavy losses. Elsewhere, after initial but brief gains, the enemy's nationwide offensive slowly sputtered out and was

BRIDGE INTERDICTION
NORTH VIETNAM

RAILROAD BRIDGE
PHU DIEN CHAU
18-58-20N 105-34-55E

PRE-STRIKE

PHU DIEN CHAU 1.6 NM

4 APRIL 1965

POST-STRIKE

17 APRIL 1965

DESTROYED SPAN

DAMAGED SPAN

HIGHWAY BRIDGE NORTHWEST
BAI DUC THON
18-04-05N 105-49-30E

PRE-STRIKE

BAI DUC THON
0.8 NM

8 APRIL 1965

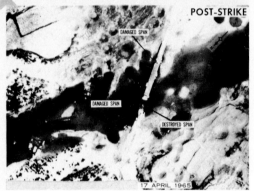

POST-STRIKE

DAMAGED SPAN

DAMAGED SPAN

DESTROYED SPAN

17 APRIL 1965

1

2

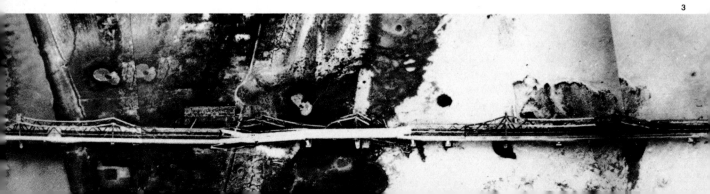

3

6

4

5

7

(2&3) USAF F-105's destroyed the Doumer Bridge on 18 December 1967. After the North Vietnamese rebuilt it, U.S. bombers destroyed it again in 1972. (4) RF-100 Voodoo pilot photographs a railroad bridge 135 miles south of Hanoi, April 1965. (5) An RF-101 casts a shadow over a missing span of the My Duc highway bridge in North Vietnam, 22 April 1965. (6) North Vietnamese highway bridge, destroyed by F-105's. (7) Destroyed highway and railroad bridge about 5 miles north-northwest of Dong Hoi, North Vietnam. (8) Destroyed bridge between Yen Bai and Bao Ha, North Vietnam, 22 May 1972.

8

1

2

3

(1&2) B-52 bombers destroyed the Kinh No railroad yard, 7 miles north of Hanoi, 27 December 1972. (3) 750- and 3,000 pound bombs impact on and near a railroad and highway bridge crossing the Canal des Rapides, 5 miles northeast of Hanoi. (4) Bomb damage caused by F-105's on the Thai Nguyen rail yard, April-May 1966. (5) An air strike on North Vietnam army supply depot, Thien Linh Dong, 16 June 1965. (6) B-52 bombers destroy the Ai No warehouse 18 December 1972 in the Hanoi area. (7) An Air Force strike on the Thai Nguyen thermal power plant in North Vietnam, 29 March 1967, knocked out the boiler plant (lower l.) and the administration building.

4

THIEN LINH DONG ARMY SUPPLY DEPOT

PRE STRIKE

POST STRIKE

DAMAGED FOOD PROCESSING BUILDINGS

DESTROYED STORAGE BUILDINGS

BURNING OPEN STORAGE

DAMAGED STORAGE BUILDINGS

80 PER CENT OF BUILDINGS IN TARGET COMPLEX DESTROYED OR DAMAGED

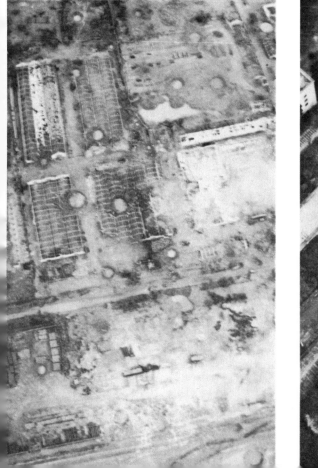

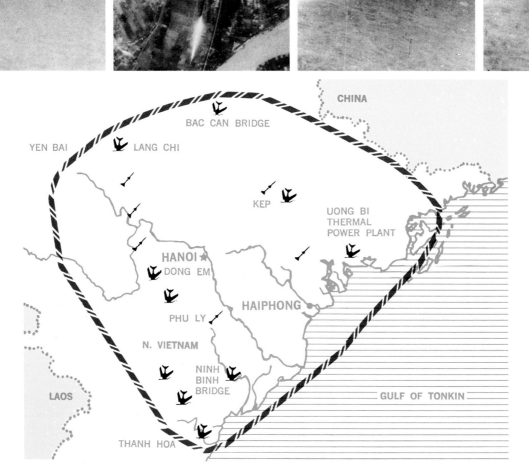

SURFACE-TO-AIR MISSILE ENVELOPE
1966

slowed, halted, and reversed. But if the North Vietnamese military campaign did not succeed, it did lead to a change in American war policies. As noted in Chapter III, President Johnson on 31 March ordered a halt to the bombing of North Vietnam north of the 20th parallel, then north of the 19th parallel. As a *quid pro quo*, the Hanoi regime agreed to meet with U.S. delegates in Paris to discuss an end to the conflict. In the meantime, the Air Force and other services virtually doubled their air strikes in the area

below the 19th parallel, interdicting enemy troop and supply movements across the DMZ into South Vietnam. They also stepped up raids against enemy positions in southern Laos.

In Paris, after many meetings and months of deadlock between the two sides on how to bring the war to an end, American and North Vietnamese representatives agreed on a certain "essential understanding" enabling President Johnson on 31 October 1968 to end all air, naval, and artillery bombardment of North Vietnam as of

A sequence of frames showing the destruction of a USAF RF-4C reconnaissance plane by an SA-2 missile, 12 August 1967. The 2-man crew, Lt. Col. Edwin L. Atterberry and Maj. Thomas V. Parrott successfully ejected and were captured and interned. Colonel Atterberry died in captivity.

A North Vietnamese SAM missile.

0800 hours Washington time, 1 November. The understanding, as Mr. Johnson expressed it, was that the other side intended "to join us in deescalating the war and moving seriously towards peace."

Ninety minutes before the President's order was issued, Maj. Frank C. Lenahan of the 8th Tactical Fighter Wing made the last target run in an F-4D against a target near Dong Hoi. Thus, 3 years and 9 months after it began, Rolling Thunder operations came to an end. The Air Force and the other services had flown approximately 304,000 tactical and 2,380 B-52 sorties and dropped 643,000 tons of bombs on North Vietnam's war-making industry, transportation net, and air defense complex. Notwithstanding the variety of constraints imposed on air power, the post-1965 aerial assault on North Vietnam helped to reduce the movement of manpower and supplies going southward and contributed to the 1968 diplomatic efforts to lower the tempo of combat.

Except for Air Force and Navy reconnaissance missions, which were permitted in a separate understanding between the Americans and North Vietnamese in Paris, all air operations over the North ceased. Later—after President Nixon assumed office—U.S. retaliatory air strikes were launched against enemy air defense units which began firing at U.S. reconnaissance aircraft in violation of the above "un-

derstanding." In February 1970, after the North Vietnamese again fired upon U.S. reconnaissance aircraft, the President authorized certain "protective reaction" strikes against NVA antiaircraft and SAM sites and also enemy airfields. When U.S. aircraft continued to receive ground fire, the President ordered "reinforced protection reaction" strikes on the enemy's air defense system.

The first of these latter missions were flown during the first 4 days in May 1970. Nearly 500 Air Force and Navy aircraft hit missile and AAA sites and NVA logistic facilities near Barthelemy pass, Ben Karai pass, and a sector north of the DMZ. During the next 6 months interim smaller strikes were flown. On 21 November the Air Force launched two major operations over the North. The first involved a joint Air Force and Army commando attempt to rescue American prisoners of war (POW's) believed confined at the Son Tay prison compound, about 20 miles northwest of Hanoi. Planned by Air Force Brig. Gen. Leroy J. Manor and Army Col. Arthur D. Simons, the volunteer commando force flew 400 miles from bases in Thailand to Son Tay in HH-53 helicopters, with A-1E Skyraiders and specially equippped C-130E's providing support. As it landed, Air Force and Navy aircraft launched heavy diversionary strikes in the area to distract the North Vietnamese. Members of the commando force

1

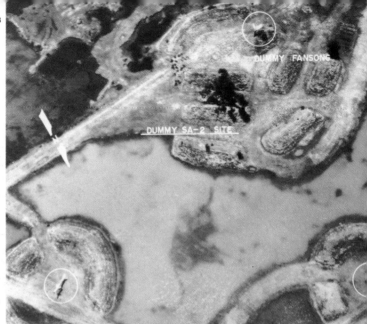

3

(1) Enemy mobile AAA units near Haiphong. (2) An alert sends North Veitnamese pilots scrambling for their MIG aircraft. (3) A dummy SA-2 site in North Vietnam. (4) Soviet ships delivered not only thousands of trucks to the North Vietnamese but also tanks, rockets, and other implements of war. (5) North Vietnamese 37-mm gunners fire at U.S. jets, August 1965. (8) An SA-2 site in the Hanoi area.

DUMMY FANSONG

DUMMY SA-2 SITE

2

4

USSR MER SHIP VITIM
ENROUTE TO HAIPHONG
10 JAN 69

DECK CARGO 51 ZIL-151 TRUCKS

SA-2 IN FLIGHT

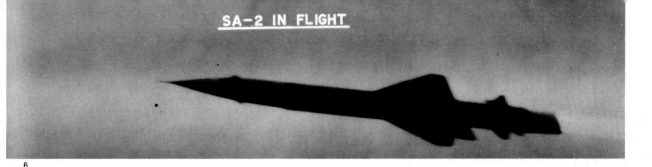

6

7

SHADOW OF SA-2 DETONATION

8

20X

FAN SONG RADAR

SA 2 MARK II
GUIDANCE SUPPORT VANS

BAMBOO MATTING

CHINA

quickly discovered, to their dismay, that the prison compound contained no prisoners. During the 28 minutes the rescuers were on the ground, they killed about 25 North Vietnamese defenders. The only American causualty was an enlisted man who suffered a broken ankle. One helicopter was destroyed on landing.

About 6 hours later, the second operation of the day was launched after an RF-4 aircraft was lost. An armada of 200 Air Force and Navy strike aircraft —supported by 50 other planes— launched a major retaliatory strike in the vicinity of the Mu Gia and Ban Karai passes and the DMZ. Their targets included SA-2 missile sites, enemy trucks, and supply and transportation facilities. All aircraft returned safely to their bases.

During the 2 years after Rolling Thunder operations ended on 1 November 1968, the United States had flown more than 60 separate strike missions in retaliation to ground fire. When the North Vietnamese continued to fire at U.S. reconnaissance aircraft, Washington officials authorized stepped up "reinforced protective reaction" strikes. In February 1971, the Air Force launched Operation Louisville Slugger. Flying 67 sorties, USAF crews destroyed 5 SAM sites, 15 SAM missile transporters, and 15 vehicles in the Ban Karai pass area. On 21-22 March, the Air Force teamed up with the Navy in Operation Fracture Cross Alpha during which they flew 234 strike and 20 armed reconnaissance sorties against enemy SAM sites. In August 1971, in an effort to curb enemy road construction across the DMZ into Military Region I* in South Vietnam, Air Force jets flew 473 sorties, seeding the road with munitions and sensors. On 21 September, flying in poor weather, 196 U.S. tactical aircraft hit three POL storage areas

south of Dong Hoi, destroying about 350,000 gallons of fuel. It was the first all-instrument air strike, employing exclusively the long-range electronic navigation (LORAN) position fixing bomb system.

These intermittent protective reaction strikes—launched mostly in the southern panhandle of North Vietnam —did not affect Hanoi's efforts to rebuild and reconstitute its air force. By late 1971, it had an inventory of about 250 MIG's, 90 of them MIG-21's, and once more it prepared to challenge American operations over the North and, to a limited extent, over Laos. By this time the North Vietnamese Air Force was operating out of 10 MIG-capable bases, 3 of them located in the panhandle area. USAF and Navy pilots, who over the years had achieved roughly a 2 1/2 to 1 victory ratio over MIG fighters in aerial battles, saw the odds drop. However, this was attributed to the U.S. rules of engagement, which again exempted MIG air bases and to the geographical and electronic advantages possessed by the defenders rather than to the superiority of enemy pilots.

To counter the enemy air threat, EC-121 aircraft—which had redeployed from Southeast Asia after Rolling Thunder operations ended in 1968—were returned to the theater to resume their "MIG watch." Once again, as in 1967 when the NVAF last posed a serious threat to air operations over the North, USAF commanders urged that MIG air bases be attacked. Washington officials agreed, and on 7-8 November USAF and Navy pilots bombed airfields at Dong Hoi, Vinh, and Quàn Lang. After neutralizing these air bases, U.S. pilots on 26-30 December launched the heaviest

Capt. Lawrence H. Pettit, 55th Tactical Fighter Squadron, discusses his MIG kill with his crew chief, Sgt. Horace G. McGruder.

---

*The four corps tactical zones were redesignated Military Regions in July 1970.

USAF Linebacker II Offensive Against North Vietnam
December 1972

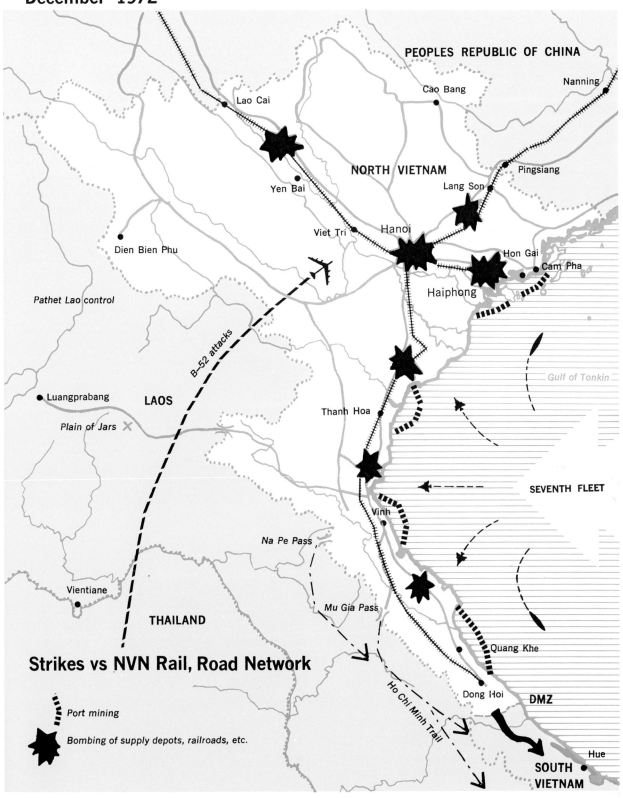

Strikes vs NVN Rail, Road Network

Port mining

Bombing of supply depots, railroads, etc.

air strikes since 1968—1,025 sorties—against a variety of military targets south of the 20th parallel.

The Communist Spring Offensive, 1972

Still hoping to end the war through negotiations, the Nixon administration kept a tight rein on its principal bargaining card—air power. Hanoi, however, was thinking in terms of another military offensive. By late 1971 evidence began to accumulate that Hanoi was planning a large-scale invasion of South Vietnam. Gen. John D. Lavelle,* who in August 1971 succeeded Gen. Lucius D. Clay, Jr., as Seventh Air Force commander, requested the recall of certain USAF units to the theater. By the spring of 1972, North Vietnam had assembled a force of about 200,000 men for a push into the South.

The invasion began on 29-30 March 1972, with some enemy forces rolling directly across the DMZ into Military Region I while others penetrated into Military Region II from Laos. All were supported by considerable numbers of tanks and other armored vehicles. The South Vietnamese army, although greatly improved since 1968, was still plagued by poor leadership and morale and was forced to retreat. U.S. air power—plus the strengthened Vietnamese Air Force—was thrown into the battle. Air Force F-105's, F-4's, A-7's, AC-130's and B-52's were joined by Navy and Marine aircraft in pounding the enemy daily between the 20th parallel in the North and the battle lines inside South Vietnam. Bolstered by aircraft reinforcements from the United States and elsewhere, attack sorties over the extended battlefield averaged 15,000 per month, almost two-thirds of the peak monthly rate in 1968.

---

* General Lavelle was recalled from his post in April 1972, charged with having authorized certain "protective reaction" strikes beyond those permitted by the rules of engagement. He was succeeded as Seventh Air Force commander by Gen. John W. Vogt.

A gun camera sequence shows the destruction of an enemy MIG-17, 3 June 1967, by an F-105 crew, Maj. Ralph L. Kuster and Capt. Larry D. Wiggins.

With Hanoi's forces ensconced inside South Vietnam and determined, despite heavy casualties, to maintain their positions below the DMZ, President Nixon on 8 May suspended the peace talks in Paris and authorized the launching of Operation Linebacker. For the first time, the United States imposed a naval blockade and mined the waters of Haiphong and other North Vietnamese ports. Simultaneously, the President authorized a renewal of air strikes throughout North Vietnam above the 20th parallel. Old and new targets were struck, including the rebuilt Paul Doumer bridge in Hanoi, bridges along the northwest and northeast rail lines from China, fuel dumps, warehouses, marshalling yards, rolling stock, vehicles, power plants, and a POL pipeline running from China. All recently emplaced SA-2 missile sites in or near the DMZ were destroyed as were many SA-2 and AAA sites further north.

To degrade or neutralize North Vietnam's rebuilt or new bristling air defenses, the Air Force made full use of its electronic technology. It employed EB-66's, Wild Weasel F-105's, and EC-135's to augment electronic countermeasure equipment used by most fighter aircraft. It also employed a profusion of laser and optically-guided bombs, which had been developed in the late 1960's. Mostly 2,000 pounders, the guided bombs enabled fighter crews to strike targets with great accuracy. Thus, the spans of the strongly defended Than Hoa bridge—which had withstood U.S. bombs for years and had cost the Air Force and Navy a number of downed aircraft—were dropped in one strike by an F-4 with guided bombs.

By June 1972 North Vietnam's offensive had stalled outside of Hue and elsewhere as South Vietnamese ground forces began to fight back. On 29 June, President Nixon reported that with the mining of the harbors and bombing of military targets in the North—particularly the railroads and oil supplies—the situation "has been completely turned around... The South Vietnamese are now on the offensive." He reiterated his proposal of 8 May for an international ceasefire and the return of American prisoners of war, warning that the United States intended to bargain from strength. The peace talks resumed in Paris on 13 July. In the ensuing weeks, Saigon's forces, heavily supported by U.S. and VNAF air strikes, continued their offensive against the 200,000 enemy troops who had seized control of large portions of the South Vietnamese countryside.

Meanwhile, North Vietnamese pilots were reacting aggressively in the Hanoi-Haiphong area in an effort to drive American pilots out of the skies over their heartland. The renewed American-North Vietnamese air battles shortly produced several Air Force aces. On 28 August 1972, Capt. Richard S. Ritchie, flying an F-4C Phantom, participated in his fifth shootdown and became the nation's second ace. (The U.S. Navy produced the first.) His weapon systems officer, Capt. Charles DeBellevue, who had flown with Ritchie in three previous "kills," became an ace on 9 September when he destroyed his fifth and sixth MIG's, becoming the first weapon systems officer to achieve this status. Capt. Jeffrey S. Feinstein, also an F-4 weapon systems officer, became an ace on 13 October when he helped bag his fifth MIG. These were the only Air Force aces of the war. Two Navy pilots likewise became aces.

The 11-Day Air Campaign

On 23 October 1972, when it seemed that the Paris talks were leading to an agreement to end the war, the United States again halted air operations above the 20th parallel. Soon after, however, the negotiations

(1) Six F-4C crews pose before their planes in April 1966, following destruction of six MIG aircraft over North Vietnam. (2) The first MIG downed during the war was credited to Capts. Kenneth E. Holcombe and Arthur C. Clark, 10 July 1965. (3) After their 3 June 1967 shootdown of a MIG-17, Capt. Larry D. Wiggins and Maj. Arthur L. Kuster review the tactics they used. (4) Col. Robin Olds, commander of the 8th Tactical Fighter Wing, and other airmen pose on the occasion of the unit's 15th air victory over enemy MIG's. (5) Capt. Jeffrey S. Feinstein, a weapons system officer was credited with five aerial victories over enemy MIG's.

1

4

2

(1) 1st. Lt. Clifton P. Dunnegan, of the 8th Tactical Fighter Wing, shot down 1 of 7 enemy MIG's destroyed over North Vietnam on 2 January 1967 (2) Capt. Charles B DeBellevue, credited with six aerial victories, poses with Col. Scott G. Smith and Capt. Richard S. Ritchie, who became the first USAF ace in Southeast Asia. (3) The five general officers shown below are World War II aces with five or more enemy aircraft "kills" to their credits, for a total of 41½ victories, directed USAF operations in Southeast Asia during 1966-1967. They are: Lt. Gen. (later General) William W. Momyer (center, front), 7th Air Force commander. The others are (l. to r.). Maj. Gen Gordon M. Graham, vice commander; Brig. Gen. Franklin A. Nichols, chief of staff; Brig. Gen. Donavon F. Smith, chief of the Air Force Advisory Group in Vietnam; and Brig. Gen. William D. Dunham, deputy chief of staff for operations. (4) Maj. Robert G. Dilger, F-4C commander (r.) and his pilot, 1st. Lt. Mack Thies (center) report to their CO, Lt. Col. Hoyt S. Vandenberg, Jr., how they destroyed a MIG-17 during a dogfight over North Vietnam, 1 May 1967.

3

stalled amid indications that Hanoi might renew its offensive in South Vietnam. Whereupon, President Nixon ordered a resumption of air strikes above the 20th parallel. There followed a final 11-day bombing campaign, nicknamed Operation Linebacker II, which resulted in the heaviest aerial assault of the war. The Air Force dispatched F-105's, F-4's, F-111's, and—for the first time, B-52's—over the heavily defended enemy capital and the adjacent Haiphong port. The tactical aircraft flew more than 1,000 sorties, the B-52's about 740, most of them against targets previously on the restricted list. They included rail-yards, power plants, communication facilities, air defense radars, Haiphong's docks and shipping facilities, POL stores, and ammunition supply areas. They repeatedly bombed the principal NVAF MIG bases and transportation facilities.

The North Vietnamese responded by launching most of their inventory of about 1,000 SAM's and opening up a heavy barrage of AAA fire against the attackers but USAF electronic countermeasures helped keep losses to a minimum. Of 26 aircraft lost, 15 were B-52's which were downed by SAM's. Three others were badly damaged. However, by 28 December the enemy defenses had been all but obliterated and during the last 2 days of the campaign, the B-52's flew over Hanoi and Haiphong without suffering any damage.

Deprived of most of their air bases, North Vietnamese pilots were able to launch only 32 aircraft of which 8 were shot down, 2 by B-52 tail gunners. Hanoi claimed the strikes on Hanoi-Haiphong produced substantial collateral damage and more than 1,000 fatalities. Considering the size of the air assault, the bombing was well controlled and not indiscriminate. Impacting fragments from enemy SAM's contributed to the destruction.

(Above) B-52 unloads its bombs.

(1) Weather observer SSgt. Ronald L. Galy and equipment repairman Sgt. George F. Hammett, Jr., inflate a weather balloon in South Vietnam. (2) Weathermen played a key role throughout the war. Maj. John A. Lasley, the unit commander (l.), discusses the day's activities with Sgt. Hammett. (3) Sgt. William E. Collins, chief observer of the weather detachment at Phu Cat AB, South Vietnam; SSgt. William S. Grady checks weather observation charts. (4) Sgt. Grady checks weather observation charts and satellite photograph.

On 30 December 1972, President Nixon announced in Washington that negotiations between Dr. Kissinger and North Vietnam's representative, Le Duc Tho, would resume in Paris on 8 January. While the diplomats talked, American air attacks were restricted to areas below the 20th parallel. Air Force, Navy, and Marine jets flew about 20 sorties per day with B-52's adding 36 to the daily total. On 15 January the United States announced an end to all mining, bombing, shelling, and other offensive actions against North Vietnam. On 23 January, the Paris negotiators signed a nine-point cease-fire agreement effective 28 January, Saigon time.

Thus, air power had played a significant role in preventing the complete takeover of South Vietnam by the northerners and in extracting an agreement to end the war. Between 1968 and 1972, only 51,000 tactical and 9,800 B-52 sorties were flown

against the North, most during the two Linebacker campaigns. The tactical aircraft dropped about 124,000 tons of bombs and the B-52's about 109,000 tons with their "Sunday punch" missions of late December 1972 being perhaps the most noteworthy. An even heavier rain of bombs pounded enemy forces in South Vietnam's Military Regions I and II.

In addition to the cease-fire, the 23 January 1973 agreement provided for the return of all American and allied POW's within 60 days, establishment of a commission to supervise truce and territorial disputes, the rights of the Vietnamese people to determine their own future peacefully, a promise of U.S. economic aid for the Indochina states, and an affirmation of the neutrality of Laos and Cambodia. The United States tacitly recognized the presence of about 100,000 North Vietnamese troops still entrenched in northern South Vietnam.

Aircraft Carrier, USS *Kitty
Hawk,* (CVA-63) launching F4
H-2 Phantom fighters.

VII U.S. Navy Task Force 77 in Action Off Vietnam

The floating airfields of the U.S. Navy in the Western Pacific, the carriers of Task Force 77, first saw action in Vietnam on 2 August 1964 in response to an emergency call from the destroyer *Maddox* (DD-731) following an unprovoked attack by North Vietnamese torpedo boats. Task Force 77's aircraft also initiated the bombing effort of North Vietnam on 7 February 1965.

It was the beginning of a 37-month long carrot-and-stick campaign to persuade Hanoi to cease its aggression against South Vietnam. It was always to be a restrained, graduated, strategic bombing effort on carefully selected targets, a stop—listen—and talk interdiction campaign. Until President Johnson's dramatic announcement on 31 March 1968 that there would be no more bombing of North Vietnam above the 20th parallel, the carriers of Task Force 77 would cruise in the waters of the Gulf of Tonkin as close as 60 miles to the enemy's coast.

This article will analyze the actions and accomplishments of Task Force 77, the attack aircraft carrier force at "Yankee" and "Dixie" Stations, beginning with the punitive attacks in August 1964 and closing with the start of the bombing curtailment on 1 April 1968, from which point

Reprinted from May 1972 *Naval Review* issue of the U.S. Naval Institute *Proceedings*. Copyright © 1972, U.S. Naval Institute.

the U.S. withdrawal from Vietnam can be measured.

The U.S. military strategy to preserve South Vietnam had two interlocking objectives: inside that country, a ground and air campaign to defeat the enemy, or force their withdrawal; and, outside that country, an air and naval offensive against North Vietnam to force her to stop her aggression. In the beginning, it was fondly hoped and believed that Ho Chi Minh would conclude that, against such American military involvement, he could not succeed.

The air bombing campaign against North Vietnam was initiated on the assumption that most North Vietnamese and Viet Cong war-making material came overland into South Vietnam; until February 1965, it was not believed that much of it came by sea. With the use of highly selective air power and, very shortly, by creating an effective anti-infiltration barrier along the South Vietnamese coast, the belief was that North Vietnam would be prevented from sustaining the war inside South Vietnam. The United States hoped that the aggression could be choked off by selective and gradually increasing attacks on North Vietnam's military installations and power plants, her petroleum products, her logistic storage areas, her war-supporting industrial facilities, and the vehicles, roads, and bridges by which war material moved south.

F-4J Phantom fighter being readied for catapult launch from USS *Constellation* (CVA-64).

F-4Js and A-7 Corsairs launched from the USS *Constellation* for missions over North Vietnam.

Throughout the campaign a fundamental principle was to avoid damaging nonmilitary targets and to avoid harm to noncombatants.

From the beginning, the air interdiction effort was inhibited by major restrictions. One of these was the unpredictability of the weather in the monsoon season of Southeast Asia, which greatly favored the enemy. Since Washington maintained control of the war from afar, the fighting forces' ability to react to changes in the weather was severely handicapped. The other major restrictions were political and they were self-imposed. The sanctuaries, base camps, and supply depots in Cambodia were declared off limits to our aircraft. Immediate pursuit of the enemy was forbidden. Haiphong, the key port of North Vietnam, through which

85% of North Vietnam's imports flowed, was never mined or blockaded or made to suffer major or crippling damage from air attacks. Instead, during the days the weather was good enough for such precision attacks, and often at night in hazardous low-level attacks under the flickering illumination of flares, shiploads of materials which had been unloaded at Haiphong were sought out and bombed on their journey south. Truck by truck and storage site by storage site—if they could be found under the dense canopy of jungle and camouflage—they were destroyed.

The Initial Involvement

Task Force 77's involvement against North Vietnam can be dated from 2 August 1964, the day North Vietnamese torpedo boats attacked the destroyer *Maddox* while that ship was on a routine reconnaissance patrol in international waters.

On 3 August the *Maddox,* now accompanied by the *Turner Joy* (Commander R. C. Barnhart), again entered the Gulf of Tonkin with orders to fire only in self-defense and with restrictions against immediate pursuit. But there was no response.

On the night of 4 August 1964, however, while the destroyers were proceeding easterly at a speed of about 20 knots, the *Maddox* spotted and tracked at least 5 high-speed radar contacts 36 miles away. Because of the high closure rate, and a similarity to the 2 August attack, the "blips" were evaluated as probable torpedo boats. The *Maddox* and the *Turner Joy* changed course and increased speed.

To those watching the radar, it soon became evident from the maneuvers of the approaching blips that they were pressing an attack. On Commodore Herrick's command, both destroyers opened fire at a range of 6,000 yards. Torpedo noises were then heard on the *Maddox*'s sonar and this information was immediately passed to her companion. In the nick of time, both ships twisted to avoid the torpedo, and seconds later a wake was sighted passing 300 feet to port of the *Turner Joy.*

Less than half an hour after the second attack, Admiral U.S.G. Sharp, Jr., Commander-in-Chief, Pacific, recommended immediate punitive air strikes by TF 77 against the North Vietnamese torpedo boat bases. Two hours later, a Presidential decision, relayed from Secretary of Defense Robert S. McNamara through the Joint Chiefs of Staff, ordered strikes at first light the following day. The assigned targets were four North Vietnamese torpedo boat bases plus the oil storage facilities at Phuc Loi and Vinh.

At 2340 on 4 August, Washington time (1140 on 5 August in the Gulf of Tonkin) the President announced to the public that the United States was making a measured response to the North Vietnamese aggression:

"My fellow Americans," he said, "as President and Commander in Chief, it is my duty to the American people to report that renewed hostile actions against United States' ships in the high seas in the Gulf of Tonkin have today required me to order the military forces of the United States to take action in reply. . . ."

Commencing at approximately 1230 local time, 64 strike aircraft were launched from the *Ticonderoga* and *Constellation* and were over their targets about 1315. Ten of the *Constellation*'s A-1s, led by Commander H. F. Griffith, plus two F-4s and 8 A-4s from the same ship, struck PT boat bases at the northernmost target, at Hon Gai. Further south, 5 other "Connie" A-4s, 3 F-4s, and 4 A-1s struck the PT boat bases at Loc Chao. Six F-8s from the "Tico" led by Commander Mohrhardt (VF-53) hit the PT boats at Quang Khe, and 26 other Tico aircraft attacked the two oil storage dumps at Vinh. This attack, led by Commander Wesley L. McDonald (Commanding Officer, VA-56), and Commander W. E. Carman (Commanding Officer, VF-53), was over in minutes.

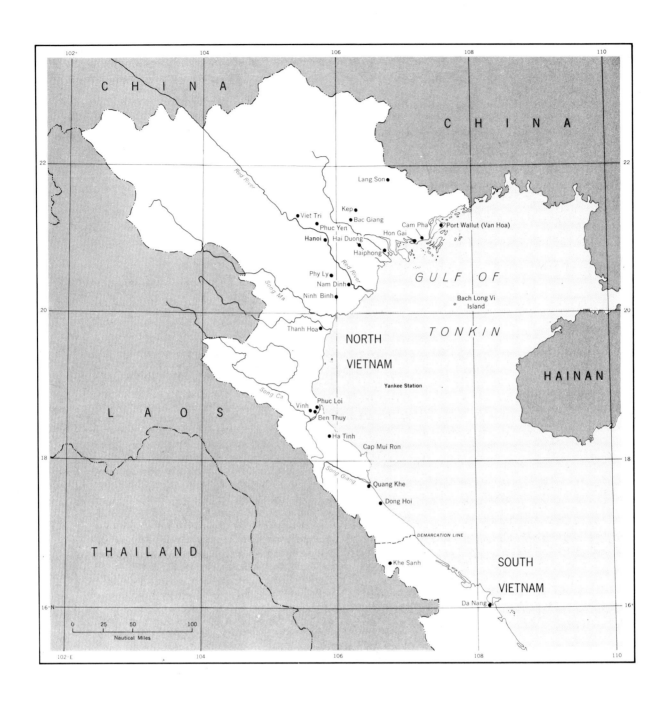

CHINA

CHINA

Lang Son

Viet Tri
Kep
Bac Giang
Cam Pha
Port Wallut (Van Hoa)
Phuc Yen
Hon Gai
Hanoi
Hai Duong
Haiphong

Phy Ly
Red River
Nam Dinh
Bach Long Vi
Island
Ninh Binh

Song Ma

Thanh Hoa
NORTH
GULF OF
VIETNAM
TONKIN

Yankee Station
HAINAN

Song Ca

Vinh
Phuc Loi
Ben Thuy

Ha Tinh
Cap Mui Ron

Song Giang
Quang Khe
Dong Hoi

DEMARCATION LINE

THAILAND
Khe Sanh
SOUTH

VIETNAM

Da Nang

LAOS

0   25   50   100
Nautical Miles

A Vietnamese torpedo boat
photographed from the USS
Maddox.

An RF-8 Crusader rolls in for a photo run over South Vietnam.

Smoke from the 10 Vinh petroleum storage tanks rose to 14,000 feet and damage was estimated at 90%. Eight gunboats and torpedo boats were destroyed and 21 damaged. Thus, the North Vietnamese Navy paid a high price for the ineffective efforts of their torpedo craft. Significantly, U.S. retaliation had come from the sea, where American power was all powerful and unhampered by the need to coordinate the response with foreign states.

But the retaliation was not without cost. Two of the *Constellation*'s aircraft were lost to AAA fire at Hon Gai. Lieutenant (j.g.) Richard Sather, flying a VA-145 Skyraider, was shot down and killed over Loc Chao; Lieutenant (j.g.) Everett Alvarez, flying an A-4C, was shot down over Hon Gai and became the first U.S. pilot to be captured by the North Vietnamese.

Six days later, on 10 August 1964, Congress passed a joint resolution—later to be called the Gulf of Tonkin resolution—that termed the attacks on the destroyers a part of a "deliberate and systematic campaign of aggression that the Communist regime in North Vietnam had been waging against its neighbors and the nations joined with them."

"For the next six months (until the retaliatory strikes beginning 7 February 1965)," said Rear Admiral H. L. Miller, CTF 77, "the operations of Task Force 77 consisted of standing by for retaliatory strikes over North Vietnam with various bomb loads and missiles. Photographic flights were made over South Vietnam and Laos watching for buildups of Viet Cong and the infiltration of North Vietnamese along the Ho Chi Minh trail. Strikes by small groups of carrier aircraft were made on trucks and material storage areas in South Vietnam whenever they were found."

The Start of Naval Air Interdiction (1965)

The attacks just described were punitive. The routine bombing of North Vietnam by TF 77 aircraft did not begin until 7 February 1965. The original nickname, Flaming Dart, was given to a plan for retaliatory air strikes if overt acts of Viet Cong aggression against American forces in South Vietnam continued. Such attacks did continue. On 7 February, the Viet Cong launched a heavy mortar attack on United States forces and billets at the Pleiku Airbase and nearby Camp Holloway. Eight Americans were killed and 109 were wounded.

Following this attack, TF 77 was alerted and Flaming Dart was readied for execution. Rear Admiral Miller, embarked in the *Ranger* (CVA-61), received orders at 0621 on 7 February 1965 to assemble TF 77 and to prepare for retaliatory strikes on North Vietnam. Two other carriers, the *Coral Sea* (CVA-43) and the *Hancock* (CVA-19), then en route to Cubi Point in the Philippines, reversed course and joined the *Ranger* in the early afternoon. The pace was intense aboard the three ships as magazines were opened, pilots were briefed, and bomb racks loaded. Commander Warren H. Sells, Commander Carrier Air Wing 21, aboard the *Hancock,* would be airborne coordinator for the strike.

At 1240, orders to attack were received. Despite very poor weather over the targets, the *Coral Sea* and *Hancock* catapulted off 20 and 29 aircraft, respectively, for strikes against the North Vietnamese army barracks and port facilities at Dong Hoi, just north of the Demilitarized Zone (DMZ).

Simultaneously, the *Ranger* launched a 34-plane strike against the Vit Thu Lu barracks, 15 miles inland and 5 miles north of the Demilitarized Zone, but the northeast monsoon prevented her attacks, as well as others by the U.S. Air Force and the South Vietnamese Air Force, from being carried out.

At Dong Hoi, ten buildings were destroyed, two others heavily damaged, and an undetermined number left burning by aircraft from the *Coral Sea* and the *Hancock*. One A-4E from the *Coral Sea* was lost, three others were damaged, and five of the *Hancock*'s aircraft were also damaged.

The enemy's response was not long in coming. On 10 February the enemy blew up a United States enlisted men's billet at Qui Nhon, killing 23 men and wounding 21 others. Again, Admiral Sharp recommended prompt and emphatic retaliation.

Flaming Dart Two began on 11 February. The *Coral Sea, Hancock,* and *Ranger* were ordered to strike the Chanh Hoa barracks. The selected times-over-target (0900 for CVW-9, 0915 for CVW-21 and 0930 for CVW-15) were chosen at the Washington level in order to coincide with a statement made by President Johnson in Washington announcing the retaliation. Tactically, the choice of time was poor, for in February, the "crachin" fog, rain, and low visibility characteristic of the northeast monsoon would almost certainly be present in the early morning.

Ninety-nine aircraft were launched by the three carriers. The predictably bad weather was present, with clouds as low as 500 feet and visibility less than a mile, and it gave the pilots trouble. The knowledge that the weather would be bad determined the choice of weapons. In this case "Snakeye," a retarded bomb, had to be used in order to provide bomb-blast escape distances. Moreover, the precise numbers of attacking and support aircraft, and the number, types, and fuzing

of weapons were specified by Washington. The use of napalm was forbidden. The *Ranger, Coral Sea,* and *Hancock* made their attacks in scud clouds at 500 feet, with a cloud layer at 1,000 feet and the visibility less than a mile. Three aircraft from the *Coral Sea* were lost and several others were hit by antiaircraft artillery. Two of the three pilots were recovered, but the third was captured when his F-8D was crippled by ground fire. The accuracy and vigor of North Vietnamese antiaircraft defense response was clearly evident.

It was evident, too, that such tight tactical restrictions on bombing, together with tactical operational decisions made at long distance for political purposes, would not achieve the desired result. This type of tit-for-tat response was not likely to deter the Communists from further attacks inside South Vietnam. Indeed, it did not. The Viet Cong continued and increased their hit-and-run attacks on U.S. forces and bases. On 30 March, for example, they bombed the U.S. Embassy in Saigon.

As Viet Cong pressure mounted in South Vietnam, Washington deemed it appropriate to provide more and better protection for U.S. installations ashore. Accordingly, on 8-10 March 1965, Marines from the Seventh Fleet were landed at Da Nang. CTF 77 provided combat air patrol and photographic coverage for this landing.

Early Rolling Thunder Raids

The bombing of North Vietnam, no longer limited to punitive raids, now began under a new notion (at this stage of the war it could not yet be called a concept) called Rolling Thunder and, like thunder, it was to be spasmodic. In the beginning the general thinking was to draw a bombing line somewhere across the southern part of North Vietnam and move the line northward very slowly. As the line neared Hanoi, it was believed that the North Vietnamese would capitulate to save their capital. As we shall see, however, this scheme was never followed. As the months rolled by and the war drew nearer to Hanoi, a sanctuary zone was placed around both Hanoi and Haiphong. Strikes in these sanctuaries were permitted only on special occasions.

Rolling Thunder operations were always conducted under strict controls and with specific guidance from the highest levels of government—targeting by remote control. As on the previous occasions, commanders were told on which day to strike; in many cases they were told the hour of attack (which ignored weather conditions). They were told by Washington the number of sorties by task and by target; the type, number, and fuzing of weapons to be used; and, sometimes, even the direction of attack. Attacks were limited to primary targets or one of two alternates. Unexpended ordnance had to be dumped into the South China Sea. Pre-strike reconnaissance was not permitted. Bomb damage assessment (photographic) aircraft were to accompany strike aircraft or follow them immediately; subsequent bomb damage assessment was to be conducted by these aircraft, unescorted, flying at medium altitudes only. No aircraft was to be re-loaded and returned for a second attack. If the target weather was bad on the approved day, the mission could not be rescheduled without repeating the elaborate process of gaining approval from Washington. Enemy aircraft had to be positively identified before shooting, a tough requirement for aircraft flying at Mach 1. Rules were so stringent that only military trucks could be hit, and these had to be moving on highways, not parked in villages. (Later this rule was relaxed to allow trucks within 100 meters, and later still, within 300 meters, of the roads to be attacked, but never in the village sanctuaries.)

A geographic point in the Gulf of Tonkin was selected as the locus of operations for TF 77 and was given the code name Yankee Station.

As the air campaign progressed, Admiral Sharp reminded his operational commanders and pilots that Rolling Thunder was unusual. "It does not seek to inflict maximum damage on the enemy," he said. "Instead, it is a precise application of military pressure for the specific purpose of halting aggression in South Vietnam."

On 18 March 1965, aircraft from the *Coral Sea* and the *Hancock* hit supply buildings at Phu Van and Vinh Son army supply depots. Several aircraft sustained light damage from antiaircraft artillery, but none was lost.

Eight days later, on 26 March, 70 aircraft from the same two carriers struck four North Vietnamese radar sites at Vinh Son, Cap Mui Ron, Ha Tinh, and Bach Long Vi Island, causing heavy damage. Both pilots were safely recovered from an A-4 and an F-8 which were hit.

On 29 March, the two carriers again launched 70 aircraft. This time they struck radar and communication facilities on Bach Long Vi, a small island strategically located in the Gulf of Tonkin. Weather and visibility were poor. Four of the first six aircraft over the target—three of them squadron commanders—were hit and three of them shot down. Commander Jack H. Harris, Commanding Officer of VA-155, had a flameout and ejected into the sea, but was rescued. Commander W. N. Donnelly, Commanding Officer of VF-154, was also hit and landed in the water four miles north of the island. The low altitude and upside-down ejection at 400 knots dislocated his shoulder and fractured a neck vertebra. (He spent 45 hours in a raft before being rescued by an Air Force HU-16 Albatross. Twice during the first night, Commander Donnelly crawled painfully under his life raft when an unidentified destroyer type vessel without flag or running lights passed as near as 300 yards to him.) Lieutenant Commander Kenneth E. Hume, also from VF-154, was killed during a run on the target. The fourth, Commander Peter Mongilardi, Commanding Officer of VA-153, took a hit in his wing and was "towed" home by a tanker aircraft, pumping fuel overboard as fast as the tanker could give it to him.

However, he was recovered aboard the *Coral Sea* safely.

In the closest attack yet to Hanoi, on 3 April, the two carriers conducted two strikes—one in the morning, one in the afternoon, hitting and wrecking a bridge at Dong Phuong Thong, 70 miles south of the enemy capital, with 60 tons of ordnance.

As a result of this early interdiction effort, the countermoves of the North Vietnamese soon became apparent. Instead of moving by companies, battalions, or regiments, the enemy soldiers traveled in small units along what formerly were little-used roads and trails hidden beneath the heavy jungle foliage. Collectively these are called the Ho Chi Minh trail.

Establishment of Dixie Station

In April 1965, Task Force 77 pilots drew still another role—a role which for the nth time reflected their value—flying regular close support missions against the Viet Cong in South Vietnam. The initial effort by aircraft from the *Midway* and the *Coral Sea,* plus Marine F-8Es from VMF-212 flying from the *Oriskany* with CVW-16, was so successful that General Westmoreland requested the permanent assignment of a carrier stationed off the northern half of South Vietnam to support his ground forces. Since land bases for tactical air were not available and could not be produced quickly enough, CinCPacFlt directed on 16 May the establishment of Dixie Station, about 100 miles southeast of Cam Ranh Bay. This assignment would last for 15 months until land based aviation had been established sufficiently so as to be able to handle the bombing load within South Vietnam.

The Growth of the Enemy's Defenses

In the fall of 1964, the air defense system of North Vietnam was weak. As the war became hotter, however, a dramatic and ominous buildup was observed in all four parts of North Vietnam's air defense system—radar networks, surface-to-air missile (SAM) defenses, MiG fighter aircraft, and automatic antiaircraft (AAA) guns.

On 5 April 1965, photography revealed the first North Vietnamese surface-to-air missile site under construction, some 15 miles southeast of Hanoi. The pictures came from the cameras of an RF-8 Crusader from the *Coral Sea* on an early reconnaissance mission. The wet prints were rushed to Rear Admiral Edward C. Outlaw, who had relieved Admiral Miller as CTF 77.

Said Admiral Outlaw: "It was the first confirmation of the enemy missile buildup, which we had expected for some time. I immediately flew to Saigon to show the pictures to Major General J. H. Moore, Commanding General, Seventh Air Force, and his staff."

The second SAM-occupied site appeared about a month later and, by mid-July 1965, several more sites were photographed in various stages of construction, forming an irregular ring around Hanoi and Haiphong. But still the authority to attack them could not be obtained.

An A-6 attack aircraft off the USS *Constellation* in flight to targets in South Vietnam.

The hesitation in Washington was partly due, of course, to a fear that if the missile sites were attacked, Russian technicians might be killed. Others insisted that the SAM batteries were defensive only; that if American aircraft did not attack Hanoi and Haiphong, the enemy would not fire at them. Still others feared that such attacks might be regarded as U.S. escalation.

Permission to attack the missile sites did not come for many weeks, until after a SAM had destroyed an Air Force F-4C on 24 July, by which time numerous sites were under construction. Three days later the Air Force was authorized to hit two SAM sites northwest of Hanoi in retaliation. The attacks were to be made on one day only, and the pilots were specifically forbidden to attack any air base from which enemy MiGs might oppose the mission.

Fifty-five Air Force aircraft attacked the SAM sites and the guns protecting them; the price paid was four aircraft lost. Another strike was ordered by Washington, and while photography taken on 8 August showed the mobile SAMs still in place at the two sites, the strike group found the sites empty the following day. It was an early and convincing demonstration of the mobility of the Soviet SA-2 missiles, and a preview of how the enemy would move his weapons in the months ahead.

The use of missiles by Hanoi led to the establishment on 12 August 1965 of Operation Iron Hand, an anti-SAM campaign using the Navy-developed Shrike missile, which could identify and home on a SAM battery's guidance radar.

On the night of 11-12 August, in fact, the Navy lost its first aircraft to SAMs. Two A-4Es, from VA-23, flying off the *Midway,* were at 9,000 feet, on a road recce mission 60 miles south of Hanoi. The flight leader, Lieutenant Commander D. Roberge, and his wingman, Lieutenant (j.g.) Donald H. Brown, Jr., observed what appeared to be two flares glowing eerily beneath the clouds 15 miles north of their position. They watched what ap-

peared to be two "hunting" spots of light come out of the clouds and move closer and closer. In sudden recognition of danger, both pilots pushed over and added full power. It was too late. Seconds later the SAMs exploded, destroying Lieutenant (j.g.) Brown's aircraft and damaging Lieutenant Commander Roberge's. Although his plane was on fire, the latter managed to limp back and land aboard the *Midway,* his Skyhawk's belly scorched, wrinkled, and peppered with more than 50 holes.

A new era of warfare for naval aviation had begun.

Task Force 77 reacted promptly in an effort to find and destroy the enemy missile batteries. As directed, on 12 and 13 August, 76 missions searched at low levels for the sites. Five planes and two pilots were lost to AAA, and seven other planes were damaged, but no SAMs were found. It was truly a black Friday the 13th for TF 77.

It was not until the morning of 17 October 1965, in fact, that an Iron Hand flight of four A-4Es, led by an A-6 Intruder from the *Independence*'s CVW-7 (flown by Lieutenant Commander Cecil E. "Pete" Garber, VA-75), destroyed the first occupied and operational SAM site, one near Kep airfield 52 miles northeast of Hanoi.

Naval air's first MiG kills came in June 1965—the first on 17 June when F-4s from the *Midway*'s VF-21 flown by Commander Louis C. Page and his radar intercept officer (RIO), Lieutenant John C. Smith and Lieutenant Jack E. D. Batson and his RIO, downed two MiGs 50 miles south of Hanoi. At 1026, while headed northeast, Commander Page picked up bogies on his radar miles ahead. The two Phantoms and four MiGs approached each other head-on at a 1,000-knot closure speed—a mile every three and one-half seconds. The F-4s were ready to fire their long-range Sparrows. Commander Page finally spotted the characteristic huge nose intakes, mid-wings and prominent bubble canopies of the silver MiG-17 "Frescoes" and pickled off his missile at the second of the four MiGs which were flying in a ragged single file. Lieutenant Batson fired at the third—and both MiGs burned in puffs of orange flame and black smoke.

On 20 June, the third MiG was bagged —this time by propeller-driven A-1 "Skyraiders." The flight of four "Spads," led by Lieutenant Commander E. A. Greathouse from VA-125, also aboard the *Midway,* were on a rescue combat air patrol (ResCAP) mission when jumped by two MiG-17s. Maintaining tight air discipline, the Skyraiders dove for the deck and "scissored" defensively just above the treetops. In a series of truns and reverses, during a dogfight which lasted five minutes, the four prop pilots succeeded in out-turning and outmaneuvering the MiGs. Two of them, Lieutenant Clinton B. Johnson and Lieutenant (j.g.) Charles W. Hartman, finally got a tail-on shot—and watched one MiG go down under their chattering 20-mm guns. (Back at Yankee Station all ears in every ready room and CIC were glued to the Tactical Air Control net listening to the four Spad pilots' account of their unusual but successful air encounter.)

1965 Results

The Rolling Thunder air operations expenditure in 1965 would grow eightfold in 1966, as more lucrative targets were authorized. Ten different attack carriers had participated in operations at Yankee Station. Eight hundred trucks and 650 pieces of railroad rolling stock had been damaged or destroyed. The Navy had flown more than 30,993 combat and combat support sorties over North Vietnam and 25,895 more over South Vietnam. Over one hundred Navy aircraft were lost, and 82 crewmen had been killed, captured, or reported missing. Forty-six others had been rescued after the loss of their aircraft. Attacks had largely been concentrated on military barracks, rails, roads, and bridges, but not on the really worthwhile targets.

Cdr. L. C. Page and Lt. J. C. Smith shot down a MIG-17.

These first 11 months of combat of 1965 revealed the development of the strategy of gradualism—applying military pressure in small doses—a strategy which was to continue for 26 more months, interspersed with other self-imposed bombing pauses, self-inflicted restrictions, and self-designated sanctuaries. This stragegy assumed that our direct military involvement in South Vietnam, and our selective use of our overwhelming airpower against North Vietnam, would force the North Vietnamese to the peace table. By applying gradual military pressure, we believed we could "get the signal through to Hanoi," to use a favorite State Department term, to convince North Vietnam to stop attacking its neighbor, and in so doing, we would not risk escalating the conflict.

The year 1965 saw another result which would become a way of life for the entire war—the tendency to measure effort and accomplishment by the number of sorties flown. "We tried to counter this unfortunate tendency," said Admiral Roy L. Johnson, then Commander Seventh Fleet, "by emphasizing quality of effort based on the best possible BDA [bomb damage assessment]. Admittedly, BDA was often difficult to obtain. But we recognized that Secretary McNamara had to have some way of measuring effort, and in particular, for controlling the air effort. Controlling and limiting the number of missions was his method."

One of the final 1965 strikes against North Vietnam was to be a big one, and the next to the last for almost seven weeks. On 22 December, the *Enterprise, Kitty Hawk,* and *Ticonderoga* launched more than 100 planes in a combined strike against the Uong Bi thermal power plant, 15 miles north-northeast of Haiphong, the first industrial target authorized by the JCS. The three carriers' aircraft were assigned times to be over target which were 30 minutes apart, beginning at 1500.

The attacks by the *Enterprise* came in from the north, while the *Kitty Hawk*'s and *Ticonderoga*'s aircraft approached from the south. Flak was heavy, especially at 3,000 feet and two A-4s from the *Enterprise* were lost to ground fire. But the attack caused severe damage to the boiler house, and the pilots saw smoke pouring from both ends of the generator hall, observed the fuel oil supply burning, and saw the administration building collapse. The petroleum storage area was engulfed in flames, the coal treatment center demolished, and the twelve storage buildings were struck. Uong Bi would supply little electrical power to the Hanoi-Haiphong electrical power network for many weeks.

The year ended with a U.S. suspension of the bombing commencing Christmas Day which, Secretary of State Rusk said, could lead to peace negotiations if the enemy would show constraint.

1966

As 1966 opened, and during the 37-day bombing standdown which followed, a massive attempt was made to bring Hanoi to the peace table. Hanoi, however, stood fast, spurned every peace

effort, and responded to the U.S. presentation before the United Nations by saying that any resolutions made by that body would be considered null and void. Also, the United States was being bombarded from all sides not to resume the bombing—from the U.N., from allies in Europe, and from doves at home. Hanoi applauded every such effort.

During the standdown, Admiral Sharp told the JCS that if the bombing effort was to succeed, North Vietnam must be denied access to external assistance from Russia, Communist China, and other Bloc nations, whether by sea or by rail. Military supplies already stockpiled in North Vietnam had to be destroyed, he said. All known military material and facilities should be destroyed and military activities and movements should be continuously harassed and disrupted. All this, he said, would require air bombing operations quite different from those in 1965.

"It was obvious," said Admiral Sharp, "that our air operations in 1965 had not achieved their goal and that the nature of the war had changed since the air campaign began. We had not forced Hanoi to the peace table. We had not scared Hanoi out of the war. We had not caused any diminution whatsoever of his carrying the war into South Vietnam. In fact, the reverse was true. It was evident to me that Ho Chi Minh intended to continue to support the Viet Cong until he was denied the capability to do so.

"I felt that a properly oriented bombing effort could either bring the enemy to the conference table or cause the insurgency to wither from lack of support. The alternative would be a long and costly war—costly in lives and material resources—a long war which even in early 1966 was already becoming distasteful to some Americans."

Rolling Thunder Operations Resumed

When Rolling Thunder operations

were resumed on 31 January, however, the same pattern as before Christmas was followed, not the revised strategy recommended by CinCPac. Targets were still largely limited to the southern portion of North Vietnam. The airfields, the MiGs, the closure of Haiphong, the industrial tragets in the northeast, the electrical and petroleum targets, all remained off limits. However, the objective of Rolling Thunder was slowly shifting (perhaps not consciously) from punishment to interdiction in order to shut off the supply of men and materials to South Vietnam, which should induce Hanoi to seek a political settlement at the peace table.

The buildup of SAM missiles, radars, MiGs, and AAA guns began to take an increasingly heavy toll of American aircraft, with AAA guns taking the most. Six aircraft and five crewmen were lost in January 1966 (two over South Vietnam, one over North Vietnam, and three at sea) and ten aircraft and ten air crewmen in February. From time to time, the flurries of SAMs damaged or downed an airplane. On 9 February, an A-4C from the *Ticonderoga* was damaged 20 miles southwest of Thanh Hoa, but the pilot, Commander Jack L. Snyder, the air wing commander of CVW-5, managed to get over the Gulf before ejecting, to be picked up by the USS *England* (DLG-22). Pilots described the SAMs as looking like telephone poles, slightly tapered at the nose, and trailed by a bright orange flame.

At first, the best defense against the Soviet supplied SA-2 missiles (which were now arriving in North Vietnam in abundance) was to fly below their envelope. However, such low altitude flight required more fuel and placed the aircraft within the kill envelope of small arms, automatic weapons, and light antiaircraft artillery.

An early set of rules for defending against SAMs was developed by Air Wing 21 aboard the *Hancock* (CVA-19), of which perhaps the most important was that pilots should not operate at mid- or high altitudes in a SAM environment.

Pilots from TF 77 flew 6,500 sorties in March in North and South Vietnam. Eleven aircraft were lost, with ten air crewmen lost or missing.

April was to be TF 77's worst month yet—21 aircraft lost with 15 air crewmen. Much of the carriers' effort was in the Vinh-Ben Thuy complex because of poorer weather farther north. However, for the first time since the Christmas bombing pause, the Northeast quadrant could be hit when weather permitted.

On 18 April, as the northeast monsoon eased off, TF 77 got a chance to hit an important industrial target for the second time—the Uong Bi thermal power plant near Haiphong. The plant supplied one-third of Hanoi's power and nearly all of Haiphong's. Since the first attack by TF 77 on 22 December, extensive repairs had been made to the plant, and it was time for another visit.

Just before midnight, two A-6As from the *Kitty Hawk,* flown by Commander Ronald J. Hays and Lieutenant John T. Been, and Lieutenant Eric M. Roemish and his RIO, all of VA-85, executed an imaginative low-level radar attack. Each of the A-6s carried 13, 1,000-pound bombs.

The approach to the target was one which would both optimize the radar return from the power plant and avoid much of the enemy defenses.

Commander Hays and Lieutenant Roemish were launched near midnight. The two A-6s joined up, updated their navigation systems, verified the operation of their weapon systems, and set course to the target. The attack plan called for remaining below the enemy's radar envelope as long as possible from Yankee Station to landfall.

The landfall was made exactly as planned and the two aircraft then took lateral separation. Each pilot acquired the target separately and made his own run. Both aircraft were on and off the target within seconds of one another. The 26 one-thousand-pound bombs hit the power plant. The success of the mission was readily apparent as huge secondary explosions occurred and showers of flashes from the resulting electrical shorts could be seen. It was not until after the crews released their bombs that the enemy started firing, lighting the night sky and filling the air with flak. The attack was not only a complete success but also a complete surprise. Subsequent photographs showed all 26 bombs had impacted inside the perimeter fence of the power plant. In fact, one or two bombs had hit the 250-foot-high smoke stack and leveled it.

The next day, three previously restricted targets at Cam Pha—only 35 miles from the Red China border—were hit by the *Kitty Hawk*—the railroad yards, the water pumping station, and a coal treatment plant. Some 50 tons of ordnance were delivered by 24 aircraft in three surprise raids. There were many hits on the web of railroad tracks, the large repair building, the coal treatment plant, and the approaches to the coal loading piers: the largest building in the area disintegrated with a large secondary explosion. A score of fires was started and smoke and debris soared above 2,000 feet. Flak suppression F-4 Phantoms quickly silenced most enemy opposition and there were no aircraft losses.

However, this strike on Cam Pha, a small and insignificant harbor, stirred up a hornet's nest in Washington.

"We had launched the strike against Cam Pha within 90 minutes after its appearance on the target list," said Rear Admiral J. R. Reedy, once again Commander TF 77, "for it was a key target we had repeatedly asked to hit and, always before, the answer had been no."

Between 13 and 19 April, *Kitty Hawk* and *Ticonderoga* aircraft dropped two important bridges—each over 1,000 feet long—at Haiphong and Hai Duong.

Commander David B. Miller, CO of VA-144 on the *Ticonderoga*, was strike leader of 11 A-4s and four F-8s against the Haiphong highway bridge, one of the largest bridges leading into that city from Red China. Earlier in the day, Commander Miller had flown a mission in the same area and had observed the mar-

ginal weather and enemy defenses. He became convinced that a small, "clean wing," maximum-load attack could be successful. The drop tanks were removed from the A-4s and the ship's launch point was moved well to the north by Captain Robert Miller, the *Ticonderoga*'s skipper.

As the strike group approached the target from behind the ridge to the north, two SAMs were fired at them from Haiphong; but the flight avoided them. Climbing again after the missiles passed, the group came under heavy flak. Two aircraft were hit—an F-8 escort, piloted by Commander Mohrhardt of VF-53, and Commander Miller's A-4. A 37-mm. projectile had hit the dorsal fin of Miller's aircraft, leaving a large hole. Despite this damage, and two more SAMs fired at the group, Commander Miller and the *Ticonderoga* flight pressed their attack and dropped five of the twenty-one spans of the bridge. Commander Mohrhardt was able to fly his burning F-8 out to sea where he was picked up safely by helicopter.

April also saw a modification of the manner in which Rolling Thunder targets were assigned. Until this time, the Air Force and the Navy had shared the air over North Vietnam on a time basis, alternating the six areas every week. But this system of fixed times on target didn't work well for the carriers, which were launching and recovering aircraft every 90 minutes. So the six route package areas were now permanently divided. This placed the coastal areas, including Haiphong, in the Navy's area, leaving the area north of the DMZ, Hanoi, and the country to the west for the Air Force. However, some route package areas were major off-limit sanctuaries which contained the most lucrative targets. In addition, there was a buffer zone along the entire border between North Vietnam and Red China, which was kept immune from bombing.

The assignment of permanent areas of responsibility to the Air Force and the Navy had one immediate effect, a reduction in aircraft and aircrew losses. This was because pilots became very familiar with their assigned target areas, since they flew over them repeatedly and got to know the enemy's defenses and the best directions for attack. Furthermore, pilots became so familiar with the areas that they could detect meaningful changes.

Throughout May, the four TF 77 carriers kept flying hard, the *Ranger,* the *Hancock,* and the *Enterprise* at Yankee Station, with the *Intrepid* (CVS-11) at Dixie Station supporting General Westmoreland's four search-and-destroy operations then underway: Lexington, Hardihood, Reno, and Makiki. The *Intrepid* (Captain G. Macri) had arrived at Dixie Station on 15 May to relieve the *Hancock.* On her decks were 32 A-4s and 24 A-1s of CVW-10, but no fighters. Once an attack carrier, but an ASW carrier since 1964, she temporarily resumed her old role and, as the U.S. Navy's 16th attack carrier, helped to ease the strain of keeping five attack carriers continuously deployed to WestPac and two in the Mediterranean. It was a killing deployment schedule for the 16 ships, 7 months out, 5 months at home at the best, a schedule which would slowly erode the reenlistment rate and depress the pilot retention rate.

With five attack carriers on station in Western Pacific, three of them constantly at Yankee Station, the air war had now reached a high level. Attack sorties on North Vietnam continued to grow.

	Attack Sorties		Aircraft/ Pilot Losses
	NVN	SVN	
March	1923	3474	11/9
April	2780	3184	21/15
May	2568	2810	9/2
June	3078	2597	9/9

By the end of May, the enemy's SAM network had been extended south and west, and more than 100 SAM sites protected North Vietnam. Hanoi and Haiphong had become the most heavily defended targets in the world.

MiG activity was also growing. TF 77's electronic warning aircraft, EA-3Bs, supported by EC-121M Big Look aircraft based at Da Nang, issued 141 SAM warnings and 38 MiG warnings. The presence of all-weather MiG-21 Fishbeds at North Vietnamese airfields was also confirmed. A total of 70 MiGs was now credited in the enemy's air order of battle, plus 6 IL-28 Beagles.

The number of supply ships arriving in Haiphong harbor was also growing. Nineteen ships arrived in April, 25 in May, and 28 in June. Pilots circling in the Gulf of Tonkin flew past loaded Soviet ships and tankers. On their decks could be seen trucks, missile equipment, and oil drums. The pilots knew they would be hunting these same trucks and missile trailers, one by one, in subsequent weeks.

It was during this period that an effective method of attacking North Vietnamese trucks was perfected, the use of flares for visual night attacks at low level. "The pioneer of this technique was Commander Harry Thomas, Commanding Officer, VA-153," said Commander David E. Leue. "He had had considerable night attack experience during the Korean War. He taught us in mid-1965 how to find and destroy trucks at night—at ferry crossings and at downed bridges." Commander Thomas was later killed on Black Friday, 13 August 1965, during the SAM hunt.

The tactic called for pairs of A-4 Skyhawks, one flying 1,000 feet above the other and carrying flares, the second and lower aircraft watching the roads, ferry crossings and bridges, and calling for flares.

"Using this tactic," said Commander Leue, "we finished out *Coral Sea*'s 1965 cruise by burning trucks on most nights of our last two line periods."

During the 1966 period, two squadrons, VA-153 and VA-155, continued and expanded the technique, and were aided by the E-2 Hawkeye aircraft, for navigational assistance, as well as by the new Mk 4 gun pod. It was risky but effective work, and demolished trucks could be seen by daylight on many of North Vietnam's principal roads.

One of the most unorthodox recoveries in the history of aircraft carriers occurred on 3 June 1966. Commander Milton J. Chewning, Commanding Officer of VA-55, while on his eleventh strike mission over North Vietnam, took a burst of AA fire just forward of the starboard wing. The exploding shell peppered the cockpit with fragments, and several of them hit and incapacitated Commander Chewning's right arm. He calmly locked his throttle and adjusted his cabin environmental controls to compensate for the loss of air pressure in the cockpit. He then flew 150 miles to the *Ranger* left-handed, reporting by radio once or twice that he felt "woozy."

On board the *Ranger,* there was a hurried conference. Should a landing be tried? Was the pilot so badly wounded he couldn't make it? Might not his landing endanger men on the flight deck? After listening to Mike on the radio, and assessing his condition, it was quickly decided to give him the chance to land aboard.

While Commander Chewning was making the 20-minute flight to the carrier, Captain Leo B. McCuddin, the *Ranger*'s Commanding Officer, ordered the flight deck cleared of all unnecessary equipment. A flight surgeon was launched in a helo in case Commander Chewning chose to eject, and a second doctor was positioned on the flight deck with all emergency equipment.

"I stood in CIC monitoring Mike's voice," said Commander Fred Palmer, Commander Air Wing 14, "and I was prepared to order him to eject if he again reported that he felt 'woozy.' He didn't, however. As Mike got within sight of the ship, Commander Paul Russell, *Ranger*'s operations officer, stood in the doorway between CIC and CATTC

monitoring his approach on the scopes, and at the same time talking directly by telephone to Captain McCuddin on the bridge. Captain McCuddin had already begun turning the ship into the wind, and when Mike's A-4E appeared on the CATTC radar astern of *Ranger,* even before Mike's plane could be seen from the ship, Captain McCuddin stopped the turn. The ship was still 30 degrees out of the wind, but this way Mike got a 'straight-in' approach to the deck.

"Mike rolled out in the groove and headed for the deck with a locked throttle," continued Commander Palmer. "The LSO, Lieutenant Commander 'Pon' Johnson, spoke gentle words to him. Mike's pass was actually FAB [Fast as a bastard], but Lieutenant Commander Johnson's LSO record book said, 'O.K. pass, #3 wire.'

"Who says LSOs—and ship's skippers—don't have a heart?"

Rushed to sickbay, Commander Chewning was operated on for the removal of the several chunks of shrapnel in his arm, and later flown ashore for further treatment.

For his courage and airmanship, Commander Chewning was awarded the Silver Star Medal.

The Hai Duong bridge, a major link between Hanoi and Haiphong, was dropped by a single A-6 crew on a night raid. Lieutenant Commander Bernie Deibert and his B/N, Lieutenant Commander Dale Purdy, executed the imaginative strike on 12 August 1966 while operating with VA-65. The Intruder crew caught the North Vietnamese completely by surprise in one of their most highly defended areas. The five Mk-84, 2,000-pound bombs they released demolished the center span of the bridge.

It was also during this period that Lieutenant R. S. Williams and his B/N, Lieutenant J. E. Diselrod, developed a unique air-to-air defense tactic for night Intruder strikes. While retiring from their target area 40 miles into North Vietnam, Lieutenant Diselrod noted indications of an enemy fighter. When evasive maneuvers appeared futile, the A-6 crew intentionally overflew Nam Dinh, an area noted for its intensive AAA fire. The barrage discharged at the unidentified aircraft proved sufficient to discourage the trailing North Vietnamese pilot, and a successful termination of intercept tracking was achieved. This particular tactic became known as the "Willard Egress" to the flight crews of VA-65 and CVW-15.

THE POL CAMPAIGN

By Asian standards, North Vietnam possessed a good petroleum, oil, and lubricants (POL) storage and distribution system to meet the needs of its industrial, transportation, and military consumers. Its wartime POL requirements were estimated to be 15,000 to 20,000 metric tons a month, an amount which two small tankers or 170 railroad tank cars bringing oil from Red China, could supply.

As the American bombing effort stepped up, Hanoi only had to look at history—World War II in Germany and Japan—to anticipate the bombing of their POL system, which was above ground and exposed. By June 1966 air bombing in the southern part of North Vietnam had eliminated Nam Dinh and Phu Qui as POL storage centers, and the storage capacity at Vinh had been cut by two-thirds.

But the major part of the POL system, located near Hanoi and Haiphong, remained untouched. In late 1965 and early 1966, new POL farms with buried or bunkered tanks were sighted or photographed all over the country, the majority of them in or near the major military and industrial centers. Also, extremely large numbers of 55 gallon-type petroleum drums were visible.

Navy pilots attacking the Haiphong POL storage area were ordered not to make attacks on any craft in the harbor unless they were first fired on, and "only if the craft is clearly of North Vietnam registry." In addition, "piers servicing the Haiphong POL storage will not be attacked if a tanker is berthed off the end of the pier."

At the very last minute, still another delay developed: a news leak. In the United States, newspaper stories appeared which said that North Vietnam's POL system would be struck very soon and giving essential strike details. This publicity, appearing at almost the same time that the POL strikes were being authorized, caused another week's postponement.

Finally, on 29 June 1966, more than a year after Rolling Thunder had commenced, the bombing program against POL facilities got underway with strikes on Hanoi and Haiphong. Twenty-eight of the *Ranger*'s aircraft, including anti-MiG, anti-SAM and anti-flak elements, led by Commander Frederick F. Palmer, Commander Air Wing 14, went against the Haiphong POL complex, the country's largest, and turned it into three huge fireballs and many columns of smoke which rose to 20,000 feet. "I put the A-4Cs, slowest of the jets in the attack group, in the van," said Palmer. "Commander Al 'Shoes' Shaufelberger, Commanding Officer of VA-146 (Blue Diamonds), did a perfect job of navigating to the target area, and the fireball from his bombs provided an interesting obstacle for subsequent attackers during their pull-out. Commander Bob Holt, leading the War Horses of VA-55, peppered and ignited several tanks with his load of 2.75-inch Mighty Mouse rockets. The flak was heavy, initially, in the target area, but flak suppressors—F-4s of VF-142 led by Commander Jim Brown—were so accurate in placing their bombs that it seemed as if a switch had suddenly 'turned off' the heavy caliber antiaircraft fire. Finally, Fighting 143, led by Commander Walt Spangenberg, positioned their Phantoms between the MiG bases and the attack group. There were no takers."

The Vinh POL storage was hit on 23 July, resulting in a spectacular fire with four large fireballs. During this attack,

Commander Wynne F. Foster, Commanding Officer of VA-163, flying an A-4E, took a 57-mm. hit through the starboard side of the cockpit, which almost severed his right arm below the shoulder. Radioing that he was bleeding badly, he managed to steer the crippled Skyhawk with his knees while holding the stump of his shattered arm and restricting the gush of blood. When over water near the USS *Reeves* (DLG-24), and growing faint, he succeeded in making a left-handed ejection and was rescued by the ship's whaleboat, then evacuated to the *Oriskany* by helicopter where his arm was amputated. (His change of command ceremony, held on the *Oriskany* in Subic Bay a few days later, was conducted from a stretcher, concluding with the traditional, but left-handed, salute.) Commander Foster later received a prosthetic arm and, after a long administrative battle, was continued on active duty.

By the end of July, the first effects of the POL strikes were becoming apparent. No Soviet tankers arrived at Haiphong in July. They showed up again in August but, then and thereafter, were loaded with drums rather than bulk fuel.

Oil tanks near Haiphong burn after being hit by USS *Oriskany*-based aircraft.

Two Soviet tankers, scheduled to unload at Haiphong, unloaded instead in Red China and their cargo was transshipped to North Vietnam by tank car.

After the attacks on the Haiphong POL storage and oil tank barges, the North Vietnamese quickly realized that though their diesel-powered barges, each able to carry 600 metric tons, were fair game, ships of other nations were not. Thereafter it became a contest between the pilots and the barge crews. The latter would nestle their 150-foot craft alongside tankers of other nations anchored in the roadsteads off Haiphong and Hon Gai. When darkness or bad weather came, these barges would dash for the ports which were off limits to U.S. aircraft. Thus it remained for the A-6 crews, with their all-weather attack systems, and the A-4 crews, working under flares at night, to prevent or inhibit the "last mile" of transport for vital petroleum to North Vietnam.

Strikes on 1 and 4 August 1966 destroyed or damaged four, and possibly six, of the ten tank barges owned by North Vietnam.

By Christmas 1966, the long POL campaign had wrecked all the above ground POL storage sites, including the largest facility, in Hanoi. The Haiphong receiving terminal had been reduced to marginal levels, from a capacity of four tanker shiploads to less than one-third of one shipload per month. Most of the oil barges and oil tank cars had been destroyed. Notwithstanding this damage, North Vietnam retained sufficient oil reserves dispersed in drums and buried or hidden in caves to maintain its military and economic activity for up to four months.

The POL campaign had come too late. The 15-month delay, and the 37-day bombing pause following Christmas, 1965, had given the enemy time to disperse his stocks and to shift from transporting oil by rail to moving it in trucks, and even to commence the construction of an underground pipeline system.

As 1966 ended, it was evident that the interdiction campaign was causing Hanoi extreme hardships. The effect of heavier air strikes was reflected in North Vietnam's public outcries and their insistence that "stop the bombing" was a first prerequisite to any negotiations. The entire population of North Vietnam had been mobilized to support the war effort, and it was estimated that more than 300,000 people were required just to keep the lines of communication open.

Task Force 77 counted up the year's effort: more than 30,000 attack sorties against North Vietnam and 20,000 against the enemy in South Vietnam. Eighty-nine airmen had been killed, captured, or reported missing, and over 120 aircraft had been lost on combat missions.

1967

As 1967 opened, Admiral Sharp made a fresh attempt to have the character of the air interdiction campaign changed. Since the objective of the U.S. military effort was neither to defeat nor to destroy North Vietnam but to cause North Vietnam to stop supporting, controlling, and directing insurgencies in Southeast Asia, three tasks had to be accomplished: (1) to deny North Vietnam access to the flow of external assistance, primarily from Communist China and Russia, (2) to curtail the flow of men and supplies from North Vietnam into Laos and South Vietnam, and (3) to destroy in depth those resources in North Vietnam that contributed to support of the aggression.

"There were six basic target systems in North Vietnam," said Admiral Sharp, "electric power, war supporting industry, transportation support facilities, military complexes, petroleum storage, and air defense."

In mid-April, ten targets were authorized by Washington, a power transformer station, a cement plant, three bridges, a rail repair shop, an ammunition depot, a POL storage area, and two

MiG airfields near Hanoi. Certain targets within ten miles of Hanoi were authorized for attack.

On 2 May, ten more targets were added—targets along the highway and railroad transportation systems from Communist China, and enemy aircraft at their home bases.

On 23 May, a ten mile no-bombing circle was placed around Hanoi.

On 20 July 1967, 16 new targets in the Northeast sector, mostly railroad and highway bridges, were added, bringing the approval total to 46. Of the 46, thirty were in the Hanoi-Haiphong area.

In August, several targets in the so-called Chinese buffer zone, some only eight miles from the border, were authorized: the Port Wallut naval base, the Lang Son railroad bridge, and the Na Phuoc railroad yard, were naval targets. However, that same month all targets in the central Hanoi area were again placed off limits, a restriction that continued for two months.

On 30 August, the coal handling resources at Cam Pha and the Hon Gai port facilities were authorized for attack whenever foreign shipping was not present. The Communists quickly took advantage of this rule, and only on rare occasions thereafter was a foreign ship *not* tied up to the Cam Pha coal piers.

The restrictions placed against North Vietnam's coal loading port of Cam Pha are indicative of Washington's sensitivity to attacks on third country shipping. The TF 77 attack on Cam Pha in April 1966, which resulted in a charge that a Polish ship had been bombed, has been described. This attack put Cam Pha back on the restricted list until August.

Meanwhile, in June 1967, another bombing incident occurred at Cam Pha. The Soviets charged that their merchant vessel *Turkestan* had been attacked on 2 June, killing one crewman and injuring others. A full scale investigation of the incident revealed that two flights of Seventh Air Force F-105s had attacked Cam Pha on 2 June, but Washington flatly denied that these aircraft had attacked the

Turkestan. Indeed, they had not. But about two weeks later, new information arrived in Washington that a third flight of Seventh Air Force fighters, after attacking Bac Giang rail yard 65 miles from Cam Pha, and while en route home, had passed over the harbor, had been fired upon by Cam Pha gun batteries, and had attacked the guns. Apparently the Soviet ship had been struck by this fire. Premier Kosygin later brought a 20-mm. projectile with U.S. Air Force markings from the *Turkestan* to the United States for his meeting with President Johnson at Glassboro, New Jersey.

In any case, the coal mines and mining facilities of North Vietnam, which supplied coal to the electric power plants of North Vietnam, were never authorized for attack.

August passed. In September, 17 new targets were added, and in October, eight more, seven in the Haiphong port area, including three shipyards. In November, 14 new targets were added, bringing the approved total to 85.

Combat SAR—the Rescue of Pilots

One of the truly great success stories of TF 77 operations in the Gulf of Tonkin is the development, by Rear Admiral J. R. Reedy and his staff, of a combat Search and Rescue (SAR) capability for rescuing pilots not only from the water, but from the enemy's territory.

The overriding reasons for a well developed and aggressive combat SAR capability in Southeast Asia were, of course, to prevent pilots from being captured and to sustain pilot morale. To fly day after day deep into the high threat areas of Vinh, Thanh, Hoa, Hanoi, Haiphong, and the Red River Valley, to dodge SAMs and endure history's heaviest and most accurate barrage of gunfire, often in marginal weather or at night, demanded the highest order of courage, airmanship, devotion to duty, and self-discipline on the part of the aviators. If

they were shot down and survived, but could not be rescued, they knew that they faced unnumbered years of prison, isolation, and hunger—even torture or death.

Thus, the pilots looked upon the combat SAR machinery as the best life insurance they could have. If they knew (and they *did* know) that every possible effort would be made to rescue them, their morale would be strengthened and their fortitude increased.

At first, in 1965-66, the SAR system consisted of an Air Force Grumman amphibian aircraft which remained airborne in the Gulf from sunrise to sunset. To this the Navy added an armed two-plane A-1 Skyraider rescue patrol (ResCAP), and a roving SAR destroyer. The Skyraiders were ideally suited for SAR and helo escort duty. They could fly slowly enough to remain with the rescue helos, and their ordnance lifting capacity enabled them to carry a heavy load of bombs and ammunition for suppressing enemy ground fire.

In April 1965, Rear Admiral M. F. Weisner established a second SAR station using a UH-2A/B Seasprite helicopter from the *Ranger* in the destroyer *England.* The northern station, lacking a helo, had a Tacan-equipped DDG and an accompanying Shotgun destroyer. The southern, or combat, SAR station was east of Vinh with a DD and a DLG, the latter fitted with both Tacan and a helo platform. The UH-2 helo (then nicknamed "Angel") aboard the DLG had no armor plating, but the pilots and crew wore flak jackets and had a .30 caliber machine gun mounted in the cabin.

The first overland rescue from North Vietnam of a Navy pilot by a Navy helo occurred on 20 September 1965 when an A-4E flown by Lieutenant (j.g.) John R. Harris of VA-72, aboard the *Independence,* was downed 20 miles east of Hanoi. Harris was recovered by a UH-1B helo which landed aboard the cruiser *Galveston* (CLG-3)

In November 1965, as a result of a recommendation by Rear Admiral E. P. Aurand to Rear Admiral Reedy, the first SH-3 Sea King helicopter arrived at Yankee Station.

In May 1966, specially equipped and armored SH-3s, known as "Big Mothers," arrived in the Gulf, armed with two M-60 machine guns. Prior to each in-country air strike, one or more Big Mothers would be dispatched to combat SAR station nearest the assigned targets. In 1966, whenever an actual rescue was in progress, four A-1 Skyraiders always accompanied each UH-2 or SH-3 to give suppressive ground support to a downed pilot and to protect the rescue helicopter.

Prearranged airborne teams of rescue helicopters and armed escorts (A-1s initially, A-4s or A-7s) flew near the egress routes of the Alfa strikes. When a pilot was shot down, the strike leader, or wingman, became "on-scene commander" to coordinate and direct the rescue attempt.

How well did the system work? From the start of the war until October 1966, 269 naval and Air Force pilots and air crewmen were shot down or forced to abandon their aircraft over North Vietnam. Of these, 103 (more than half of them from the Air Force) were recovered, 75 were known to have been killed, 46 were made prisoners, and the fate of the remaining 45 is not known.

It became evident that speed in rescues was all important, for after 30 minutes a downed pilot's chances of rescue began dropping rapidly. It also became apparent that any SAR effort which lasted for several hours, or which continued the following day, could be converted into an ambush for rescue aircraft and helos. The enemy often spread parachutes to attract attention and get pilots to fly low. The enemy also made use of captured "beeper" radios carried by all pilots to decoy a rescue helo into an ambush.

The night rescue of Lieutenant Commander John W. Holtzclaw and his RIO Lieutenant Commander John A. Burns, both of VF-33, took place on 19 June 1968. The rescue helo pilot was Lieutenant Clyde E. Lassen of HC-7.

Ten minutes after midnight on 19 June 1968, an F-4B from the USS *America* (CVA-66) was destroyed by a SAM-missile. Its two crewmen, Lieutenant Commander Holtzclaw and Lieutenant Commander Burns, were able to eject from the tumbling wreckage, but they were down 20 miles inland, south of Hanoi, and in a densely inhabited area. Their parachutes fell into a rice paddy area between two villages. During the next 45 minutes, Holtzclaw and Burns slowly made their way across the rice paddies to a small densely foliaged karst hill nearby. The hill was flanked on three sides by rice paddies and on the fourth by a mountain range.

The rescue attempt started from southern SAR station when a UH-2A Seasprite helicopter lifted off the deck of the USS *Preble* (DLG-15) and headed through the dark, moonless night. Its crew consisted of pilot Lieutenant Clyde E. Lassen, co-pilot Lieutenant (j.g.) Clarence L. Cook, and crewmen AE2 Bruce B. Dallas and ADJ3 Donald West.

"For the first hour," said Holtzclaw, "we heard no airplanes overhead. We made our way up the hill to an extremely dense section of jungle, where we first heard the sound of airplanes. We used our walkie-talkies and were told "Clementine Two" was on the way to get us. Lieutenant Commander Burns and I tried to find a clear area on the hillside for pickup but couldn't find one."

As the Seasprite neared the rescue area, two "balls of flame," possibly SAMs, streaked past the helicopter. A minute later, Lieutenant (j.g.) Cook sighted the flaming wreckage of the F-4 and located the general position of the survivors who were now about three miles from the crashed aircraft. Difficult terrain, a dark, overcast night, and heavy enemy small arms and automatic weapons fire were factors making the rescue of the F-4 crew extremely difficult.

Lieutenant Lassen made his first landing in a rice paddy below the hill and 600 feet from the downed pilots.

As the helo touched down, the waiting

LCdr. Thomas Tucker is hauled up from Haiphong Harbor.

enemy opened up with small arms and automatic weapons fire. Lassen immediately lifted off and orbited the area.

Meanwhile, other aircraft had arrived from TF 77 and began dropping flares.

"The survivors were between two large trees about 150 feet apart," said Lieutenant Lassen, "and other fairly tall trees were also in the area, but I decided that by the light of the flares, I'd try to pick them up from the hillside."

As Lieutenant Lassen approached, in a 50-foot high hover between the trees, Petty Officer Dallas began lowering the rescue sling.

Suddenly the flares burned out, leaving the area in pitch darkness and Lieutenant Lassen with no visual ground reference.

"Dallas yelled that we were going to hit a tree," Lieutenant Lassen said. "I added

power and was just starting a climb when I hit it. The jolt was terrific. The helo pitched nose down and went into a tight starboard turn. I regained control and waved off. I then told the rescue aircraft orbiting overhead that we had struck a tree and that I was experiencing fairly heavy vibration. We requested more flares and were told that no more were available but that some were on the way. Also, I told the survivors that they would have to get down off that hill and into the clearing.".

In the rear of the helicopter, the crewman, Dallas, was also having his troubles in recovering the hoist.

"I started retracting the hoist as fast as possible," he said, "and in the process the helo hit a tree on the right side. I was leaning out of the open door at the time, and I was hit on the face as the tree went by. As soon as the limb hit me, I yelled 'Get up! Get up!'—and we were out of there and climbing. Nothing but Mr. Lassen's skill and experience saved us from crashing."

The helicopter developed a fairly heavy vibration immediately after the collision which damaged the horizontal stabilizer, the tail rotor, the antenna, and the door.

Shaken but undeterred by the narrow escape, Lieutenant Lassen made pass after pass over the area while Cook and Dallas fired at the gun flashes below.

In the darkness of the tangled, vine-covered hillside, Holtzclaw and Burns, the latter hampered by a sprained left ankle and an injured knee as a result of the ejection, were stumbling downhill toward the rice paddy area below. As they reached the flat area, Lieutenant Lassen made his second approach for the pick-up. As the UH-2 touched down, he spotted the survivors struggling across the rice paddies but still too far away. Enemy fire was also steadily increasing. He took off again, circled the area and headed in for his third landing. Another SAM went by, narrowly missing the UH-2, but the pilot continued to drop lower until finally he held the helo in a hover with the wheels just touching the soft ground.

"While we were on the edge of the clearing," said Burns, "we both could hear the North Vietnamese search party noisily crashing through the jungle a short distance away."

For three minutes the helicopter hung there with its floodlight on as Holtzclaw and Burns frantically stumbled and fell their way across the paddy with its criss-crossing dikes. The UH-2 was under fire from two sides at first, and then from a third, as the enemy closed in on the area vacated a minute before by the men being rescued. Returning the fire, the helicopter crew silenced at least one position and managed to keep the enemy down until the exhausted, mud-spattered survivors clambered aboard.

Lieutenant Lassen immediately lifted off and headed the badly damaged and vibrating helicopter for the sea. The helicopter had been overland for 56 minutes and under fire for 45 minutes while pressing the rescue attempt. Even yet, they were not out of danger, for as Lieutenant Lassen neared the coast, the Seasprite once again ran into heavy flak and automatic fire, and during subsequent evasive maneuvers, the damaged door was torn off.

Finally over the water, the success of the rescue now depended on how much fuel remained. With every available radio in TF 77 listening and all hands praying, the Seasprite finally landed aboard the *Jouett* (DLG-29) with only five minutes of fuel remaining.

For his intrepidity and conspicuous gallantry, Lieutenant Lassen was later awarded the Medal of Honor by President Johnson.

The Effects of the Weather

One of the key factors in the bombing interdiction effort against North Vietnam was the monsoon weather, which often precluded full-scale attacks on fixed targets and greatly reduced armed reconnaissance.

The heavy, often torrential rain, low clouds, and poor visibility, served to hide the enemy's missiles and guns, and to provide early concealment for the lauching and inflight trajectory of the missiles. This forced our aircraft below the cloud layers and down into the effective range of radar controlled guns and small arms. When these weather handicaps were added to the cover of night, when the only aircraft which could find a target without the use of flares, fly low enough to hit it, and maneuver to avoid the mountain tops, missiles, and flak, was the A-6 Intruder, it can be understood why bombing aircraft usually could locate their targets over North Vietnam less than one-third of the time.

In summary, the uncertainty, unpredictability, and caprice of the Vietnamese weather was a factor heavily favoring the enemy. "The nature of the weather in Vietnam was also a vital factor in the interdiction campaign that was never fully appreciated by Washington," said Vice Admiral David C. Richardson, CTF 77 in 1966-67. "With the centralized control of the war from afar," he said, "Washington could not keep in touch with the ever-changing weather which often required on-the-scene changes in target and weapon assignments."

Mining of North Vietnamese Waters

It was never fully appreciated in Washington that about 50% of the enemy's cargo moved on the internal waterways.

During 1966, as the road and rail systems of North Vietnam were attacked by TF 77, the enemy made increasing use of barges and sampans (waterborne logistic craft) to transport men and supplies southward. This trend had first been noted early in 1966, and recommendations had been made to close the river mouths to the barges by mining. Finally, on 23 February 1967, the mining from the air of selected areas of North Vietnam—not Haiphong, of course—was authorized by higher authority. The use of

Heavy rains lash the flight deck of the *Oriskany.*

air-delivered mines in selected river areas was determined to be an effective method of reducing North Vietnamese coastal traffic.

The first use of mines commenced on 26 February when seven A-6As from the carrier *Enterprise,* led by Commander A. H. Barie, Commanding Officer of VA-35, planted two fields in the mouths of the Song Ca and South Giang rivers. The mines were dropped from a very low altitude, and although some flak was noted in the vicinity of Vinh, no SAMs were fired.

In March, three new minefields were sown in the mouths of the Song Ma, Kien Giang, and Cua Sot rivers, this time by A-6s from the carrier *Kitty Hawk,* In view of the need to make very precise drops, the aircraft had to make straight-in, low-level passes. This necessitated nighttime runs using a radar-significant target. Though moonlight was a help when it was available, most missions were flown in bad weather. It was a demanding and dangerous assignment.

By mid-April, all the minefields authorized, five in number, had been planted. North Vietnam's three main deep water ports of Haiphong, Hon Gai, and Cam Pha, however, were not authorized.

A careful watch was made to see what effect the mining campaign had.

The first indication came in April, in the Song Giang, when several boats conducting minesweeping operations were photographed. Soon it became apparent that little, if any, traffic was entering or leaving the river mouths. Three sunken boats were noted in the Song Giang on 23 May.

The traffic across the river mouths slowly dried up. And just as the enemy had abandoned truck and rail traffic on the exposed coastal highway, so now did he stop moving war supplies by coastal barges. The enemy simply accepted his losses and the fact that in this area he was beaten. He moved inland, using more trucks, mainly at night, over the unpaved roads hidden under the heavy canopy of the jungle.

The Effort to Isolate Haiphong

The quick and easy way to snuff out the war would have been to blockade Haiphong—or to use the term of the 1962 Cuban missile crisis, to "quarantine" it. But this recommendation was repeatedly rejected because of the risk of damage to third-country shipping.

But, if closing Haiphong harbor from seaward by mining or blockading was forbidden, could not the port city be isolated by bombing? To do this would require the destruction of the major bridges, the mining of the transshipment points near the city, and the cutting of the rail lines between Hanoi and Haiphong.

The effort got underway on 30 August 1967, as a result of a visit to Washington by Admiral Sharp which included discussions with key members of Congress.

The Haiphong highway bridge, south-southeast of the city, was the initial isolation target. The *Oriskany's* air wing, led by Commander Burton H. Shepherd, dropped it into the river.

This strike was a prime example of the discipline and the expertise which strike groups had gained in conducting multiple "Alfa" strikes.

Approaching Haiphong with 24 planes, the strike group evaded a covey of SAMs and maintained their flight integrity. Nearing Haiphong proper, intense 37-mm., 57-mm., and 85-mm. fire was encountered, but the strike group pressed on. Execution was such that every bomb detonated within a period of 10 to 12 seconds. When the smoke cleared, three of the four bridge spans had disappeared. As the strike group retired, it strafed barge traffic in the nearby canals and rivers.

In a matter of weeks, all the main bridges around the two cities were made unserviceable for varying lengths of time. For example, TF 77 hit Haiphong's four major bridges in September. The North Vietnamese made intense efforts to repair them and by the next month they were in service again. Then TF 77 hit all four of them again.

The enemy responded to the isolation effort in several ways. Increasingly, shipments were made into Sihanoukville, Cambodia, whence by truck, barge, and sampan, war supplies were surreptitiously moved into the sanctuaries along the border with South Vietnam.

The Soviets increased their deliveries. During the first six months of 1967, almost 400,000 tons were delivered into Haiphong, despite the delays in unloading. This was a 38% increase over the corresponding period in 1966.

The enemy also responded by building numerous bypasses. Truck and supply boat activity increased. Boats were moored near foreign ships in order to lessen the chance of their being attacked. The number of boats on the waterways from Haiphong to Hanoi doubled in the last half of September, and tripled by the middle of October. Large open storage areas near the Haiphong docks and throughout the city multiplied as the full weight of the campaign became evident.

It was during this period that Haiphong ran out of missiles and low on AAA ammunition. On the fifth successive day of striking targets in the Haiphong area, for example, Navy pilots were amazed to arrive over Haiphong without being greeted by the usual SAMs and intense AAA. The electronic signals were there to spoof aircrews, but no SAMs rose from the sites and only sporadic 37-mm. antiaircraft fire was observed, and then only at relatively low level. One flak suppression section circled over Haiphong for 15 minutes looking for an active AAA site and finally dropped their flak suppression weapons on the primary target. This phenomenon lasted for two days, when heavy rain and clouds from the tail end of a typhoon terminated all "Alfa" strike activity over North Vietnam for the next three days.

When the weather cleared and strike groups again returned to Haiphong, the enemy's defenses had been restored and there were many SAMs and heavy AAA fire. As always, North Vietnam had resourcefully used the respite to replenish depleted stocks.

The almost continuous attacks on Haiphong began to have other effects. On 25 August, for example, an evacuation order was issued. All civilians except those vital to the defense of Hanoi and Haiphong and to the subsistence of those who defended it were ordered to leave. Women, children, and the elderly assembled, with their suitcases, at collection points where buses, trucks, and pedicabs picked them up. Workshops, offices, and institutions near military targets were moved out of the two city areas.

It was also in August that there began to appear unconfirmed reports that Hanoi was considering an agreement to negotiate as a device to stop the bombing and relieve pressure on its forces.

THE FIRST WALLEYE ATTACKS

In March 1967, a new Navy weapon called Walleye—a TV-guided air-to-surface glide bomb—was introduced into combat. This weapon represented a long stride forward in the accurate delivery of air-dropped ordnance, since Walleye could be locked on to its target by the pilot prior to drop, and after release, its TV eye would continue to direct the bomb toward the pre-selected aiming point without further help from the pilot, who could then devote his full attention to avoiding missiles and gunfire.

The first Walleye attacks were conducted under the supervision of Rear Admiral Thomas J. Walker, Commander Carrier Division Three, who was charged with their combat introduction. Rear Admiral Walker carefully selected six targets. Attack Squadron 212, commanded by Commander Homer Smith aboard the *Bon Homme Richard,* made the first attacks.

The first launch went against a large military barracks complex at Sam Son on 11 March 1967. Commander Smith launched the weapon, and he and the accompanying pilots watched the TV bomb fly straight and true into a window of the barracks, exploding within—exactly like the brochure said it would.

The second attack went against the Phu Dien Chau highway bridge, and the third and fourth against other parts of the Sam Son barracks complex. The next day three more Walleyes were dropped against the Thanh Hoa bridge. Again, all were direct hits but damage to the bridge was assessed as minor.

It was the beginning of a new era in aerial warfare and the first use of what soon became known as "smart bombs."

THE INTERDICTION EFFORT PEAK—1967

During the better weather months of May through October 1967, the interdiction campaign reached its peak of intensity—with the Iron Triangle receiving the maximum attention. An unprecedented barrage of major "Alfa" strikes was directed against this region. With a sufficient supply of Walleye weapons now available, several major strikes were directed against the Ngoc Kuyet railroad siding, a nearby bridge, and a bypass between Hanoi and Haiphong. One of the most important attacks went against the Hanoi Thermal Power Plant, which early

in May was released as a target, for Walleye only. This indicated the high degree of confidence that Washington had gained in the new "smart bomb" for the reason that collateral damage in downtown Hanoi could be avoided.

"Bonnie Dick" was called out of Subic Bay with orders to hit the Hanoi Thermal Power Plant with Walleye as soon as possible. The weather cleared, and on 19 May 1967 the first attack was made. Once again, Commander Homer Smith led the strike, with Lieutenant Mike Cater as his only wingman. Six F-8Es from VF-24 were flak suppressors. Air Wing 11 aboard the *Kitty Hawk* was scheduled to strike the Van Dien Truck Park located five miles southwest of the city simultaneously. The two air wings rendezvoused at sea and went "feet dry" (i.e., overland) well to the south. Some MiG-17 fighters were observed attempting to intercept the flight southwest of the city and Lieutenant Phil Wood of VF-24 shot one down at this time. The Walleye attack group maintained integrity and dropped down to a lower altitude to dash the last ten miles, over flat country, to the city. The MiGs were outdistanced at this time but the flight encountered a severe barrage of SAMs and AAA. The two Walleye A-4s pitched up to roll-in from west to east over the lake and delivered their weapon directly on target in the thermal power plant. Gunfire and SAMs continued to lace the sky, as evidenced by Japanese news film taken from within the city and later shown on U.S. television. During this attack, two F-8s were shot down—one en route to target and the second during the attack.

The remainder of the flight retired at low level back toward the mountains to the southwest. At this point, the MiG-17s joined in earnest, attempting to get to the two A-4s. A major dogfight erupted just southwest of the city between the remaining F-8s and ten MiG aircraft. The fight ranged from treetop level up to 4,000 feet. Commander Paul Speer, Commanding Officer of VF-211, bagged a MiG-17 in a turning encounter behind the A-4s, followed a few seconds later by Lieutenant (j.g.) Joe Shea, his wingman, who bagged a second MiG-17. The fight continued moving southwest and Lieutenant Bob Lee of VF-24 got another one. With the A-4s safely over the mountains the engagement broke off and thus ended the Navy's largest jet air battle so far. Four MiGs were accounted for in this brief, furious encounter.

As TF 77's efforts intensified between May and October, the enemy's AAA fire was especially heavy. July, in fact, was a record month, with 233 SAMs being launched at TF 77 aircraft and, while 19 planes were lost, most of them were lost to antiaircraft fire.

The search for SAMs continued. On 19 July, the *Constellation*'s Reconnaissance Squadron 12 brought home pictures of a SAM site in a most unusual place; inside a soccer stadium between Haiphong and Hanoi. During the day several attacks on the SAM missile battery, the missiles, the vans, transporters, and the stadium itself were made. Commander Robin Mc-Glohn, Commanding Officer, VF-142, and Commander Robert Dunn, Commanding Officer, VA-146, led the first attack. They damaged three missiles on their launchers and watched orange smoke rise out of the stadium. Later in the day, Commander Gene Tissot, Commander Carrier Wing 14, led a second strike that totally demolished the installation.

On 21 July 1967, a fierce seven-minute engagement occurred as the airplanes from the "Bonnie Dick's" Carrier Wing 21 approached for an attack on the petroleum storage area at Ta Xa. Eight MiG-17s attacked the F-8E/C fighter cover provided by VF-211 and VF-24 and the Shrike-armed "Iron Hand" A-4s of VA-76 and VA-212. One MiG was destroyed by a Sidewinder fired by Commander Marion H. Isaacks; a second was downed by the 20-mm. fire of Lieutenant Commander Robert L. Kirkwood; a third was destroyed by an air-to-ground Zuni rocket and 20-mm. guns fired by Lieutenant Commander Ray Hubbard, Jr.; and a

"probable" fourth was damaged by another Sidewinder launched by Lieutenant (j.g.) Philip W. Dempewolf which hit but never exploded. Two other MiGs were damaged. Commander Isaacks and Lieutenant Commander Kirkwood's F-8s were damaged, but both got home safely.

During the Phy Ly railroad yard attack on 16 July, an F-8E from the *Oriskany* (Lieutenant Commander Demetrio A. Verich of VF-162) was hit by a SAM after dodging two others. Verich "punched out" and reached the ground safely in a karst area, a steep hillside covered with brush, tangled trees, and vines. It was only an hour before dark, however, and too late for a rescue effort to be started. So Verich laid low, covered himself with branches and sweated out the long night, hearing voices of a nearby searching party. He was 30 miles south of Hanoi and about 50 miles from the coast. Early the next day a Big Mother helo flown by Lieutenant Neil R. Sparks and Lieutenant (j.g.) Robin Springer, with crewmen ADJ1 Masengale and AE3 Ray, made the extremely hazardous trip. The SH-3 spent two hours and 23 minutes over North Vietnam under continuous attack before snatching Verich from the clutches of the nearby North Vietnamese searching party. Sparks won the Navy Cross for his heroic rescue.

Such rescues deep within North Vietnam and close to villages and cities were becoming increasingly difficult and risky. Not far from the incident just described, two A-4Es from the *Oriskany*'s VA-164 were shot down on 18 July. Lieutenant (j.g.) Larrie J. Duthie was saved by a U.S. Air Force "Jolly Green Giant" helicopter in another hazardous rescue. But the attempt to rescue the second pilot was not successful. In this instance, the Big Mother SAR helo from the *Hornet* (CVS-12) was hit by ground fire as it approached the scene, killing one crewman. A second Clementine helo, flown from the *Worden* (DLG-18), was also hit by the heavy automatic weapons fire, which damaged the main rotor, cut six inches off one blade of the tail rotor, and hit in the fuselage. Later in the day, in a third attempt, an SH-3 helicopter was shot down and four crewmen were killed. In addition, during the intensive SAR effort, still another A-4E (Lieutenant Barry T. Wood, VA-164) from the *Oriskany* was struck by antiaircraft fire over the scene. Low on fuel, Wood managed to reach the ocean, where he ejected and was rescued by a boat from the *Richard B. Anderson* (DD-786).

Obviously the North Vietnamese were rushing antiaircraft guns into any rescue area, perhaps even allowing downed pilots to remain free while they set up flak traps. In many cases they used captured radios to send false messages.

The furious pace continued. In August 1967, 16 naval aircraft were shot down, six of them by SAMs. This was the highest loss to missiles in a single month. Two hundred and forty-nine SAMs were counted by the pilots, exceeding the previous high reached in July. During the single day of 21 August, 80 missiles were fired by the enemy, a record for the war.

An example of one day's heavy work occurred on 21 August 1967, the day the 80 missiles were fired. The *Constellation, Intrepid,* and *Oriskany* were at Yankee Station, and the weather over North Vietnam was excellent.

Air Wing Ten on the *Intrepid* sent two major "Alfa" strikes against Port Wallut, 23 aircraft on the first attack, 21 three hours later on the second. A third "Alfa" strike by the *Intrepid*'s aircraft also struck the Van Dien army supply depot. Pilots saw at least seven secondary explosions and watched balls of black smoke rising to 1,000 feet. Eight buildings and warehouses were destroyed, seven others were damaged, the marine railway was lightly damaged, and one span of the bridge was knocked down. Fourteen SAMs were fired, but no aircraft were hit.

The *Constellation*'s Air Wing 14, meanwhile, was attacking two major targets, the Duc Noi railroad yard and Kep airfield. Both antiaircraft and SAMs were very heavy, and three A-6s of VA-196

were lost. At Kep airfield, one revetted Colt (transport aircraft) was destroyed, another damaged, the runway was cratered, and heavy damage was inflicted on three barracks. The pilots from the *Constellation* counted 51 SAMs fired at their aircraft.

Commander Bryan W. Compton, Commanding Officer of VA-163 aboard the *Oriskany,* led an attack on the Hanoi thermal power plant, the same one that had been battered on 19 and 21 May. With typical determination, the enemy had made repairs, and recently smoke had been seen issuing from the generator plant. In anticipation of further attacks, the enemy had brought in several additional 85-mm. and 57-mm. guns to protect it.

Once again, Walleye weapons were used. On this occasion, five Walleyes were fired and five bullseyes resulted, three striking the generator hall and two the boiler house. Dense black and white smoke from the entire complex rose high in the air. Thirty SAMs were fired at the strike aircraft. The 85-mm., 57-mm., and small arms flak was the heaviest seen to date, but no planes were lost. Two were badly damaged. One, flown by Lieutenant Commander Dean A. Cramer, returned with 53 holes in it, while the second, flown by Lieutenant Commander James B. Busey, landed aboard with 127 holes, a fire in the starboard wing, the end of the starboard horizontal stabilizer gone, and all of the starboard elevator shot off.

As the weather began to turn sour in October 1967, the A-6 Intruders once again came into their own as they had done during the 1966 northeast monsoon season, for at night and in bad weather they were the only aircraft in the American inventory able to find, strike, and destroy point targets in the heavily defended northeast quadrant. The Intruders became the scourge of the Iron Triangle.

On 27 October, six A-6s executed individual night time attacks on the Hanoi ferry slips, each successive aircraft encountering increasing opposition.

On the night of 30 October 1967, a single A-6A Intruder launched from the deck of *Constellation* successfully completed one of the most difficult single-plane strikes in the history of air warfare. Once again, the purpose of the strike was to drop eighteen 500-pound bombs on the all-important Hanoi railroad ferry slip, and to keep it inoperative. The A-6 mission was flown by Lieutenant Commander Charles B. Hunter with Lieutenant Lyle F. Bull, bombardier navigator, from VA-196. This mission will be described in some detail since it is typical of the capability of the A-6 and of the courage, tenacity, and airmanship of the A-6 Intruder crews.

By late 1967, Hanoi had become the most heavily defended city against air attack in the history of warfare. It was defended by fifteen "hot" or occupied SAM sites, at least 560 known anti-aircraft guns of various calibers, and some MiG 17s or 21s at nearby airfields. The mission called for making a low-level, instrument approach across the rugged karst mountains surrounding the Red River Valley. It would then be necessary to drop a string of eighteen 500-pound bombs along an impact line of 2,800 feet. By using maximum concealment and by flying at low level, it was hoped that the plane could remain below the effective SAM envelope. However, this approach would require Lieutenant Commander Hunter to maintain a constant bombing course and altitude for several seconds during a highly vulnerable period of the attack.

The mission was routine until Hunter was about 18 miles from Hanoi, still navigating by radar between and over the karsts. At this point, his instruments and earphones indicated that the enemy's missile search radar had detected his presence. He immediately descended to hide himself below the radar horizon. Shortly thereafter Lieutenant Bull acquired the "IP" (initial point—a recognizable location) on his radar and immediately commenced to make his bombing solution of the aircraft's computer and bombing equipment. While he was doing so, Hunter's instruments and earphones indicated that a second SAM-battery was preparing to fire at him, so he descended once again. To those who have not flown a plane, it is difficult to describe the courage and skill required to fly a heavily loaded aircraft at 460 knots, on instruments, at night, above unfamiliar terrain, while maintaining a very low altitude.

It was now time to turn to the bombing heading. As he did so, Hunter caught sight of the first of 16 SAMs that would be fired at him. "When I first saw it, it was dead ahead and above me," he said, "and it appeared that it would pass overhead. However, just as it got overhead, I could see it turn directly downward and head for us. To me, the rocket exhaust looked like a doughnut." At this point, he might have jettisoned his bombs, aborted the mission, and headed for home. Instead, with 9,000 pounds of bombs under his wings, he executed a high "G" barrel-roll to port from a very low altitude—an exceedingly dangerous maneuver. The SAM exploded within 200 feet, shaking the aircraft violently. Hunter's roll took him to 2,000 feet, inverted, but he continued rolling and leveled out again, flying low within a few degrees of the desired inbound heading. By keeping on course to target while making this violent maneuver, he was able to maintain Lieutenant Bull's accurate work on the computer so that the radar cursors could continue tracking the target and making the bombing solution.

The actual bombing run on the Hanoi ferry slip now began. "At this time," said Hunter, "the AAA fire was so heavy that it lit up the countryside and I could see details on the ground pretty well." As the sky lit up with flak, Bull spotted two SAMs approaching at 2 o'clock (to the right of his nose) and Hunter saw three more SAMs between 10 and 11 o'clock (to the left of his nose). At least five missiles were now airborne and aimed at the Intruder.

There was no chance to avoid them, if the attack was to be pressed. So, for the last seven miles, the aircraft was flown at deck level on the radar altimeter in the hope that during the on-the-deck approach the SAMs would be unable to guide on the fast-moving Intruder. As each successive SAM exploded directly overhead, approximately 400 feet above the canopy, it filled the cockpit with an orange glow and made the aircraft shudder. "During the run-in to target a continuous barrage of flak lit the sky around the aircraft as if it were daylight," said Hunter. Numerous searchlights also illuminated the aircraft for the benefit of small arms and automatic weapons sites.

Despite all the flak, SAMs, and searchlights, the A-6 bored in and released its bombs whereupon Hunter made a seven-"G" turn to starboard. During this turn, four additional SAM explosions were experienced aft and above the aircraft. In the amply flak-lit sky, it was easy to see the intended target clearly visible next to the Red River and to watch the string of bombs fall on the assigned target. Hunter rolled out, heading southeast at various altitudes, some of them high, and commenced heavy jinking to cope with a cockpit indication that a MiG-17 was not on his tail. Sporadic flak was encountered until the coast was reached.

It was missions like this, night after night over Haiphong and Hanoi, which caused Vice Admiral William F. Bringle, Commander Seventh Fleet, to say, "The low-level night missions flown by the A-6 over Hanoi and Haiphong were the most demanding missions we have ever asked our aircrews to fly. Fortunately, there is an abundance of talent, courage, and aggressive leadership in these A-6 squadrons."

ATTACKS ON SHIPYARDS AND RAILROADS

While the A-6s continued their nocturnal, single-plane raids, and the attempt to isolate Haiphong by multi-plane day attack was maintained, a new target system was struck: shipyards and barge-building yards. On 12 October 1967, the *Oriskany*'s pilots, led by Commander

Elbert Lighter (Executive Officer, VA-163), conducted an Alfa strike on the Haiphong Shipyard, with excellent results. A power boat and five barges (one of which was in the graving dock) were sunk, and all support buildings within the yard were destroyed. A few minutes later, pilots from the *Intrepid* attacked the boat yard at Lach Tray and heavily damaged it. One A-4C sustained four 6-inch holes in its wing, but the pilot was able to return safely to the "Fighting I." The third yard, Haiphong West, was rendered completely unserviceable by the *Intrepid*. All support buildings, the fabrication shops, and the two marine railways were destroyed, and seven shipways were heavily damaged.

In November 1967, other shipyards were struck. On 7 November, the *Constellation*'s Air Wing 14 scored numerous direct hits on the Ninh Ngoai boat works and the An Ninh Noi boat yard. Three A-6s from the "Connie" made visual runs on the Yen Cuong boat repair yard, dropping fifty-four 500-pound bombs. Five vessels were destroyed, the building ways interdicted, and four barges under construction heavily damaged. Simultaneously, the *Intrepid*'s pilots attacked the Uong Bi barge yard and reported that their bombs produced several large fireballs. On 13 November, the *Intrepid*'s air wing attacked the Phui Nighai Thuong boat yard and the Uong Bi barge yard, while on the 16th, airplanes from the *Coral Sea* (CVA-43) attacked Haiphong shipyard number two. Photography showed excellent results—severe damage to one graving dock, the slipway destroyed, ten support buildings demolished, and six others damaged. Flak was heavy, and the *Coral Sea* pilots counted 8 SAMs during the attack. On 17 November 1967, the aircraft of *Intrepid*'s Air Wing 10 heavily damaged the Hanoi barge yard. The strike consisted of 26 aircraft, led by Commander Richard A. Wigent, Commanding Officer of VA-34. "There were many SAMs in the air," he said, "the most I've ever seen." One of them demolished a Skyhawk; the pilot ejected from his burning aircraft and was immediately captured.

No attempt was made by the North Vietnamese to repair these damaged shipyards. Instead, the enemy took advantage of the sanctuaries of Haiphong and Hanoi. Photographs taken in January 1968 revealed four new barge construction sites in Haiphong, two along the streets and plazas, and two in heavily inhabited areas where attacks were forbidden. Thus, the Communists maintained their double standard, putting military targets in known sanctuaries, pulling every propaganda stop to call for a bombing cease-fire, and at the same time waging an unceasing campaign of assassination and terror against the civilian populace of the South. All this was suffered to pass with little criticism from the world community.

In December 1967, whenever the monsoon weather abated, the northeast quadrant was struck and the cordon around Haiphong was kept taut. The major rail lines of the Iron Triangle received particular attention. The *Oriskany*'s pilots caught a 40-car train southeast of Phy Ly on 14 December and destroyed eight cars and damaged eight more. Pilots from the *Ranger* (CVA-61) located and struck a 30-car train south of Hanoi and wrecked the engine and several cars.

The *Ranger* had arrived on station on 3 December, bringing two new aircraft, the A-7A Corsair II, flown by Attack Squadron 147, and the EKA-3B Tacos. The A-7A Corsair, a single place, light attack jet aircraft, featured advanced radar, navigation and weapons systems, and could carry a 15,000-pound bomb load. The EKA-3B Tacos was a much-modified model of the A-3 Skywarrior, rebuilt especially for the electronic warfare environment of North Vietnam.

As the year closed and the holidays approached, the aerial mining of the coastal and inland waterways was intensified, for previous experience had shown that the Communists would make a maximum effort to move supplies during the holiday standdowns.

In 1966, in fact, the Joint Chiefs of Staff had taken a position of strong opposition to any cessation of military operations during the Christmas and Tet holiday seasons. But, if a cease-fire had to be made, the Joint Chiefs said, it should be limited to a maximum of 48 hours in order to minimize the military advantages given the enemy. In every previous case of a Tet or other holiday standdown, the enemy had conducted major resupply operations and had replenished his forces, all of which cost the United States greater casualties. For example, between 8 and 12 February 1966, aerial reconnaissance revealed significant logistic movement of material by water, truck, and rail transport—between 22,300 and 25,100 tons of supplies were moved from the north into the area below 19 degrees North Latitude.

Prior to the 24-hour Christmas and 36-hour New Year standdowns in 1967, there were many indications that the enemy planned once more to take full advantage of these periods. Later events proved that he conducted a massive and well organized resupply of his forces. Almost 1,300 trucks were noted in the Panhandle by pilots and photo-interpreters during Christmas and about 1,800 during the slightly longer New Year standdown. This compared with a daily average of only 170 for the other days between 22 December 1967 and 4 January 1968. Pilots of the *Kitty Hawk* flying over the coastal highway during the Christmas standdown counted 560 trucks bumper to bumper over a seven-mile section of road. During the New Year's standdown, more than 1,000 trucks were counted moving south. Pilots reported that the coastal road looked "like the New Jersey turnpike."

By October 1967, some 200,000 tons of goods imported by sea had piled up and were stacked in mountainous piles in open storage areas near the Haiphong docks. There was some uncertainty whether the enemy considered these stockpiles "safe" by our own self-imposed restrictions forbidding attack on them, or whether they were jammed up because the supplies could not be moved south. In any event, authority was never granted to attack these huge stockpiles or the Haiphong docks and warehouses.

On the positive side, early in November intelligence indicated that the frequent night and day air alerts were slowing work on the Haiphong docks as workers took shelter. Absenteeism among stevedores increased because of the dangers of coming to work. It was also reported that dock workers suffered from hunger and weariness. Ship unloading times increased from 13 days to 42 days. A shortage of trucks and lighters slowed down the unloading of ships and the clearing of cargo from the port. The mere presence of U.S. aircraft in the area reduced effective dredging of the approaches to Haiphong, and foreign merchant ships were unable to take advantage of their full load capacity.

The key rail line running south from Hanoi and Haiphong to Thanh Hoa was kept cut in several places along its 100-mile length. These frequent cuts often provided opportunities for attacks on trains trapped between cuts—58 cars were destroyed in the Ninh Binh railroad siding in November. Also, with bridges along the key rail line down, the enemy was forced to offload at every crossing, ferry the cars and supplies across (usually at night), and reload them on tthe other side. Aircraft from the *Coral Sea* and the *Intrepid* caught another train at a river crossing in November and destroyed 25 rail cars.

Although Secretary McNamara in late August 1967 had testified voluminously before Senator Stennis' Preparedness Committee against expanding the bombing, the first public expression of doubt that the bombing wasn't accomplishing what was expected reached the pilots in combat on 10 October 1967 when the Secretary voiced disappointment.

"I do not think [the bombing] has in any significant way affected their war making capability," he said. ". . . the North Viet-

namese still retain the capability to support activities in South Vietnam and Laos at present or increased combat levels and force structure.

"All of the evidence is so far that we have not been able to destroy a sufficient quantity [of war material in North Vietnam] to limit the activity in the South below the present level, and I do not know we can in the future."

To the pilots who were risking their lives daily under the restrictive targeting system and flight rules imposed by Secretary McNamara, who were not allowed to destroy the supplies where they could be seen, it was a disheartening judgment.

Despite the bad weather, the missiles, the MiGs, and the flak, and despite all the bombing restrictions, the 1967 accomplishments of Task Force 77 *were* impressive. Thirty SAM sites and 187 AAA/AW gun batteries had been destroyed. Nine hundred fifty-five bridges were destroyed and 1,586 others were damaged. Seven hundred thirty-four motor vehicles, 410 locomotives and rail cars, and 3,185 watercraft had been destroyed.

During the year, eleven carriers had participated in operations as part of Task Force 77—the *Bon Homme Richard, Constellation, Coral Sea, Enterprise, Forrestal, Hancock, Intrepid, Kitty Hawk, Oriskany, Ranger,* and *Ticonderoga.* Many thousands of attack sorties had been flown over North Vietnam. Fourteen MiG aircraft had been destroyed in the air, 32 others on the ground. One hundred thirty-three aircraft had been lost in combat. This was a 9% increase over losses in 1966. Approximately one-third of the crews of aircraft shot down by the North Vietnamese had been recovered by the courageous and resourceful rescue units.

Five hundred thousand civilians in North Vietnam were engaged in air defense or repair activities on the lines of communication. This diversion of manpower from other pursuits, particularly agriculture, had raised the cost and difficulty of the war for Hanoi.

As 1967 closed, and the northeast monsoon intensified, it was apparent that the war in Southeast Asia had become very much a war of determination, Communist determination to conduct and support aggression in the South versus the determination of the Free World to halt that aggression through the application of controlled air power.

1968

The final three months of effort before the 31 March bombing halt was drastically curtailed owing to the northeast monsoon. During January, February, and March, the weather was even worse than predicted. In the Iron Triangle, there was an average of only three days per month during which visual strikes could be accomplished. The weather in February 1968, in fact, was the poorest experienced during any month since the beginning of air interdiction, with only three percent of the days having flying weather. In March, it was six percent.

The campaign against lines of communication around Haiphong forced the North Vietnamese to adopt extraordinary efforts to maintain a flow of material over existing lines. Distribution problems for Hanoi were further aggravated by the arrival of a near-record number of foreign ships in Haiphong: over 40 in January, and a similar number in March. The port of Hon Gai was pressed into service by the Communists as a discharge point in an effort to reduce the pressure on Haiphong. Normally this port served only the nearby coal mining area and did not contribute significantly to the flow of imports into the country.

Expansion of the road networks continued as North Vietnam sought to gain flexibility by adding bypasses and constructing new segments of road. Of particular significance was the route being built to connect Red China with the Haiphong region, a development which would make it possible to add 1,000 metric tons of supplies to the quantity enter-

ing North Vietnam each day. Repair efforts elsewhere in the country were vigorously pursued. The Paul Doumer bridge, located immediately north of Hanoi, was the object of numerous air attacks by the U.S. Air Force and suffered heavy damage. Along with repairs to that bridge, several bridge bypasses and ferry landings were built near the bridge, a testimony to the importance of the route to the enemy, who used it to move material coming from both Communist China and Haiphong.

1968 STANDDOWNS

There were two brief standdown periods in January—New Year's and Tet. As they had always done before, the North Vietnamese took full advantage of the ceasefire to move a great amount of supplies as far south as possible. In Route Package II alone, 378 trucks were seen and photographed, 337 of them moving south, and it was estimated that 9,000 tons of war materials had been moved in these vehicles. Reconnaissance sorties flown during the 36-hour New Year's standdown located a total of 800 trucks, 130 boats, and 159 railroad cars, 90% of which were headed south. Air strikes against these targets during the 24 hours immediately following New Year's accounted for 24 trucks destroyed and 13 damaged, 28 boats destroyed and 47 damaged, and 41 railroad cars destroyed and 47 damaged.

The second January cease-fire, for Tet, was also scheduled for 36 hours (1800 on 29 January to 0600 on 31 January). But on the first day of the cease-fire, 29 January, the North Vietnamese launched their powerful Tet offensive against selected military installations and provincial capitals throughout South Vietnam. The most spectacular of these took place in and around Saigon, where the enemy attacked the President's Palace, the U.S. Embassy, and Tan Son Nhut Air Base, but were unsuccessful in their attempts to capture or destroy any of these. The main purpose of the attacks was psychological rather than political, to show that the Communists still had effective combat capabilities, that South Vietnam had not been made secure by the presence of more than a half million Americans, and that the bombing effort against North Vietnam was a failure.

As a result of this Communist offensive, the Tet cease-fire was cancelled and all forces resumed intensified operations. Moreover, U.S. forces were permitted to use armed reconnaissance aircraft south of Vinh, which forced the North Vietnamese to use fewer and smaller truck convoys. Aircraft of Task Force 77 saw only 300 trucks in the Tet period, less than one-third of those sighted during the New Year's standdown period.

THE THANH HOA RAILROAD AND HIGHWAY BRIDGE

On 28 January, during a break in the northeast monsoon, several major Alfa strikes were directed against North Vietnam. One of the targets was the seemingly indestructible Thanh Hoa railroad and highway bridge. For three years, U.S. Navy, Air Force, and Marine aircraft attacked this steel bridge which carries both highway 1A and the main east coast rail line. In 1965, 277 sorties had struck it; 135 in 1966; 204 in 1967. More than 1,250 tons of all types of heavy ordnance had been dropped on this bridge, and eight aircraft had been lost in the nearly 700 attack sorties, but the rugged, heavily trussed stone bridge, built into an outcropping of solid rock, while often damaged, was still intact and is still in use.

"The enemy had long since built several bypasses around the Thanh Hoa bridge," said Rear Admiral David C. Richardson, the Commander of Task Force 77, "and it had lost a great deal of its importance in the interdiction effort.

"For this reason, I placed the bridge off-limits and would only occasionally approve attacks on it. To the pilots of TF 77,

the psychological importance of that bridge far exceeded its tactical importance. Every air wing out in WestPac wanted the honor of knocking it down and it gave the pilots a real boost to occasionally go after it."

In November, on the last strike of their 1966 deployment aboard the *Constellation,* CVW-15 received approval from Rear Admiral Richardson for a final try at the Thanh Hoa bridge before returning home. Hopes ran high and the first post-strike reports of smoke, vapor, and dust obscuring the target kept open the possibility that this symbol of the North Vietnam transportation network was at last destroyed. In fact, the carrier's skipper, Captain Bill Houser, rushed the optimistic pilot reports to Rear Admiral Richardson. "We got it, we got it!" he exclaimed. Unfortunately, subsequent photography confirmed the fact that this narrow horizontal steel birdcage had once again withstood Yankee attack.

Five more strikes by the Navy and Air Force went against the heavily defended bridge in January 1968. Carrier Air Wing 15, including attack squadrons VA-153 and VA-155, this time aboard the *Coral Sea,* made attacks on 28 January. Direct hits were achieved on the span with 2,000-pound bombs, two holes were punched in the bridge decking, the truss structure at the eastern end of the bridge was damaged, and the western approach was closed. But, once again, the bridge did not go down, and by 8 February it was again in service.

It was the one target in North Vietnam that nobody could destroy.

TF 77 PROVIDES RELIEF TO KHE SANH

During January 1968, TF 77 flew 811 attack sorties in support of the U.S. Marines at Khe Sanh, striking at enemy troop concentrations, artillery and rocket positions, and storage areas. On 31 January, TF 77 was requested to provide 1,000 sorties per day to help the embattled Marines in Operation Niagara. In February, almost 1,500 attack sorties were flown in support of the Marine base. Another 1,600 attack sorties were flown in March, attacking weapon sites, troop concentrations, rocket positions, base camps, tanks, and trucks. In many instances, TF 77 pilots dropped ordnance on enemy trenches within 100 meters of the defending Marines.

In February 1968, with Washington calling for increased bombing pressure against Hanoi to coerce the North Vietnamese to the conference table, and in the face of the monsoon season's worst weather the burden fell again on the A-6 Intruders. The *Kitty Hawk*'s VA-75, commanded by Commander Jerrold Zacharias, led the way. On 1, 2, 5, 9, 10, 13, 14, 16, and 18 February, A-6s attacked a variety of targets in the Iron Triangle: airfields, power plants, the Hanoi-Haiphong bridge, barge construction facilities, the Hanoi radio communication facility, and railroad yards.

The A-6 mission flown on 24 February against the Hanoi port facility deserves mention. This was a newly authorized target on the southeast corner of the city, lying along the Red River and immediately south of Gia Lam airfield. Three aircraft were launched, with Commander Zacharias and his B/N, Lieutenant Commander M. R. Hall, leading the way.

"There was no moon," said Commander Zacharias, "and we used our terrain avoidance radar to fly at 400 to 500 feet above the peaks. When I knew we were clear of the mountains, I descended to the deck so the SAM radars couldn't pick us up. With no moonlight, I was strictly 'on the gauges' although I could just discern some ground texture at this altitude. After about a minute in the flat lands, we saw a SAM launch at twelve o'clock. The bottom of the overcast was 1,000 feet and the light from the SAM booster rocket reflected off the bottom of the overcast and from every rice paddy between the missile and the aircraft, providing a very nice horizon. The missile

was about 10 miles away and had been fired directly toward us. I descended somewhat, but overshot a little and Mike called level at 40 feet. That was too low and so I went back up a way. A few seconds later we saw the second SAM headed our way—it was off our nose to the right, so I made a slight course change to the right to place the missile on the left side of the aircraft where I could see it at all times. About five seconds later, I saw the missile make a course change to compensate for our alteration of heading and it resumed its course toward us. I waited until I thought it was the right time and then changed both our course and altitude. The first missile exploded under us, right where we had been, and buffeted the aircraft quite a bit. On our inbound run they fired no more missiles, perhaps because they were afraid one would land in the city. At about six miles, every gun in town opened up and they were really awake by now. Mike picked up the target. As we got near it, I popped up and delivered 24 bombs. Although Hanoi was completely blacked out by the time we got there, there was enough light from all the flak so that I could see the river banks and determine that we were on our target. At bomb release I broke down and left and crossed the downtown part of Hanoi at 530 knots just to wake up the heavy sleepers. We then altered course frequently to avoid the many flak sites which were really hosing the sky. I could see it all going up and could pick the holes where it looked the lightest to go between."

Summary

Vice Admiral Ralph W. Cousins, Commander Task Force 77 during the height of the interdiction effort, summed up in his farewell speech perhaps the major lesson of the war:

A U.S. Navy aircraft handler directs an A-7 Corsair pilot to release his hook after catching an arresting wire and being abruptly stopped while landing on the USS *America*, after a bombing mission over North Vietnam. The support personnel as well as the pilots did yeoman duty on the carriers, as elsewhere in the Southeast Asian War.

"In these years," he told the Fleet on his departure, "we have seen Task Force 77 take the war to the enemy—into the very heart of North Vietnam —'downtown' Hanoi and Haiphong, as the pilots say—into an area where by general consensus the flak and the surface-to-air missiles presented our aircrewmen with the most hostile environment in the history of warfare. In late 1967, in a single day, as many as 80 SAMs were fired at our air wings over Haiphong. We lost aircraft and aircrewmen—and several hundred of the finest men in the world are now in prison in Hanoi.

"But in all that time, the morale of our aircrewmen never wavered. There was never any doubt in anyone's mind but that we could continue to dish it out—and take it—as long as necessary.

"If there were ever a force—a fleet that came to stay—this is it.

"The fact is that we hit North Vietnam so hard during the fall of 1967—and during the first few months of 1968 with A-6s—that Hanoi decided they had better go to the conference at Paris and see what relief—and concessions—they could win by negotiation.

"I am certain that the United States has never fought a war in which our young men have been as courageous—as competent—as they have in this one."

VIII The Vietnamese Air Force

From the beginning of U.S. involvement in Southeast Asia, Washington officials undertook to strengthen South Vietnam's armed forces so they could deal with their Communist opposition themselves. Thus, shortly after his inauguration President Kennedy approved a buildup of the Vietnamese armed forces along with an increase in the size of the U.S. Military Assistance Advisory Group. In the case of the Vietnamese Air Force, the Defense Department was authorized to replace its obsolete American-supplied aircraft with better aircraft—A-1's, T-28's and H-34's.

When the Farm Gate detachment arrived at Bien Hoa in November 1961, Vietnamese airmen were in the process of activating their first T-28 squadron. In January 1962, as noted earlier, Farm Gate instructors began training 25 Vietnamese pilots to fly the T-28 and methods of day and night operations. The training effort went well and, in the spring of 1962, the first T-28 squadron was declared operational. When a second squadron was activated, Farm Gate pilot instructors again helped with its training. The Vietnamese proved to be apt pupils and soon were flying combat strikes in their new aircraft. By mid-1962, the Vietnamese Air Force had grown to a force of about 5,700 officers and airmen with an operational inventory of 140 aircraft.

As the VNAF buildup continued, the Air Force found itself carrying a heavy training burden both in Vietnam and the United States. Thus, Air Training Command dispatched several mobile detachments to South Vietnam to instruct VNAF personnel how to maintain and operate the new aircraft. For example, in May 1962 it sent a 45-man team to Vietnam for 6 months TDY to teach Vietnamese maintenance personnel the intricacies of the T-28. Other mobile training teams taught VNAF personnel RT-28 reconnaissance procedures and others how to fly the U-17A, an off-the-shelf Cessna aircraft provided South Vietnam under the military assistance program. In the spring of 1963 TAC dispatched 20 USAF L-19 pilots to Vietnam to augment VNAF liaison squadrons so that Vietnamese pilots could begin upgrade training in the A-1E.

By mid-1963 approximately 1,800 Vietnamese airmen out of a total VNAF strength of 7,736 personnel were students, most of them pilots. Of that number, 459 were being trained in the United States. One hundred fourteen attended U.S. Army and Navy training courses since several of the new aircraft in their inventory came from those services.

The Language Problem

Throughout the war the language barrier was a factor that inhibited all U.S. training programs. In early 1962 the Farm Gate detachment—to partly resolve the problem—produced an English-Vietnamese list of basic words for voice communications. Vietnamese airmen studied this as part of their curriculum at the VNAF FAC school at Tan Son Nhut. Also, in October 1962, the Air Force instituted an 8-week language school for Vietnamese airmen in training at Hurlburt Field, Fla.

In July 1963, in a further effort to overcome the language barrier, the Air Force dispatched a 5-man English language training detachment to Vietnam, which it later augmented with five more instructors. These men helped organize three English lan-

Maj. George T. Bennett, adviser to the 524th Squadron (VNAF), checks a target map with a VNAF pilot at Bien Hoa AB.

guage schools in South Vietnam, two of them operating on two 6-hour shifts per day. One school was located in Saigon, the others at Tan Son Nhut and Nha Trang. By 31 January 1964, a total of 994 Vietnamese students had begun language training and 514 had completed the course.

Subsequently, VNAF personnel sent to the United States for pilot training were required to complete a 15-week English language course at Lackland Air Force Base, Tex. The Lackland school—later assigned to the Defense Language Institute—became the first stop for thousands of Vietnamese airmen trained in the United States. To facilitate the training effort both in Vietnam and the United States, the Air Force also began translating a number of its on-the-job training publications into the Vietnamese language. In South Vietnam, the Air Force used both uniformed and civilian contractor personnel in the OJT program until such time as Vietnamese noncommissioned officers were qualified as instructors. However, the language barrier was never entirely overcome and remained a problem which handicapped all USAF training efforts throughout the war.

As the buildup of the Vietnamese Air Force continued, it reached a December 1964 strength of 10,592 personnel. They manned four tactical fighter squadrons, four helicopter and four liaison squadrons, two troop carrier squadrons, plus other miscellaneous units. In 1965 modernization was accelerated when the single-seat A-1H fighters and the two-seat A-1G began replacing the VNAF's T-28's. The A-1's were faster and carried a larger bomb load. The transition to the A-1's was completed by April 1965. During the year the VNAF O-1 liaison fleet more than doubled in size, going from 37 in January to 84 in December. Its U-17 inventory rose from 25 to 46 aircraft. In all, during the year, the VNAF acquired 108 additional aircraft, a 38 percent increase over the previous year.

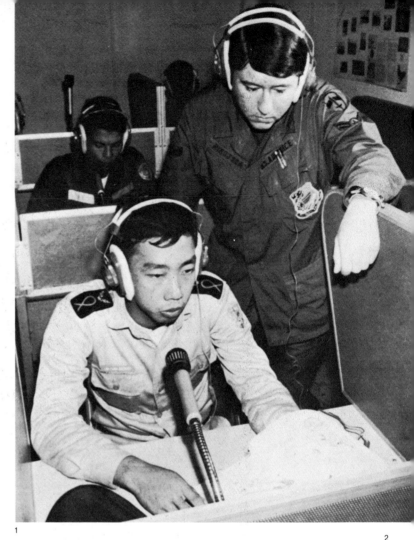

1

2

3 © N.G.S.

Throughout 1965 Air Force training efforts were aimed at increasing the number of VNAF fighter, helicopter, and liaison pilots, while also producing mechanics, communication specialists, and other support personnel. A substantial portion of this growing training took place in Vietnam, with 1,232 VNAF personnel completing OJT and 320 language training in 1965. The Air Force continued to make extensive use of ATC field training detachments and mobile teams (including one from the U.S. Navy), and civilian contract technical service personnel. The last-mentioned group, assigned to the Air Force Advisory Group in Vietnam, taught a variety of technical subjects to the Vietnamese, e.g., engines, communications, and radio navigation aids. At Bien Hoa, the 6251st Combat Support Wing, USAF, provided VNAF pilots A-1 transition training, while the 19th Tactical Air Support Squadron taught Vietnamese

airmen to fly the O-1F. A U.S. Marine element provided H-34 helicopter upgrade training for Da Nang-based VNAF helicopter pilots.

As the air war escalated, South Vietnamese officials—particularly the new Premier, Nguyen Cao Ky (he continued to head the VNAF)—pressed the United States to provide Vietnam with jet aircraft. They argued that the North Vietnamese, Cambodians, and Thais already possessed jet aircraft. American officials subsequently approved their request, and on 9 August 1965 the first of four B-57's were turned over to the Vietnamese Air Force. Transition training was begun in the Philippines and initially involved 6 pilots, 4 navigators, 4 maintenance officers, and 16 aircraft mechanics. By year's end, four combat-ready VNAF crews began flying training missions with the Air Force B-57 unit at Da Nang.

Meanwhile, the Air Force Advisory

199

1

2

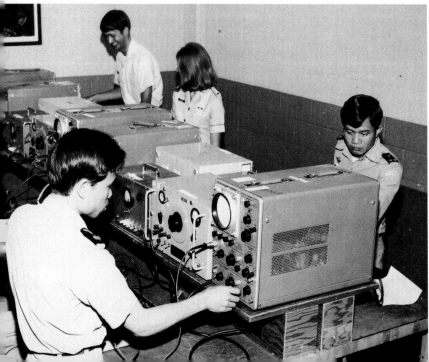

3

4

5

(1) VNAF students in a classroom at Sheppard AFB, Tex. (2) Vietnamese officers were trained on oscilloscope sets, its chief use being to serve as an indicator in a radar set. (3) VNAF pilot, Lt. Van Lich Hien, prepares for a mission in his A-1 Skyraider at Bien Hoa AB. (4) An A-37A light ground attack aircraft (in foreground) was turned over to the VNAF in October 1970. (5) Maj. Dang-Duy Lac, commander of the VNAF 524th Squadron makes a final adjustment in his equipment, while Lt. Col. Walter V. Woods, 604th SOS commander, starts up the A-37 engine. (6) Air Force T/Sgt Bruce A. Miller, a 604th Special Operations Squadron aircraft maintenance technician, shows a VNAF mechanic how to install a canopy safety clamp.

6

Group studied other options to provide the VNAF an additional jet capability. It focused on the F-5, a new jet aircraft which the Air Force had sent to South Vietnam in October 1965 to begin combat field tests. The Advisory Group recommended, and Secretary McNamara approved, conversion of one A-1 squadron to F-5's. Thirty-two VNAF pilots departed in August to begin F-5 conversion training at the Combat Crew Training Center, Williams AFB, Ariz. Ten of these men, however, were first required to take 9 weeks of language training before entering flight training.

In December 1966, after the first F-5 crews returned from combat crew training in Arizona, an F-5 training detachment arrived at Bien Hoa to continue VNAF pilot training in the jet. The following month 10 USAF noncommissioned officers and a civilian contract engineer were dispatched to Vietnam to provide further training to F-5 officers and airmen. By the spring of 1967 the Vietnamese had flown hundreds of training sorties in their new jet aircraft. On 1 June, at a formal VNAF-USAF ceremony held at Bien Hoa, the planes were officially turned over to the 522d VNAF Fighter Squadron, which immediately began flying combat sorties.

In 1967 USAF personnel also assisted the Vietnamese to modernize their transport fleet. VNAF C-47 officers and airmen were sent to the United States to begin transition training in the C-119. After completing ground courses at Lackland and Sheppard Air Force Bases, they were sent to Clinton County AFB, Ohio, the Air Force's C-119 training center. There they were taught engine and airframe maintenance by ATC's 614th Field Training Detachment and C-119 crewmen of the Air Force Reserve. The first seven VNAF C-119 crews—six pilots, eight copilots, and seven flight engineers— returned home in September 1967. They were followed to Vietnam in October by an Air Force C-119G detach-

3

4

© N.G.S.

(1) An Air Force captain briefs a Vietnamese airman prior to flying a gunship mission. (2) A VNAF gunner performs maintenance on a UH-1's miniguns at Bin Thy AB, South Vietnam. (3) A Vietnamese student checks out a night observation scope at Phan Rang AB as his instructor, Capt. William H. King, looks on. (4) With an Air Force adviser looking on, a Vietnamese navigator in a flare plane radios defenders below to learn the location of enemy troops.

ment, which continued their training there. By mid-March 1968, more than 200 Vietnamese airmen had completed all C-119 training.

Air Force modernization plans also called for converting three VNAF A-1 fighter squadrons to A-37 jets and one C-47 squadron into an AC-47 gunship unit. During 1967 the Vietnamese Air Force assigned 103 pilots to three squadrons scheduled to receive the A-37's. On 1 January 1968 the first squadron to receive the A-37's stood down to prepare for the conversion, and the following month the first 18 pilots departed for the United States to begin transition training. In May, an A-37 mobile training detachment arrived at Nha Trang to begin maintenance training.

Actual squadron conversion began in November 1968 with delivery of the first A-37 jets from the United States. By May 1969 the full complement of 54 A-37B jets were on hand and assigned to the 524th, 520th, and 516th Fighter Squadrons. The first A-37 jet squadron was declared operationally ready in March 1969, the last one in July. During 1969 VNAF personnel strength grew to about 29,000 officers and airmen, an increase of more than 5,000 over the previous year.

Shortly after becoming President in January 1969, Mr Nixon announced that one of the primary goals of his administration would be to end U.S. combat in Southeast Asia while simultaneously strengthening South Vietnam's ability to defend itself. In March Secretary of Defense Melvin R. Laird, after visiting officials in Saigon, ordered an accelerated "Vietnamization" program aimed at turning over combat operations to the South Vietnamese. In May Mr. Laird informed the Joint Chiefs that Vietnamizing the war was the Defense Department's highest priority. In June 1969, after conferring with South Vietnamese officials on Midway Island, the President announced plans to withdraw the first U.S. troops from South Vietnam. In

203

1

2

3

(1) VNAF students in a classroom at Sheppard AFB, Tex. (2) Two Vietnamese Air Force Captains stand at attention before the first of 40 A-37 jets were turned over to the VNAF in October 1970. (3) Aboard a VNAF UH-1 helicopter gunship, a Vietnamese gunner fires a minigun during a training mission in South Vietnam. An Air Force adviser, Sgt. Isidro Arroyo, Jr., looks on. (4) Two VNAF crewmen check out the Forward-Looking Infrared (FLIR) sensor system. Their instructors were members of the 17th Special Operations Squadron at Phan Rang AB, South Vietnam. (5) An Air Force staff sergeant, member of an air weather unit, instructs a VNAF airmen in plotting weather maps.

4

5

support of this action, the South Vietnamese requested further assistance for Vietnamization. Among other things, they asked for F-4 Phantoms, C-130 transports, and air defense missiles.

In August 1969 Secretary Laird directed the JCS and the services to prepare plans and programs to develop a South Vietnamese capability to cope successfully with a combined Viet Cong/NVA attack. In response, the Air Force began intensive planning on ways to speed the Vietnamization program. A joint Seventh Air Force-USAF Advisory Group Ad Hoc Committee was established in South Vietnam for that purpose. In Washington, an office for the Special Assistant for Vietnamization was organized within Headquarters USAF on 3 November 1969 to monitor all actions concerning transfer of Air Force combat responsibilities to the Vietnamese Air Force.

Integrated VNAF Training

An important innovation in the Vietnamization program took place in 1970 with the start of on-the-job integrated training conducted by USAF C-123 operational crews for their South Vietnamese counterparts. The project was undertaken when it became clear to the Air Force that the VNAF airmen would be completing C-123 combat crew training in the United States about 9 months before activation of the first VNAF C-123 squadron. To maintain VNAF pilot proficiency in the interim, the Air Force decided to integrate the Vietnamese airmen into USAF C-123 units in Vietnam, pending transfer of those aircraft to the VNAF. This was a reversal of the 1962 assignment of 30 U.S. Air Force pilots (the "Dirty Thirty") as crewmen flying with VNAF C-47 transport units. The ensuing on-the-job training by USAF C-123 crews gave Vietnamese pilots current operational experience, reduced the

need to train them in the United States, and also lessened Air Force C-123 pilot requirements in South Vietnam.

The idea of both integrated and OJT training for VNAF officers and airmen subsequently was adopted at all bases where Vietnamese and American air units were collocated. Conventional OJT methods were used with courses tailored to fit VNAF requirements. Special emphasis was given to training the Vietnamese in base support operations, a subject not previously given high priority. Individual skill upgrading resulted from this integrated program but it was designed primarily to achieve VNAF self-sufficiency as soon as possible. By 31 January 1970, more than 900 trainees were enrolled in this integrated training program. By mid-year, more than 1,240 officers and airmen were being taught more than 30 different specialties at Bien Hoa, Nha Trang, Binh Thuy, Pleiku, Da Nang, and Tan Son Nhut. Many of the VNAF airmen were trained in security, fire protection, weather, communications/electronics, air traffic control, and civil engineering.

Meanwhile, Secretary Laird approved further increases in VNAF strength—to 35,786 officers and airmen in 1970 and 44,712 in 1972 to support a VNAF force of 34 squadrons. To support this major expansion, the Vietnamese Air Force was completely restructured. It emerged in 1970 with 5 air divisions, 10 tactical wings, 5 maintenance and supply wings, and 7 air base wings. The VNAF Air Logistics Wing was transformed into an Air Logistics Command, equipped with a modern computer and given control of all VNAF inventory assets. Also with the help of ATC, the Vietnamese began expanding their Nha Trang Training Center, which was the location of six military schools and the English Language School. In the military schools, all instructors were Vietnamese.

To further speed VNAF self-sufficiency, 243 Vietnamese technicians were sent to the United States in 1970 to be trained as instructors to serve in the Nha Trang schools. This training consisted of a basic mechanics course tailored to their specific needs, instructor training, and follow-on training in ATC classrooms or with ATC field training detachments. The first instructor course began in March 1970. By mid-1971 more than 5,500 Vietnamese instructors had graduated and returned to Vietnam, while another 1,330 remained in training in the United States. In addition to this program, the Air Force sent ATC mobile training teams to Nha Trang to teach 37 specialized skills. The Air Force Advisory Group also provided teams at each VNAF base to assist the Vietnamese wherever possible.

During 1971 the VNAF flew more combat sorties in Vietnam than the U.S. air arms combined—63 percent of all such missions. It constituted a 69.8 percent increase over the VNAF's 1970 operations. In September 1971 the Air Force transferred a second AC-119G gunship squadron to the VNAF. During the year the VNAF transport fleet was increased to five squadrons following turnover of three USAF squadrons of C-123's. In addition, 3 C-119's were added to the 16 already being flown by the Vietnamese. In November, the VNAF took control of three direct air support centers at Pleiku, Bien Hoa, and Da Nang. By year's end, the Vietnamese also were solely responsible for operating air navigation facilities at eight bases—Binh Thuy, Ban Me Thuot, Bien Hoa, Nha Trang, Da Nang, Chu Lai, and Phu Cat.

Meanwhile, a plan was adopted to phase out most Vietnamese training in the United States. As part of this plan, the Air Force turned its attention to translating technical orders into Vietnamese and building training aids so that all instruction could be performed in South Vietnam. Additional mobile training teams were sent to Southeast Asia equipped with specially built training aids to expedite the teaching of VNAF maintenance personnel.

The partial success of Vietnamization of the air war was demonstrated during North Vietnam's 1972 spring invasion of the south. Responding to the enemy attack, the VNAF began flying the first of more than 20,000 strike sorties, which helped blunt the North Vietnamese advance. VNAF transports carried more cargo and troops than ever before, while fighters, gunships, and helicopters provided close air support to ARVN ground forces. In March and July, the VNAF activated its first C-7A Caribou squadrons and subsequently also acquired its first C-130 Hercules transports. The first VNAF C-130 instructor aircrew took its final check in December 1972.

The turnover of all training programs to the Vietnamese continued throughout 1972. English language training went from an almost entirely USAF effort to an almost entirely VNAF responsibility. In May 1972 the VNAF established a communications and electronics school at Bien Hoa. Also, with the aid of USAF mobile training teams, the VNAF took over maintenance training for the C-130, T-27B, and other aircraft systems. An AC-119K mobile training team started cross-training VNAF AC-119G and C-119G aircrews and maintenance crews into the AC-119K.

By December 1972 the Vietnamese Air Force had almost doubled in size over its June 1969 strength. From an organization of about 29,000 men, 20 squadrons, and an inventory of 428 aircraft in 1969, it had grown to 42,000 officers and airmen (with another 10,000 in training), organized into 49 squadrons equipped with about 2,000 aircraft (22 different types). In terms of numbers of aircraft, it had emerged as the fourth largest Air Force in the world—behind Communist China, the United States, and the Soviet Union.

IX Air Operations in Laos

On 3 April 1965 an Air Force C-130—equipped with flares and accompanied by two B-57's—flew a night mission over routes 12, 23, and 121 in the southern panhandle of Laos. The crews of the three aircraft searched for Communist vehicles and other enemy targets moving down the Ho Chi Minh trail toward South Vietnam and Cambodia. The mission marked the beginning of Operation Steel Tiger, a limited U.S. air campaign against enemy troop and supply movements within the panhandle of southern Laos. It had been preceded by Operation Barrel Roll, another limited interdiction effort aimed principally against Communist Pathet Lao and North Vietnamese troops which began in December 1964 (see Chapter VI). Both were supported by U.S. reconnaissance missions inaugurated in May 1964 to obtain target information.

The Ho Chi Minh trail, consisting of numerous winding roads and pathways, had served for many years as an infiltration route between the northern and southern sectors of Vietnam. During World War II and after, Vietnamese insurgents used it to fight the Japanese and later the French. After Hanoi launched a guerrilla war against the Saigon government, the trail was used by South Vietnamese "returnees" and indigenous North Vietnamese personnel sent to South Vietnam to aid the Viet Cong effort at unseating President Diem and unifying the country. By 1964, the trail had developed into a system of many dry-season truck roads and smaller paths for bicycles and human portage. By early 1965 the trail had become the principal artery by which Communist personnel and

supplies reached the northern sectors of South Vietnam.

The first Steel Tiger strikes—initiated a month after the start of Rolling Thunder attacks against North Vietnam—were directed against enemy personnel and supplies moving into South Vietnam through the DMZ or into the Laotian panhandle. Steel Tiger's mission was one of complementing Rolling Thunder. In both campaigns, political considerations were dominant and affected the tempo of the air strikes, which were generally limited in scope.

In undertaking these operations, Washington's primary concern was to avoid involving Communist China and the Soviet Union in the war, while maintaining the "neutral" status of Laotian Prime Minister Souvanna Phouma's government in Vientiane. This had been guaranteed in the 23 July 1962 Declaration on the Neutrality of Laos, signed by the Peoples Republic of China, the Soviet Union, the United States, France, Great Britain, and other nations. Thus, U.S. officials desired to avoid a large-scale air or ground campaign in Laos by any of the big powers which might undermine Souvanna Phouma's fragile regime. Another constraint on USAF operations in Laos was the Vientiane government's desire not to subject its people or troops to the hazards of unrestricted aerial warfare. Accordingly, the number of U.S. strike sorties, the areas where they could be flown, and the use of ordnance initially were severely restricted.

Because of this, command and control arrangements for Steel Tiger (and other air operations over Laos) were

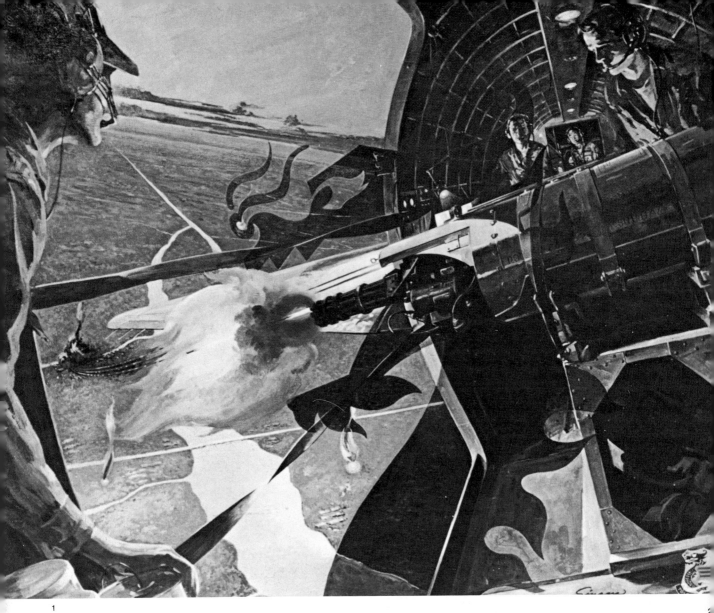

1

(1) A gunship in action (2) Interior of an AC-119 gunship (3) Aerial mines are dropped to interdict an enemy ferry and ford near Tchepone, Laos, 1968 (4) AC-119 gunship over Tan Son Nhut, 1969

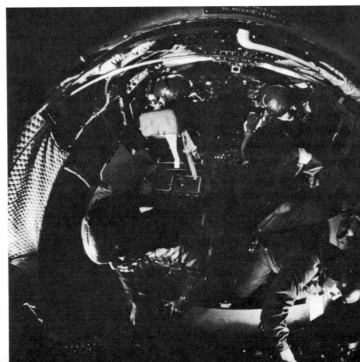

3

28 NOV 68

FERRY AND FORD

4

highly complex. The JCS relayed high-level Washington target authorizations to USAF and Navy commanders through CINCPAC in Honolulu and MACV in Saigon. Because USAF planes flying over Laos were based in South Vietnam and Thailand, the U.S. ambassadors in Saigon, Bangkok, and Vientiane also played important roles in controlling air operations. The position of the American ambassador in Vientiane was, however, unique. In the absence of a formal U.S. military command in Laos (such as MACV in South Vietnam), he became the principal American military as well as political authority there. On air operational matters, he normally exercised his authority through the office of the Air Force Attache.

In Saigon, General Moore's 2d Air Division, a MACV component, coordinated Air Force and other U.S. service air units employed in Steel Tiger. To meet political requirements arising from the use of Thai-based Air Force aircraft operating over Laos, General Moore had a Deputy Air Commander located at Udorn RTAFB. In April 1966, when the division was replaced by the Seventh Air Force, he became Deputy Commander, 7th AF/13th AF, reporting to the Seventh on operational matters and to the Thirteenth on administration and logistic matters.

At the start of Steel Tiger operations, the Air Force relied chiefly on the RF-101 and RB-57 for target detection and bomb damage assessment. For air strikes, it employed the F-100, the F-105, and the B-57 bomber—the last normally in conjunction with a C-130 Hercules flareship for night armed reconnaissance. As in the case of operations over northern Laos and North Vietnam, SAC KC-135 tankers were indispensable for refueling aircraft heading to or from targets or target areas. Air Force and Navy strikes initially concentrated on cutting roads and bombing traffic "choke points", particularly along routes leading from

the Mu Gia and Nape passes, two principal entry points from North Vietnam into Laos. They also struck trucks, bridges, and troop and storage areas. The Air Force averaged 9 to 10 sorties per day, the Navy a slightly higher number.

Soon after Steel Tiger operations were launched in April 1965, the annual May to October southwest monsoon began sweeping over Laos, sharply curtailing Air Force and Navy operations. Enemy personnel, on the other hand, adept at using jungle growth to conceal their troop and supply movements southward, continued their logistic activities. If the monsoon rains washed out roads and trails, they used watercraft on swollen streams and rivers to transport their men and supplies.

Introduction of New Tactics

By mid-1965, despite the poor weather, Air Force and Navy pilots were flying more than 1,000 Steel Tiger sorties per month. To improve their operations against targets of opportunity, the Air Force placed several F-105's on "strip alert" at a Thai air base. The use of the Thunderchiefs on strip alert (nicknamed "Whiplash") became an enduring Steel Tiger tactic against fleeting targets. Another measure undertaken was to send South Vietnamese ground reconnaissance teams—trained and led by U.S. Army personnel — into the border areas of the Laotian panhandle to locate and determine the extent of enemy traffic along the trail. The first team was flown in and removed by helicopter in October 1965. Other ground reconnaissance teams followed and soon began contributing to Steel Tiger operations by directing strikes on enemy positions, truck parks, and POL, supply, and ammunition stores normally concealed by the jungle growth or bad weather.

As the southwest monsoon subsided in late 1965, the Communists stepped up their infiltration, exceeding earlier U.S. estimates that they would send 4,500 men and 300 tons of supplies monthly into Vietnam. As a result, American and Lao authorities agreed to concentrate more air power on a segment of the Ho Chi Minh trail most contiguous to South Vietnam and used extensively by the infiltrators. Air Force Col. John F. Groom drew up the operational, command, communications, and support requirements for the new air program. Nicknamed Tiger Hound, it began in December 1965. Tiger Hound required more resources than the Air Force had employed in Laos up to that time. An airborne battlefield command and control system was established, involving initially C-47's which were later replaced by C-130's, for overall control of air operations within the strike area. Air Force O-1's and A-1E's, along with Royal Laotian Air Force (RLAF) T-28's, served as FAC's. RF-101's and the newly-arrived RF-4C aircraft, which were equipped with the latest infrared and side-looking radars, also were employed for target detection. UC-123 spray aircraft defoliated jungle growth along roads and trails to improve visibility. The principal strike aircraft were B-57's, F-100's, F-105's, and AC-47 gunships. Substantial Marine, Navy, and Army air joined in the operation. The Army provided additional O-1's for FAC missions while its OV-1 Mohawks, which were equipped with infrared and side-looking radar, were used mostly at night and often flew with Air Force C-130 flareships.

To facilitate the search for and destruction of targets, Tiger Hound rules of engagement were somewhat less stringent than elsewhere in Laos. By the end of December, the Air Force had logged 384 strike sorties in Tiger Hound, 51 of them at night; the other services flew an additional 425 sorties. The chief targets were trucks, storage and bivouac areas, bridges, buildings, and enemy antiaircraft sites. A substantial number concentrated on cutting roads and creating traffic choke points. On 11 December, B-52's struck the Mu Gia pass area, marking their first use in Laos.

In January 1966, the Air Force launched another air program in Laos called Cricket. It involved the use of O-1 and A-1E aircraft, based at Nakhon Phanom RTAFB near the Laotian border, to fly visual reconnaissance or to serve as FAC's in the northern Steel Tiger and southern Barrel Roll sectors. In the Barrel Roll area, the mission was primarily to support friendly ground units; in Steel Tiger, it was armed reconnaissance. Air Force aircraft ranged outward about 300 nautical miles from Nakhon Phanom, concentrating on roads to the south of Mu Gia pass—Routes 12, 23, and 911. RLAF observers flew with some U.S. FAC's to validate targets before allowing the F-100's, F-105's, and AC-47's to strike. The FAC pilots worked with both ground air liaison officers and road reconnaissance teams inside Laos who helped pinpoint targets. Although Cricket was a relatively minor operation, it proved quite effective in destroying or · damaging enemy trucks and supplies.

In early 1966 Tiger Hound operations gathered momentum with each passing month. In March, for example, tactical air strikes destroyed an estimated 210 trucks and damaged about 278 more. SAC B-52's flew more than 400 sorties in the first half of the year, conducting saturation strikes on roads to block enemy traffic and to hit troop encampments, supply dumps, and truck parks. By May, Tiger Hound attacks had destroyed or damaged an estimated 3,000 structures, 1,400 trucks, scores of bridges, and more than 200 automatic weapon and antiaircraft positions.

Recognizing the need for aircraft with a long loitering capability to help

1

2

3

5

8

6

(1) View of an AC-119 20-mm cannon (2) AC-119 gunship (3) Mini-gun firing (4) Loading 20-mm ammunition on a gunship (5-6) 15,-000 lb. bomb used to create jungle landing zones (7) An AC-130 gunship at Nha Trang AB (8) Servicing a 20-mm cannon

7

locate and attack an enemy concealed by jungle or weather, the Air Force deployed eight slow, nonjet A-26's (of World War II vintage which were re-equipped) to Nakhon Phanom in June 1966. Used in both a hunter and killer role against trucks, these aircraft replaced the older-model AC-47 gunships (which were later succeeded by improved AC-119 and AC-130 gunships). Also in June, the Air Force installed an MSQ-77 Skyspot radar at the base. Its 200-mile range permitted more accurate bombing day or night and in poor weather. The enemy reacted to the increased tempo of air operations by deploying more AAA weapons which took a steady toll of the attacking aircraft.

By May 1966 they had downed 22 U.S. aircraft in the Steel Tiger/Tiger Hound areas. With the onset of the annual southwest monsoons in the spring, air effectiveness again diminished as did the pace of infiltration. To maintain their supply flow southward, the Communists shifted to roads in North Vietnam (route package 1) above the DMZ.

In October 1966, when drier weather returned, the enemy resumed large-scale supply movements and Steel Tiger and Tiger Hound operations intensified once more. From January through April 1967, the dry months of the year in the Laotian panhandle, American pilots flew 2,900 to 3,400 strike sorties per month. In February, in undertaking one of the largest sustained air assaults in Laos, they flew 500 sorties against enemy concentrations opposite Kontum province in South Vietnam, thereby aiding considerably Allied operations against the Communists in that threatened province.

Subsequently, air operational rules were changed following the division of the Steel Tiger/Tiger Hound areas into four zones. In zone one, closest to South Vietnam, pilots had relative freedom to strike targets of opportunity. However, there were progressively more stringent strike rules governing the three zones westward. In those areas targets could not be hit unless authorized by Laotian officers, low-flying U.S. FAC's, or by the office of the American ambassador in Vientiane. In bad weather, all missions had to be under Skyspot radar control.

To maintain an umbrella of air power over the Ho Chi Minh trail, USAF commanders tried new tactics and introduced more specially-equipped aircraft. They also inaugurated the practice of having FAC pilots fly over "target boxes" in the same geographical area on a daily basis. This enabled them to become familiar with the terrain, aided in the detection of the enemy's presence, and simplified the command and control of strike aircraft. The use of additional ground reconnaissance teams led to the discovery of numerous concealed targets or target areas for air strikes. SAC B-52 bombers stepped up their operations, flying 1,718 sorties in the Laotian panhandle in 1967, nearly triple the 617 sorties flown in 1966. The Royal Laotian Air Force flew more T-28 FAC and strike missions, although its main effort continued to be in the Barrel Roll area of northern Laos.

The Air Force's most effective "truck killers" were the AC-119 and AC-130 gunships, the B-57, a few C-123's equipped with special detection devices and BLU bomblet cannisters, and the A-26. Carrying flares and detection devices, these aircraft flew mostly at night when Communist truck travel was heaviest. They also could serve as FAC's, calling in "fast movers" such as F-4C Phantoms for additional strikes. Other aircraft with a FAC capability included Air Force A-1E's, Navy P-1's. and RLAF T-28's. In 1967 O-2's began replacing O-1's and in 1968 the Air Force introduced the larger OV-10 Forward Air Control aircraft. The nighttime detection capability of a few tactical aircraft was enhanced by equipping them with the Starlight Scope, originally developed by the Army for its M-16 rifle. During the last 2 months of 1967 an important advance was made in the Allies' ability to detect enemy movements through the Laotian panhandle. This was a rudimentary, air-supported electronic anti-infiltration system, which consisted of "strings" of seismic and acoustic sensors dropped from aircraft in designated jungle areas. These devices, planted along a number of infiltration roads and trails, almost at once began picking up the sounds and movements of enemy vehicular traffic and personnel movements. The information was transmitted to a high-flying EC-121 which, in turn, retransmitted it to an Air Force infiltration surveillance center at Nakhon Phanom. There data were collated with other intelligence information.

The anti-infiltration detection system had a succession of nicknames, with Igloo White being best known and used the longest. It was another technological innovation for locating an enemy shielded by terrain or bad weather. A unit organized under the command of Air Force Brig. Gen. William P. McBride, named Task Force Alpha, built and operated the infiltration surveillance center. To dispense the sensors, the Air Force relied upon a small number of A-1E's, CH-3 helicopters, and also some F-4D's. Navy OP-2E aircraft also were employed to dispense the sensors. In January-February 1968, after the Communists laid siege to the Marine base Khe Sanh, General Westmoreland diverted Task Force Alpha resources to its defense. Dropped in the vicinity of the base, the sensors in one instance were able to detect North Vietnamese troop movements and preparations for a large-scale ground assault against the Marine positions. Thus alerted, the threat was thwarted and beaten back by heavy air strikes and Marine artillery fire.

Commando Hunt Operations

As was noted in Chapter III, the Tet offensive and siege of Khe Sanh triggered changes in U.S. policy in Southeast Asia. On 31 March 1968, President Johnson ordered an end to all bombing of North Vietnam above the 19th parallel to facilitate peace negotiations, hopefully paving the way for withdrawal of American troops from the theater while simultaneously strengthening Saigon's military forces. While U.S. air power hit hard at enemy infiltration through the DMZ, the annual southwest monsoon once again reduced Communist traffic in the Laos panhandle and air action against it.

In November 1968, on the basis of an "understanding" reached with Hanoi, the President ended all attacks upon North Vietnam. The enemy threat to South Vietnam, however, remained undiminished. Abatement of the rainy season in Laos, which coincided with the end of all bombing of the North, found infiltration down the Ho Chi Minh trail heavier than ever. To reduce it, the Air Force, Navy, and Marines launched a new air campaign nicknamed Commando Hunt. Its major objectives were to destroy as many supplies as possible being moved down the trail, to tie down enemy manpower, and to further test the effectiveness of the sensor system. Initial operations were confined roughly to a 1,700 square-mile sector of Laos contiguous to South Vietnam. The Air Force employed an array of FAC, strike, and reconnaissance aircraft, B-52's, C-130 airborne battlefield command and control centers, and AC-47 and AC-130 gunships. The gunships proved especially valuable in interdicting enemy truck traffic. In 1969, AC-119 gunships—some manned by Air Force reservists mobilized by President Johnson in May 1968—also flew missions against the trail.

Initially, about 40 percent of all sorties attempted to block narrow road passes, 35 percent hit truck parks and storage areas, 15 percent truck traffic, and 10 percent enemy AAA positions. By the end of April, after 6 months of these operations, U.S. analysts believed that the Commando Hunt operations had destroyed or damaged enough vehicles and supplies to force the Communists to rely more heavily on water routes including the Cambodian port of Kompong Som (apparently with the acquiescence of Cambodian officials). As the pace of the aerial assault quickened, the number of tactical sorties rose from about 4,700 in October 1968, to 12,800 in November, and 15,100 in December. B-52 sorties jumped from 273 in October to more than 600 for each of the last 2 months of the year. During 1968 SAC bombers logged 3,377 sorties over the Laotian panhandle, nearly double the total for 1967. Somewhat greater operational flexibility allowed air commanders in early 1969 facilitated the upward sortie trend. Notwithstanding their rising materiel losses, the Communists doggedly continued to send a substantial flow of supplies through Laos into South Vietnam.

Commando Hunt II, begun in May 1969, coincided with the beginning of the annual southwest monsoon and the usual reduction of enemy movements and U.S. operations over southern Laos. American pilots nonetheless continued to harass or hamper the efforts of the Communists to repair roads and trails washed out by floods. Within North Vietnam, the enemy assembled more manpower, trucks, and watercraft and stockpiled supplies near the Laos border to prepare for the next infiltration surge through Laos after the monsoon abated. They also built a POL pipeline into the southern Laotian panhandle and augmented considerably their antiaircraft defenses. This activity was facilitated greatly, of course, by the end of the bombing of the North and the continued, unrestricted flow of trucks,

(1) A Chinese built truck, captured in Laos. 1971 (2) U. S. Army helicopters supported Lam Son 719 in early 1971. (4) Captured Soviet PT-76 amphibious tank (5) A North Vietnamese antiaircraft gun captured in Laos by Saigon's troops in 1971

ENEMY TRUCKS
22 MILES NORTH OF
MU GIA PASS

guns, equipment, and supplies from China or through Haiphong and other seaports. Gen. George S. Brown, Seventh Air Force commander (August 1968 to September 1970), observed that the enemy had a "free ride" to the borders of Laos and South Vietnam.

Commando Hunt III, launched as the dry season began in November 1969, again witnessed more intense air operations against an expanded flow of enemy troops and supplies southward. The use of many seismic and acoustic sensors, unaffected by darkness and weather, provided considerable data on NVA movements and resulted more frequently in more timely air strikes. The AC-119 and AC-130 gunships, and C-123's equipped with bomblet cannisters continued to be the best truck killers. Of the total number of trucks claimed destroyed or damaged between late 1969 and early 1970 (one estimate ranged upwards to 10,000 trucks), the gunships and C-123's were credited with about 48 percent, although they flew a relatively small number of total Commando Hunt sorties. Some analysts believed that no more than 33 percent of the supplies that entered the Ho Chi Minh trail reached South Vietnam while the rest were destroyed, damaged, or consumed en route.

During Commando Hunt III, the tempo of air operations declined gradually. Washington authorities, confident that American objectives in Southeast Asia were being achieved, imposed budgetary limits on the overall U.S. war effort which led to some reduction in Air Force and Navy sortie ceilings. Sortie requirements were reduced beginning 26 February 1970 when enemy traffic in southern Laos suddenly dropped to half of the volume observed in the preceding weeks. Meanwhile, there were requests to use air assets elsewhere. In February 1970, for example, numerous tactical and B-52 missions—the latter for the first time—were diverted to the Barrel Roll

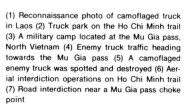

(1) Reconnaissance photo of camoflaged truck in Laos (2) Truck park on the Ho Chi Minh trail (3) A military camp located at the Mu Gia pass, North Vietnam (4) Enemy truck traffic heading towards the Mu Gia pass (5) A camoflaged enemy truck was spotted and destroyed (6) Aerial interdiction operations on Ho Chi Minh trail (7) Road interdiction near a Mu Gia pass choke point

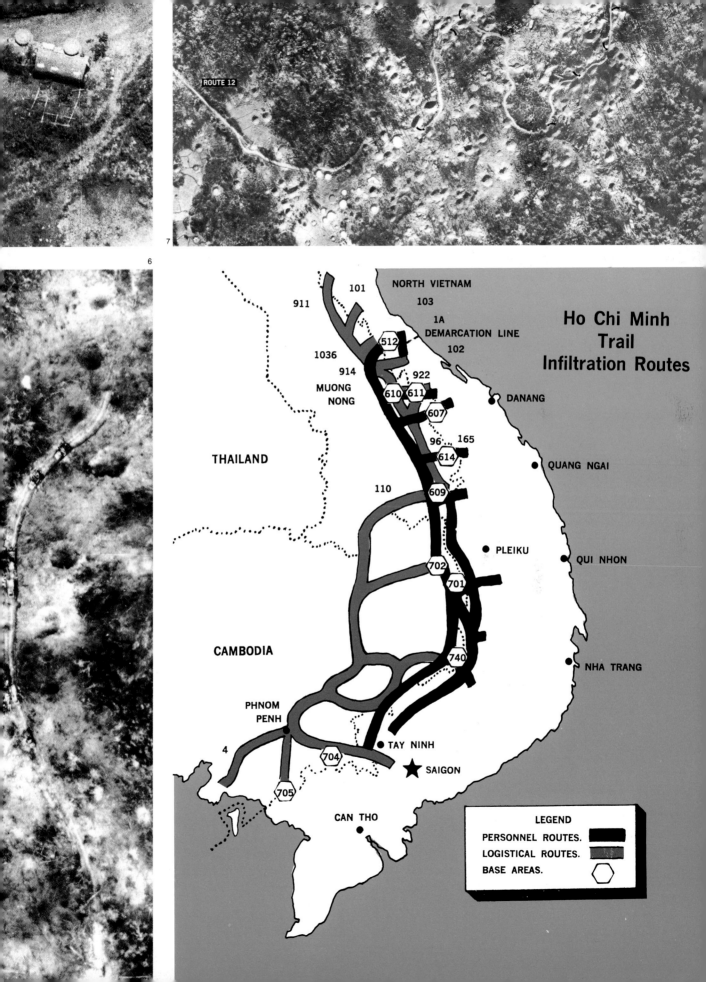

ROUTE 12

7

6

Ho Chi Minh Trail Infiltration Routes

NORTH VIETNAM

101
911
103
1A
DEMARCATION LINE
102
512
1036
922
914
610 611
MUONG NONG
607
DANANG
96 165
614
QUANG NGAI
110
609
PLEIKU
702
QUI NHON
701
THAILAND
CAMBODIA
740
NHA TRANG
PHNOM PENH
4
704
TAY NINH
705
SAIGON
CAN THO

LEGEND
PERSONNEL ROUTES.
LOGISTICAL ROUTES.
BASE AREAS.

sector of northern Laos to counter stepped up Pathet Lao-North Vietnamese activity there. Other diversions occurred in April and May 1970, when U.S. and South Vietnamese troops invaded the "Parrot's Beak" and "Fishhook" regions of Cambodia to attack Communist base areas and supply concentrations. In fact, air requirements in Cambodia, South Vietnam, and northern Laos for the time being took precedence over those in southern Laos.

Lam Son 719

Late in 1970, attention again was directed to an upsurge of Communist movements in the Laos panhandle. There was evidence of considerable stockpiling around Tchepone, a supply hub on the upper end of the Ho Chi Minh trail, not far from the DMZ. The enemy seemed to be preparing for a major ground offensive into South Vietnam's two northernmost provinces, Quang Tri and Thau Thien.

As the enemy buildup grew, U.S. and South Vietnamese authorities decided to conduct a military thrust across a portion of the Ho Chi Minh trail toward Tchepone with the objective of thwarting the NVA attack and cutting a segment of the infiltration route. As in the earlier invasion of Cambodia, the incursion into Laos promised to "buy time" to insure success of Vietnamization and the withdrawal of U.S. and Allied troops from South Vietnam. Because Congress had prohibited the use of American ground forces in Laos, only South Vietnamese troops were committed to the invasion, supported primarily by U.S. air power. Nicknamed Lam Son 719, the operation was conducted between January and April 1971. Air assets earmarked earlier for Commando Hunt V (October 1970 to April 1971) were diverted to Lam Son 719.

The first phase of the joint South Vietnamese-American undertaking began on 30 October when U.S. ground troops in Quang Tri province cleared an area near the Laotian border in order to establish logistical bases at Khe Sanh and the Vandegrift (Marine) camp. Construction of a new assault air strip and stockpiling of fuel and supplies followed. Air Force C-123 and C-130 transports played a major preparatory role, flying about 1,900 sorties to airlift 12,846 personnel, mostly South Vietnamese troops, and 19,900 tons of cargo to the jump-off areas.

The invasion was launched on 8 February 1971. South Vietnamese troops—drawn from a ranger, airborne, and ARVN infantry division and including some mechanized elements —fought for the first time without accompanying U.S. advisors. Initially, a mechanized unit rolled across the border to establish and secure land lines, while other ARVN troops were airlifted by helicopter to the A Loui area, south of Route 9 leading to Tchepone. In support of the Vietnamese, the Air Force operated a tactical air control system from the forward direct air support center (DASC) set up and collocated with the U.S. XXIV Corps forward command post at Quang Tri. It also provided most of the O-2 and OV-10 FAC aircraft.

English-speaking Vietnamese flew with the Air Force FAC pilots and aboard C-130 aerial command posts to bridge language difficulties between Vietnamese commanders and ground personnel. Other participating USAF aircraft included F-100's, F-4C's, AC-119's, AC-130's, and B-52's—all for direct support or interdiction purposes. Also supporting the operation were RF-4C's for reconnaissance, A-1E's for air cover rescue missions, and KC-135's for air refueling. C-130, C-123, and C-7 transports airlifted more than 30,000 tons during the invasion. U.S. Marine and Navy aircraft provided considerable tactical support and the Army employed helicopter gunships and hundreds of other helicopters for troop and supply airlift. The VNAF also provided combat and airlift support.

By the end of the first day, 6,200 South Vietnamese troops were in Laos, most of them airlifted to predetermined locations. They built fire bases, conducted patrols, and uncovered numerous supply and ammunition caches. The bodies of many NVA troops were found, killed by air strikes. By 12 February about 10,000 South Vietnamese were in Laos and shortly after their strength peaked at about 17,000. Enemy resistance initially was light to moderate. Meanwhile, U.S. aircraft continued to strike heavily at NVA positions and their LOC's. At night Air Force FAC's, flareships, and gunships provided cover for friendly troops; on 14 February the B-52's launched their first close air support strike. By the 23d, the B-52's had flown 399 sorties, which helped clear the path for the advancing Vietnamese and to prepare helicopter landing zones. Air Force C-130's joined in, unloading 15,000-pound bombs on suspected enemy concentrations and using them to create instant helicopter landing areas.

On 25 February 1971, the North Vietnamese launched a counter offensive. They first attacked the forward support base at A Loui and expanded their operations in the ensuing 5 days. The size and intensity of their response proved greater than anticipated. Some 24,000 NVA combat troops —supported by about 11,000 support personnel—reached the vicinity of the forward elements of the South Vietnamese force moving westward. The NVA troops were equipped with about 120 tanks, considerable artillery, and a profusion of antiaircraft automatic weapons. The AA guns soon began taking a heavy toll of low-flying U.S. Army helicopters.

With the help of fixed-wing air power, the South Vietnamese briefly contained the enemy assaults and, on 3 March, they resumed their westward drive. On the 7th three battalions reached the area around the logistic hub of Tchepone, the principal objective, where they were joined by two other battalions. Enemy resistance, at first relatively light, grew stiffer between 3-10 March as NVA reinforcements arrived in the Tchepone area. Other NVA attacks of growing strength began to hit the ARVN troops and fire-bases stretching from South Vietnam's border to Tchepone. A number of enemy ambushes inflicted heavy casualties on the invaders.

Faced with mounting personnel and equipment losses, Lt. Gen. Hoang Xuan Lam, the commander of the invasion forces, decided to cut short the operation and ordered a withdrawal. In the hasty retreat that followed, with many personnel being evacuated by helicopter, the South Vietnamese abandoned large quantities of armor, tanks, trucks, and other military hardware. Intense enemy ground fire made helicopter missions extremely dangerous and scores were shot down or seriously damaged, leading to panic among many ARVN troops. However, under massive tactical and B-52 air cover, virtually all South Vietnamese troops were extricated by 24 March. A number of ground reconnaissance units fought a rearguard action as Lam Son 719 officially ended on 6 April.

The cost was high to both sides. The North Vietnamese suffered an estimated 14,500 personnel killed, about 4,800 by air strikes, and unknown numbers of wounded. Aircraft were credited with destroying the greatest part of about 20,000 tons of food and ammunition and 156,000 gallons of fuel. About 1,530 trucks were destroyed and 480 damaged and a NVA tank regiment—with about 74 tanks destroyed and another 24 damaged—was virtually wiped out. The enemy also lost an estimated 6,000 weapons. The South

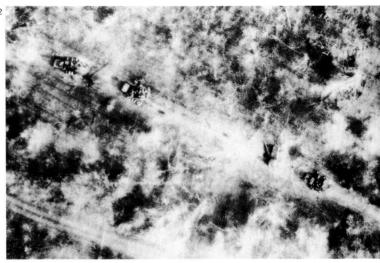

Vietnamese suffered 1,519 killed, 5,423 wounded, and 651 missing in action. ARVN equipment destroyed or captured included about 75 tanks, many armored personnel carriers, 198 crew-served weapons, and about 3,000 individual weapons.

American air support had been massive. More than 8,000 tactical air sorties were flown and some 20,000 tons of ordnance dropped. The B-52's flew 1,358 sorties in direct support of the South Vietnamese troops. U.S. Army helicopters flew thousands of sorties in airlifting troops into and out of Laos, resupplying units, and evacuating casualties. Considering the magnitude of the air effort and the North Vietnamese response to it, aircraft losses were relatively small. The Air Force lost six aircraft, the Navy one. U.S. Army helicopters suffered the heaviest attrition. At least 107 were destroyed and upwards of 600 damaged, many so badly that they would not fly again. American casualties totalled 176 killed, 1,042 wounded, and 42 missing in action. One lesson of Lam Son 719 was that neither the invasion nor the withdrawal would have been possible without the extensive use of air power.

Following the operation, both sides were forced to reconstitute and re-

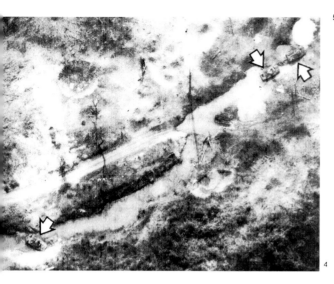

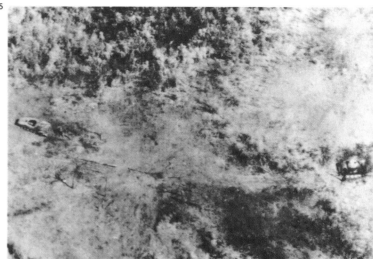

(1) U. S. fighter bombers destroy enemy truck in Laos (2) Four enemy trucks damaged by U. S. aircraft in vicinity of the Mu Gia pass (3) Air Force fighter-bombers attacked enemy petroleum drum cache on the Ho Chi Minh trail (4) Three Soviet PT-76 tanks damaged by Air Force fighter bombers (5) Enemy tanks destroyed in Laos

equip many of their units. Having suffered by far the largest number of casualties, the North Vietnamese had to replace and retrain many personnel. They also had to repair roads, trails, bridges, and restock stores of food, POL, and ammunition in the battle area. As a consequence, Hanoi's plans for a new major offensive against South Vietnam suffered a temporary setback and bought additional time for Washington and Saigon to advance the on-going Vietnamization program.

Additional Commando Hunt Campaigns

During the annual May to October monsoon in 1971, when Commando Hunt operations diminished, the North Vietnamese maintained an above normal level of activity in southern Laos. They added about 140 miles of new roads to the Ho Chi Minh trail which, by October, brought the total to 2,170 miles—including single lanes, multiple parallel routes, by-passes, and spur roads. They also expanded their air defenses. By late 1971, about 344 antiaircraft guns and thousands of smaller automatic weapons defended vital points along the trail. A number of SA-2 missile sites on the North Vietnamese border and in Laos posed a

new threat, as did rebuilt air bases in southern North Vietnam. The latter enabled MIG pilots to challenge or harass Commando Hunt aircraft. As more North Vietnamese troops arrived, American officials estimated enemy strength in Laos—south and north—at about 96,000. In Cambodia there were about 63,000 North Vietnamese and in South Vietnam about 200,000.

Thus, with the onset of the dry season in late 1971, the Communist threat again was formidable. To counter it, the Air Force launched Commando Hunt VII, extending it beyond the Steel Tiger area of southern Laos. However, there were fewer U.S. aircraft available for Laos because of competing requirements in Cambodia, for North Vietnam where "protective reaction" strikes were under way, and because of U.S. budget cutbacks and the consequent withdrawal of U.S. air and ground units. To compensate for fewer U.S. aircraft, USAF officials called for greater participation in Commando Hunt VII by the indigenous air forces of Laos, Cambodia, and South Vietnam, more flexible employment of U.S. tactical and B-52 aircraft, and the use of the newest technological advances for interdiction.

By 1971, U.S. research and development activities had wrought many changes in interdiction techniques and ordnance. OV-10 FAC aircraft were now able to direct laser-guided bombs dropped by fighter aircraft flying day or night missions, and also were more effective in assisting air rescue operations. The target-detection and truck-killing capability of the B-57G and the AC-119 and AC-130 gunships had been upgraded. The AC-130 was equipped with a variety of target acquisition devices, including low-light-level television, illuminators, beacon-tracking radar, and infrared sensors. LORAN-equipped F-4's could lead other aircraft not so equipped to targets at night or in bad weather. The Task Force Alpha infiltration center at Nakhon Phanom assumed a more direct operational role while continuing to collect, analyze, and disseminate sensor-gathered data on enemy movements. And pilots had available more deadly types of cluster bombs, more accurate laser-guided bombs, and improved aircraft guns.

Commando Hunt VII operations in the Steel Tiger area of Laos were conducted in three phases. Beginning with Phase I on 1 November 1971, strike aircraft concentrated on hitting several entry points from North Vietnam into Laos, principally the Mu Gia, Ban Karai, and Ban Raving passes and the western end of the DMZ at the 17th parallel. During Phase II, as the North Vietnamese moved supplies further southward along roads and trails in the Laotian panhandle, strike aircraft shifted attacks to those routes in order to create "blocking belts" at key transportation points or areas. These were formed first by cutting a road with laser-guided bombs and then seeding the road area with air-dropped land mines. When ground sensors detected the enemy clearing minefields or bypassing the belt area, aircraft were quickly dispatched to the scene. During Phase III operations in early 1972, U.S. tactical and B-52 aircraft

HIGHWAY BRIDGE, ROUTE 9
TCHEPONE AREA, LAOS
16-42N 106-13E

shifted their attacks to seven principal exit points from Laos into South Vietnam and Cambodia.

Commando Hunt VII operations were completed at the end of March 1972. By then, since Steel Tiger operations began in the Laotian panhandle in April 1965, U.S. tactical aircraft had flown about 31,500 sorties, with the Air Force flying more than half of the this total. As previously, the B-52's participated, flying 3,176 strikes. About 70 percent of the tactical missions were directed against interdiction points, trucks, and storage areas. Many of the strikes triggered explosions and secondary fires and analysts estimated that the enemy lost many of his trucks and a substantial part of about 31,000 tons of supplies moving through southern Laos during the 5-month campaign. Despite intense enemy AAA fire in some areas, the United States lost only 13 aircraft in the Steel Tiger sector during Commando Hunt VII.

This bridge in the Tchepone areas of Laos, destroyed in early 1964, was rebuilt by enemy forces and later downed again.

226

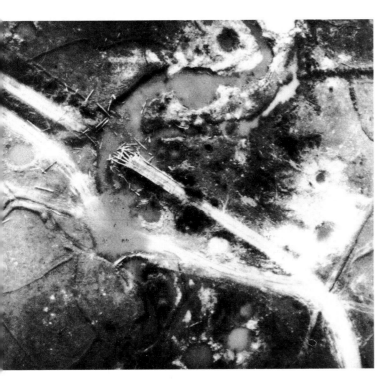

aircraft interdicted this
e in Laos in 1969.

Air Power Shifts Again

While absorbing its losses in Laos, the Hanoi regime remained free from air attacks north of the DMZ, except for occasional protective reaction air strikes, to build up its troop strength and supplies. In April 1972, as the northeast monsoon began to abate, the North Vietnamese launched their "spring offensive," sending about 100,000 men into northern South Vietnam. The United States responded forcefully, with President Nixon ordering a naval blockade of the North for the first time, renewed regular strikes above the DMZ, and a buildup of U.S. units to provide air support to South Vietnamese forces. Augmented by 50 more B-52's, American air units again pounded the enemy. By July, the NVA offensive had been contained but the North Vietnamese had succeeded in seizing large portions of South Vietnamese territory in the northern and western portions of the Republic of Vietnam. As a result of Hanoi's spring invasion of South Vietnam, air strikes in Laos dropped to the lowest level since 1965. In September the tempo increased with B-52's concentrating on the Steel Tiger area and tactical aircraft hitting enemy troops in the northern part of the country. In October, as the southwest monsoon declined, the North Vietnamese for the first time in several years did not step up drastically their infiltration activity in southern Laos. The Air Force, in turn, did not launch another Commando Hunt campaign. It continued, however, to fly air strikes against segments of the Ho Chi Minh trail, employing for the first time the A-7D Corsair II for close air support of friendly Lao units and the swept-wing F-111 for armed reconnaissance. Both aircraft possessed sophisticated radar equipment for poor weather operations.

These air missions continued at a low but steady pace until 18 December 1972, when Linebacker II operations were launched against the North Vietnamese capital area, including the port of Haiphong. The 11-day Linebacker II campaign was followed on 23 January 1973 by the signing of an accord, effective on the 28th, Saigon time, between the United States and North Vietnam providing for the release of all American and allied prisoners of war in exchange for a U.S. withdrawal of all combat forces from South Vietnam. However, tactical and B-52 sorties continued to be flown in the Laotian panhandle until 21 February 1973, when the rival Laotian factions reached a ceasefire agreement. The bombing, halted the next day, was renewed on 23 February at the request of the Vientiane government because of ceasefire violations. The B-52's returned to action in April, again in connection with a breakdown in the ceasefire. With the completion of these strikes against targets on the Plain of Jars, all American air operations in Laos ceased.

227

After nearly 9 years of operations over northern Laos, the Air Force on 17 April 1973 flew its last combat sortie in support of the Royal Laotian Government (RLG). Unlike the Steel Tiger interdiction strikes against North Vietnamese traffic on the Ho Chi Minh trail in the Laotian panhandle discussed above, the northern operations known as Barrel Roll primarily supported friendly government ground forces—the Royal Laotian Army and Neutralist troops but especially the army of Maj. Gen. Vang Pao, consisting of about 5,000 CIA-trained Meo tribesmen, a mountain people living within Laos. Operating mostly as irregulars, the Meos did much of the fighting, helping to defend an area which included the capital at Vientiane and the politically important Plain of Jars. Northeast of the plain was Sam Neua province, the Pathet Lao capital of the same name, and major east-west roads leading to and from North Vietnam.

Air Force operations over northern Laos had origins in the failure of the Geneva Accords of 23 July 1962. Signed by the United States, the Soviet Union, the two Vietnams, and eight other countries, the agreement recognized Laos as a neutral, independent country to be ruled by a tripartite government divided among Rightists, Neutralists, and the Pathet Lao. Foreign military personnel—other than accredited military attaches— were prohibited from being stationed in Laos. Thus, the 750-man U.S. Military Assistance Advisory Group— which had been in Laos for about 2 years before the accords were

signed—had to leave, its departure being monitored by the International Control Commission. But on the other side, North Vietnamese forces lingered on in Pathet Lao territory and prevented the ICC from inspections by obstructive tactics which were abetted by the Communist member of the Commission.

When efforts by Prime Minister Souvanna Phouma to form a tripartite coalition government proved unsuccessful, he requested American economic and military aid, including supplies, spare parts, and aircraft for the Royal Laotian Air Force. T-28 fighter-bombers were subsequently delivered to the RLAF, replacing worn-out T-6's. To manage the increased materiel flow, the United States maintained in its embassy in Laos a small contingent of civilians (most of them retired military men). In the spring of 1964, after Pathet Lao and NVA forces launched attacks against Neutralist forces on the Plain of Jars, government troops evacuated the area. This prompted the Neutralist general, Kong Le, to warn RLG officials that without immediate air support all would be lost to the Communists.

Thereafter, with Washington's approval, Leonard Unger, the U.S. ambassador in Vientiane, released the fuzes for the bombs previously delivered and allowed the Laotian Air Force to attack with live ordnance. He also proposed, and Souvanna Phouma approved, low-level reconnaissance aircraft in early June 1964. Soufanna authorized the use of tactical fighters to accompany the unarmed jets after

229

one of the reconnaissance aircraft was lost on 6 June. Following the second loss of a Yankee Team aircraft, President Johnson ordered a retaliatory strike by eight F-100's on 9 June against a Communist AAA installation at Xieng Khouang on the Plain of Jars.

Three months earlier, in response to Souvanna Phouma's request for help to the RLAF—the Air Force deployed Detachment 6, 1st Air Commando Wing, to Udorn, Thailand. Two of its major jobs were to establish a T-28 flight checkout system for Laotian pilots and to assist with aircraft maintenance. Forty-one airmen, along with four aircraft, opened for business at Udorn in April 1964. Subsequently, as support of friendly ground operations increased, Air Force personnel were assigned to work as ground controllers or forward air guides in Laos, since few Laotians could speak English and none were familiar with procedures for directing air strikes against enemy positions. In early 1965, Detachment 6 began training English-speaking Lao and Meo personnel to direct air strikes from the ground. As these personnel became proficient, USAF airmen withdrew from this role.

When Barrel Roll operations got under way in December 1964, the U.S. ambassador in Vientiane as head of the "country team"—that is, all Americans officially assigned to the embassy—assumed responsibility for the direction, coordination, and supervision of U.S. military activities—almost entirely air—in support of the government. The Air Force attache and a small contingent of military and CIA personnel assisted him.

Although Unger and his successors—Ambassadors William H. Sullivan and G. McMurtrie Godley—did not concern themselves with details of operations (the number or types of planes employed), they validated all targets and none could be bombed without their permission. Strikes were limited to specific areas and conduct-

ed under strict rules of engagement.

As the tempo of operations increased, the Air Force in November 1965 established Headquarters 2d Air Division/Thirteenth Air Force at Udorn, some 45 miles from Vientiane to serve as a focal point for Laotian air support requests. The commander, a major general, as the senior Air Force representative in Thailand, had multiple responsibilities: he reported to the American ambassadors in Thailand and Laos on military matters in their respective areas; to the Commander, Thirteenth Air Force for administrative and logistic matters involving USAF units in Thailand; and to the Commander, Second Air Division in Saigon for the combat operations of those units. Thus, the Second Air Division actually issued the directives (the daily "frag" orders) for Barrel Roll missions in the Laotian panhandle. The Udorn headquarters in April 1966 was redesignated as 7th/13th Air Force following establishment of Seventh Air Force at Tan Son Nhut AB, South Vietnam.

The Effects of Weather

As elsewhere in Southeast Asia, the seasonal weather was a major factor in the ground struggle between government forces and the Pathet Lao-NVA in northern Laos. Enemy troops normally became active during the dry season between October and April. In the 6 months of the wet season that followed, the weaker government forces became active. Thus, with the onset of the dry season in the fall of 1965, enemy troops launched their largest offensive up to that time in an attempt to eliminate all government outposts on the Plain of Jars and establish secure lines of communication. The expanded fighting brought a sizable increase in the embassy workload and led the Secretary of Defense to increase the attaché staff to 117 military and 5 civilian personnel—42 of them from the Air Force.

The number of Air Force personnel continued to increase during the next several years until it totaled 125 in 1969. They helped establish Air Operations Centers within the five military regions of Laos, which were jointly manned by Laotian and USAF airmen to manage air support requests. In addition, the Air Force assigned forward air controllers to Royal Laotian Army units and Vang Pao's Meo forces as a means of overcoming the language barrier between them and the strike aircraft crews. Operating under the designation of Raven, these FAC's flew O–1's, U-17's, and T-28's on 6-month tours of duty. And, as necessary, the Air Force deployed a C-47 airborne battlefield command and control center to the area.

Despite the American air assistance, enemy forces overran a number of government posts in Sam Neua province in early 1966, including the key airfield at Na Khang—known as Lima Site 36 (LS-36)—which fell on 17 February. On 20 March a two-battalion enemy force seized a Neutralist stronghold and induced defection of its troops. To ease the pressure on friendly forces, USAF pilots flew 32 strike sorties daily, some with aircraft diverted from North Vietnam and the Ho Chi Minh trail.

The air strikes gradually took a heavy toll of enemy resources, destroying large quantities of supplies patiently built up over the previous year and slowing down his offensive. This success enabled Vang Pao's irregulars to take the offensive with the start of the wet season and recover a number of government posts, including Lima Site 36. By August 1966, the irregulars had reached Nam Bac, only 45 miles from the North Vietnamese border and a major point on the historic invasion corridor from the north. In effect, the Communist Pathet Lao dry season offensive of 1965-1966 had been a failure.

North Vietnam reacted to this turn of events by dispatching 14,000 first-line troops to northern Laos, bringing the total Communist strength to about 50,000 men for the start of the next dry season offensive. As the weather improved during the fall of 1966, enemy forces moved against government-controlled Lima Sites in northern Laos. By early January 1967 they had advanced to Na Khan where the Meo, supported by Thai T-28 pilots (trained by USAF instructors), drove them back. When the enemy tried to overrun LS-52, located some 20 miles from the Pathet Lao capital at Sam Neua, allied air power again saved the day. Frustrated by these setbacks, the Communists on 2 February mortared the Luang Prabang airfield, destroying eight aircraft and badly damaging three others as well as the air operations center. The attack was unprecedented, since both sides had always considered the royal capital immune.

The airfield attack had major impact on the opposing forces. The government troops became demoralized while the enemy appeared to gain a new momentum. On 4 April, he again struck at LS-52, attacking from three sides. Adverse weather deprived the government troops of their air support and they quickly fled, only to fall into an ambush, and were severely mauled by the North Vietnamese. For the next 2 months, operations were at a low level. Then, on 16 July, the enemy again struck the airfield at Luang Prabang, destroying 10 or 11 T-28's along with a major portion of the government's ammunition supply. The raid left the RLAF with only 38 T-28's. Pending delivery of additional aircraft, Seventh Air Force in July diverted sorties from Rolling Thunder to take up the slack.

After slowly rebuilding his forces, Vang Pao on 2 August 1967 attacked and captured Muong Ngan, depriving the enemy of the year's rice harvest in that area. Both sides then built up

1

2

3

4

5 6

7

(1) Munitions storage area at Vientiane, Laos, 1970 (2) 20,000 Laotian refugees were evacuated from Saravane in 2 1/2 days by three American C-46 transports (3) A C-7A Caribou delivered supplies to remote Laotian bases (4) An Air Force F-111 takes off from a base in Thailand on a bombing mission against enemy targets in North Vietnam (5-6) Damage caused by an enemy rocket attack which destroyed six aircraft and damaged three others at the Vientiane airport on 2 February 1967. (7) Royal Laotian forces captured this Soviet PT-76 tank on the Plain of Jars

their forces in the Nam Bac valley in anticipation of the dry season offensive. The government tried to move first, but weather and inadequate logistic support produced costly delays. Then, in early September, the T-28's inadvertently bombed their own troops, who promptly fled. Subsequent air strikes were poorly coordinated and controlled and by mid-October the situation at Nam Bac was critical. A relief operation proved far too complicated to succeed, although Vang Pao's guerrilla force gradually fought its way way toward Nam Bac. Finally, during the night of 14-15 January—with Vang Pao's force only 12 kilometers away—the Royal Laotian garrison abandoned the town and fled into the jungle. Of the 4,000-man garrison, only 1,400 were eventually accounted for. They left behind seven 105-mm howitzers, thirty-six 60-mm mortars, forty-two 57-mm recoilless rifles, and more than 1 million pounds of ammunition.

The Loss of Lima Site 85

Following this success, the enemy turned his attention to Lima Site 85, isolated on a 5,200-foot mountain 25 miles west of Sam Neua and 160 miles west of Hanoi, deep within Pathet Lao territory. Accessible from only one side of the mountain, LS-85 was near a 700-foot dirt landing strip which had been scratched out in a narrow valley several hundred feet below. In 1966 the Air Force installed a tactical air navigation system there, primarily for the direction of aircraft headed for North Vietnam and northern Laos. Late in 1967 the Air Force replaced the original facility with an all-weather navigation system, operated and maintained by 19 USAF personnel.

The increased activity on the mountain's heights aroused North Vietnamese suspicions and, on 12 January 1968—in one of the bizarre air actions of the war—Soviet-manufactured, sin-

gle engine NVAF Colt aircraft (AN-2's) attacked the site, the crews firing machineguns out the windows. At this point an American helicopter with security forces aboard returned fire and shot down one Colt. A second NVAF plane crashed while attacking the site, and a third Colt was chased toward North Vietnam by the U.S. helicopter. The third aircraft was forced to crash land some 18 miles north of the site in Laos. Whereupon, the North Vietnamese sent units to seize LS-85. By 10 March they had captured the landing strip and then advanced up a supposedly invulnerable side to the top of the mountain, where they defeated in hand-to-hand combat some 100 Meo guarding the site. Once there, they methodically destroyed the radar equipment. Of the 19 Air Force personnel operating the equipment, 12 managed to escape and were rescued by helicopters, 4 bodies were seen in the ruins of the facility, and 3 remained unaccounted for.

Following the loss of Lima Site 85, the enemy launched a drive against Vang Pao's troops. Friendly outposts fell one by one while most Air Force and RLAF planes remained grounded by weather. By early May the Communists had massed five battalions at Na Khang, which was defended by some 1,500 men. At this point the weather improved, enabling Allied airmen to fly several hundred sorties which blunted the enemy thrust. In June Vang Pao went over to the offensive and drove the enemy back towards Sam Neua. Before the summer was over, his forces and other friendly troops--supported by some 700 Air Force sorties--had recaptured most of the posts and territory previously lost to the enemy.

At the beginning of the 1968 dry season, when the enemy normally launched his offensive, Vang Pao decided to seize the initiative by heading straight for Lima Site 85. In December, as his troops reached the mountain site, they received heavy mortar fire from the enemy. Whereupon, Air Force FAC's directed numerous strikes against the Communist positions. Seventh Air Force allocated 250 sorties for the operation, 50 being flown daily for 5 days. After the enemy guns fell silent, the Meo recaptured the airstrip. It proved a transitory success; on Christmas Day three fresh Communist battalions from Sam Neua counterattacked and drove the Meo from the area. Lima Site 85 remained in enemy hands.

NVA troops also moved to regain control of Route 7 and the Plain of Jars. By late February they were threatening Lima Site 36, the scene of repeated fighting and the location of the only tactical air control system in northeast Laos. An all-out air effort was launched to save the site. However, so many aircraft were diverted to the scene that the FAC's found it necessary to return some to their original targets because they could not properly handle them. Unfortunately, the enemy troops had dispersed in small groups and the FAC's—assuming they were hidden in the jungle—directed most of the ordnance there. An AC-47 gunship also went to the support of the badly battered government troops. On 1 March, however, after all their officers had been killed, the Laotian troops abandoned LS-36 and withdrew under cover of USAF aircraft.

Following their capture of the site, the Communists turned their attention to Vang Pao's headquarters at Long Tieng (Lima Site 20A). As a countermove, Vang Pao proposed a three-pronged preemptive attack with air cover to seize the main towns on the Plain of Jars (including the provincial capital of Xieng Khouang), interdict Route 7 east and west of Ban Ban, and capture Tha Thom south of the plain. However, his American advisors urged a less ambitious offensive, which he

accepted and which began on 23 March 1969. It involved a two-pronged attack with air support along the plain's western rim with separate advances to the enemy's rear. In advance of the attack, on 17 March Seventh Air Force and RLAF units launched the first of a series of attacks against enemy targets. During the first 4 days, 261 Air Force and 43 RLAF sorties struck more than 600 enemy structures, including bunkers and trenches. Of 345 targets in the Xieng Khouang area, 192 were knocked out.

By the time these air operations ended on 7 April, the Allied air forces had flown 730 sorties. They were credited with causing hundreds of secondary explosions and fires but, more importantly, they enabled Vang Pao's troops to walk virtually unopposed into Xieng Khouang in late April, a feat thought impossible at the start of the campaign. There they found large caches of supplies, including trucks, jeeps, 37-mm guns, and armored personnel carriers.

Following the capture of Xieng Khouang, the Meo leader launched diversionary attacks on Routes 61 and 7 to force the enemy to withdraw from Routes 4 and 5 south and east of Muong Soui, the old Neutralist headquarters and gateway from the Plain of Jars to the major north-south road between the two Laotian capital cities of Vientiane and Luang Prabang. The Air Attaché in Vientiane requested an augmentation of 50 sorties a day for 5 days in addition to the 70 regular Barrel Roll sorties to support the operation. Unfortunately, bad weather interfered with bombing some 150 targets, and Vang Pao's troops met stiff resistance from enemy units sent from Sam Neua.

At the same time, NVA troops opened their offensive against Muong Soui. About 4,000 Neutralist troops backed by a 300-man Thai artillery unit, defended the town. Both sides

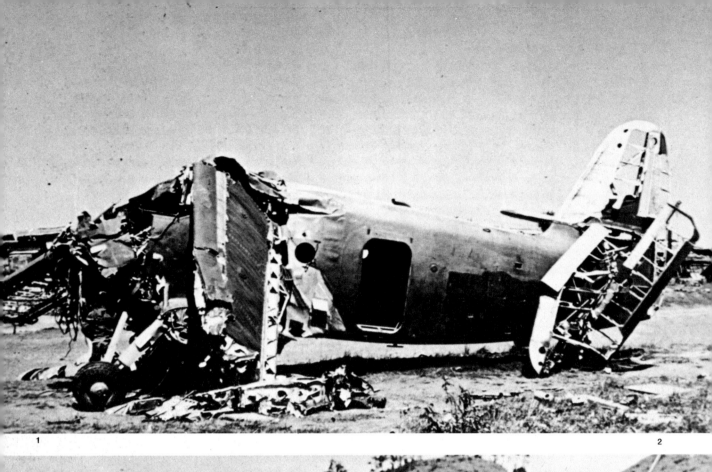

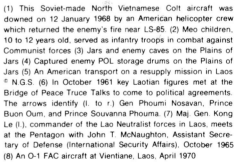

(1) This Soviet-made North Vietnamese Colt aircraft was downed on 12 January 1968 by an American helicopter crew which returned the enemy's fire near LS-85. (2) Meo children, 10 to 12 years old, served as infantry troops in combat against Communist forces (3) Jars and enemy caves on the Plains of Jars (4) Captured enemy POL storage drums on the Plains of Jars (5) An American transport on a resupply mission in Laos © N.G.S. (6) In October 1961 key Laotian figures met at the Bridge of Peace Truce Talks to come to political agreements. The arrows identify (l. to r.) Gen Phoumi Nosavan, Prince Buon Oum, and Prince Souvanna Phouma. (7) Maj. Gen. Kong Le (l.), commander of the Lao Neutralist forces in Laos, meets at the Pentagon with John T. McNaughton, Assistant Secretary of Defense (International Security Affairs), October 1965 (8) An O-1 FAC aircraft at Vientiane, Laos, April 1970

realized that its capture would be a serious blow to Souvanna Phouma's government. Although the Neutralist force outnumbered the NVA troops by three to one, the latter had been ordered to take Muong Soui at all costs. At first light on 24 June 1969, as the NVA launched a tank-led attack, Raven FAC's directed air strikes which destroyed three and damaged a fourth tank. But the NVA pressed on and captured three 155-mm and five 105-mm guns, plus portions of the nearby dirt strip (Lima Site 108). The fighting then died down and remained sporadic for 3 days. By this time the Neutralist troops—traditionally poor fighters to begin with—were in complete disarray and an evacuation was ordered. Sixteen American helicopters covered by support aircraft managed to extract the Thais and Neutralists, including 200 families of the latter. Air strikes destroyed stores and equipment left behind, including nineteen 105-mm guns, 84 trucks and 1 helicopter previously shot down.

The loss of Muong Soui was a heavy blow to the Royal Government. Despite the general gloom, Vang Pao decided to go over to the offensive in an effort to retake the town. On 1 July 1969 the Air Force flew 50 strikes against Communist forces in Muong Soui, destroying 30 bunkers and producing 18 secondary explosions. Helped by their "flying artillery," the Meo met little resistance until they neared the town, when Vang Pao's plans went awry. Some 1,000 Neutralist troops committed to the operation did not move as planned and adverse weather hampered vitally needed air operations. On 8 July only six sorties could be flown; on the 12th, there were none. Without air support, the government advance slowed to a virtual standstill. On 12 July the enemy launched a counteroffensive which overran the government forces, inflicting heavy casualties and ending the operation.

A Major Government Victory

Vang Pao next proposed an operation which one embassy official called the "first major victory in the history of the Royal Government." His plan called for RLG troops to reestablish the government's presence on the southern fringes of the Plain of Jars, while his Meo guerrillas—operating from several Lima Sites (LS-2, ! S-6, LS-32, and LS-201) in enemy-held territory—disrupted supply lines to the rear, particularly on Route 7. Poor weather again restricted air support. Thus, although Seventh Air Force scheduled 200 Barrel Roll sorties a day, less than half were executed. The weather improved somewhat in mid-August, and both the Meo and Royal Army forces were able to chalk up some good progress. The latter cleared an area along both the southeastern and southwestern edges of the plain. Vang Pao's guerrillas, supported by heavy air strikes, gathered momentum far beyond what was originally expected, cleared sizable areas around the Lima sites, and cut enemy lines of communication, particularly on Route 7. The jubilant general pressed his advantage, assisted by some 200 Barrel Roll sorties daily.

Aerial reconnaissance soon disclosed that Allied air operations had deprived the enemy of fuel and ammunition and caused him to abandon his tanks and trucks in major portions of the Plain of Jars. Government troops moved in quickly and on 12 September reoccupied Xieng Khouang, meeting no opposition. They captured enormous caches of supplies, including more than 3 million rounds of ammunition, 150,000 gallons of gasoline, 12 tanks, 30 trucks, and 13 jeeps. On 28 September government forces retook Muong Soui, again without opposition.

But with the start of the 1969-1970 dry season, the enemy once again became active, particularly along

Route 7 and the northern portions of the Plain of Jars, where battalion and company-sized engagements increased. Air sorties in the region declined as the Air Force shifted its attention to the Ho Chi Minh trail. Taking advantage of the air lull, fresh NVA troops moved back into northern Laos, and their construction crews set about repairing roads leading southward. By December, a vigorous North Vietnamese offensive was well under way. On the other hand, the Meo—untrained in conventional warfare—were weary. Indeed, after more than 8 years of fighting, they had suffered so many casualties that 13- and 14-year old boys formed a substantial portion of their force.

The results of the expanding fighting were predictable. On 12 January 1970, NVA forces captured Phou Nok Kok, the northeast entry point to the Plain of Jars on Route 7. In February Xieng Khouang and its airstrip fell as the youthful Meo panicked and fled at the sight of the advancing tanks. The town's garrison of 1,500 men also walked away.

At this point, the United States resorted to the B-52, using it for the first time to attack enemy positions in northern Laos. CINCPAC had earlier proposed such an operation when Communist forces had threatened the royal capital. But it was not until 7 months later that Washington authorities approved the use of the B-52's to support the Laotian government. The first raid took place on 17-18 February 1970. In 36 sorties, the B-52's dropped 1,078 tons of munitions on NVA and Pathet Lao positions on the Plain of Jars, causing many secondary explosions and inflicting numerous casualties. Thereafter, until 1973, the Stratofortresses flew several thousand sorties against enemy targets in northern Laos.

With the momentum gained from the easy capture of Xieng Khouang, the NVA moved on Muong Soui. On 24

February, at the first sign of the approaching enemy, the town's 120-man defending force fled. Thus, almost overnight the government position on the plain had collapsed and the positions of the two sides were back to that of a year earlier. At this point, Vang Pao's immediate concern was to secure his main headquarters at Long Tieng (LS-20A). He deployed his troops along a string of hilltop sites, forming them into a crescent-shaped line around the southwest corner of the plain. USAF crews supported him with numerous interdiction strikes along Route 7 in an attempt to hinder enemy supply movements. Additionally, after sunset each day, other aircraft seeded the road with antipersonnel mines to delay repair of the bombed roadbed. AC-47, AC-119, and AC-130 gunships flew nightly, attacking truck traffic. Despite these efforts, the enemy managed to circle undetected to the rear of Vang Pao's troops and, on 17 March 1970 appeared around Sam Thong and Long Tieng. Early on the 18th, the Communist troops were spotted only 2 miles from the camp, and the airstrip at Sam Thong came under heavy attack. Despite poor weather, Seventh Air Force dispatched strike aircraft but thick haze and smoke interfered with the pilots' ability to locate communist positions.

Just when things appeared darkest, Thai reinforcements arrived and positioned themselves on the south ridge. Other government reinforcements were airlifted in on the 19th, increasing friendly forces to about 2,000 men. The enemy, who had occupied portions of the skyline ridge overlooking the airstrip, began firing into the valley. RLAF T-28 strikes on their position initially had little effect. USAF A-1's and T-28's during the next 2 days joined in the attacks on the NVA troops.

On 24 March, with the weather clearing, USAF and RLAF sorties plus ground artillery pounded the enemy

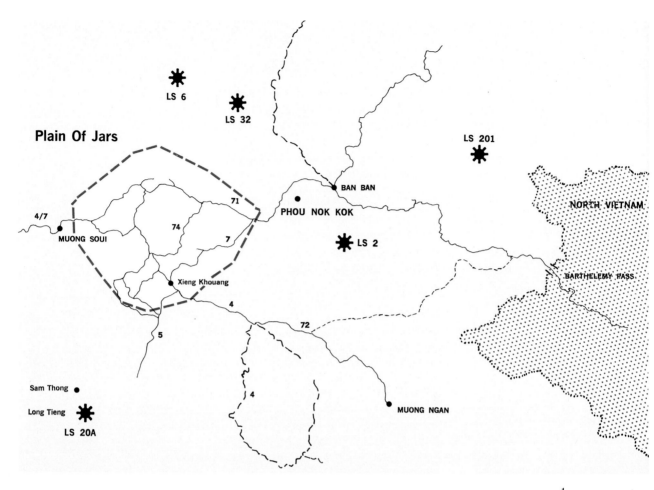

Plain Of Jars

LS 6

LS 32

LS 201

4/7

MUONG SOUI

71

74

7

PHOU NOK KOK

BAN BAN

NORTH VIETNAM

LS 2

Xieng Khouang

4

5

72

BARTHELEMY PASS

Sam Thong

Long Tieng

LS 20A

4

MUONG NGAN

1

XW-PGV

N. Laos & Plain Of Jars

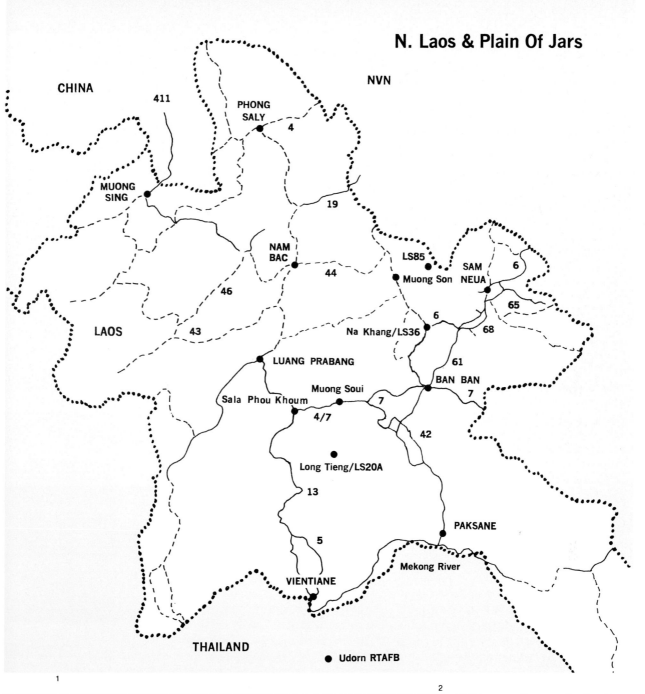

CHINA

411

PHONG SALY

4

NVN

MUONG SING

19

NAM BAC

LS85

Muong Son

SAM NEUA

6

44

46

LAOS

43

Na Khang/LS36

6

65

68

61

LUANG PRABANG

BAN BAN

7

Muong Soui

Sala Phou Khoum

7

4/7

42

Long Tieng/LS20A

13

PAKSANE

5

Mekong River

VIENTIANE

THAILAND

● Udorn RTAFB

(1) Refugees awaiting evacuation from Lima Site 32 in Laos (2) Lima Site 15 at Ban Na, Laos

241

on the ridgeline. During the afternoon the Meo moved out to clear the NVA from the ridge, succeeded, and then beat off an enemy counterattack. The next day, as more Royal Army reinforcements arrived, the RLAF flew 43 sorties even though the weather again deteriorated. On 26 March, after Seventh Air Force launched 185 sorties, the NVA departed the area, with Vang Pao's troops following cautiously behind. Long Tieng had been saved.

During the next 2 years the struggle between government and Communist forces continued to swing back and forth with the monsoon seasons, but the enemy clearly was on the ascendancy. Thus, by March 1971—a year after Long Tieng had survived the enemy's 1970 offense—Communist troops returned to the skyline ridge and seized new positions, although this time they did not try to capture Vang Pao's headquarters. The Meo leader's subsequent wet season offensive, launched in April, initially was successful in driving NVA forces from the Long Tieng

area. However, by late August the offensive had stalled.

The government had managed to hang on to certain positions on the northern portion of the Plain of Jars but, by year's end they had been virtually eliminated by five NVA regiments, which were equipped with 130-mm guns. These units then moved out against Long Tieng once more. To try to stop the enemy's advance, the Royal government in January 1972 brought in reinforcements and launched some 1,500 strike sorties. The Seventh Air Force flew almost as many. Despite these attacks, the enemy by mid-March were back in the vicinity of Long Tieng and began employing their 130-mm guns to batter government positions. The guns, difficult to spot from the air, were even more difficult to hit. Several were finally destroyed by USAF laser-guided bombs, but the enemy replaced them and continued long distance shelling. At the start of the wet season in mid-April, the Communists again withdrew from the Long Tieng area but this time

(1) LS-161 area of Laos (2) Gen. Vang Pao, commander of Meo forces (3) An American transport lands at a Laotian base © N.G.S. (4) The Command Post Center at Vientiane, Laos, coordinated air operations against Pathet Lao and North Vietnamese forces (5) T-28 aircraft at Vientiane, Laos, 1970.

no further than a day's march.

In August, after recovering from this latest siege, the government undertook a new offensive, but it was poorly coordinated and ran into stiff enemy resistance. By November 1972 the Communists were a scant 16 miles from Long Tieng, the best position they had ever had prior to launching their annual dry season offensive. To ease the threat, the Air Force launched a heavy B-52 and F-111 air attack against enemy troop and artillery positions, which also came under fire from other USAF aircraft. This intensive air campaign completely overwhelmed the North Vietnamese and Pathet Lao, who broke off the siege.

Meanwhile, peace talks between the contending Lao factions had gotten under way. On 10 November 1972 Premier Souvanna Phouma received the ranking member of the Pathet Lao delegation, Phoumi Vongvichit, in Vientiane. Anticipating an in-place ceasefire in the near future, the Communist forces undertook to eliminate the last government enclaves in the northern portions of the Plain of Jars, rather than try another offensive against Long Tieng. By year's end, some of these posts had managed to hold out with the help of aerial resupply and tactical strikes.

On 21 February 1973, less than a month after North Vietnam and the United States signed a ceasefire agreement, the Laotians followed suit. U.S. bombing operations were promptly halted, only to be renewed on 23 February at the request of the Vientiane government after Communist ceasefire violations. On that date, the B-52's launched a heavy attack against enemy positions near Paksong on the Bolovens Plateau. A second enemy ceasefire infringement brought the Stratofortresses back in April with a final strike south of the Plain of Jars. When the dust settled, some 9 years of USAF operations over Laos came to an end.

X Air War in Cambodia

One of the issues that troubled American military leaders was the Presidential prohibition against allied operations into North Vietnamese and Viet Cong sanctuaries in Cambodia and Laos. As early as January 1964, General Taylor, then chairman of the Joint Chiefs of Staff, noted to Secretary McNamara that the war was being fought entirely on Communist terms. The enemy, he said

> ...has determined the locale, the timing and the tactics of the battle while our own actions are essentially reactive. One reason for this is the fact that we have obliged ourselves to labor under self-imposed restrictions with respect to impending external aid to the Viet Cong. These restrictions include keeping the war within the boundaries of South Vietnam.

But in January 1965 President Johnson hoped to avoid a major expansion of the war. However, aware that a serious problem existed, he approved a series of small, covert cross-border military operations. Initiated on 1 February, they involved small-scale American and Vietnamese hit-and-run raids against enemy lines of communication in southern North Vietnam and the Laotian panhandle. These initial cross-border operations proved so successful that Secretary McNamara on 16 March recommended their continuance on a larger scale. He reiterated, however, that the existing "in-country" war strategy was "generally sound and adequate." But there were contrary views. For example, the Director of Central Intelligence, John A. McCone, argued that the allied program would never be completely satisfactory "so long as it permits the Viet Cong a sanctuary in Cambodia and Laos and a continuing uninterrupted and unmolested source of support and reinforcement from North Vietnam through Laos."

Periodically, the Joint Chiefs of Staff would suggest specific measures to take the initiative from the enemy. Thus, in August 1964 they proposed breaking up Viet Cong sanctuaries in the Cambodia-South Vietnam border area "through the conduct of 'hot pursuit' operations...as required." The President rejected the recommendation at that time and again in 1965 and 1966. In early 1966 Premier Ky pressed U.S. officials for action against the Cambodian sanctuaries. The administration, however, continued to forbid such operations except for self-defense in emergency situations, such as "shooting across the border." In September 1966 General Westmoreland became increasingly concerned about the threat of large enemy forces in Laos, Cambodia, and North Vietnam. His staff studied possible courses of action to counter them, but there was no change in the President's policy prohibiting border crossings.

In March 1967 South Vietnam's leaders met with President Johnson on Guam and again expressed their frustration over the enemy sanctuaries. The President replied that he was just as concerned as they were but did not pursue the issue further. Five months later, Admiral Sharp raised the subject while appearing before a Senate Special Investigating Subcommittee examining restrictions imposed on the air war against North Vietnam. Sharp complained that the allies were limited to essentially "defense" actions, but the enemy attacked "from sanctuaries across the DMZ, from Laos, and from Cambodia, and moves his forces at will across these borders." Political restraints, the admiral noted, had ruled out ground operations to deprive the enemy of those sanctuaries.

Capt. Laird Johnson, 8th Tactical Fighter Wing, checks his F-4 ordnance prior to flying the unit's last combat mission in Southeast Asia.

245

1

2   3

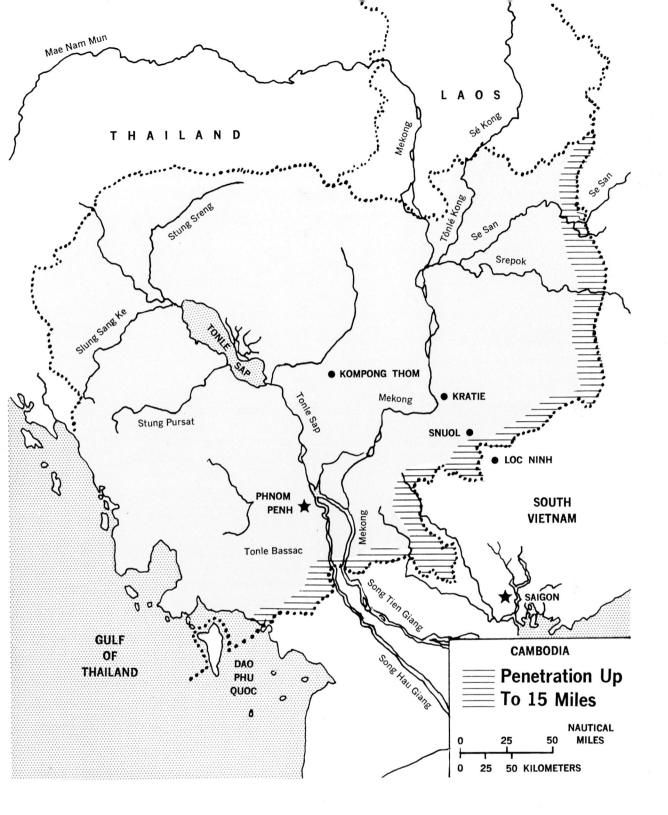

LAOS

THAILAND

Mae Nam Mun

Mekong

Sé Kong

Stung Sreng

Tônlé Kong

Se San

Se San

Srepok

Slung Sang Ke

TONLÉ SAP

● KOMPONG THOM

Mekong

● KRATIE

Stung Pursat

Tonle Sap

SNUOL ●

● LOC NINH

PHNOM PENH ★

SOUTH VIETNAM

Tonle Bassac

Mekong

★ SAIGON

Song Tien Giang

GULF OF THAILAND

DAO PHU QUOC

Song Hau Giang

CAMBODIA

| | Penetration Up |
| | To 15 Miles |

NAUTICAL MILES

0   25   50

0   25   50 KILOMETERS

(1) Allied forces seized enemy rice supplies; (2) a cache of enemy rifles and other weapons in Cambodia; (3) an Air Force F-4 of the 366th Tactical Fighter Wing, Da Nang AB, sweeps through smoke of a previous strike to lay its ordnance on an enemy bunker complex in the Fish Hook area of Cambodia.

247

Some 4 months later a prestigious voice was heard on the subject. From his retirement home at Gettysburg, Pa., former President Eisenhower on 24 November 1967 publicly advocated "hot pursuit, even in the air," into Cambodia and Laos "to remove a thorn in our sides." Apparently as a direct result of Eisenhower's remarks —endorsed by Gen. Omar N. Bradley, a former chairman of the JCS—the Department of State on 4 December dispatched a diplomatic note to Cambodia complaining about the use of its territory by the Communists. "The root cause of incidents affecting Cambodia territory," the department said, "is the Viet Cong and North Vietnamese presence in the frontier region and their use of Cambodian territory in violation of the neutrality of Cambodia."

Cambodia's leader, Prince Norodom Sihanouk, on 24 December officially denied that "foreign armed forces" were implanted on Cambodian soil. However, in an interview appearing in the *Washington Post* on 29 December, Sihanouk conceded that "small units" of Communist forces had entered Cambodia "under pressure from American forces." He went on to suggest that "if limited combat breaks out between American and Vietnam [Communist] forces" in uninhabited areas of Cambodia, "it goes without saying that we would not interfere militarily." The Cambodian chief suggested that President Johnson send an emissary, preferably Sen. Mike Mansfield, to Phnom Penh to discuss possible U.S. military actions against Communist forces inside his country.

On 1 January 1968, responding to a press conference query, President Johnson said that he had read the account "with a great deal of interest —and I might say pleasure," and that Sihanouk's remarks were being studied. Three days later the White House announced the U.S. ambassador to India, Chester A. Bowles, would soon meet with Sihanouk. Secretary of State Dean Rusk, asked whether Sihanouk's message indicated the door was open for "hot pursuit into his territory," responded that it was a "hypothetical question." He said that if the Cambodian government could assure its own neutrality and territorial integrity with the aid of the International Control Commission, then the question would not arise.

On 8 January the first of several meetings between Ambassador Bowles and Prince Sihanouk took place in Phnom Penh. The envoy also met with the Cambodian prime minister and other government officials. During subsequent discussions with Sihanouk, the ambassador assured him that the United States had no desire to conduct military operations inside his country. Sihanouk accepted these assurances and later told Bowles that "he would not object to the United States engaging in 'hot pursuit' in unpopulated areas of Cambodia." He added that he could not say this publicly or officially.

What President Johnson thought of Bowles' report and what operations he planned to authorize is not known. Whatever these plans, they were aborted at the end of January when Communist forces—operating out of Cambodia, Laos, and North Vietnam— launched their famous Tet offensive throughout South Vietnam. In the early weeks of fighting, NVA and Viet Cong troops temporarily occupied dozens of South Vietnamese cities and towns, including portions of the ancient capital of Hue. As noted in Chapter II, the 1968 Tet offensive killed and injured thousands of people and wreaked enormous physical damage in South Vietnam. Among its victims, politically, was President Johnson. On 31 March he announced that he would not seek re-election and invited Hanoi to negotiate a settlement of the war. As an inducement, he ordered a halt to bombing of most of North Vietnam. In May 1968 the negotiations got under way in Paris, but quickly bogged down. On 31 October, in a final effort to obtain a settlement before he left office, Mr. Johnson ordered a total ban on air, naval, and artillery bombardment of North Vietnam. But he also warned Hanoi that the end of U.S. operations above the DMZ "must not risk the lives of our men and that the United States would react in such a situation."

President Nixon Orders the Bombing of Cambodia

The North Vietnamese claimed credit for the "overthrow" of the Johnson administration by the U.S. electorate. They also apparently decided to keep up the pressure on the new President, Richard M. Nixon. Thus, the new chief executive had scarcely assumed office in January 1969 when the enemy launched another, if smaller, nationwide offensive on 23 February, shelling Saigon, scores of other cities and towns, and numerous military bases. Not surprisingly, the President concluded that North Vietnam had no intention of going along with the understanding which ended the bombing of North Vietnam. He had before him at this time an 11 February 1969 request from General Abrams, Westmoreland's successor as MACV commander, for authority to bomb enemy bases in Cambodia using B-52's. Whereupon, Mr. Nixon authorized the use of the big bombers against the enemy's rear bases in Cambodia and directed that the bombing be kept secret.

Thus, on 18 March 1969—operating under cover of special security and reporting procedures—the B-52 campaign was launched against NVA-Viet Cong sanctuaries inside Cambodia. To insure secrecy—required to protect Prince Sihanouk's position (in July 1969 he agreed to restore diplomatic relations with the United States,

broken off since 1965)—the Defense Department announced these B-52 strikes as being against targets in South Vietnam. The sorties, all of which were flown at night, were directed by ground control radar units. During pre-mission briefings, pilots and navigators of the aircraft were told to react to all directions for bomb release from the ground control personnel. In all, between 18 March 1969 and 26 May 1970, the B-52's flew 4,308 sorties and dropped 120,578 tons of munitions on enemy base camps and headquarters in Cambodia.

Four months after the bombing began, the Cambodian parliament in August 1969 elected a new government headed by Lt. Gen. Lon Nol, the Army Chief of Staff. During the next several months, he and Prince Sihanouk tried unsuccessfully to secure international assistance in removing the North Vietnamese and Viet Cong troops from Cambodian soil. In March 1970, while Prince Sihanouk was visiting Europe, the Cambodian government boldly demanded withdrawal of all North Vietnamese. Shortly after, on the 18th, Lon Nol announced the overthrow of Prince Sihanouk and the establishment of the Khmer Republic. Sibanouk subsequently formed a government-in-exile in Peking. The Lon Nol government soon found itself threatened by an estimated 40,-000 North Vietnamese and Viet Cong troops and appealed for arms assistance. By 20 April 1970 enemy forces had taken control of large areas of the country and had cut roads within 15 miles of Phnom Penh. This apparent threat triggered an American-South Vietnamese invasion of Cambodia to root out and destroy the NVA/Viet Cong forces. From the U.S. viewpoint, the operation was long overdue and essential to safeguard the withdrawal of the bulk of American forces from South Vietnam under President Nixon's Vietnamization policy.

The operation began on 24 April when USAF and VNAF tactical aircraft launched strikes against enemy targets in Cambodia. On 29 April and 1 May, 48,000 South Vietnamese and 42,000 American troops drove across the border. Initially, the tactical air strikes, like the operations of the ground troops they were supporting, were limited to areas within 18 miles of the South Vietnamese-Cambodian border. On 14 May, however, a special tactical air strike was launched against a major truck park and storage area in Cambodia beyond the 18-mile zone, along the Xe Kong river near the Laotian border. In addition to the numerous tactical sorties, there were hundreds of B-52 strikes against the enemy.

By 29 June all American and most South Vietnamese troops had withdrawn from Cambodia. In just 60 days the allied ground forces had penetrated up to 20 miles beyond the border and overrun an area totally dominated by the North Vietnamese Army and the Viet Cong. During the operation, the allies killed more than 11,300 troops and captured 2,300 prisoners. They also captured 22,892 individual weapons; more than 15 million rounds of ammunition; 143,000 rockets, mortars, and recoilless rifle rounds; over 199,000 antiaircraft rounds; 5,500 mines, 62,000 grenades, and 83,000 pounds of explosives. They also seized more than 430 vehicles and destroyed 11,600 bunkers and other military structures.

On 30 June 1970, the day after the allied withdrawal, Air Force tactical aircraft began flying air strikes against enemy forces west of the Mekong River, which were menacing the town of Kompong Thom. When attempts by Lon Nol's troops to advance overland to the town failed despite air support, USAF crews turned their attention to roads leading from enemy-occupied Laos toward Kompong Thom. This interdiction attempt failed, however, because the flat terrain permitted the enemy to bypass cratered segments of the highway. Aerial efforts to defend Kompong Thom finally bore fruit, when 182 fighter-bomber and 37 gunship strikes between 31 July and 9 August 1970 finally forced the enemy to fall back. Similar aerial support—60 tactical and 15 gunship sorties—enabled Lon Nol's troops to recapture Skoun, an important highway junction west of the Mekong.

To improve communications between air and ground forces in Cambodia, the Air Force initially assigned an airborne radio relay station (a modified transport) to the combat zone. Later, an elaborately equipped airborne battlefield command and control center was positioned over Cambodia to direct close air support strikes. Problems of language, however, interfered with operations. Some Cambodian officers understood English, but few Americans could speak the local languages. Since the nearest thing to a common tongue was French, a carry over from colonial days, the Air Force used French-speaking volunteers to fly with FAC's and serve as interpreters. The Cambodians also made an effort to find and assign English-speaking officers as forward air guides with infantry units, thereby permitting direct communication between Cambodian ground commanders and Air Force forward air controllers.

By early November 1970 Communist forces had seized perhaps one-half of Cambodia's territory, including several uninhabited regions, despite the tremendous air support provided the Cambodian Army. When the latter proved unable to keep the highway open between the capital and Kompong Som, the nation's major seaport, allied attention turned to the use of river transport to deliver supplies to Phnom Penh. Delivery of supplies via the Mekong River from Vietnam to Cambodia became essential because of costs and the limited capacity of airlift. Whereupon, Communist forces began interdicting river traffic along a stretch of the Mekong, about 70 miles in length, where it cuts through an area of open flatlands. By January 1971 the enemy had achieved sufficient control of the region to strike almost at will against river traffic, firing from ambush with rocket launchers and recoilless rifles. To ensure the capital's survival, the allies instituted a convoy system, with as many as 46 ships and small craft of the South Vietnamese Navy escorting 10 or more merchantmen and tankers at a time.

USAF planes and Army helicopters assisted Cambodian and South Vietnamese airmen in providing air cover for the convoys. Later, U.S. Navy planes and helicopters also escorted the convoys. Because so many villages dotted the Mekong's banks, a forward air controller had to be present during such air escort operations. During an ambush, the FAC solicited strike clearance from officers familiar with the area so as not to endanger noncombatants. Only after the FAC received strike authorization could the aerial escort expend their munitions. Similarly, when friendly troops were involved in clearing operations along river banks, tight control over allied aircraft strikes was necessary.

During the summer of 1971 U.S. air units supported Cambodian operations to reopen the Phnom Penh-Kompong Som highway and the road to Kompong Thom. The latter drive occurred in September and was judged a success. The most important USAF action was taken against an enemy force deployed in a rubber plantation near Chamkar Andong. The aerial attack forced the enemy to abandon his entrenchments there. A napalm strike upon the village of Kompong Thmar routed the defenders and destroyed their munitions stockpile. On the other hand, the enemy got close enough to

Phnom Penh to bombard the airport with artillery shells and rockets, causing extensive damage to Cambodian Air Force planes. Communist rockets also hit an oil depot near the capital in September, destroying about 40 percent of Cambodia's fuel storage capacity and millions of gallons of petroleum. The United States replaced the loss with increased POL shipments.

During 1971 the Lon Nol government continued to require the military assistance of South Vietnam and U.S. air power. On several occasions, Saigon forces ventured across the border to attack NVA bases and supply dumps. During one such operation in June, the NVA badly mauled an ARVN task force which fell back in confusion. Because of poor flying weather, the troops initially lacked air support. As the skies cleared, hundreds of sorties were launched against the North Vietnamese. In September and October, ARVN troops were more successful. After stopping an enemy attack upon their positions along the Cambodian border, ARVN troops on 20 September went over to the offensive and reopened the highway between Tay Ninh, South Vietnam, and Krek, Cambodia. While the Vietnamese did the fighting, 1,500 U.S. troops moved behind them in a supporting position inside South Vietnam. Enemy targets in the Tay Ninh-Krek area took a battering from the air, with B-52's dropping 1,000 tons of bombs on the first day of the operation. As the sweep was ending, however, an American fighter-bomber accidentally attacked a South Vietnamese unit, killing 18 and wounding 7.

In Peking, where he was living in exile, Prince Sihanouk claimed that Lon Nol clung to power "only through the intervention of the U.S. Air Force." While somewhat exaggerated, the fact was that air power had influenced those battles in which trained and motivated Cambodian troops had

Among the Soviet and Chinese manufactured weapons seized during the allied incursion into Cambodia were 22,800 individual weapons, more than 15 million rounds of ammunition, and 143,000 rockets, mortars and recoilless rifle rounds.

proved successful. On the other hand, allied air power could not save ill-trained, poorly led units from defeat. As the Cambodians suffered repeated setbacks, their reliance on South Vietnamese ground forces increased. Early in 1972, ARVN troops were withdrawn in anticipation of an enemy attack on the South Vietnamese capital. When it failed to materialize, the troops were sent back to Cambodia where they launched several operations into enemy-held territory.

One of these ARVN incursions in March 1972 proved especially successful. The South Vietnamese, supported by B-52 strikes, seized enough rice from the enemy to feed 10,000 men for 3 months. Also, one B-52 raid caused spectacular damage; the advancing infantry found the bombs had made a direct hit, shattering bunkers of reinforced concrete, killing the occupants, and destroying supplies stored inside. Nevertheless, the enemy still remained in control of large portions of Cambodia east of the Mekong, but still proved incapable of capturing the capital and ousting Lon Nol. U.S. aircrews continued to fly missions against them, even after the ceasefire in South Vietnam became effective in January 1973.

By this time a major portion of the enemy forces threatening the capital were local insurgents of the Khmer Rouge. When they launched an assault on Phnom Penh early in 1973, Cambodia's government quickly requested American help and a massive bombardment got under way. By May an armada of USAF aircraft—including B-52's, F-111's, A-7's, and AC-130's —were launching repeated strikes against enemy targets on the outskirts of the capital. At times, crowds gathered on the west bank of the Mekong to watch them hit Khmer Rouge forces on the opposite shore. Eighty percent of these strikes were against local insurgents and apparently thwarted their plan to capture the capital in the summer of 1973. At one point, when it appeared the enemy might block river traffic again, the Air Force launched

(1) Cambodian troops were trained by the South Vietnamese at the Lam Son Training Center; (2) U.S. Army engineers examine supply crates left behind by fleeing enemy troops; (3) In March 1970, the Cambodian Defense Minister Lt. Gen. Lon Nol, seized control of the government and announced the overthrow of Prince Sihanouk, then visiting in Europe; (4) Lon Nol visited Cambodian troops in September 1970.

1

2

3

(1) Cambodian troops trained in Vietnam prepare to board U.S. Air Force transports at Nha Trang for the flight back to Cambodia. (2) Sihanouk visited Communist China in October 1965. Shown (l. to r.): Chairman Mao Tse-Tung, Peng Chen, Sihanouk, and China's Chief of State, Liu Shao-chi. (3) Prince Sihanouk met with North Vietnamese Premier Pham Van Dong in Peking in November 1971.

an emergency C-130 airlift from U-Tapao to Phnom Penh's airport. It delivered munitions, rice, military equipment, and occasionally POL. This C-130 resupply effort was temporarily halted, however, when the river convoys succeeded in forcing their way to the capital with the help of aerial escort.

Congressional Criticism

The continuing bombing of Cambodia in the spring and summer of 1973 stirred renewed Congressional criticism at home of the war. Members of the House of Representatives tacked on amendments to several administration bills prohibiting the use of appropriated funds for bomb-

ing Cambodian targets. On 27 June the President vetoed one such bill and the House sustained the veto. Later, President Nixon informed Congress that he would not oppose legislation calling for a halt in the bombing within 45 days (on 15 August 1973) instead of requiring an immediate bombing halt. Congress accepted this compromise and on 1 July passed Public Law 93-52 cutting off all funds "to finance directly or indirectly combat activities by United States military forces in or over or from off the shores of South Vietnam, Laos or Cambodia." Mr. Nixon signed the bill into law on 1 July.

As the deadline drew near, the Air Force became involved in two tragic accidents. On 6 August a B-52 mistakenly dropped 20 tons of bombs on the friendly town of Neak Luong, 38 miles southeast of Phnom Penh. The raid killed or wounded more than 400 people. Two days later, American bombs hit a village on an island in the Mekong, just 3 miles from Neak Luong, causing at least 16 casualties. The last U.S. air strike in Cambodia occurred on the morning of 15 August 1973, when an A-7 Corsair, piloted by Capt. Lonnie O. Ratley, returned to its home base in Thailand, marking an end to the nation's longest war. USAF C-130's, however, continued to deliver needed supplies to the Cambodians after that date.

255

XI American POW's and Operation Homecoming

On 23 January 1973 Dr. Henry Kissinger, Assistant to the President for National Security Affairs, and Special Adviser Le Duc Tho of North Vietnam reached agreement in Paris to end the war in Vietnam and restore the peace. Four days later the four major combatants—the United States and South Vietnam on the one side and North Vietnam and Viet Cong (the Provisional Revolutionary Government of the Republic of South Vietnam) on the other—signed the cease-fire agreement. It required the release of all American prisoners of war held by the Communists simultaneously with withdrawal of all U.S. forces from South Vietnam, these actions to be completed within 60 days.

For the 591 American POW's, the 27 January agreement meant freedom after many years of captivity in North Vietnamese, Viet Cong, Laotian, and Chinese prison camps. Three hundred and twenty-five were USAF personnel, mostly combat pilots. Two were Korean war aces—Lt. Col. James L. Kasler and Col. Robinson Risner—who had spent 6½ and 7 years in captivity, respectively. A third Air Force pilot, Col. John P. Flynn, who was shot down in October 1967, was the senior American POW in North Vietnam. Promoted to brigadier general while in captivity (to protect him against harassment, no announcement was made), Colonel Flynn helped to organize and command the "4th Allied POW Wing" in the last years of the war.

USAF officials did not have much information about the prisoners' living conditions or their treatment during the early years of their captivity. What was known was not encouraging. As early as 25 June 1965, Hanoi radio reported that the Viet Cong had executed Sgt. Harold G. Bennett, an adviser to an ARVN unit, who was captured on 29 December 1964, in retaliation for the execution of Communist terrorists by the Saigon government. In August 1965—after Hanoi radio broadcast the tape-recorded statements of two recently captured Air Force pilots praising their captors for their "humane" treatment—fears were expressed that they had been tortured. These fears eventually were confirmed.

Beginning in late 1965 and during the next 7 years, the U. S. government worked to bring international pressure to bear on Hanoi to insure that the rights of the prisoners under terms of the 1949 Geneva Convention were being observed. Although North Vietnam had signed the convention in 1957, it announced that captured American pilots were not entitled to POW status. According to Hanoi, there had been no formal declaration of war between the United States and North Vietnam (the Geneva convention made no such distinction) and the pilots were "criminals" who could be convicted "under the principles established by the Nuremburg war crime trials."

In its efforts to ease the plight of the POW's, the Johnson administration solicited the assistance of the International Red Cross and friendly nations to use their influence in obtaining proper treatment. On 29 April 1966, at the request of the White House, the State Department established a Committee on Prisoner Matters which included representatives from several Department of Defense agencies. On 10 May the President designated W. Averell Harriman as his Special Representative and Ambassador to negotiate an exchange of prisoners. The United States also asked the Soviet Union to intervene with North Vietnam to allow Red Cross representatives to visit the POW's, but Moscow referred the Americans to Hanoi.

Hanoi Threatens "War Crimes" Trials

During the early summer of 1966, following increased U. S. airstrikes against oil facilities in the Hanoi-Haiphong area, North Vietnam initiated a propaganda campaign leading to the scheduling of "war crime" trials for the captured airmen. As part of this campaign, 52 American POW's handcuffed in pairs were paraded through the streets of Hanoi while agitated crowds stoned, beat, and reviled them. On 7 July 1966 Hanoi radio read depositions from several pilots (they had been tortured) denouncing American war operations and asking for Vietnamese "forgiveness." On 12 July two East European Communist press agencies reported that 60 American military men would be brought to trial later in the month or in early August.

The United States took North Vietnam's plans for war crime trials seriously. President Johnson made no public threats but warnings about his reaction should the trials actually take place were soon dispatched around the world. In Washington, 19 senators who strongly opposed Johnson's Vietnam policies on 15 July issued "a plea for sanity" to Hanoi. Violence against the captured Americans, they warned,

would "incite the public demand for retaliation swift and sure." The next day Sen. Richard B. Russell, chairman of the Senate Armed Services Committee, warned that North Vietnam would be made "a desert" if the trials were held. Sen. George D. Aiken predicted "complete destruction of North Vietnam" if the POW's were killed. The *New York Times* reported that there was little doubt that "Lyndon Johnson's reaction would be severe."

These warnings had a salutary effect on Hanoi, which abruptly ceased its propaganda campaigns about the trials. Its treatment of the captured airmen, however, remained severe. Their lot included torture—ranging from being trussed up by ropes and hung on rafters to being beaten severely by prison guards or having their fingernails pulled out. Some POW's were tortured to persuade them to meet with American antiwar and other visiting delegations and recite dictated statements about their "humane" treatment. Many prisoners—especially senior officers—were placed in solitary confinement for years and fed a bare subsistence diet. Except in certain serious cases, medical care was minimal. Mail privileges were nonexistent for most prisoners. During the Christmas season of 1966, 457 of 467 packages sent to them by their families were returned with the stamp: "Refused by the Postal Authorities of Vietnam."

During 1967 the U. S. government continued its search for ways to persuade Hanoi to allow Red Cross representatives to visit the prison camps in the North. The South Vietnamese government cooperated by opening its camps for Viet Cong and North Vietnamese prisoners to inspection by the International Committee of the Red Cross and allowing mail privileges. Still Hanoi refused to budge. On 26 July 1967 the Department of Defense established a Prisoner of War Policy Committee. Chaired by Paul C. Warnke, Assistant Secretary of Defense (International Security Affairs), it had the job of coordinating all POW matters and planning the eventual recovery and repatriation of the prisoners.

Information about the living conditions and treatment of POW's held by the Viet Cong in jungle camps in South Vietnam or Cambodia came to light from the infrequent successful escapee or from the American captive occasionally released by the enemy for political purposes. Living conditions were extremely primitive, with many POW's succumbing to disease and starvation.

In the case of North Vietnamese camps, the first authoritative information became available in February 1968, when Hanoi released three American pilots shot down 4 to 6 months earlier. They were Lt. Col. Norris M. Overly, USAF; Capt. John D. Black, USAF; and Lt. (jg.) David P. Matheny, USN. The North Vietnamese announced their impending release on 27 January, noting that they would be handed over to the U. S. National Mobilization Committee to End the War. Two of its members—the Rev. Daniel Berrigan and Dr. Howard Zinn —flew to Hanoi, where the release took place on 16 February.

The entire affair may have been a North Vietnamese ploy related to the 1968 Tet offensive, launched on 1 February. If, as seems likely, the enemy thought that the 3-man release might ward off U. S. retaliatory strikes in the Hanoi-Haiphong area, they were correct. In Washington, Assistant Secretary Warnke—serving as a member of a working group created by the newly designated Secretary of Defense, Clark Clifford, to prepare new military recommendations for the President— argued against JCS proposals for such bombings. He recommended that the existing bombing ban "should be continued pending the return of the 3 American PWs."

When the three released captives reached the United States several weeks later, U. S. officials learned for the first time that many of the American POW's were in prison camps in the Hanoi area. The airmen also identified 40 men as prisoners who had been listed as missing in action. Citing their testimony, Warnke argued that heavy and "indiscriminate" attacks in the Hanoi area "would jeopardize the lives of these prisoners and alarm their wives and parents."

Subsequently, the President on 31 March 1968 announced a halt to all bombing of North Vietnam (except for the area immediately north of the DMZ) and invited Hanoi to begin peace talks in Paris. The North Vietnamese accepted and, in May 1968, the first meetings got under way in Paris. Apparently, in an effort to further encourage an end to all bombings of North Vietnam, in August 1968 Hanoi released three more captured pilots, all members of the Air Force and recent captives. They were Maj. James F. Low, a Korean War ace shot down in December 1967; Maj. Fred N. Thompson, captured in March 1968; and Capt. Joe V. Carpenter, captured in February 1968. Turned over to members of the U. S. antiwar movement in Hanoi on 18 July, they were escorted back to the United States.

During the waning months of the Johnson administration in late 1968, little progress was made in the Paris talks. The next major event affecting the POW's involved the efforts of the new administration of President Richard M. Nixon, who took office in July 1969. Within days of his inauguration, the President sent Ambassador Henry Cabot Lodge to Paris to head the U.S. delegation to the peace talks. Mr. Lodge very early proposed to the North Vietnamese the release of POW's held by both sides as part of any peace agreement. Hanoi, however, demanded that the United States end its support of Saigon. As the talks deadlocked over this issue, the administration in early 1969 abandoned quiet diplomacy in dealing with the

2

(1-2) POW's were driven to the Gia Lam Airport preparatory to their turnover to American officials. (3) Col. Emil J. Wengel, USAF greets Maj. Hubert K. Flesher (I.), who was shot down on 2 December 1966. (4) Happy former POW's after boarding a C-141 transport taking them back to the United States. (5) The end of a long journey for Army Sgt. Edward W. Williams, greeted by close relatives at Scott AFB, Ill. (6-7) Welcome signs greet returned POW's.

4

1

3

5

6

7

POW issue and proposed discussing it "openly, candidly, forcefully, and repeatedly." In the dozens of meetings with the North Vietnamese during 1969, the Americans repeatedly brought up the subject. They cited "disturbing evidence" that the prisoners were being held "in solitary confinement and being subjected to physical and mental duress." They repeatedly proposed a prisoner exchange, repatriation of the sick and wounded, and inspection of the camps by impartial outsiders. They pressed the North Vietnamese for lists of all POW's so that their families could know "who is dead and who is alive."

Although it rejected all these proposals, Hanoi on 3 July 1969 announced that "in recognition of the American Independence Day," it would release a third group of prisoners. They were: Capt. Wesley L. Rumble, USAF, a captive 15 months; Seaman Douglas Hegdahl, imprisoned more than 2 years; and Lt. Robert F. Frishman, USN, a prisoner for about 20 months. Prior to their turn-over to another U. S. antiwar group in Hanoi on 18 July, the North Vietnamese warned Lieutenant Frishman not to cause them any "embarrassment" since they would retaliate against those left behind. The other POW's, however, had urged him to speak out about their ill-treatment when he got home.

He did several weeks later, with the encouragement of the administration. On 3 September 1969, Frishman and Hegdahl held a press conference at the Bethesda Naval Hospital, during which the lieutenant reported that POW's had been beaten, tortured, placed in solitary confinement, provided minimal medical care, and otherwise mistreated. Frishman, for example, almost lost his injured right arm, which became shorter than his left arm for lack of adequate medical aid. Based upon these statements and other available information, the U. S. government on 13 September report-

ed to the International Conference of the Red Cross meeting in Istanbul, Turkey, on Hanoi's gross violations of the Geneva Convention.

The publicity about the harsh treatment had a galvanizing effect on the families of the prisoners. Starting in September-October 1969, delegations of wives and relatives of POW's descended on the North Vietnamese delegation in Paris to plead for information about their men. The spectacle produced widespread headlines and television coverage and adversely affected North Vietnam's position in the eyes of the world. On 12 November the United States also took its case to the United Nations General Assembly, where it denounced Hanoi's torture and treatment of the prisoners and its refusal to allow mail privileges to the POW's.

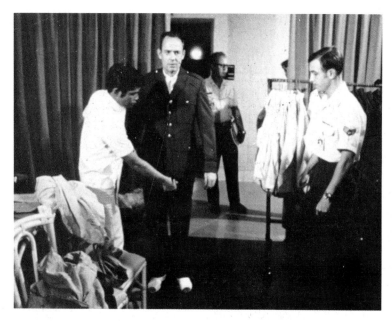

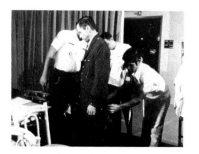

191 came from new writers, whose fate for the most part had remained unknown to their families. This was an important break-through for the prisoners and was followed by noticeable improvement in their living conditions.

The administration continued to hammer away at the POW issue in various forums. In early 1970 both houses of Congress adopted a resolution expressing concern about the prisoners' fates. During the summer President Nixon appointed Col. Frank Borman (he and two companions orbited the moon in December 1968) as his Special Representative on Prisoners of War. Borman traveled to 14 countries (including the Soviet Union) seeking assistance in persuading Hanoi to exchange American prisoners for the thousands of captured North Vietnamese troops. Although the trip was unsuccessful, it helped to focus the spotlight on the plight of the POW's. After his return to the United States in September 1970, Colonel Borman reported to a joint session of Congress on his efforts.

In October the National League of Families of American Prisoners and Missing in Southeast Asia held its first annual convention in Washington, D.C., attended by more than 450 family members. The League grew out of the activities of a group of wives on the West Coast in 1966. In November the U.S. government received—via the antiwar Committee of Liaison—the first news from Hanoi about the death in captivity of six POW's. The committee also turned over a North Vietnamese list of 339 American captives, which included 4 new names.

In late November 1970—as a direct result of the daring U.S. raid on the Son Tay prison camp west of Hanoi—the North Vietnamese evacuated all outlying prisons and brought the POW's—352 of them—to the Hoa Lo prison (Vietnamese for "hell hole" but usually called the "Hanoi Hilton" by the POW's). This consolidation

These events finally produced a North Vietnamese reaction. Responding to the unfavorable publicity, Hanoi requested members of the American peace movement to form a "Committee of Liaison With Families of Servicemen Detained in North Vietnam" to transmit letters from the POW's to their families in the United States. Subsequently, on 14 December 1969, North Vietnamese prison officials suddenly directed the POW's: "Everyone will write home for Christmas." There followed a dramatic change in the number of letters sent and received. For example, in the 4½ years ending in January 1969, American families had received only 620 letters from 103 prisoners. During the next 11 months, the number climbed to 940 from 294 writers, most of the additional 320 letters being written in November and December. Of those,

opened a new era for the prisoners. For the first time they were placed in large open-bay rooms housing 20 to 50 men, enabling them to organize to a greater extent than ever before. Their senior officers, although still kept in isolation by the North Vietnamese, were able to issue policy guidance and directives to the younger men via a variety of clandestine communication methods and maintained effective command of the "4th Allied POW Wing" despite efforts to halt this activity.

During 1971-1972 perhaps the most important influence on Hanoi—and the final peace settlement—was President Nixon's state visits to North Vietnam's major military suppliers—Communist China in February 1972 and the Soviet Union in May. Within months after Dr. Kissinger's secret trip to Peking in July 1971 which led to arrangements for the President's trip to China, a North Vietnamese delegate at Paris offered to release all POW's if the United States promised to withdraw all its forces from Vietnam by a fixed date. The proposal became the foundation for reaching a final agreement between Kissinger and Tho in 1972. There were several setbacks and interruptions in their negotiations, including Hanoi's major offensive in the spring of 1972 to seize territory in South Vietnam and defeat the Saigon government. The heavy bombardment of Hanoi and Haiphong in December 1972—following Hanoi's procrastination over the settlement—apparently was a factor leading to the 27 January 1973 agreement and set the stage for Operation Homecoming, the return of all American prisoners.

Planning the POW Recovery

Operation Homecoming plans, refined over a period of several years, called for each returning POW to remain in medical channels from the time he returned to American control

until he had completed all post-captivity processing in a hospital in the United States. Representatives of the Office of the Secretary of Defense, the military services, and the State Department attended the final planning conference, held in Honolulu, Hawaii, during August 1972. Among the attendees were physicians, surgeons, lawyers, escorts, consular officials, chaplains, public affairs officers, and others. The Commander, 9th Aeromedical Evacuation Group (PACAF), was appointed overall aeromedical evacuation coordinator for the recovery operation.

The operation was divided into three phases. First, there was to be the initial reception of prisoners at three release sites: prisoners held by the Viet Cong were to be flown to Saigon by helicopter; those in North Vietnam, the majority of the prisoners, would be released at Hanoi; and finally, three American POW's held in China—two U.S. pilots and a CIA agent imprisoned during the Korean War—would be set free at Hong Kong. All would be flown to Clark AB in the Philippines for the second phase of the operation—processing through the Joint Homecoming Reception Center. Then the POW's would fly to 1 of 31 military hospitals

WILLIAM ARCURI

two Canadians, two Filipinos, two Thais, and one South Vietnamese. The total number of Americans returning home—including the three released by China—was 591.

Under provisions of the cease-fire agreement, POW's were to be released simultaneously with the withdrawal of American troops, at approximately 15-day phased intervals. The first release took place almost on schedule and was followed by another North Vietnamese "good will" release a few days later. When the North Vietnamese fell behind the release schedule, the President ordered a halt in American force withdrawals from the South to make clear the importance the United States attached to prompt and full compliance with the agreement. North Vietnam responded by releasing additional prisoners, the last of them on 29 March. In the South, Saigon officials released 26,508 North Vietnamese and Viet Cong prisoners while the Communist side released about 5,000 South Vietnamese POW's.

For the American people the return of the nation's captured military men was a moment of tears and joyous celebration as they watched the arrival of their servicemen at Clark and then at air bases throughout the United States. A State Department official, Frank A. Sieverts, Special Assistant to the Deputy Secretary of State for Prisoner of War/Missing in Action Matters, told a congressional committee in May 1973 of being at Hanoi's Gia Lam airport on 12 February and his joy when the first group of POW's arrived there for their flight to freedom. He said:

> The guards ordered the men off the bus. Suddenly, the senior American officer of the group took command away from the guards and gave the orders for the men to march in formation to the release point. The guards tried to intervene but fell back. It was clear then that, despite the grim experience of their captivity, our men had endured and prevailed. They deserve our thanks and commendation.

in the United States for detailed medical assistance and processing, the third phase of the operation.

In late September 1972 a realistic rehearsal for Operation Homecoming took place after North Vietnam released three more American POW's: Maj. Edward K. Elias, USAF; Lt. Norris A. Charles, USN; and Lt. Markham L. Gartley, USN. Their release gave Homecoming personnel the opportunity to exercise and refine their procedures. The 9th Aeromedical Evacuation Group, for example, responded five times, sending a C-9A aeromedical aircraft to potential release sites, including Vientiane, Laos.

On 27 January 1973, as specified in the cease-fire agreement, North Vietnam and the Viet Cong provided the United States with a list of 587 American POW's of whom 566 were military personnel and 22 civilians. On 1 February the "Lao Patriotic Front" provided the names of nine other American prisoners—seven military and two civilians. Finally, an additional POW in Viet Cong hands also was reported, bringing the overall total of American personnel to be released to 588. The Communist side also listed nine non-U.S. personnel: two West Germans,

Glossary

AAA	antiaircraft artillery	FAC	forward air controller
AB	air base		
AD	air division	GPES	Ground Proximity Extraction System
ADVON	advanced echelon		
AFB	Air Force Base		
AFLC	Air Force Logistics Command	I&C	installation and checkout
AFROTC	Air Force Reserve Officer Training Corps	ICC	International Control Commission
AFSC	Air Force Systems Command	IFF/SIF	Identification Friend or Foe/ Selective Identification Feature
AID	Agency for International Development		
ALCC	Airlift Control Center		
ALO	air liaison officer	JCS	Joint Chiefs of Staff (U.S.)
ANG	Air National Guard	JGS	Joint General Staff (South Vietnamese)
AOC	Air Operations Center		
APOE	Aerial Port of Embarkation		
ARVN	Army of Republic of South Vietnam	LAPES	Low-Altitude Parachute Extraction System
ATRC	air traffic regulation center	LBR	local base rescue
		LCM	landing craft, medium
BLU	bomb, live unit	LOC	line of communication
		LORAN	long-range electronic navigation
CAP	combat air patrol		
CBU	cluster bomb unit (anti-personnel weapon)	LS	Lima Site - Temporary aircraft landing sites in Laos
CCC	Combat Control Center	LZ	landing zone
CCK	Ching Chuan Kang (AB, Taiwan)	MAAG	Military Assistance Advisory Group (U.S.)
CCTW	combat crew training wing		
CIA	Central Intelligence Agency (U.S.)	MACV	Military Assistance Command, Vietnam (U.S.)
CIDG	Civilian Irregular Defense Group	MAF	Marine Amphibious Force
		MAC	Military Airlift Command
CINCPAC	Commander in Chief, Pacific	MSTS	Military Sea Transportation Service
CINCPACAF	Commander in Chief, Pacific Air Forces		
COSVN	Central Office for South Vietnam (Vietnamese Communist headquarters)	NCP	National Campaign Plan (South Vietnamese)
		NLF	National Front for the Liberation of Vietnam
CRAF	Civil Reserve Air Fleet		
CRP	control and reporting post	NORS	not operationally ready, supply
CSAS	Common Service Airlift System		
		NSC	National Security Council (U.S.)
CTZ	Corps Tactical Zone		
DASC	Direct Air Support Center	NVA	North Vietnamese Army
DMZ	demilitarized zone	NVAF	North Vietnamese Air Force
ECM	electronic countermeasure	OJT	on-the-job training
ELF	electronic location finder	OSD	Office of Secretary of Defense
EW	electronic warfare	OTS	Officer Training School

PACAF	Pacific Air Force	USAF	United States Air Force
PACOM	Pacific Command	USAID	United States Agency for International Development
PMEL	Precision Measurement Equipment Laboratory	USMACV	U.S. Military Assistance Command, Vietnam
POW	prisoner of war		
Prime Beef	base engineering emergency force	VNAF	Vietnamese Air Force (South Vietnam)

R&R	rest and recuperation
RAM	rapid area maintenance
RAPCON	radar approach control
RASS	rapid area supply support
RATS	rapid area transportation support
Recce (Recon)	reconnaissance
Red Horse	rapid engineering deployment and heavy operational repair squadron, engineering
RESCAP	rescue combat air patrol
RLAF	Royal Laotian Air Force
RLG	Royal Laotian Government
RTU	replacement training unit
RVNAF	Republic of Vietnam Armed Forces

SAC	Strategic Air Command
SAM	surface-to-air missiles
SAR	search and rescue
SARTAF	SAR Task Force
SAW	special air warfare
SEA	Southeast Asia
SEAAS	Southeast Asia Airlift System
SEAITACS	Southeast Asia Integrated Tactical Air Control System
SEATO	Southeast Asia Treaty Organization

TAC	Tactical Air Command
tac	tactical
TACC	Tactical Air Control Center
TACC(NS)	Tactical Air Control Center, North Sector
TACC(SS)	Tactical Air Control Center, South Sector
TACS	Tactical Air Control System
TDY	temporary duty
TFW	tactical fighter wing
TTF	Tanker Task Force

USA	United States Army

Index

Annam, 4
Anthis, Rollen H., 12, 17, 19, 21, 25, 29
Ap Bac, 20, 24, 26
Ap Trung, 127
Armament
    aircraft, 22
    helicopters, 18
ARC LIGHT. *See* B-52
Armed Forces Council, RVN, 35
Armstrong, Alan J., 94
Artillery assaults and support, 20
Associated States of Vietnam, Laos and
    Comboda, 5
Atomic bomb strikes, 3
Atterberry, Edwin L., 149
ATTLEBORO Operation, 51
Atsugi, Japan, 75, 76
Aurand, E. P., 179, 180
Australian forces, 46, 102, 105

B

Bac Giang, 179
Bac Ginn, 139
Bac Lieu, 41
Bach Long Vi Island, 167
Bai Duc Thon, 144
Bangkok, 3
Ban Karai pass, 149, 152
Ban Me Thout, 25, 117, 207
Bao Dai, 5
Bao Ha, N. V., 145
Bao Trai, 47
Barie, A. H., 183
Barnhart, R. C., 163
BARREL ROLL Operation, 209, 229, 230
Barrow, Robert H., 89
Base Area 604, North Vietnamese Army, 69,
    71
Batson, Jack E. D., 169, 170
Beeler, William R., 86
Ben Cat, 17, 28
Ben Het, 102, 121
Bien Hoa, 9, 12, 15, 20, 21, 26, 30, 34, 35, 58,
    65, 197, 199, 207
Big Look (EC-121M), 174
Binh Dinh Province, 24, 44, 47, 51, 53, 55, 57
Binh Duong Province, 16
Binh Long, 112, 121, 124
Binh Thuan Province, 55
Binh Thuy, 207
Blanchard, William H., 98
BOLD Operation, 142
BOMBING Operations, 3, 5, 8, 19, 20, 24, 25,
    27, 28
Bombs
    napalm, 19, 20
    Phosphorus, 22
Bon Homme Richard, USS, 185, 191
Bong Son, 47
Bong Son Plain, 54
Borman, Frank K., 262
Boxer, USS, 43, 44
Bradley, Omar N., 247
Brezhnev, Leonid, 10
Bridge Interdiction (North Vietnam), 144, 145
Bringle, W. F., 189
Brink Hotel, 35
British Commonwealth forces, 4
Brown, Donald H., Jr., 169
Brown, George S., 99, 219
Brown, James W., 13
Brown, Jim, 176
Brumett, Robert, 29
Bu Prang, 121
Bunker systems, enemy, 24
Burma, 3, 5
BURNING ARROW Operation, 20
BYRD Operation, 55

C

Ca Mau peninsula, 9, 19, 29
Caldara, Joseph D., 5
Ca Lu, 59, 60, 61
Cam Pha, 173, 178, 179
Cam Ranh Bay, 3, 64, 168
Cambodia, 3, 5, 8, 9, 16, 66, 70, 101, 109–
    112, 124, 125, 143, 159, 162, 184, 218,
    244–247
    as enemy sanctuary, 20, 24, 112, 244
Camp Evans, 63
Camp Haskins, 93
Camp Horn, 93
Can Tho, 102
Canal Des Rapides Railway, 143, 146
Cao, Huyn Van, 20
Cap Mui Lay, 117
Cap Mui Ron, 167
Cap St. Jacques (Vung Tau), 3
Capital Military District, 19
Card, USNS, 37
Card, USS, 32
Carey, John F., 73
Carl, Marion E., 77
Carman, W. E., 163
Carter, Tennis, 104
Cay Giep Mountains, 47, 50

EDITOR'S NOTE: Military Unit Designations were not included in the index because they were too numerous.